Physical Database Design

The Morgan Kaufmann Series in Data Management Systems

Series Editor: Jim Gray, Microsoft Research

Physical Database Design

The Database Professional's Guide to Exploiting Indexes, Views, Storage, and More

Sam Lightstone
Toby Teorey
Tom Nadeau

AMSTERDAM • BOSTON • HEIDELBERG • LONDON
NEW YORK • OXFORD • PARIS • SAN DIEGO
SAN FRANCISCO • SINGAPORE • SYDNEY • TOKYO
Morgan Kaufmann Publishers is an imprint of Elsevier

ELSEVIER

MORGAN KAUFMANN PUBLISHERS

Publisher	Diane D. Cerra
Publishing Services Manager	George Morrison
Project Manager	Marilyn E. Rash
Assistant Editor	Asma Palmeiro
Cover Image	Nordic Photos
Composition:	Multiscience Press, Inc.
Interior Printer	Sheridan Books
Cover Printer	Phoenix Color Corp.

Morgan Kaufmann Publishers is an imprint of Elsevier.
500 Sansome Street, Suite 400, San Francisco, CA 94111

∞ This book is printed on acid-free paper.

Library of Congress Cataloging-in-Publication Data
Lightstone, Sam.
  Physical database design : the database professional's guide to exploiting indexes,
  views, storage, and more / Sam Lightstone, Toby Teorey, and Tom Nadeau.
      p.   cm. -- (The Morgan Kaufmann series in database management systems)
  Includes bibliographical references and index.
  ISBN-13: 978-0-12-369389-1 (alk. paper)
  ISBN-10: 0-12-369389-6 (alk. paper)
  1. Database design.   I. Teorey, Toby J. II. Nadeau, Tom, 1958– III. Title.
  QA76.9.D26L54 2007
  005.74--dc22   2006102899

For information on all Morgan Kaufmann publications, visit our Web site at
www.mkp.com or www.books.elsevier.com

Printed in the United States of America
07 08 09 10 11   10 9 8 7 6 5 4 3 2 1

Contents

To my wife and children, Elisheva, Hodaya and Avishai
Sam Lightstone

To Bessie May Teorey and Bill Alton, my life mentors
Toby Teorey

To my father Paul, who was a man of integrity and compassion
Tom Nadeau

Preface

Since the development of the relational model by E. F. Codd at IBM in 1970, relational databases have become the de facto standard for managing and querying structured data. The rise of the Internet, online transaction processing, online banking, and the ability to connect heterogeneous systems have all contributed to the massive growth in data volumes over the past 15 years. Terabyte-sized databases have become commonplace. Concurrent with this data growth have come dramatic increases in CPU performance spurred by Moore's Law, and improvements in disk technology that have brought about a dramatic increase in data density for disk storage. Modern databases frequently need to support thousands if not tens of thousands of concurrent users. The performance and maintainability of database systems depends dramatically on their physical design.

A wealth of technologies has been developed by leading database vendors allowing for a fabulous range of physical design features and capabilities. Modern databases can now be sliced, diced, shuffled, and spun in a magnificent set of ways, both in memory and on disk. Until now, however, not much has been written on the topic of physical database design. While it is true that there have been white papers and articles about individual features and even individual products, relatively little has been written on the subject as a whole. Even less has been written to commiserate with database designers over the practical difficulties that the complexity of "creeping featurism" has imposed on the industry. This is all the more reason why a text on physical database design is urgently needed.

We've designed this new book with a broad audience in mind, with both students of database systems and industrial database professionals clearly within its scope. In it we introduce the major concepts in physical database design, including indexes (B+, hash, bitmap), materialized views (deferred and immediate), range partitioning, hash partitioning, shared-nothing design, multidimensional clustering, server topologies, data distribution, underlying physical subsystems (NUMA, SMP, MPP, SAN, NAS, RAID devices), and much more. In keeping with our goal of writing a book that had appeal to students and database professionals alike, we have tried to concentrate the focus on practical issues and real-world solutions.

In every market segment and in every usage of relational database systems there seems to be nowhere that the problems of physical database design are not a critical concern: from online transaction processing (OLTP), to data mining (DM), to multidimensional online analytical processing (MOLAP), to enterprise resource planning (ERP), to management resource planning (MRP), and in both in-house enterprise systems designed and managed by teams of database administrators (DBAs) and in deployed independent software vendor applications (ISVAs). We hope that the focus on physical database design, usage examples, product-specific syntax, and best practice, will make this book a very useful addition to the database literature.

Organization

An overview of physical database design and where it fits into the database life cycle appears in Chapter 1. Chapter 2 presents the fundamentals of B+tree indexing, the most popular indexing method used in the database industry today. Both simple indexing and composite indexing variations are described, and simple performance measures are used to help compare the different approaches. Chapter 3 is devoted to the basics of query optimization and query execution plan selection from the viewpoint of what a database professional needs to know as background for database design.

Chapters 4 through 8 discuss the individual important design decisions needed for physical database design. Chapter 4 goes into the details about how index selection is done, and what alternative indexing strategies one has to choose from for both selection and join operations. Chapter 5 describes how one goes about choosing materialized views for individual relational databases as well as setting up star schemas for collections of databases in data warehouses. The tradeoffs involved in materialized view selection are illustrated with numerical examples. Chapter 6 explains how to do shared-nothing partitioning to divide and conquer large and computationally complex database problems. The relationship between shared-nothing partitioning, materialized view replication, and indexing is presented.

Chapter 7 is devoted to range partitioning, dividing a large table into multiple smaller tables that hold a specific range of data, and the special indexing problems that need to be addressed. Chapter 8 discusses the benefits of clustering data in general, and how powerful this technique can be when extended to multidimensional data. This allows a system to cluster along multiple dimensions at the same time without duplicating data.

Chapter 9 discusses the problem of integrating the many physical design decisions by exploring how each decision affects the others, and leads the designer into ways to optimize the design over these many components. Chapter 10 looks carefully at methods of counting and sampling data that help improve the individual techniques of index design, materialized view selection, clustering, and partitioning. Chapter 11 goes more thoroughly into query execution plan selection by discussing tools that allow users to look at the query execution plans and observe whether database decisions on design choices, such as index selection and materialized views, are likely to be useful.

Chapter 12 contains a detailed description of how many of the important physical design decisions are automated by the major relational databases—DB2, SQL Server, and Oracle. It discusses how to use these tools to design efficient databases more quickly. Chapter 13 brings the database designer in touch with the many system issues they need to understand: multiprocessor servers, disk systems, network topologies, disaster recovery techniques, and memory management.

Chapter 14 discusses how physical design is needed to support data warehouses and the OLAP techniques for efficient retrieval of information from them. Chapter 15 defines what is meant by denormalization and illustrates the tradeoffs between degree of normalization and database performance. Finally, Chapter 16 looks at the basics of distributed data allocation strategies including the tradeoffs between the fast query response times due to data replication and the time cost of updates of multiple copies of data.

Appendix A briefly describes a simple computational performance model used to evaluate and compare different physical design strategies on individual databases. The model is used to clarify the tradeoff analysis and design decisions used in physical design methods in several chapters. Appendix B includes a comparison of two commercially available disaster-recovery technologies—IBM's High Availability Disaster Recovery and Oracle's Data Guard.

Each chapter has a tips and insights section for the database professional that gives the reader a useful summary of the design highlights of each chapter. This is followed by a literature summary for further investigation of selected topics on physical design by the reader.

Usage Examples

One of the major differences between logical and physical design is that with physical design the underlying features and physical attributes of the database server (its software and its hardware) begin to matter much more. While logical design can be performed in the abstract, somewhat independent of the products and components that will be used to materialize the design, the same cannot be said for physical design. For this reason we have made a deliberate effort to include examples in this second book of the major database server products in database server products about physical database design. In this set we include DB2 for zOS v8.1, DB2 9 (Linux, Unix, and Windows), Oracle 10g, SQL Server 2005, Informix Dataserver, and NCR Teradata. We believe that this covers the vast majority of industrial databases in use today. Some popular databases are conspicuously absent, such as MySQL and Sybase, which were excluded simply to constrain the authoring effort.

Literature Summaries and Bibliography

Following the style of the our earlier text on logical database design, *Database Modeling and Design: Logical Design, Fourth Edition*, each chapter concludes with a literature summary. These summaries include the major papers and references for the material covered in the chapter, specifically in two forms:

- Seminal papers that represent the original breakthrough thinking for the physical database design concepts discussed in the chapter.
- Major papers on the latest research and breakthrough thinking.

In addition to the chapter-centric literature summaries, a larger more comprehensive bibliography is included at the back of this book.

Feedback and Errata

If you have comments, we would like to hear from you. In particular, it's very valuable for us to get feedback on both changes that would improve the book as well as errors in the current content. To make this possible we've created an e-mail address to dialogue with our readers: please write to us at db-design@rogers.com.

> Has everyone noticed that all the letters of the word *database* are typed with the left hand? Now the layout of the QWERTY typewriter keyboard was designed among other things to facilitate the even use of both hands. It follows, therefore, that among other things, writing about databases is not only unnatural, but a lot harder than it appears.
>
> —*Anonymous*

While this quip may appeal to the authors who had to personally suffer through left-hand-only typing of the word *database* several hundred times in the authoring of this book,[1] if you substitute the words "writing about databases" with "designing data-

---

[1] Confession of a bad typist: I use my right hand for the t and b. This is an unorthodox but necessary variation for people who need to type the word "database" dozens of times per day.

bases," the statement rings even more powerfully true for the worldwide community of talented database designers.

Acknowledgments

As with any text of this breadth, there are many people aside from the authors who contribute to the reviewing, editing, and publishing that make the final text what it is. We'd like to pay special thanks to the following people from a range of companies and consulting firms who contributed to the book: Sanjay Agarwal, Eric Alton, Hermann Baer, Kevin Beck, Surajit Chaudhuri, Kitman Cheung, Leslie Cranston, Yuri Deigin, Chris Eaton, Scott Fadden, Lee Goddard, Peter Haas, Scott Hayes, Lilian Hobbs, John Hornibrook, Martin Hubel, John Kennedy, Eileen Lin, Guy Lohman, Wenbin Ma, Roman Melnyk, Mughees Minhas, Vivek Narasayya, Jack Raitto, Haider Rizvi, Peter Shum, Danny Zilio and Calisto Zuzarte. Thank you to Linda Peterson and Rebekah Smith for their help with manuscript preparation.

We also would like to thank the reviewers of this book who provided a number of extremely valuable insights. Their in-depth reviews and new directions helped us produce a much better text. Thank you to Mike Blaha, Philippe Bonnet, Philipe Carino, and Patrick O'Neil. Thank you as well to the concept reviewers Bob Muller, Dorian Pyle, James Bean, Jim Gray, and Michael Blaha.

We would like to thank our wives and children for their support and for allowing us the time to work on this project, often into the wee hours of the morning.

To the community of students and database designers worldwide, we salute you. Your job is far more challenging and complex than most people realize. Each of the possible design attributes in a modern relational database system is very complex in its own right. Tackling all of them, as real database designers must, is a remarkable challenge that by all accounts ought to be impossible for mortal human beings. In fact, optimal database design can be shown mathematically to truly be impossible for any moderately involved system. In one analysis we found that the possible design choices for an average database far exceeded the current estimates of the number of atoms in the universe (10^{81}) by several orders of magnitude! And yet, despite the massive complexity and sophistication of modern database systems, you have managed to study them, master them, and continue to design them. The world's data is literally in your hands. We hope this book will be a valuable tool for you. By helping you, the students and designers of database systems, we hope this book will also lead in a small incremental but important way to improvements in the world's data management infrastructure.

Engineering is a great profession. There is the satisfaction of watching a figment of the imagination emerge through the aid of science to a plan on paper. Then it moves to realization in stone or metal or energy. Then it brings homes to men or women. Then it elevates the standard of living and adds to the comforts of life. This is the engineer's high privilege.

—Herbert Hoover (1874–1964)

The most likely way for the world to be destroyed, most experts agree, is by accident. That's where we come in; we're computer professionals. We cause accidents.

—Nathaniel Borenstein (1957–)

Introduction to Physical Database Design

I have not lost my mind. It's backed up on disk somewhere.
—Unknown

There was a great debate at the annual ACM SIGFIDET (now SIGMOD) meeting in Ann Arbor, Michigan, in 1974 between Ted Codd, the creator of the relational database model, and Charlie Bachman, the technical creative mind behind the network database model and the subsequent CODASYL report. The debate centered on which logical model was the best database model, and it had continued on in the academic journals and trade magazines for almost 30 more years until Codd's death in 2003. Since that original debate, many database systems have been built to support each of these models, and although the relational model eventually dominated the database industry, the underlying physical database structures used by both types of systems were actually evolving in sync. Originally the main decision for physical design was the type of indexing the system was able to do, with B+tree indexing eventually dominating the scene for almost all systems. Later, other concepts like clustering and partitioning became important, but these methods were becoming less and less related to the logical structures being debated in the 1970s.

Logical database design, that is, the design of basic data relationships and their definition in a particular database system, is largely the domain of application designers and programmers. The work of these designers can effectively be done with tools, such as ERwin Data Modeller or Rational Rose with UML, as well as with a purely manual approach. Physical database design, the creation of efficient data storage, and retrieval mechanisms on the computing platform you are using are typically the domain of the database administrator (DBA), who has a variety of vendor-supplied tools available today to help design the most efficient databases. This book is devoted to the physical design methodologies and tools most popular for relational databases today. We use examples from the most common systems—Oracle, DB2 (IBM), and SQL Server (Microsoft)—to illustrate the basic concepts.

1.1   Motivation—The Growth of Data and Increasing Relevance of Physical Database Design

Does physical database design really matter? Absolutely. Some computing professionals currently run their own consulting businesses doing little else than helping customers improve their table indexing design. Impressive as this is, what is equally astounding are claims about improving the performance of problem queries by as much as 50 times. Physical database design is really motivated by data volume. After all, a database with a few rows of data really has no issues with physical database design, and the performance of applications that access a tiny database cannot be deeply affected by the physical design of the underlying system. In practical terms, index selection really does not matter much for a database with 20 rows of data. However, as data volumes rise, the physical structures that underlie its access patterns become increasingly critical.

A number of factors are spurring the dramatic growth of data in all three of its captured forms: structured (relational tuples), semistructured (e.g., XML), and unstructured data (e.g., audio/video). Much of the growth can be attributed to the rapid expansion and ubiquitous use of networked computers and terminals in every home, business, and store in the industrialized world. The data volumes are now taking a further leap forward with the rapid adoption of personal communication devices like cell phones and PDAs, which are also networked and used to share data. Databases measured in the tens of terabytes have now become commonplace in enterprise systems. Following the mapping of the human genome's three billion chemical base pairs, pharmaceutical companies are now exploring genetic engineering research based on the networks of proteins that overlay the human genomes, resulting in data analysis on databases several petabytes in size (a petabyte is one thousand terabytes, or one million gigabytes). Table 1.1 shows data from a 1999 survey performed by the University of California at Berkeley. You can see in this study that the data stored on magnetic disk is growing at a rate of 100% per year for departmental and enterprise servers. In fact nobody is sure exactly where the growth patterns will end, or if they ever will.

There's something else special that has happened that's driving up the data volumes. It happened so quietly that seemingly nobody bothered to mention it, but the change is quantitative and profound. Around the year 2000 the price of storage dropped to a point where it became cheaper to store data on computer disks than on paper (Figure

Table 1.1   Worldwide Production of Original Content, Stored Digitally, in Terabytes[*]

Storage Medium	Type of Content	Terabytes/Year, Upper Estimate	Terabytes/Year, Lower Estimate	Growth Rate, %
Paper	Books	8	1	2
	Newspapers	25	2	−2
	Periodicals	12	1	2
	Office documents	195	19	2
	Subtotal:	**240**	**23**	**2**
Film	Photographs	410,000	41,000	5
	Cinema	16	16	3
	X-Rays	17,200	17,200	2
	Subtotal:	**427,216**	**58,216**	**4**
Optical	Music CDs	58	6	3
	Data CDs	3	3	2
	DVDs	22	22	100
	Subtotal:	**83**	**31**	**70**
Magnetic	Camcorder Tape	300,000	300,000	5
	PC Disk Driver	766,000	7,660	100
	Departmental Servers	460,000	161,000	100
	Enterprise Servers	167,000	108,550	100
	Subtotal:	**1,693,000**	**577,210**	**55**
TOTAL:		**2,120,539**	**635,480**	**50**

[*] *Source:* University of California at Berkeley study, 1999.

1.1). In fact this probably was a great turning point in the history of the development of western civilization. For over 2,000 years civilization has stored data in written text—on parchment, papyrus, or paper. Suddenly and quietly that paradigm has begun to sunset. Now the digitization of text is not only of interest for sharing and analysis, but it is also more economical.

The dramatic growth patterns change the amount of data that relational database systems must access and manipulate, but they do not change the speed at which operations must complete. In fact, to a large degree, the execution goals for data processing systems are defined more by human qualities than by computers: the time a person is willing to wait for a transaction to complete while standing at an automated banking machine or the number of available off-peak hours between closing time of a business in the evening and the resumption of business in the morning. These are constraints that are defined largely by what humans expect and they are quite independent of the data volumes being operated on. While data volumes and analytic complexity are growing

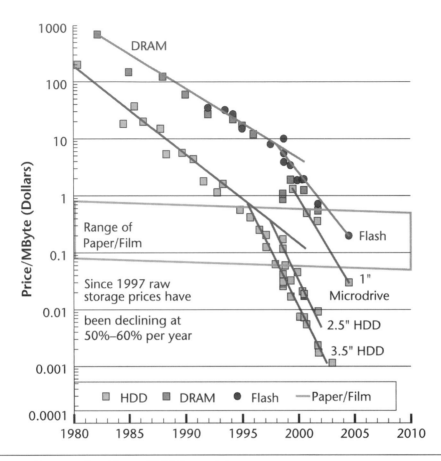

Figure 1.1   Storage price. (*Source:* IBM Research.)

rapidly, our expectations as humans are changing at a much slower rate. Some relief is found in the increasing power of modern data servers because as the data volumes grow, the computing power behind them is increasing as well. However, the phenomenon of increasing processing power is mitigated by the need to consolidate server technology to reduce IT expenses, so as a result, as servers grow in processing power they are often used for an increasing number of purposes rather than being used to perform a single purpose faster.

Although CPU power has been improving following Moore's Law, doubling roughly every 18 months since the mid 1970s, disk speeds have been increasing at a more modest pace (see Chapter 13 for a more in-depth discussion of Moore's Law). Finally, data is increasingly being used to detect "information" not just process "data," and the rise of on-line analytical processing (OLAP) and data mining and other forms of business intelligence computing has led to a dramatic increase in the complexity of the processing that is required.

These factors motivate the need for complex and sophisticated approaches to physical database design. Why? By exploiting design techniques a practitioner can reduce the processing time for operations in some cases by several orders of magnitude. Improving computational efficiency by a thousand times is real, and valuable; and when you're waiting at the bank machine to get your money, or waiting for an analysis of business trading that will influence a multimillion dollar investment decision, it's downright necessary.

1.2 Database Life Cycle

The database life cycle incorporates the basic steps involved in designing a logical database from conceptual modeling of user requirements through database management system (DBMS) specific table definitions, and a physical database that is indexed, partitioned, clustered, and selectively materialized to maximize real performance. For a distributed database, physical design also involves allocating data across a computer network. Once the design is completed, the life cycle continues with database implementation and maintenance. The database life cycle is shown in Figure 1.2. Physical database design (step 3 below) is defined in the context of the entire database life cycle to show its relationship to the other design steps.

1. *Requirements analysis.* The database requirements are determined by interviewing both the producers and users of data and producing a formal requirements specification. That specification includes the data required for processing, the natural data relationships, and the software platform for the database implementation.

2. *Logical database design.* Logical database design develops a conceptual model of the database from a set of user requirements and refines that model into normalized SQL tables. The goal of logical design is to capture the reality of the user's world in terms of data elements and their relationships so that queries and updates to that data can be programmed easily. The *global schema*, a conceptual data model diagram that shows all the data and their relationships, is developed using techniques such as entity-relationship (ER) modeling or the Unified Modeling Language (UML). The data model constructs must ultimately be integrated into a single global schema and then transformed into normalized SQL tables. Normalized tables (particularly third normal form or 3NF) are tables that are decomposed or split into smaller tables to eliminate loss of data integrity due to certain delete commands.

   We note here that some database tool vendors use the term *logical model* to refer to the conceptual data model, and they use the term *physical model* to refer

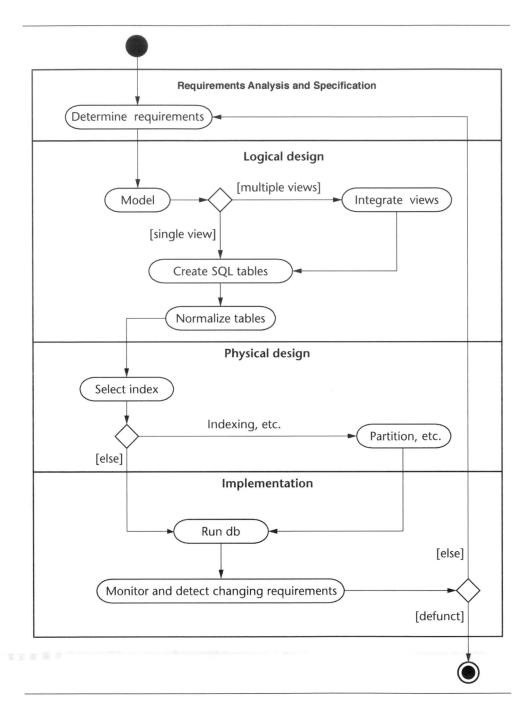

Figure 1.2   Database life cycle.

to the DBMS-specific implementation model (e.g., SQL tables). We also note that many conceptual data models are obtained not from scratch, but from the process of *reverse engineering* from an existing DBMS-specific schema [Silberschatz 2006]. Our definition of the physical model is given below.

3. *Physical database design.* The physical database design step involves the selection of indexes, partitioning, clustering, and selective materialization of data. Physical database design (as treated in this book) begins after the SQL tables have been defined and normalized. It focuses on the methods of storing and accessing those tables on disk that enable the database to operate with high efficiency. The goal of physical design is to maximize the performance of the database across the entire spectrum of applications written on it. The physical resources that involve time delays in executing database applications include the CPU, I/O (e.g., disks), and computer networks. Performance is measured by the time delays to answer a query or complete an update for an individual application, and also by the throughput (in transactions per second) for the entire database system over the full set of applications in a specified unit of time.

4. *Database implementation, monitoring, and modification.* Once the logical and physical design is completed, the database can be created through implementation of the formal schema using the data definition language (DDL) of a DBMS. Then the data manipulation language (DML) can be used to query and update the database, as well as to set up indexes and establish constraints such as referential integrity. The language SQL contains both DDL and DML constructs; for example, the "create table" command represents DDL, and the "select" command represents DML.

As the database begins operation, monitoring indicates whether performance requirements are being met. If they are not being satisfied, modifications should be made to improve performance. Other modifications may be necessary when requirements change or end-user expectations increase with good performance. Thus, the life cycle continues with monitoring, redesign, and modifications.

1.3 Elements of Physical Design: Indexing, Partitioning, and Clustering

The physical design of a database starts with the schema definition of logical records produced by the logical design phase. A *logical record* (or record) is a named collection of data items or attributes treated as a unit by an application program. In storage, a record includes the pointers and record overhead needed for identification and processing by the database management system. A *file* is typically a set of similarly constructed records of one type, and relational tables are typically stored as files. A *physical database* is a collection of interrelated records of different types, possibly including a collection of inter-related files. Query and update transactions to a database are made efficient by the implementation of certain search methods as part of the database management system.

1.3.1 Indexes

An *index* is a data organization set up to speed up the retrieval (query) of data from tables. In database management systems, indexes can be specified by database application programmers using the following SQL commands:

```
CREATE UNIQUE INDEX supplierNum ON supplier(snum);
/*unique index on a key*/
```

A unique index is a data structure (table) whose entries (records) consist of attribute value, pointer pairs such that each pointer contains the block address of an actual database record that has the associated attribute value as an index key value. This is known as an ordered index because the attribute (key) values in the index are ordered as ASCII values. If all the key values are letters, then the ordering is strictly alphabetical. Ordered indexes are typically stored as B+trees so that the search for the matching key value is fast. Once the key value and corresponding data block pointer are found, there is one more step to access the block containing the record you want, and a quick search in memory of that block to find the record.

Sometimes data is better accessed by an attribute other than a key, an attribute that typically has the same value appear in many records. In a unique index based on a key, the key has a unique value in every record. For a nonunique attribute, an index must have multiple attribute, pointer pairs for the same attribute value, and each pointer has the block address of a record that has one of those attribute values. In the B+tree index, the leaf nodes contain these attribute, pointer pairs that must be searched to find the records that match the attribute value. The SQL command for this kind of index, also called a secondary index, is:

```
CREATE INDEX shippingDate ON shipment (shipdate);
/*secondary index on non-key*/
```

In a variation of the secondary or nonunique index, it is possible to set up a collection of attribute values that you want to use to query a table. Each entry in the index consists of a set of attribute values and a block pointer to the record that contains exact matches for all those attribute values in the set. An example of an SQL command to set up this kind of index is:

```
CREATE INDEX shipPart ON shipment (pnum, shipdate);
/*secondary concatenated index*/
```

This kind of index is extremely efficient for queries involving both a part number (pnum) and shipping date (shipdate). For queries involving just one of these attributes, it is less efficient because of its greater size and therefore longer search time.

When we want to improve the query time for a table of data, say for instance the table we access via the nonunique index on ship dates, we could organize the database so that equivalent ship dates are stored near each other (on disk), and ship dates that are close to each other in value are stored near each other. This type index is called a *clustered index*. Otherwise the index is known as a *nonclustered index*. There can only be one clustered index per table because the physical organization of the table must be fixed.

When the physical database table is unordered, it can be organized for efficient access using a *hash table index* often simply known as a *hash index*. This type of index is most frequently based on a key that has unique values in the data records. The attribute (key) value is passed through a function that maps it to a starting block address, known as a *bucket address*. The table must be set up by inserting all the records according to the hash function, and then using the same hash function to query the records later.

Another variation of indexing, a *bitmap index*, is commonly used for secondary indexing with multiple attribute values, and for very large databases in data warehouses. A bitmap index consists of a collection of bit vectors, with each bit vector corresponding to a particular attribute value, and for each record in the table, the bit vector is a "1" if that record has the designated bit vector value, and "0" if it does not. This is particularly useful if an attribute is sparse, that is, it has very few possible values, like gender or course grade. It would not work well for attributes like last name, job title, age, and so on. Bit vectors can be stored and accessed very efficiently, especially if they are small enough to be located in memory.

The analysis and design of indexes are discussed in detail in Chapters 2 and 4.

1.3.2 Materialized Views

When one or more tables are queried, the result can be stored in what is called a *materialized view*. Normally, views in SQL are stored as definitions or templates, but materialized views are stored as tables in the database just like any other table. In data warehouses, materialized views are maintained as aggregates of data in the base tables. These kinds of views are very useful to speed up queries of data that have been asked before (and frequently), or queries based on aggregates of data that can build on materialized views to answer the question instead of having to go back to the original data each time. Potentially a great deal of query time savings can be realized if the proper set of materialized views is stored. It is usually impossible to store all possible views because of storage space limitations, so some means must be found to focus on the best set of views to materialize. There is also a problem with updates—when base tables are updated, this cascades into the materialized views, which are derived from the base tables. The problem of multiple updates makes the use of materialized views less efficient, and this must be taken into account in their design and usage. This is discussed in more detail in Chapter 5.

1.3.3 Partitioning and Multidimensional Clustering

Partitioning in physical database design is a method for reducing the workload on any one hardware component, like an individual disk, by partitioning (dividing) the data over several disks. This has the effect of balancing the workload across the system and preventing bottlenecks. In range partitioning, the data attribute values are sorted and ranges of values are selected so that each range has roughly the same number of records. Records in a given range are allocated to a specific disk so it can be processed independently of other ranges. The details of partitioning across disks are discussed in Chapter 7.

Multidimensional clustering (MDC) is a technique by which data can be clustered by dimensions, such as location, timeframe, or product type. In particular, MDC allows data to be clustered by many dimensions at the same time, such as ice skates sold in Wisconsin during the month of December. The clusters are meant to take advantage of known and anticipated workloads on this data. MDC is developed in detail in Chapter 8.

1.3.4 Other Methods for Physical Database Design

There are many other ways to make data access more efficient in a database. For instance, data *compression* is a technique that allows more data to fit into a fixed amount of space (on disk) and therefore accessed faster if data needs to be scanned a lot. The overhead for compression is in the algorithm to transform the original data into the compressed form for storage, and then to transform the compressed form back to the original for display purposes.

Data striping, or just *striping*, is a technique for distributing data that needs to be accessed together across multiple disks to achieve a greater degree of parallelism and load balancing, both of which makes system throughput increase and generally lowers query times. This is particularly suited to disk array architectures like RAID (redundant arrays of independent disks) where data can be accessed in parallel across multiple disks in an organized way.

Another way to improve database reliability includes data redundancy techniques like *mirroring*, in which data is duplicated on multiple disks. The downside of redundancy is having to update multiple copies of data each time a change is required in the database, as well as the extra storage space required. Storage space is getting cheaper every day, but time is not. On the other hand, data that is never or infrequently updated may lend itself nicely to be stored redundantly.

As part of the physical design, the global schema can sometimes be refined in limited ways to reflect processing (query and transaction) requirements if there are obvious large gains to be made in efficiency. This is called *denormalization*. It consists of selecting dominant processes on the basis of high frequency, high volume, or explicit priority; defining simple extensions to tables that will improve query performance; evaluating total cost for query, update, and storage; and considering the side effects, such as possible loss of integrity. Details are given in Chapter 15.

1.4 Why Physical Design Is Hard

Physical database design involves dozens and often hundreds of variables, which are difficult to keep track of, especially when their effects are very often interrelated to the various design solutions proposed. The individual computations of performance based on a given index mechanism or partition algorithm may take several hours by hand, and performance analysis is often based on the comparison of many different configurations and load conditions, thus requiring thousands of computations. This has given rise to automated tools such as IBM's DB2 Design Advisor, Oracle's SQL Access Advisor, Oracle's SQL Tuning Advisor, and Microsoft's Database Tuning Advisor (DTA), formerly known as the Index Tuning Wizard. These tools make database tuning and performance analysis manageable, allowing the analyst to focus on solutions and tradeoffs while taking care of the myriad of computations that are needed. We will look at both manual analysis and automatic design tools for physical database design in this book.

TIPS AND INSIGHTS FOR DATABASE PROFESSIONALS

- **Tip 1. The truth is out there, but you may not need it.** Every database has a theoretically perfect, or "optimal", physical design. In reality almost nobody ever finds it because the search complexity is too high and the validation process too cumbersome. Database design is really hard problem. However, the complexity is mitigated by the practical fact that at the end of the day what matters most is not whether the database performance is as good as it can theoretically be, but whether the applications that use the database perform "good enough" so that their users are satisfied. Good enough is a vague and subjective definition of course. In most cases, while the perfect database design is usually elusive, one that performs more than 85% of optimal can be achieved by mere mortals.

- **Tip 2. Be prepared to tinker.** The possibilities are endless, and you will never be able to explore them all. But with some wisdom and insight you and some playing around with possibilities you can go far. Trial and error is part of the process.

- **Tip 3. Use the tools at your disposal.** Throughout this book we will describe various techniques and methods for physcal database design. Many database design perform an order of magnitude worse than they could simply because the designer didn't bother to use the techniques available. Database designs does not begin and end with simple single column index selection. By exploiting features like memory tuning, materialized views, range partitioning, multidimensional clustering, clustering indexes, or shared nothing partitioning you can dramatically improve on a basic database design, especially for complex query processing.

1.5 Literature Summary

Database system and design textbooks and practitioners' guides that give serious attention to the principles of physical database design include Burleson [2005], Elmasri and Navathe [2003], Garcie-Molina, Ullman, and Widom [2000, 2001], Ramakrishnan and Gehrke [2004], Shasha and Bonnet [2003], and Silberschatz, Korth, and Sudarshan [2006].

Knowledge of logical data modeling and physical database design techniques is important for database practitioners and application developers. The database life cycle shows what steps are needed in a methodical approach to database design from logical design, which is independent of the system environment, to physical design, which is based on maximizing the performance of the database under various workloads.

Agarwal, S., Chaudhuri, S., Kollar, L., Maranthe, A., Narasayya, V., and Syamala, M. Database Tuning Advisor for Microsoft SQL Server 2005. *30th Very Large Database Conference (VLDB)*, Toronto, Canada, 2004.

Burleson, D. *Physical Database Design Using Oracle.* Boca Raton, FL: Auerbach Publishers, 2005.

Elmasri, R., and Navathe, S. B. *Fundamentals of Database Systems.* Boston: Addison-Wesley, 4th ed. Redwood City, CA, 2004.

Garcia-Molina, H., Ullman, J., and Widom, J. *Database System Implementation.* Englewood Cliffs, NJ: Prentice-Hall, 2000.

Garcia-Molina, H., Ullman, J., and Widom, J. *Database Systems: The Complete Book.* Englewood Cliffs, NJ: Prentice-Hall, 2001.

Oracle—SQL Tuning Advisor, at
http://www.oracle-base.com/articles/10g/AutomaticSQLTuning10g.php.

Ramakrishnan, R., and Gehrke, J. *Database Management Systems*, 3rd ed. New York: McGraw-Hill, 2004.

Shasha, D., and Bonnet, P. *Database Tuning*. San Francisco: Morgan Kaufmann, 2003.

Silberschatz, A., Korth, H. F., and Sudarshan, S. *Database System Concepts,* 5th ed. New York: McGraw-Hill, 2006.

Zilio, D.C., Rao, J., Lightstone, S., Lohman, G.M., Storm, A., Garcia-Arellano, C., and Fadden, S. DB2 Design Advisor: Integrated Automatic Physical Database Design. VLDB 2004, Toronto, Canada, 1087-1097.

Basic Indexing Methods

*If you don't find it in the index, look very carefully
through the entire catalogue.*
—Sears, Roebuck, and Co., *Consumer's Guide*, 1897

The concept of indexing for dictionaries, encyclopedias, book manuscripts, catalogs, and address lists has been around for centuries. Methods like tabs in a book volume or lists of index terms at the back of the book are used very effectively. When a computer needs to find data within a relational database it has exactly the same need. How can a small amout of data be found from within a very large sct without "looking very carefully through the entire thing catalog." For example, consider how inefficient life would be if every time you walked over to an ATM machine to withdraw money the bank's computer performed a linear search through possibly millions of customer records until it found the entry matching your bank account number. Large electronic files and databases have accelerated the need for indexing methods that can access a subset of the data quickly. In some cases the data is very small and can be accessed in a single input/output (I/O) operation.

In other cases data needs to be accessed in bulk and looked over by an analyst to determine which data is relevant to the current need. In the late 1970s, indexing for the earliest relational, hierarchical (like IMS), and CODASYL databases was done in a wide variety of ways: sequential, indexed sequential, hashing, binary search trees, B-trees, TRIE structures, multilist files, inverted files, and doubly chained trees to name a few. Many options were allowed for programmers to choose from, and the choice of the best method for a particular database was a complex decision, requiring considerable formal training. For other types of databases—object-oriented, spatial, temporal, and so on—the list of potential indexing strategies (R-trees for instance) goes on and will continue to evolve for the foreseeable future.

Fortunately, for relational databases, the B+tree has properties that span virtually all of the methods mentioned above and has become the de facto indexing method for the major relational database systems today. This chapter discusses the basic principles of indexing used in today's database systems to enhance performance.

2.1 B+tree Index

The B+tree is the primary indexing method supported by DB2, Oracle, and SQL Server. It features not only fast access, but also the dynamic maintenance that virtually eliminates the overflow problems that occur in the older hashing and indexed sequential methods. Let's take a look at a typical B+tree configuration in Figure 2.1. Each nonleaf index node consists of p tree pointers and p-1 key values. The key values denote where to search to find rows that have either smaller key values, by taking the tree pointer to the left of the key, or great or equal key values by taking the tree pointer to the right of the key. Each leaf index node consists of a series of key and data-pointer combinations that point to each row. The leaf index nodes (and the associated data blocks) are connected logically by block pointers so that an ordered sequence of rows can be found quickly. The variable p represents the *order* of the B+tree, the fan-out of pointers from one node to the next lower node in the tree.

The *height* of a B+tree is the level of the leaf nodes, given that the root node is defined as Level 1. In Figure 2.1, the order of the B+tree is four and the height is three.

The intermmediate nodes help the database find the desired leaf nodes with very few I/Os. However, what's stored within the leaf nodes is the real meat. The leaf nodes will store three very important things: the key, a record identifier (RID) and a pointer to the next leaf. For example, if the index is defined on a CITY column, the keys of the index may include NEW YORK, BOSTON, TORONTO, SAN JOSE. For each city the index will include an identifier of where to find each record in the table that matches the key. Consider a search through the index where the key value is 'NEW YORK'. If the table has 400 entries for NEW YORK, the index leaf node will include one key entry for NEW YORK and identifiers for where to find each of the 400 records in the base table. These identifier are called record identifiers, or RIDs, and will be discussed next. The key and the RIDs are the two most critical parts of the leaf content.

Keys are stored within the leaf pages in sorted order. As a result while B+tree indexes can be used by the DBMS to find a row or set or rows that match a single key, they can also be used to easily find a range of keys (i.e., a numeric range or alphabetic range) as well as implicitly return records in sorted order.

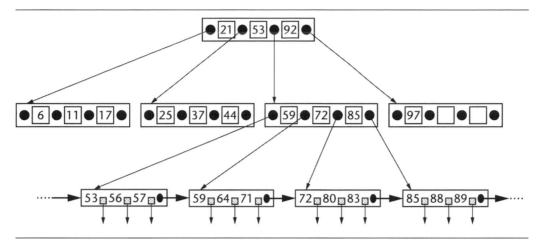

Figure 2.1   B+tree configuration (order four, height three).

Example: Determine the Order and Height of a B+tree

To determine the order of a B+tree, let us assume that the database has 500,000 rows of 200 bytes each, the search key is 15 bytes, the tree and data pointers are 5 bytes, and the index node (and data block size) is 1,024 bytes. For this configuration we have

$$\text{Nonleaf index node size} = 1{,}024 \text{ bytes} = p \times 5 + (p - 1) \times 15 \text{ bytes.}$$

Solving for the order of the B+tree, p, we get:

$$p = \text{floor}((1{,}024 + 15)/20) = \text{floor}(51.95) = 51, \qquad 2.1$$

where the floor function is the next lower whole number, found by truncating the actual value to the next lower integer. Therefore, we can have up to $p - 1$ or 50 search key values in each nonleaf index node. In the leaf index nodes there are 15 bytes for the search key value and 5 bytes for the data pointer. Each leaf index node has a single pointer to the next leaf index node to make a scan of the data rows possible without going through the index-level nodes. In this example the number of search key values in the leaf nodes is floor $((1{,}024 - 5)/(15 + 5)) = 50$, which is the same number of search key values in the nonleaf nodes as well.

The height h of a B+tree is the number of index levels, including the leaf nodes. It is computed by noting that the root index node (ith level) has p pointers, the i-1st level has p^2 tree pointers, i-2nd level has p^3 tree pointers, and so on. At the leaf level the number of key entries and pointers is $p - 1$ per index node, but a good approximation can be made by assuming that the leaf index nodes are implemented with p pointers and

p key values. The total number of pointers over all nodes at that level (h) must be greater than or equal to the number of rows in the table (n). Therefore, our estimate becomes

$$p^h > n$$
$$h \log p > \log n$$
$$h > \log n / \log p \qquad \qquad 2.2$$

In this case, for n = 500,000 rows and p = 50 pointers per node, the height (h) of the B+tree becomes $h > 3.35$ or $h = 4$.

A query to a particular row in a B+tree is simply the time required to access all h levels of the tree index plus the access to the data row (within a block or page). All accesses to different levels of index and data are assumed to be random.

$$\text{Read a single row in a table (using a B+tree)}$$
$$= h + 1 \text{ block accesses.} \qquad \qquad 2.3$$

Updates of rows in a B+tree can be accomplished with a simple query and rewrite unless the update involves an insertion that overflows a data or index node or a deletion that empties a data or index node. A rewrite of a row just read tends to be a random block access in a shared disk environment, which we assume here. For the simple case of updating data values in a particular row, assume that each index node is implemented as a block.

$$\text{Update cost for a single row (B+tree)}$$
$$= \text{search cost} + \text{rewrite data block}$$
$$= (h + 1) + 1$$
$$= h + 2 \text{ block accesses,} \qquad \qquad 2.4$$

where a block access is assumed to be an access to an individual block (or page) in a shared disk environment.

If the operation desired is an insertion and the insertion causes overflow of a data or leaf index node, additional accesses are needed to split the saturated node into two nodes that are half filled (using the basic splitting algorithm) plus the need to rewrite the next higher index node with a new pointer to the new index node (see Figure 2.2). The need for a split is recognized after the initial search for the row has been done. A split of an leaf index node requires a rewrite of the saturated leaf index node, half filled with data, plus a write of a new leaf index node also half filled, plus a rewrite of the non-leaf index node with a new pointer value to the new leaf index node.

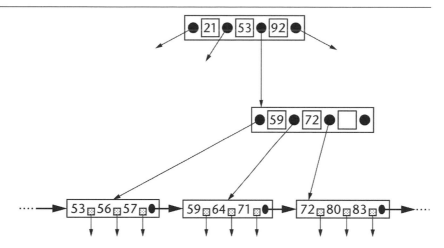

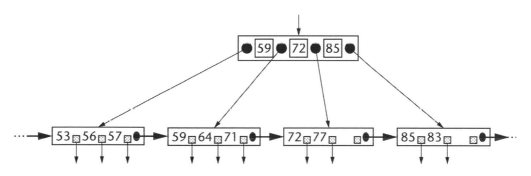

(a) B⁺- tree before the insertion of record with key value 77

(b) B⁺- tree after the insertion and split block operation

Figure 2.2   Dynamic maintenance for a B+tree row insertion.

Insert cost for a single row (B+tree)
= search cost + rewrite data block + rewrite index block
= $(h + 1) + 1 + 1$
= $h + 3$ block accesses,   2.5

plus additional writes, if necessary, for splitting.

    Occasionally, the split operation of an leaf index node necessitates a split of the next higher index node as well, and in the worst case the split operations may cascade all the way up to the index root node. The probability of additional splits depends on the type of splitting algorithm and the dynamics of insertions and deletions in the workload. Database statistics can be collected to determine these probabilities.

Deletions may result in emptying a data block or index node, which necessitates the consolidation of two nodes into one. This may require a rewrite of the leaf index node to reset its pointers. The empty data node can be either left alone or rewritten with nulls, depending on the implementation. We will assume that the node where data is deleted need not be rewritten. Occasionally the leaf or nonleaf nodes become empty and need consolidation as well. Thus, we obtain the cost of deletion:

Delete cost for a single row (B+tree)
= search cost + rewrite data block + rewrite index block
= $(h + 1) + 1 + 1$
= $h + 3$ block accesses,   2.6

plus additional writes, if necessary, for consolidation.

Example: Cost Computation

As an example, consider the insertion of a node (with key value 77) to the B+tree shown in Figure 2.2. This insertion requires a search phase and an insertion phase with one split node, which demands a rewrite of the data entry plus a rewrite of an index entry. The total insertion cost for height three on a shared disk is

Insertion cost = search cost + rewrite data block
+ rewrite index block + split rewrites
= $(h + 1) + 1 + 1 + 2$ split rewrites (for data and index blocks)
= 8 block accesses.   2.7

If we use the disk model in Appendix A, the expected time for a block access in a shared disk for a typical 4 KB block is 5.6 ms. For this situation, the insertion cost for a single row is 8 block accesses × 5.6 ms = 44.8 ms.

For large-scale updating of databases with millions of records, economy of scale can be reached in insertions and updates in general with batch processing, which takes advantage of the greater efficiency of large data access using table scans.

2.2 **Composite Index Search**

A single index can be defined on more than one table column. Specfically the index key can be composed of more than one value. For example, consider an index on both CITY and STATE. Many states have towns with the same name so city name alone is inadequate to uniquely identify a place (there are at least 24 US towns with the name

"Athens" for example). An index defined with a key that contains more than one column is known as a composite index.

Composite indexes can be used to efficiently search a database table, given a more complex SQL search criterion. As an example, the query

```
SELECT empNo, empName, empAddress, jobTitle
    FROM employee
    WHERE jobTitle = 'database administrator'
    AND city = 'Los Angeles'
    AND totalPur < 500;
```

results in the access to a set of target rows in the employee table that is typically a small subset of the entire population of rows, but usually significantly more than a single row. Using search methods based on a single attribute key will not work here, and frequent exhaustive scans of the entire base table are usually prohibitively expensive.

We can easily extend the B+tree indexing method to handle more complex queries of this type, commonly implemented in all the major database management systems (DBMSs). In Section 2.2, we used B+trees to implement the concept of a unique index based on a primary key, and accessing a single row. Now we wish to use the same general structure to implement a nonunique index capable of accessing a set of rows that satisfy a query with WHERE and AND conditions. In a unique index, the nonleaf nodes contain key-pointer pairs where the key is the primary key of the table you want to access. In a nonunique index, the key field is a concatenation of all the attributes you want to set up to access the set of rows desired. We form a nonunique index key by concatenating the secondary keys for job title, city, and total amount of purchases, as shown in the example in Figure 2.3.

The leaf nodes for unique indexes contain the complete set of primary key values, with each key value paired with a pointer to the block containing the row with the given primary key value. For the nonunique leaf nodes, we also have key-pointer pairs, but the key values are the complete set of all combinations of the composite key that actually occur in existing rows. If a composite key value occurs in k rows, then there are k key-pointer pairs required to point to those rows, with the given key value repeated k times.

The analysis of a B+tree composite index proceeds in the same way as for a simple key index, with the new definition of key fields accounting for the composite of attributes. We note that this method of accessing the k target rows once at the end of the B+tree search of concatenated keys is much faster than searching for the target rows over and over for each individual key using multiple simple indexes. It is certainly possible to do this, but for k keys in the composite index, you would have to search the index k times, and for each time, retrieve far more pointers to target rows for that key than you would for the k rows that have the specific values you are looking for in all keys. We illustrate this efficiency in the example that follows.

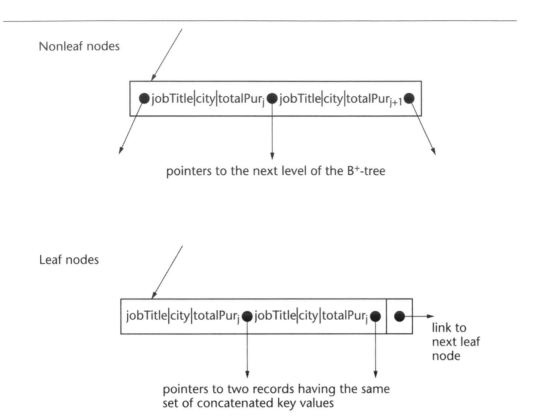

Figure 2.3   Using a B+tree for multiple indexes.

Example: Mail-order Business

Assume we have a table of 10 million rows of mail-order customers for a large commercial business. Customer rows have attributes for customer name, customer number, street address, city, state, zip code, phone number, e-mail, employer, job title, credit rating, date of last purchase, and total amount of purchases. Assume that the average row size is 250 bytes; block size is 5,000 bytes; pointer size, including row offset, is 5 bytes; and composite key for jobTitle, city, and totalPur is 35 bytes. The table of 10 million rows has 500,000 blocks since each block contains 20 rows. In general, rows tend to be variable length, but for simplicity we assume they are equal length here.

The query to be analyzed is

```
SELECT empNo, empName, empAddress, empPhone, empEmail
FROM customer
WHERE jobTitle = 'software engineer'
```

```
AND city = 'Chicago'
AND totalPur > 1000;
```

For each AND condition we have the following hit rates, that is, rows that satisfy each condition:

- Job title (jobTitle) is 'software engineer': 84,000 rows.
- City (city) is 'Chicago': 210,000 rows.
- Total amount of purchases (totalPur) > $1,000: 350,000 rows.
- Total number of target rows that satisfy all three conditions = 750.

If we were to satisfy this query with separate index searches for each individual key, we would have to locate all 85,000 pointers to job title 'software engineer', all 200,000 pointers to 'Chicago', and all 50,000 pointers to '>1000'. Then we would have the additional step of merging all three lists of pointers to find the 750 intersection rows with all three key values we want. If we assume the total of 84,000 + 210,000 + 350,000 = 644,000 pointers fit into blocks holding (5,000 bytes/35 bytes = 142) pointers each, the estimated cost of using the three index approach is:

Query cost
= three index search cost + merge pointer cost
+ final data access cost
= (h1 + 1) + (h2 + 1) + (h3 + 1) + 644,000/142
+ 750 block accesses.

If we assume $h1 = 2$, $h2 = 3$, and $h3 - 3$, then we have

Query cost = 3 + 4 + 4 + 4,535 + 750 block accesses.

Of these block accesses, the index and data accesses are individual random accesses (761), and the merging (4,535 blocks) is done with high-speed scans. If we assume an individual block access takes 2 ms for the average rotational delay and our high-speed disk scans the block at 320 MB/sec, then the total cost in terms of I/O time is:

Block access time
= 2 ms rotational delay + transfer time of 5,000 bytes/320 MB/sec
= 2.02 ms.

Query I/O time
= 761 × 2.02 ms + (4,535 blocks × 5,000 bytes/block)/320 MB/sec

$$= 1.54 \text{ sec} + .07 \text{ sec}$$
$$= 1.61 \text{ seconds.}$$

2.2.1 Composite Index Approach

First we need to find the height (h) of the multiple index. Applying Equation 2.1 and 2.2,

5,000 bytes/block >= $p \times 5$ for pointers + ($p - 1$) × 35 for index entries

$p <= 5,035 / 40 = 125.875$, or $p = 125$

$p^h > n$, where $p = 125$ and $n = 10,000,000$ rows

$h > \log 10,000,000/\log 125 = 7/2.097 = 3.34$, or $h = 4$

Number of blocks needed to hold 750 target row pointers
= 750/(5,000 bytes/block/35 bytes/pointer) = 750/142
= 5.28 blocks => 6 blocks.

Query cost
    = composite index search + pointer search for target records
       + final data access cost
    = h + 6 + 750
    = 4 + 6 + 750 block accesses.

Query I/O time
    = 754 × 2.02 ms + (6 blocks × 5,000 bytes/block)/320 MB/sec
    = 1.52 seconds.

2.2.2 Table Scan

For a full scan of this table of 10 M rows or 500,000 blocks use the simple model in Appendix A and apply it to this example. Since most disk systems use prefetch buffers to speed up table scans, we assume a 64 KB prefetch block here. Thus, the number of I/O operations is:

Number of prefetch buffer I/O operations
    = 10,000,000 rows × 250 bytes/row/64 KB = 38,147.

Query time = time to fill 38,147 prefetch buffers in a table scan
    = 38,147 × (2 ms rotational delay + 64 KB/320 MB/sec transfer)
    = 38,147 × (2 ms + .19 ms)
    = 83.5 seconds.

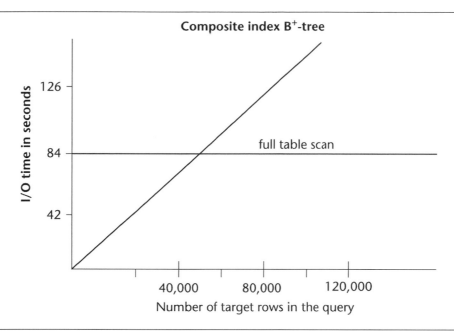

Figure 2.4   Comparison of composite index and scan I/O time for the same query.

Thus, we see that the composite index time reduces the exhaustive scan time by a factor of about 55 to 1. Multiplying 55 times 750 target rows to get a rough estimate, we see that at approximately 41,250 target rows and higher, a table scan becomes the more efficient method of satisfying this query. The overall plot of I/O time is shown in Figure 2.4.

2.3 Bitmap Indexing

One of the most basic rules of thumb for index design in data warehouses is to create indexes on each column of each of the dimension tables and all the corresponding foreign keys in the fact table. This facilitates any joins required between the fact table and the corresponding dimension tables, including multiple joins. Join indexes that map an attribute value (or a concatenation of several attribute values) of a dimension table to one or more rows in a fact table are just variations on the composite index searches we discussed in Section 2.3. Thus, a join index is really a binary precomputed join, and composite join indexes are really *n*-way precomputed joins. These techniques can greatly enhance performance of a data warehouse.

Highly analytical queries that are weakly selective can make use of bitmap (or bit vector) indexes [O'Neil 1995]. *Bitmap indexes* are particularly useful for low-selectivity queries, such as those that search based on few alternative values, like male/female

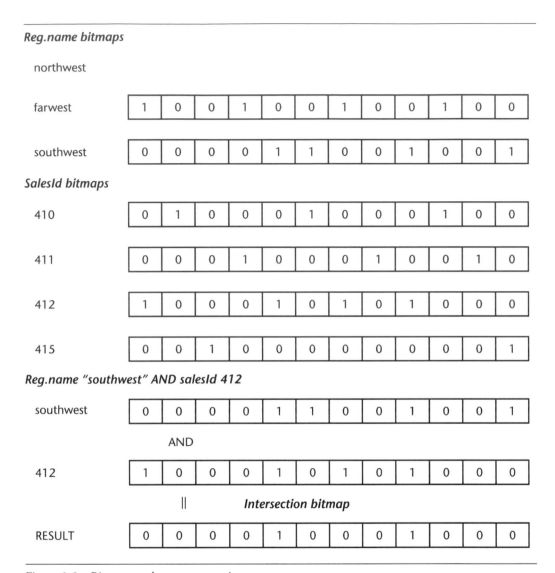

Reg.name bitmaps

northwest

farwest

1	0	0	1	0	0	1	0	0	1	0	0

southwest

0	0	0	0	1	1	0	0	1	0	0	1

SalesId bitmaps

410

0	1	0	0	0	1	0	0	0	1	0	0

411

0	0	0	1	0	0	0	1	0	0	1	0

412

1	0	0	0	1	0	1	0	1	0	0	0

415

0	0	1	0	0	0	0	0	0	0	0	1

Reg.name "southwest" AND salesId 412

southwest

0	0	0	0	1	1	0	0	1	0	0	1

AND

412

1	0	0	0	1	0	1	0	1	0	0	0

‖   **Intersection bitmap**

RESULT

0	0	0	0	1	0	0	0	1	0	0	0

Figure 2.5   Bitmaps and query processing.

attributes or salaried/hourly employee attributes. Bitmap indexes speed up special index operations such as intersection or union. In a typical B+tree, secondary index, for instance, leaf nodes have a pointer array of physical row addresses for all rows that meet a given criterion defined by the index.

In a bitmap, however, the structure is different. Each row a table is represented by a single bit in a bit vector, and each row satisfying the criterion (e.g., reg-name = 'south-west' or sales-id = 412) has its bit set in that bit vector, as shown in Figure 2.5. Here we see that each attribute value has a separate bit vector. Those rows satisfying all criteria are found by taking the AND of the bit vectors, as shown in Figure 2.5 for the intersection of reg-name = 'southwest' and sales-id = 412. Bitmap indexes are now quite common in commercial systems, for example, IBM's DB2, Oracle, and SQL Server.

However, despite their efficiency in quickly identifying records, bitmap indexes are not as easily extended to new keys as B+tree indexes. They also do not store data in sorted order that makes B+trees so valuable for range predicates and implied sorting of data. As a result they are best suited to databases where data is accessed by point values, and new data values are infrequently added to the database.

2.4 Record Identifiers

Indexes always store a reference back to where the key values can be found in the base table. These identifiers are called record identifiers, or RIDs. RIDs are needed because the index itself often does not include all the column data required to answer a query requiring the database to go back to the base table for the extra information. Thanks to the index the database knows exactly where to look in the base table, so performance is still dramatically improved compared to a table scan, but not quite as good as it would be if the query could be answered with just the data residing within the index. A simple example would be a query to a bank account. A table for a bank account table would typically have an index on the account number. When a customer or teller wants to find out information about the account the query is issued to retrieve the data for a specific account number. The database scans the index to find the key that matches the account number, but the additional information such as name, address, balance, etc is found within the base table itself. The index scan returns the RID telling the database where to find the full table record.

Of course, a composite index can be defined that includes most or all of the columns in the base table which would obviate the need to go back to the base table for information. However, creating wide indexes that include many columns is unreasonably expensive in terms of storage costs, and reduces the number of keys that can be returned in a single I/O of the index leaf pages, so it is rarely done.

Indexes can return a single RID or lists of RIDs depending on how many keys qualified for the search and how many RIDs were associated with each key value.

The classic format for RIDs (see C.J. Date 2003) used a 4 byte model. Data wthin the tables is stored on storage pages (4KB or 8KB would be typical). Each page is numbered, 1,2,3 etc. Records within each page are similarly numbered. The 4 byte model for RIDs used 3 bytes to represent a page number and one byte to represent a record number. This structure limited table size to three byte addressability (xFFFFFF or 16777215 pages). Similarly the number of records that could be addressed on a database page were limited to one byte (xFF or 256 records). The 4 byte RID design was effective in clearly locating a record on a page. However, both limits became too constrictive over time and database vendors required designs that would not limit them to 3 byte page addressing or 256 records per page. New RID designs emerged over the past decade using 6 and 8 byte designs. The specific format of RIDs varies between databases, but the humble RID remains the essential device within the database for specifying exactly where a record resides.

2.5 Summary

This chapter discussed the basic concepts in indexing, in particular the B+tree index and composite index variation of the B+tree. A simple approach to estimating database performance is used to aid in the tradeoff analysis.

TIPS AND INSIGHTS FOR DATABASE PROFESSIONALS

- **Tip 1. The B+tree is the indexing method of choice for all the major DBMSs.** Indexing should always be used for access to a small number of rows for queries.

- **Tip 2. Index tradeoff analysis can be done with a simple database performance estimation mentioned above. This helps us justify index selection decisions.** Once we understand the basic performance model (see Appendix A) it can be easily applied to any index mechanism so decisions on indexing can be based on actual time to process a set of queries.

- **Tip 3. Remember that indexes have a cost.** Indexes provide orders of magnitude benefit for query processing but that benefit comes with two significant penalties. First storage cost. Every index that is created requires disk space to store the keys, RIDs, pointers and intermmediate nodes. If several indexes are created on a table the storage needs for the index structures can rival or even exceed the storage requirements fore the data tables! Similarly indexes consume memory as well. Secondly, indexes need to be maintained as data is added deleted or updated from the table. A simple change in the table data cane require an index key to not only be modified, but to move from one leaf node to another requiring several times the I/O and CPU processing that was required to simply modify the data in the base table. As a result, while indexes have tremendous benefit for query performance, they also impose a significant penalty on write operations such as INSERT, UPDATE, DELETE, IMPORT and LOAD.

2.6 Literature Summary

The idea for extending a table for usage efficiency came from Scholnick [1980]. Comprehensive surveys of search methods can be found in Harbron [1988], Groshans

[1986], Wiederhold [1987], and brief surveys are given in Elmasri [2003] and Silberschatz [2002].

Bayer, R., and McCreight, E. Organization and Maintenance of Large Ordered Indexes. *Acta. Inf.*, 1(3), 1972: 173–189.

Date, C. J. , *An Introduction to Database Systems*, Vol. 1, 8th Ed., Addison-Wesley, 2003.

Elmasri, R., and Navathe, S. B. *Fundamentals of Database Systems*, 4th ed. Boston: Addison-Wesley, and Redwood City, CA, 2004.

Grosshans, D. *File Systems Design and Implementation*. Englewood Cliffs, NJ: Prentice-Hall, 1986.

Harbron, T. R. *File Systems Structures and Algorithms*. Englewood Cliffs, NJ: Prentice-Hall, 1988.

O'Neil, P., and Graefe, G. Multi-Table Joins through Bitmapped Join Indices. *SIGMOD Record*, 24(3), Sept. 1995: 8-11.

O'Neil, P., and O'Neil, E. *Database: Principles, Programming, and Performance*, 2nd ed. San Francisco: Morgan Kaufmann, 2001.

Ramakrishnan, R., and Gehrke, J. *Database Management Systems*, 3rd ed. New York: McGraw-Hill, 2004.

Silberschatz, A., Korth, H. F., and Sudarshan, S. *Database System Concepts,* 5th ed. New York: McGraw-Hill, 2006.

Teorey, T. J., and Fry, J. P. *Design of Database Structures*. Englewood Cliffs, NJ: Prentice-Hall, 1982.

Wiederhold, G. *File Organization for Database Design*. New York: McGraw-Hill, 1987.

Query Optimization and Plan Selection

It is a capital mistake to theorize before one has the data. Insensibly one begins to twist facts to suit theories, instead of theories to suit facts.
—Sir Arthur Conan Doyle (1859–1930)

If you ever wanted to learn to play the piano, there are many different approaches that people have tried over the past three centuries. The traditional recommended way is to sign up with a professional teacher and take lessons one-on-one. Others have tried a variety of methods of self-instruction, such as using books like *Piano for Dummies*, watching videos, or just getting some sheet music and start playing. Regardless of which method you choose, there is another variable, how to proceed to learn the piece you want to play: hands separate and then together, hands together from the beginning, learning in sections, etc. Therefore, to get to the final goal, there are literally dozens and possibly hundreds of paths one can take to get the final "correct" result. The quality of the result may vary, but you can get there many different ways. For database queries there is also a multipath possibility to get the same correct result, and it is important to be able to analyze the different paths for the quality of the result, in other words, the performance of the system to get you the correct result and choose the best path to get you there.

This chapter focuses on the basic concepts of query optimization needed to understand the interactions between physical database design and query processing. We start with a simple example of query optimization and illustrate how the input/output (I/O) time estimation techniques in Chapter 2 can be applied to determining which query execution plan would be best. We focus here on the practical tradeoff analysis needed to find the best query execution plan to illustrate the process.

3.1 Query Processing and Optimization

The basic steps of query processing are:

1. *Scanning, parsing, and decomposition of an SQL query.* This step checks for correct SQL query syntax and generates appropriate error messages when necessary. The output of this step is an intermediate form of the query known as a query tree or query execution plan.

2. *Query optimization.* This step includes both local and global optimization. Global optimization determines the order of joins and the order of selections and projections relative to the joins. It also involves restating (recasting) nested join queries into flat queries involving the same joins. This is the main concept described in this chapter. Local optimization determines the index method for selections and joins, using techniques covered in Chapters 2 and 4. Both kinds of optimization are based on estimates of cost (I/O time) of the various alternative query execution plans generated by the optimizer. The cost model is based on a description of the database schema and size, and looks at statistics for the attribute values in each table involved in queries.

3. *Query code generation and execution.* This step uses classical programming language and compiler techniques to generate executable code.

3.2 Useful Optimization Features in Database Systems

In addition to the basics of query processing and optimization described above, there are many useful features in database management systems today that aid the database administrator, application developer, and database system itself to process queries more efficiently.

3.2.1 Query Transformation or Rewrite

Modern databases (e.g., Oracle, DB2, SQL Server) transform (rewrite) queries into more efficient forms before optimization takes place. This helps tremendously with query execution plan selection. Examples of the more popular query rewrites are transforming subqueries into joins or semi-joins, pushing down the group by operations below joins, the elimination of joins on foreign keys when the tables containing the results of the join are no longer used in the query, converting outer joins to inner joins when they produce equivalent results, and replacing a view reference in a query by the actual view definition (called *view merging*).

A very common transformation is the materialized view rewrite. If some part of a query is equivalent to an existing materialized view, then the code is replaced by that view. Oracle, for instance, performs a materialized view transformation, then optimizes both the original query and the rewritten query and chooses the more efficient plan between the two alternatives.

Rewrites are especially common in data warehouses using the star schema format. In Oracle, for instance, joins of the fact table with one or more dimension tables are replaced by subqueries involving both tables, using special (bitmap) indexes on the fact table for efficiency.

3.2.2 Query Execution Plan Viewing

How do you know what plan your database chose for the most recent query? All modern database products provide some facility for the user to see the access plan. In DB2 and Oracle it is called Explain or Explain Plan (the graphical version is called Visual Explain). This facility describes all the steps of the plan, the order in which tables are accessed for the query, and whether an index is used to access a table. The optimizer selects the best plan from among the candidate plans generated.

3.2.3 Histograms

Many database systems (e.g., DB2, SQL Server, Oracle) make use of stored histograms of ranges of attribute values from the actual database to help make better estimates of selectivities for selection and join operations, so costs for query execution plans can be estimated more accurately.

3.2.4 Query Execution Plan Hints

Along with Explain, plan hints have become a major fixture in the database industry, allowing application programmers (users) to force certain plan choices, removing uncertainty in many cases. Hints are programmer directives to an SQL query that can change the query execution plan. They are supported by all of the major database systems. While made widely available, they should be used only when major performance problems are present. As an example of the use of a hint, a user can set up an experiment to compare a suboptimal index with an optimal index (and therefore an optimal plan) and see if the performance difference is worth the overhead to use the optimal index, especially if it is used only for this query.

3.2.5 Optimization Depth

Different database products have different search depth, the simplest being greedy search, but there are usually more advanced dynamic programming-based approaches as well. Often the search depth is a configurable parameter.

3.3 Query Cost Evaluation—An Example

The example in this section assumes that we have a basic query execution plan to work with, and focuses on query cost evaluation to minimize I/O time to execute the query whose plan we are given. It illustrates the benefit of applying well-known query optimization strategies to a simple real-life problem. Although the problem is elementary, significant benefits in query time can still be reached using heuristic rules, and the definition of those rules can be clearly illustrated.

Let us assume a simple three-table database [Date 2003] with the following materialization of tables: part, supplier, and the intersection table shipment.

Part (P)			Supplier (S)				Shipment (SH)			
pnum	pname	wt	snum	sname	city	status	snum	pnum	qty	shipdate
p1	bolt	3	s1	brown	NY	3	s1	p2	50	1-4-90
p2	nail	6	s2	garcia	LA	2	s1	p3	45	2-17-90
p3	nut	2	s3	kinsey	NY	3	s2	p1	100	11-5-89
							s2	p3	60	6-30-91
							s3	p3	50	8-12-91

Attribute name and size (bytes), and table name and size:

- supplier: snum(5), sname(20), city(10), status(2) => 37 bytes in one record in supplier
- part: pnum(8), pname(10), wt(5) => 23 bytes in one record in part
- shipment: snum(5), pnum(8), qty(5), shipdate(8) => 26 bytes in one record in shipment

Note: Assumed block size (bks) = 15,000 bytes.

3.3.1 Example Query 3.1

"What are the names of parts supplied by suppliers in New York City?" If we translate the query to SQL we have

```
SELECT p.pname
FROM P, SH, S
WHERE P.pnum = SH.pnum
```

```
AND SH.snum = S.snum
AND S.city = 'NY';
```

Possible join orders of three tables = 3! = 6:

1. S join SH join P
2. SH join S join P
3. P join SH join S
4. SH join P join S
5. S × P join SH
6. P × S join SH

There are six possible join orders of these three tables, given the two joins specified in the query. Orders 1 and 2 are equivalent because of the commutativity of joins: A join B is equivalent to B join A. By the same rule, orders 3 and 4 are equivalent, and orders 5 and 6 are equivalent. Orders 5 and 6 are to be avoided if at all possible because they involve the Cartesian product form of join when there are no overlapping columns. When this occurs the size of the resulting table is the product of the rows in the individual tables and can be extremely large. Also, the data in the new table is arbitrarily connected.

We are left with orders 1 and 3 as the reasonable options to consider. Within these two orders, we can also consider doing the joins first or doing the selections first. We can also consider doing the queries with indexes and without indexes. We now do a cost estimate for these four among the eight possible alternatives:

- Option 1A: Order 1 with joins executed first, selections last, without indexes.
- Option 1B: Order 1 with selections executed first, joins last, without indexes.
- Option 3A: Order 3 with joins executed first, selections last, without indexes.
- Option 3B: Order 3 with selections executed first, joins last, without indexes.

Intuitively we know that option 1B improves on 1A because joins are by far the most costly operations, and if we can reduce the size of the tables before joining them, it will be a lot faster than joining the original larger tables. In option 1B we also explore the possibility of using indexes.

In these examples we only consider queries and not updates to illustrate the efficiency of executing selections first and using indexes. In practice, query optimizers must consider updates. The reader is directed to Chapter 2 for a discussion on estimating the I/O time needed for updates.

Finally, we use sequential block accesses (SBA) and random block accesses (RBA) as estimators for I/O time since there is a linear relationship between SBA or RBA and I/O time, and I/O time is a generally accepted form of cost comparison in database operations.

Option 1A Cost Estimation: Brute-force Method of Doing All Joins First, with No Indexes

We summarize the basic sizes of records, counts of records, and counts of blocks accessed sequentially in the following table. The tables TEMPA, TEMPB, and so on. are temporary tables formed as the result of intermediate operations during the course of the query.

Table	Row Size	No. Rows	BF	Scan Table (no. Blocks)
supplier (S)	37 bytes	200	405	1
part (P)	23 bytes	100	652	1
shipment (SH)	26 bytes	100K	576	174
TEMPA (S join SH)	58 bytes	100K	258	388
TEMPB (TEMPA join P)	73 bytes	100K	205	488
TEMPC (select TEMPB)	73 bytes	10K	205	49

BF is the blocking factor or rows per block (estimated with average row size).

This approach is detailed below and summarized in Figure 3.1 using the query execution plan notation of Roussopoulos [1982]. The query execution plan dictates that the joins are executed first, then the selections. We use merge joins, so no indexes are used in this option. For each step we first estimate the number of records accessed, then sequential blocks accesses, then take a sum of SBAs. We assume each table is stored on disk after each operation and then must be read from disk to do the next operation.

Step 1. Join S and SH over the common column snum forming TEMPA (snum, sname, city, status, pnum, qty, shipdate) at 58 bytes per row (record). If a sort of a table is required before executing a merge join, the estimated cost of an M-way sort is approximately $2 \times nb \times \log_M nb$ [O'Neil 2001, Silberschatz 2006] where nb is the number of blocks (pages) in the table to be sorted. In these examples, $M = 3$. However, in this case we don't need to sort SH since table S is very small, less than one block, so we only need to scan SH and compare in fast memory with one block of S.

Number of block accesses (step 1)
    = read S + read SH + write TEMPA
    = ceiling(200/405) + ceiling(100K/576) + ceiling(100K/258)

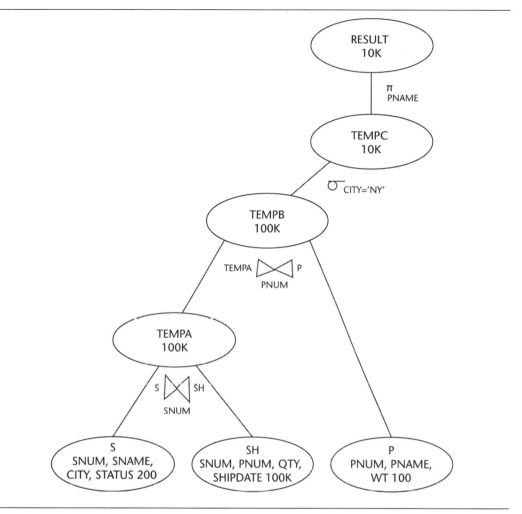

Figure 3.1   Query execution plan for option 1A.

$$= 1 + 174 + 388$$
$$= 563.$$

Step 2. Join P and TEMPA over the common column pnum forming TEMPB.

Number of block accesses (step 2)
= read P + sort TEMPA + read TEMPA + write TEMPB
= $1 + 2 \times 388 \times \log_3 388 + 388 + 488$
= $1 + 4214 + 388 + 488$
= 5,091.

Step 3. Select TEMPB where city = 'NY' forming TEMPC (same attributes as TEMPB) at 73 B per row. Assume NY has 10% of all suppliers.

Number of block accesses (step 3)
= read TEMPB + write TEMPC
= 488 + 49 = 537.

Step 4. Project TEMPC over pname forming RESULT (pname) at 10 B per row.

Number of rows = 10K (read TEMPC)
Number of block accesses (step 4)
= read TEMPC
= 49.

In summary, for the entire query (option 1A) we have the following totals:

Number of block accesses for query (option 1A)
= 563 + 5,091 + 537 + 49 = 6,240.

Option 1B Cost Estimation: Do All Selections (Including Projections) before Joins, without Indexes (and an Exploration of the Potential Use of Indexes)

Table	Row Size	No. Rows	BF	Blocks to Scan Table
supplier (S)	37 B	200	405	1
part (P)	23 B	100	652	1
shipment (SH)	26 B	100K	576	174
TEMP1 (select from S)	37 B	20	405	1
TEMP2 (project over SH)	13 B	100K	1,153	87
TEMP3 (project over P)	18 B	100	833	1
TEMP4 (TEMP1 semi-join TEMP2)	13 B	10K	1,153	9
TEMP5 (TEMP4 semi-join TEMP3)	18 B	10K	833	13

This approach is detailed below and summarized in Figure 3.2.

Step 1. We first select S where city = 'NY' forming TEMP1 (snum, sname, city, status) at 37 B per row. Because this is a very small table, we avoid creating an index and just scan the table instead.

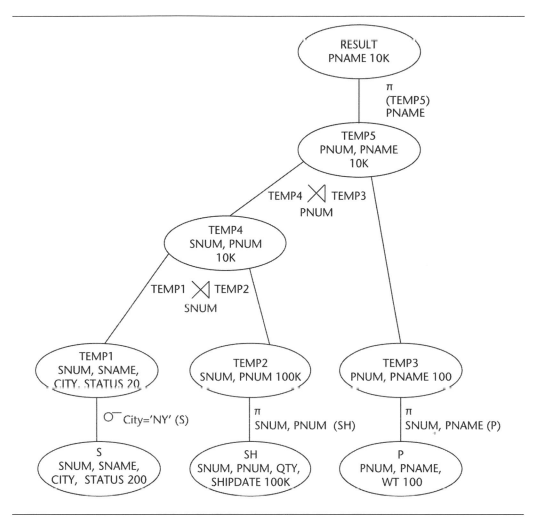

Figure 3.2 Query execution plan for option 1B.

Number of block accesses (step 1)
= read S + write 10% of rows to TEMP1
= 1 + 1
= 2.

Step 2. We then project SH over snum, pnum forming TEMP2 (snum, pnum) at 13 bytes per row. No indexes are required since a projection operation requires a full table scan.

Number of block accesses (step 2)

   = read SH + write TEMP2

   = 174 + 87

   = 261.

Step 3. Next we project P over pnum, pname forming TEMP3 (pnum, pname) at 18 bytes per row. Again, no index is required for a projection operation.

Number of block accesses (step 3)

   = read P + write TEMP3

   = 1 + 1

   = 2.

Step 4. Now we want to do a semi-join (a combined join and projection) with TEMP1 with TEMP2 (essentially joining smaller versions of S and SH), forming TEMP4 (snum, pnum) at 13 bytes per row, which has the same scheme as TEMP2. Note that sorting of TEMP2 is not required here because TEMP1 is a very small table (much less than one block). Even with 10% hit rates of records in TEMP2, virtually every block will be accessed because of the very large blocking factor. Therefore, we don't need an index in this situation.

Number of block accesses (step 4)

   = read TEMP1 + read TEMP2 + write TEMP4

   = 1 + 87 + 9

   = 97.

Step 5. Now we have TEMP4 (snum, pnum) and TEMP3 (pnum, pname) that need to be joined over pnum. To accomplish this with a minimum of I/O cost we do a semi-join with TEMP4 projected over pnum before joining with TEMP3 and forming TEMP5 (pnum, pname) with 18 bytes per row. No sorting of TEMP4 is required because TEMP3 is very small (less than one block).

Number of block accesses (step 5)

   = read TEMP4 + read TEMP3 + write TEMP5

   = 9 + 1 + 13

   = 23 a.

Step 6. Finally we project TEMP5 over pname for the final result.

Number of rows = 10K (read TEMP5)

Number of block accesses (step 6)

= read TEMP5

= 13.

In summary, the total cost of answering the query using this approach is as follows:

Number of block accesses for the query (option 2A)

= 2 + 261 + 2 + 97 + 23 + 13

= 398.

We now compare the two approaches:

	Block Accesses
Option 1A	6,240 executing joins first
Option 1B	398 executing joins last

It is clearly seen that the use of table reduction techniques (early selections and projections) has the potential of greatly reducing the I/O time cost of executing a query. Although in this example indexes were not required, in general they can be very useful to reduce I/O time further.

3.4 Query Execution Plan Development

A query execution plan is a data structure that represents each database operation (selections, projections, and joins) as a distinct node. The sequence of operations in a query execution plan can be represented as top down or bottom up. We use the bottom-up approach, and Figures 3.1 and 3.2 are classic examples of the use of query execution plans to denote possible sequences of operations needed to complete SQL queries. An SQL query may have many possible execution sequences, depending on the complexity of the query, and each sequence can be represented by a query execution plan. Our goal is to find the query execution plan that finds the correct answer to the query in the least amount of time. Since the optimal solution to this problem is often too difficult and time consuming to determine relative to the time restrictions imposed on database queries by customers, query optimization is really a process of finding a "good" solution that is reasonably close to the optimal solution, but can be quickly computed.

A popular heuristic for many query optimization algorithms in database systems today involves the simple observation from Section 3.3 that selections and projections should be done before joins because joins tend to be by far the most time-costly operations. Joins should be done with the smallest segments of tables possible, that is, those segments that have only the critical data needed to satisfy the query. For instance in Example Query 3.1, the supplier records are requested for suppliers in New York, which represents only 10% of the supplier table. Therefore, it makes sense to find those records first, store them in a temporary table, and use that table as the supplier table for the join between supplier and shipment. Similarly, only the columns of the tables in a join that have meaning to the join, the subsequent joins, and the final display of results need to be carried along to the join operations. All other columns should be projected out of the table before the join operations are executed.

To facilitate the transformation of a query execution plan from a random sequence of operations to a methodical sequence that does selections and projections first and joins last, we briefly review the basic transformation rules that can be applied to such an algorithm.

3.4.1 Transformation Rules for Query Execution Plans

The following are self-evident rules for transforming operations in query execution plans to reverse the sequence and produce the same result [Silberschatz 2006]. Allow different query trees to produce the same result.

Rule 1. Commutativity of joins: R1 join R2 = R2 join R1.

Rule 2. Associativity of joins: R1 join (R2 join R3) = (R1 join R2) join R3.

Rule 3. The order of selections on a table does not affect the result.

Rule 4. Selections and projections on the same table can be done in any order, so long as a projection does not eliminate an attribute to be used in a selection.

Rule 5. Selections on a table before a join produce the same result as the identical selections on that table after a join.

Rule 6. Projections and joins involving the same attributes can be done in any order so long as the attributes eliminated in the projection are not involved in the join.

Rule 7. Selections (or projections) and union operations involving the same table can be done in any order.

This flexibility in the order of operations in a query execution plan makes it easy to restructure the plan to an optimal or near-optimal structure quickly.

3.4.2 Query Execution Plan Restructuring Algorithm

The following is a simple heuristic to restructure a query execution plan for optimal or near-optimal performance.

1. Separate a selection with several AND clauses into a sequence of selections (rule 3).

2. Push selections down the query execution plan as far as possible to be executed earlier (rules 4, 5, 7).

3. Group a sequence of selections as much as possible (rule 3).

4. Push projections down the plan as far as possible (rules 4, 6, 7).

5. Group projections on the same tables, removing redundancies.

Figure 3.1 illustrates a query execution plan that emphasizes executing the joins first using a bottom-up execution sequence. Figure 3.2 is the same plan, transformed to a plan that executes the joins last using this heuristic.

3.5 Selectivity Factors, Table Size, and Query Cost Estimation

Once we are given a candidate query execution plan to analyze, we need to be able to estimate the sizes of the intermediate tables the query optimizer will create during query execution. Once we have estimated those table sizes, we can compute the I/O time to execute the query using that query execution plan as we did in Section 3.3. The sizes of the intermediate tables were given in that example. Now we will show how to estimate those table sizes.

Selectivity (S) of a table is defined as the proportion of records in a table that satisfies a given condition. Thus, selectivity takes on a value between zero and one. For example, in Example Query 3.1, the selectivity of records in the table supplier that satisfies the condition WHERE city 'NY' is 0.1, because 10% of the records have the value NY for city.

To help our discussion of selectivity, let us define the following measures of data within a table:

- The number (cardinality) of rows in table R: $card(R)$.
- The number (cardinality) of distinct values of attribute A in table R: $card_A(R)$
- Maximum value of attribute A in a table R: $max_A(R)$
- Minimum value of attribute A in a table R: $min_A(R)$

3.5.1 Estimating Selectivity Factor for a Selection Operation or Predicate

The following relationships show how to compute the selectivity of selection operations on an SQL query [Ozsu 1991].

The selectivity for an attribute A in table R to have a specific value a in a selected record applies to two situations. First, if the attribute A is a primary key, where each value is unique, then we have an exact selectivity measure

$$S(A = a) = 1/card_A(R). \qquad\qquad 3.1$$

For example, if the table has 50 records, then the selectivity is 1/50 or 0.02.

On the other hand, if attribute A is not a primary key and has multiple occurrences for each value a, then we can also use Equation 3.1 to estimate the selectivity, but we must acknowledge that we are guessing that the distribution of values is uniform. Sometimes this is a poor estimate, but generally it is all we can do without actual distribution data to draw upon. For example, if there are 25 cities out of 200 suppliers in the supplier table in Example Query 3.1, then the number of records with 'NY' is estimated to be $card_{city}(supplier) = 200/25 = 8$. The selectivity of 'NY' is $1/card_{city}(supplier) = 1/8 = 0.125$. In reality, the number of records was given in the example to be 10%, so in this case our estimate is pretty good, but it is not always true.

The selectivity of an attribute A being greater than (or less than) a specific value "a" also depends on a uniform distribution (random probability) assumption for our estimation:

$$S(A > a) = (max_A(R) - a)/(max_A(R) - min_A(R)). \qquad\qquad 3.2$$

$$S(A < a) = (a - min_A(R))/(max_A(R) - min_A(R)). \qquad\qquad 3.3$$

The selectivity of two intersected selection operations (predicates) on the same table can be estimated exactly if the individual selectivities are known:

$$S(P \text{ and } Q) = S(P) \times S(Q), \qquad\qquad 3.4$$

where P and Q are predicates.

So if we have the query

```
SELECT city, qty
FROM shipment
WHERE city = 'London'
AND qty = 1000;
```

where P is the predicate city = 'London' and Q is the predicate qty = 1000, and we know that

S(city = 'London') = .3, and

S(qty = 1000) = .6, then the selectivity of the entire query,

S(city = 'London' OR 'qty = 1000') = .3 × .6 = .18.

The selectivity of the union of two selection operations (predicates) on the same table can be estimated using the well-known formula for randomly selected variables:

$$S(P \text{ or } Q) = S(P) + S(Q) - S(P) \times S(Q) \qquad 3.5$$

where P and Q are predicates.

So if we take the same query above and replace the intersection of predicates with a union of predicates, we have:

```
SELECT city, qty
    FROM shipment
    WHERE city = 'London'
    OR qty = 1000;
```

$S(\text{city} = \text{'London'}) = .3$
$S(\text{qty} = 1000) = .6$
$S(\text{city} = \text{'London'} \text{ or } \text{qty} = 1000) = .3 + .6 - .3 \times .6$
       $- .72.$

3.5.2 Histograms

The use of average values to compute selectivities can be reasonably accurate for some data, but for other data it may be off by significantly large amounts. If all databases only used this approximation, estimates of query time could be seriously misleading. Fortunately, many database management systems now store the actual distribution of attribute values as a *histogram*. In a histogram, the values of an attribute are divided into ranges, and within each range, a count of the number of rows whose attribute falls within that range is made.

In the example above we were given the selectivity of qty = 1000 to be .6. If we know that there are 2,000 different quantities in the shipment table out of 100,000 rows, then the average number of rows for a given quantity would be 100,000/2,000 = 50. Therefore, the selectivity of qty = 1000 would be 50/100,000 = .0005. If we have stored a histogram of quantities in ranges consisting of integer values: 1, 2, 3, 4, ..., 1,000, 1,001,......2,000, and found that we had 60,000 rows containing quantity values equal to1,000, we would estimate the selectivity of qty = 1000 to be .6. This is a huge difference in accuracy that would have dramatic effects on query execution plan cost estimation and optimal plan selection.

3.5.3 Estimating the Selectivity Factor for a Join

Estimating the selectivity for a join is difficult if it is based on nonkeys; in the worst case it can be a Cartesian product at one extreme or no matches at all at the other extreme. We focus here on the estimate based on the usual scenario for joins between a primary key and a nonkey (a foreign key). Let's take, for example, the join between a table R1, which has a primary key, and a table R2, which has a foreign key:

$$\text{card}(R1 \text{ join } R2) = S \times \text{card}(R1) \times \text{card}(R2), \qquad 3.6$$

where S is the selectivity of the common attribute used in the join, when that attribute is used as a primary key. Let's illustrate this computation of the selectivity and then the size of the joined table, either final result of the query or an intermediate table in the query.

3.5.4 Example Query 3.2

Find all suppliers in London with the shipping date of June 1, 2006.

```
SELECT supplierName
    FROM supplier S, shipment SH
    WHERE S.snum = SH.snum
    AND S.city = 'London'
    AND SH.shipdate = '01-JUN-2006';
```

Let us assume the following data that describes the three tables: supplier, part, and shipment:

- $\text{card}(\text{supplier}) = 200$
- $\text{card}_{\text{city}}(\text{supplier}) = 50$
- $\text{card}(\text{shipment}) = 100,000$
- $\text{card}_{\text{shipdate}}(\text{shipment}) = 1,000$
- $\text{card}(\text{part}) = 100$

There are two possible situations to evaluate:

1. The join is executed before the selections.
2. The selections are executed before the join.

Case 1: Join Executed First

If the join is executed first we know that there are 200 suppliers (rows in the supplier table) and 100,000 shipments (rows in the shipment table), so the selectivity of supplier number in the supplier table is 1/200. Now we apply Equation 3.6 to find the cardinality of the join, that is, the count of rows (records) in the intermediate table formed by the join of supplier and shipment:

card(supplier join shipment)
    = S(snum) × card(supplier) × card(shipment)
    = (1/200) × 200 × 100,000
    = 100,000.

This is consistent with the basic rule of thumb that a join between a table R1 with a primary key and a table R2 with the corresponding foreign key results in a table with the same number of rows as the table with the foreign key (R2). The query execution plan for this case is shown in Figure 3.3(a). The result of the two selections on this joined table is:

card(result) = S(supplier.city = 'London') × S(shipment.shipdate
    = '01-JUN-2006') × card(supplier join shipment)
    = (1/50) × (1/1,000) × 100,000
    = 2 rows.

Case 2: Selections Executed First

If the selections are executed first, before the join, the computation of estimated selectivity and intermediate table size is slightly more complicated, but still straightforward. We assume there are 50 different cities in the supplier table and 1,000 different ship dates in the shipment table. See the query execution plan in Figure 3.3(b).

S(supplier.city = 'London') = 1/card$_{city}$(supplier) = 1/50.
S(shipment.shipdate = '01-JUN-2006') = 1/card$_{shipment}$(shipment)
    = 1/1,000.

We now determine the sizes (cardinalities) of the results of the two selections on supplier and shipment:

card(supplier.city = 'London') = (1/50) × (200 rows in supplier)
    = 4 rows.

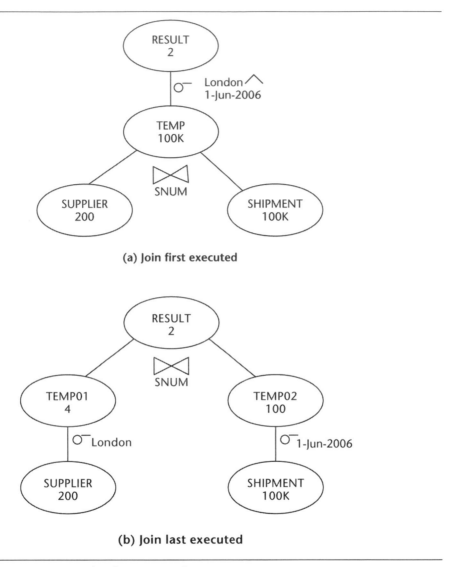

(a) Join first executed

(b) Join last executed

Figure 3.3   Query execution plan for cases 1 and 2.

card(shipment.shipdate = '01-JUN-2006') = (1/1,000) × (100,000)
  = 100 rows.

These two results are stored as intermediate tables, reduced versions of supplier and shipment, which we will now call 'supplier' and 'shipment':

card('supplier') = 4 (Note: 'supplier' has 4 rows with city = 'London'.)

card('shipment') = 100 (Note: 'shipment' has 100 rows with shipdate
    = '01-JUN-2006'.)

Now that we have the sizes of the two intermediate tables we can now apply Equation 3.6 to find the size of the final result of the join:

card('supplier' join 'shipment')
    = S(snum) × card('supplier') × card('shipment')
    = (1/200) × 4 × 100
    = 2.

The final result is 2 rows, that is, all the suppliers in London with the ship date of 01-JUN-2006.

We note that both ways of computing the final result have the same number of rows in the result, but the number of block accesses for each is quite different. The cost of doing the joins first is much higher than the cost for doing the selections first.

3.5.5 Example Estimations of Query Execution Plan Table Sizes

We now revisit Figures 3.1 and 3.2 for actual table sizes within the query execution plan for Example Query 3.1.

Option 1A (Figure 3.1)

For the query execution plan in Figure 3.1 we first join supplier (S) and shipment (SH) to form TEMPA. The size of TEMPA is computed from Equation 3.6 as

card(TEMPA) = S × (card(supplier) × card(shipment))
    = 1/200 × 200 × 100,000 = 100,000 rows,

where S = 1/200, the selectivity of the common attribute in the join, snum.
    Next we join TEMPA with the part table, forming TEMPB.

card(TEMPB) = S × card(TEMPA) × card(part)
    = 1/100 × 100,000 × 100 = 100,000 rows,

where S = 1/100, the selectivity of the common attribute in the join, pnum.
    Finally we select the 10% of the rows from the result that has city = 'NY', giving us 10,000 rows in TEMPC and the final result of the query. We note that the 10% ratio holds through the joins as long as the joins involve primary key–foreign key pairs (and do not involve the attribute city).

Option 1B (Figure 3.2)

In Figure 3.2 we look at the improved query execution plan for option 1B.

TEMP1 is the result of selecting city = 'NY' rows from supplier, with selectivity .1 using Equation 3.1, giving us 200 rows (supplier) × .1 = 20 rows in TEMP1.

TEMP2 is the result of projecting columns snum and pnum from shipment, and therefore has the same number of rows as shipment, 100,000. Similarly, TEMP3 is the result of a projection of pnum and pname from the part table, and has the same number of rows as part, 100.

TEMP4 is shown as the semi-join of TEMP1 and TEMP2 over the common attribute, snum. We note that a semi-join can be represented by a join followed by a projection of pnum and snum from the result. Applying Equation 3.6 to this join:

$$\text{card(TEMP4)} = S \times \text{card(TEMP1)} \times \text{card(TEMP2)}$$
$$= 1/200 \times 20 \times 100,000$$
$$= 10,000 \text{ rows,}$$

where S = 1/200, the selectivity of the common attribute of the join, snum.

TEMP5 is shown as the semi-join of TEMP4 and TEMP3 over the common attribute, pnum. Again we apply Equation 3.6 to this join:

$$\text{Card(TEMP5)} = S \times \text{card(TEMP4)} \times \text{card(TEMP3)}$$
$$= 1/100 \times 10,000 \times 100$$
$$= 10,000 \text{ rows,}$$

where S = 1/100, the selectivity of the common attribute of the join, pnum.

The final result, taking a projection over TEMP5, results in 10,000 rows.

3.6 Summary

This chapter focused on the basic elements of query optimization: query execution plan analysis and selection. We took the point of view of how the query time can be estimated using the tools developed in Chapter 2, where the I/O time can be estimated from the sequential and random block accesses needed to execute a query. We also looked at the estimation of intermediate table size in a query made up of a series of selections, projections, and joins. Table size is a critical measure of how long merge joins take, whereas index definitions help determine how long indexed or hash joins take to execute.

> ## TIPS AND INSIGHTS FOR DATABASE PROFESSIONALS
>
> • **Tip 1. Indexes can greatly improve query time and should be an integral part of a query optimizer.** Automated tools used by Microsoft and IBM integrate index design with query optimization. Some basic estimates for query time for a given query execution plan can be manually estimated, with or without indexes.

3.7 Literature Summary

Burleson, D. *Physical Database Design Using Oracle*. Boca Raton, FL, Auerbach Publishers, 2005.

Date, C. J. *An Introduction to Database Systems*, vol. 1, 8th ed. Boston: Addison-Wesley, 2003.

Elmasri, R., and Navathe, S. B. *Fundamentals of Database Systems*, 4th ed. Boston: Addison-Wesley, and Redwood City, CA, 2004.

Garcia-Molina, H., Ullman, J., and Widom, J. *Database Systems: The Complete Book*. Englewood Cliffs, NJ: Prentice-Hall, 2001.

O'Neil, P., and O'Neil, E. *Database: Principles, Programming, and Performance*, 2nd ed. San Francisco: Morgan Kaufmann, 2001.

Ozsu, M. T., and Valduriez, P. *Principles of Distributed Database Systems*. Englewood Cliffs, NJ: Prentice-Hall, 1991.

Roussopoulos, N. View Indexing in Relational Databases. *ACM Trans Database Systems* 7(2), 1982: 258–290.

Ramakrishnan, R., and Gehrke, J. *Database Management Systems*, 3rd ed. New York: McGraw-Hill, 2004.

Selinger, P. G., Astrahan, M. M., Chamberlin, D. D. Lorie, R. A., and Price, T. G. Access Path Selection in a Relational Database Management System. *ACM SIGMOD Conference*, 1979, pp. 23–34.

Silberschatz, A., Korth, H. F., and Sudarshan, S. *Database System Concepts*, 5th ed. New York: McGraw-Hill, 2006.

Selecting 4 Indexes

Give no decision till both sides thou'st heard.
—Phocylides (6th century B.C.)

The B+tree, as we described in detail in Chapter 2, has evolved to become the most popular indexing method for relational databases, replacing many other methods used in the past. However, the task of index selection for a database is still a complex one, walking the fine line between art and science. Decisions still must be made re-garding which keys and non-key attributes to index, equality vs. range queries, composite indexes with many keys, and index main-tenance. This chapter helps clarify these decisions.

4.1 Indexing Concepts and Terminology

Indexes are one of the primary tools used in database management systems (DBMSs) to deliver high performance (i.e. low response time) for the wide range of queries typically requested of these sys-tems. Indexes have a wide range of purposes in terms of perform-ance: fast lookup for specific data and ranges of data, uniqueness enforcement, and so on.. After a database has gone through the logical design of the schema to make sure it is clean and coherent, it is implemented using a commercial system. Soon after that point, when the system has been running and monitored, performance tuning is often done to increase the database system throughput and reduce the database response time, includ-ing service time and queuing delays, for a set of transactions—queries and updates. The most direct way to achieve these improvements is to find and eliminate bottlenecks in the system resources that occur during the execution of the transactions.

The first (lowest) level of database performance tuning is at the hardware level [Silberschatz 2006]. Bottlenecks can be reduced or eliminated by increasing the resources; for example, making the CPU faster, increasing memory size (buffer space), adding disks, using RAID systems of disks, or striping (partitioning) the data across disks to increase the potential of parallelism.

The second level of tuning is in the database system itself. System performance can sometimes be improved by increasing the buffer size or changing the checkpoint intervals.

The third (highest) level of tuning is done at the schema and transaction level. Transactions can be redesigned for speed in addition to the normal query optimization done by the system. Developers must carefully write SQL queries because the optimization engines of the DBMSs are imperfect. Tables can be denormalized for higher performance at some risk of delete and update anomalies. Finally, decisions about materialized views, partitioning, and index selection are made at this level. We will focus our attention on indexing decisions in this chapter.

Let us first do a quick review of the basic types of indexes for individual relational tables before we discuss index selection decisions.

4.1.1 Basic Types of Indexes

1. **B+tree index:** Basic table index based on one or more attributes, often used to enforce uniqueness of primary keys.

2. **Hash table index:** An index that maps primary key values to block data addresses in the database for otherwise unordered data.

3. **Composite index:** An index based on more than one attribute or key (i.e., a concatenated key).

4. **Clustered index:** Any index structure having the data accessed in the same way the index is organized so that data with similar or the same key values is stored (or clustered) together. Clustering tends to greatly reduce input/output (I/O) time for queries and sorting.

5. **Covering index (index only):** An index with enough information to satisfy certain queries by itself, in other words, the query can be satisfied merely by searching the index and not the database.

6. **Bitmapped index:** A collection of bit vectors to form an index that can be used to quickly search secondary indexes or to search data warehouses. Each bit vector represents a different value of an attribute, and the length of each vector is the number of rows (rows) in the table.

7. **Dense versus sparse index:** A dense index has a pointer to each row in the table; a sparse index has at most one pointer to each block or page in the table.

This list contains different types of index structures: B+tree, hash index, bitmap, and sparse/dense. It also contains different of ways of using these index structures: composite index, clustered index, covering index. These can be combined in certain ways. For in-stance, a user can create a composite index for a B+tree index. Similarly, a user can create a unique index using a B+tree or hash index structure.

Indexes for join operations are the same types as those used for single table indexes—they are simply applied in turn for each table involved in a join. Most joins requiring indexing use the B+tree or hash table indexes because they compare attribute values between tables, working within the data storage arrangements for the individual tables. Details about join indexing are in Section 4.5.

4.1.2 Access Methods for Indexes

Each database system has built-in access methods that are used to scan indexes and data, and each is set up to optimize the searching of data for each particular type of query. Basic access methods commonly used include:

- *Table scanning:* when an index is not needed.
- *Index scanning:* for clustered or nonclustered indexes.
- *Index-only scanning:* scanning a covering index.
- *Block or row index ANDing:* for merging index entries for multipoint queries.
- *List prefetch:* a sort on record IDs (RIDs) followed by a fetch of sorted rows from the data blocks or pages, enabling future sequential operations on this data to be prefetched.

4.2 Indexing Rules of Thumb

This section contains practical rules for indexing that have been found extremely useful for database practitioners. The succeeding sections contain a more in-depth analysis of indexing based on types of queries and types of indexes.

Rule 1. Index every primary key and most foreign keys in the database. Most joins occur between primary keys (PKs) and foreign keys (FKs), so it is important to build indexes on all PKs and FKs whenever possible. This is part of the basic infrastructure that should be set up before considering the workload. The workload can prove to be difficult to predict and often changes quickly during the use of an application. This basic infrastructure also includes a clean and coherent logical design and careful design of queries, including the avoidance of certain pitfalls such as nested selects.

We note that in most DBMSs, when PKs are explicitly declared in SQL, indexes are formed as a side effect. FKs should be looked at in terms of their use as a search field, and also their use during primary key deletes. In particular, when there are a small number of possible values (like in gender or state located), indexes could be quite large and vulnerable to primary key deletes.

Indexes should also be used in small tables, contrary to popular belief. Many DBAs have found circumstances when lack of indexes, even for tables with a few dozen rows, have resulted in very bad performance.

Rule 2. Attributes frequently referenced in SQL WHERE clauses are potentially good candidates for an index. The SQL WHERE clause is used for search attributes in a query and is the most likely set of candidates for indexing when the predicate is an equality. These search attributes are either used for restricting the set of target rows or for joins of two tables. In either case, indexes should be considered to speed up the operations.

An exception to this rule occurs when the predicate is an inequality like "WHERE cost <> 4". Indexes are seldom useful for inequalities because of the high selectivity involved.

Rule 3. Use a B+tree index for both equality and range queries. For both equality queries and range queries that return any number of target rows, B+tree indexes can be set up to find all the target rows very efficiently. Clustered indexes can also be easily set up with B+tree formats. Queries that always return at most one row are theoretically best served using a hash index. However, most systems don't offer hash indexes, and since B+trees are almost as efficient, they are highly recommended in all such cases.

Rule 4. Choose carefully one clustered index for each table. A clustered index dictates how data is to be physically stored for a specific table. Any other index on that table will not be as efficient in accessing data within that table when many target rows need to be accessed, so it is important to create a clustered index on the most important query or closely related queries on that table.

It is also important to build a clustered index on a primary key that allows range searches or maintains an order that makes batch processing efficient. DB2, SQL Server, Oracle, and Sybase all support-clustered indexes.

Rule 5. Avoid or remove redundant indexes. Indexes that use the same columns or almost the same columns make query optimization more complicated and often do not take advantage of many composite indexes that could be used efficiently for a variety of queries. Also, some database generation tools produce duplicate indexes, so an application developer should be careful to inspect a tool's output to see if any performance problems exist. Caution should be exercised when removing indexes; make sure that there is no performance degradation due to these removals.

Rule 6. Add indexes only when absolutely necessary. When redesigning indexes, either you have too many or too few indexes already. You have too few indexes and need more when you are doing unnecessary table scans for certain queries that return only a fraction of the rows in the table [Hubel 2001].

Rule 7. Add or delete index columns for composite indexes to improve performance. Do not alter primary key columns. Multiple-column composite indexes can be very efficient for certain complex queries. For one thing, they reduce the number of sorts and merges required for multiple single-index searches. Also, additional columns can help with the execution of joins across tables. On the other hand, the more columns used in the index, the more restrictive the applicability and usefulness of the index for queries that don't specify exactly the attributes defined in the index. Performance tradeoffs must be carefully considered when adding or deleting columns.

For primary keys, adding or deleting columns will tend to change the uniqueness of the key and affect the integrity of any applications that use it. Therefore, in general, avoid altering primary key columns.

Rule 8. Use attributes for indexes with caution when they are frequently updated. Some expert developers simply index all FKs regardless of how often they are updated and only make adjustments if serious bottlenecks appear. In general, when attributes (columns) are frequently updated, both the indexes and stored rows containing those attribute values must be updated. If the cost (I/O time) of those updates, when using an index, is significantly larger than the benefit (I/O time) of faster queries using that index, then the index should not be created.

Rule 9. Keep up index maintenance on a regular basis; drop indexes only when they are clearly hurting performance. Index maintenance is needed constantly when table rows are constantly updated with insertions, deletions, and changes. However, as we mentioned in Chapter 2, index maintenance can significantly hurt performance of many writing commands such as INSERT, UPDATE, DELETE, IMPORT, and LOAD. When performance data collection indicates that an index has become the bottleneck, either reorganize the index or delete it. If updates are done during the day and queries are done at night, it may be useful to delete the indexes at the beginning of the day and rebuild them at the end of the day when queries are done. Again, caution should be observed when deleting indexes—serious problems could arise when foreign key constraints are involved.

DBAs are known to sometimes drop indexes before a large data import, and then rebuild the indexes afterward. The incremental cost of adding an index can actually be greater than the cost of mass building the index. For mass building, we assume that most DBMSs sort the data using more efficient algorithms, and then build the actual index.

Rule 10. Avoid extremes in index cardinality and value distribution. Database users with experience in performance tuning often find that they need to avoid index distributions that are extremely skewed. Don't allow just a few index values to have much higher levels of frequency than other values. When this occurs, you need to redesign the index to get a more balanced distribution and avoid costly CPU and I/O delays for certain types of updates.

Also, you want to avoid extremes in index cardinality. For example, you want to avoid indexes with only one entry, particularly for tables with over 1,000 rows. You also want to avoid indexes so large that they begin to approximate (above 75%) the number of rows in the table you are indexing.

Rule 11. Covering indexes (index only) are useful, but often overused. Index-only usage can often be very useful to search indexes and avoid I/Os within the database. However, as with most indexing features, they can also be overused, resulting in extremely query-specific indexes with very long keys and fewer keys per index page, thus more I/O.

Rule 12. Use bitmap indexes for high-volume data, especially in data warehouses. Large data stores, such as in data warehouses, that involve terabytes or petabytes, tend to have extremely large (B+tree) indexes. Indexes can be effectively compressed with bitmap structures, which save space and time for many queries.

4.3 Index Selection Decisions

Now that we have enumerated the basic rules for indexing, we shall consider the design decisions the practitioner will face when tuning a database. In general, we want to consider additional indexes incrementally and see whether we could have a better plan, for example, whether the performance (throughput and response time) significantly improves for each new index. There is no standard rule here, but they must be set up individually for each database system and user.

We also need to consider updates. Sometimes a new index improves query performance but severely degrades update performance. It is the combined performance for query and update that will determine whether a new index is useful. This is a common tradeoff in index design, and requires that we document what updates are needed, what their frequencies are, and which tables they apply to.

Many of the following critical design questions were defined in the excellent database book by Ramakrishnan [2004]. They have been modified and extended here.

Design Decision 1: Does this table require an index or not, and if so which search key should I build an index on? A reasonable starting point for index design is to first declare the PKs and index the FKs, regardless of the query mix you are given. For applications that are very demanding in terms of frequency, heavy volume of data accessed, and/or priority, adding or modifying indexes may need to be considered if bottlenecks appear.

If you decide you need an index, look at the WHERE (and AND) clause of a query to determine which attributes can be used for index search keys. Each query may involve different attributes, and indexes should be chosen for each query that can significantly improve the database performance. Queries that require full table scans may not need any indexing. Indexes that speed up more than one query will be the most valuable.

Design Decision 2: When do I need multi-attribute (composite) search keys, and which ones should I choose? A multipoint query involves a WHERE clause with multiple attributes. When this type of query occurs, a composite B+tree index should be used to efficiently access the set of rows that satisfies all the search criteria in the query. It was shown in Chapter 2 that a single composite index on n attributes can be significantly faster than n separate indexes on the same attributes because the separate index approach must include a merge step to find the intersection RIDs for the query. Tradeoff analysis between full table scans and multi-attribute B+tree indexes is shown in Section 2.5 (see Figure 4.1 for a summary).

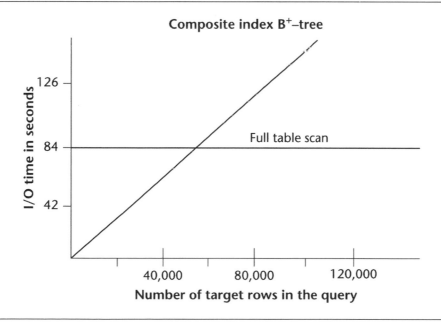

Figure 4.1   Comparison of composite index and scan I/O time for the same query.

Design Decision 3: Should I use a dense or sparse index? When rows are small relative to page size, sparse indexes are favored. A dense index will have many more entries and will often require one more level of indexing to access data than that for a sparse index. On the other hand, dense indexes can be effectively merged to make composite indexes efficient for multipoint queries. When rows are large relative to page size, a sparse index is rarely more efficient than a dense index. Another advantage of a dense index is that it can often become a covering index for certain queries.

Design Decision 4: When can I use a covering index? Sometimes a composite index can be used as a covering index for certain queries that can be satisfied by only searching the index. For example, an index on an attribute's feature, make, and model in that order could be used to completely satisfy a query:

```
SELECT make, model, vin, year
FROM carOnLot
WHERE feature = 'catalytic converter';
```

Design Decision 5: Should I create a clustered index? The basic rules for clustered indexes are:

1. Only one clustered index can be created for a given table, otherwise there would be major conflicts among the rows satisfying multiple queries using different indexes.

2. If an index can be used as a covering index, then no clustering is needed because the query can be satisfied by accessing the index only.

3. Range queries, multipoint queries, and single-point queries on nonprimary key values may all benefit from clustering. Each type of query involves accessing multiple rows, and any clustering would improve performance. If you have several choices of which rows to cluster, a tradeoff analysis may be needed to determine which choice optimizes performance (see Chapter 2).

Design Decision 6: Is an index still preferred when updates are taken into account? What are the tradeoffs between queries and updates for each index chosen? Once the indexes are chosen to improve performance for known queries, consider all the updates (inserts, deletes, updates) on the target tables. Looking at the tradeoffs from a cost/benefit perspective, consider the I/O time for all transactions involving queries and updates of each target table for a given index, taking into account the frequency of each query and update over a fixed time period:

Benefit of the index
= I/O time (all queries without index) −
I/O time (all queries with index).

Cost of the index
= I/O time (all updates with index) −
I/O time (all updates without index).

Note that each update has two components: the query to access the row(s) to be updated and the actual update itself. Clustered indexes tend to have higher update costs than nonclustered indexes and should be looked at carefully.

Basic rule: Create the index if the benefit is greater than the cost. This rule has exceptions that must be considered, since it is based only on I/O time. The priority of queries may be much higher than the priority of updates, especially if updates can be batch processed at noncritical hours in the day, which assumes that you can live with a few hours' delay in updates. In this case, the benefit may actually be less than the cost, as measured by I/O time, since priority may be a more important factor.

On the other hand, if updates must immediately be posted, but queries can be delayed, then the balance of priority shifts to the updates and the benefit must be significantly greater than the cost to justify the use of the index.

Design Decision 7: How do I know I made the right indexing choice? After one has made a decision about choice of index, it is important to investigate whether the right choice has been made or not. The original decision itself should have been done using some analytical performance tradeoff analysis that estimates the I/O time needed to answer a set of known queries on that table or set of tables and index. The design decision is very often made on this well-established, but theoretical basis.

Once the new index is set up, new queries are often established to take advantage of it, and data needs to be collected both before the index is implemented and afterward to determine whether or not the index is making the database perform better. Data collection facilities are now common to the major vendors. IBM uses the DB2 Instrumentation Facility to collect performance trace data for analysis; Microsoft uses data collection and analysis tools for SQL Server 2005, such as Performance Monitor and PSSDIAG; and Oracle uses the Automatic Workload Repository (AWR) in the Common Manageability Infrastructure to collect, maintain, and provide access to key statistics for performance self-tuning. If there is no improvement in performance, or if there is a degradation in performance, then the search needs to continue for a better solution. Automated tools are most useful here (see Chapter 11).

4.4 Join Index Selection

Up to this point, index selection has assumed simple queries based only on selection criteria, e.g.

```
SELECT lastName
FROM employee
WHERE empNo = 45678;
```

However, most queries involve at least one or more joins, and in-dexes are commonly used to speed up the join operations. This sec-tion discusses the index selection tradeoffs involved in join opera-tions using our simple mathematical model in Appendix A.

The basic join implementations we will consider are:

- Nested-loop join
  - Block nested-loop join
  - Indexed nested-loop join
- Sort-merge join
- Hash join

All these basic join implementations are supported by DB2, SQL Server, and Oracle, as well as many other systems.

Our analysis is based on the assumption that if the join is between a table whose foreign key matches another table's primary key, then m represents the number of rows in the table with the primary key and n represents the number of rows in the table with the foreign key. If the join is not between two such tables, then the designations of which table has m rows and which one has n rows is arbitrary.

4.4.1 Nested-loop Join

The nested-loop strategy is the basic method of join. The outer loop is a sequential scan of the first table R, and for each row in table R scanned, the inner loop is executed, a sequential scan of the second table S. Our basic parameters are the number of rows, m and n, in the two tables to be joined and the physical order of rows in each table. The complexity is $O(mn)$ because of the double loop. We assume that each table is stored in physically contiguous disk space to facilitate table scans. The time cost of executing this strategy also depends on which table we select for the outer and inner loops.

As an example, let us assume that we have three tables in the database: an employee table (emp) with 10,000 rows, a project table with 250 rows, and an assignedTo table with 50,000 rows. Two of these tables, project and assignedTo, are involved in the query below (see Figure 4.2). The common join column is projectName. We omit the time required to display the results of the join since it is constant for all the strategies and depends heavily on the display medium.

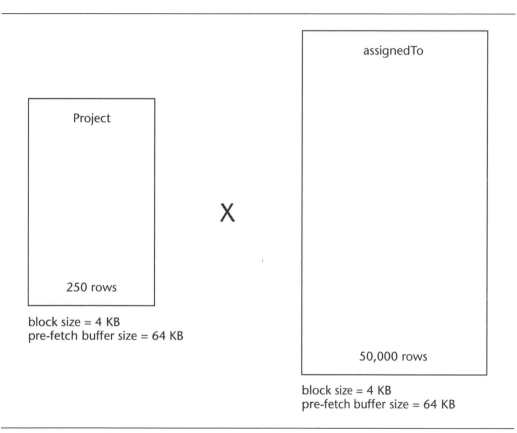

Figure 4.2   Two table join configuration.

Example Query 4.1

```
SELECT p.projectName, p.projectLeader, a.empId
    FROM project AS p, assignedTo AS a
    WHERE p.projectName = a.projectName;
```

m = 250 rows in the project table (each row is 200 bytes).

n = 50,000 rows in the assignedTo table (each row is 100 bytes).

We use the 4 KB block size and 64 KB prefetch buffer size described in Appendix A, and we use the block access times derived there from the IBM U320 hard drive: average seek time is 3.6 ms, average rotational delay is 2 ms, and transfer speed is 320 MB/sec. We also assume a shared-disk environment and the use of prefetch buffers for all table scans.

Number of 64 KB prefetch buffers needed to hold the assignedTo table
= ceiling((50,000 rows × 100 bytes/row)/64 KB)
= ceiling (5,000,000/65,536)
= 77.

Number of 64 KB pre-fetch buffers needed to hold the project table
= ceiling((250 rows × 200 bytes/row)/64 KB)
= ceiling (50,000/65,536)
= 1.

Nested-loop Case 1: assignedTo is the outer loop table.

join I/O time = scan assignedTo once, scan project n times
= (77 buffers + 50,000 scans × 1 buffer) × 5.8 ms
= 290.4 seconds.

Nested-loop Case 2: Project is the outer loop table.

join I/O time = scan project once, scan assignedTo m times
= (1 buffer + 250 scans × 77 buffers) × 5.8 ms
= 19,251 buffers × 5.8 ms
= 111.7 seconds.

In general the smaller table is usually chosen to be the outer table as the more efficient implementation of the query.

The nested-loop strategy can obviously improve its performance by a proper selection of outer and inner loop tables, but for this example both cases result in a long query (approximately 112–290 seconds). Note that this strategy does not take advantage of any row ordering or indexing methodology.

In general, one should avoid joins based on nonkeys. They are likely to produce very large tables, thus greatly increasing storage and update costs. For example, if two tables have 100 and 200 rows, respectively, then a join based on the key of either one results in a maximum of 200 rows, but a join based on a nonkey of either one can result in a maximum of 100 × 200, or 20,000 rows. Null values are also restricted to nonkey attributes so that they will not be used inadvertently in join operations.

4.4.2 Block Nested-loop Join

The block nested-loop join is a variation of the nested-loop join where the inner loop table is scanned once per block of the outer loop table instead of once per row. Once a block of the outer loop table is held in the buffer, the algorithm can scan all the rows in that block as a main memory operation with no I/Os. This process can greatly reduce the number of I/O operations required for the join and is generally preferred over the basic nested-loop approach. We look again at Example Query 4.1 and evaluate the two possible cases for the outer loop table.

Nested-loop Case 1: assignedTo is the outer loop table.

join I/O time = scan assignedTo once, scan project 77 prefetch
    buffer times
    = (77 buffers + 77 scans × 1 buffer) × 5.8 ms
    = .89 seconds.

Nested-loop Case 2: Project is the outer loop table.

join I/O time = scan project once, scan assignedTo m times.
    = (1 buffer + 1 scan × 77 buffers) × 5.8 ms
    = .45 seconds.

The block nested-loop configurations are both dramatically faster than the basic nested-loop configurations. We also note that making the project table the outer table is the better strategy for either set of configurations.

4.4.3 Indexed Nested-loop Join

The indexed nested-loop join is a useful alternative to the block nested-loop join when the join selectivity is low so that only a small subset of rows of the joined tables need to be accessed. Let's take another look at Example Query 4.1 and modify it by adding a WHERE condition to reduce the selectivity.

Example Query 4.2

This is a variation of Example Query 4.1 for low-selectivity joins.

```
SELECT p.projectName, p.projectLeader, a.empId
    FROM project AS p, assignedTo AS a
    WHERE p.projectName = a.projectName
    AND p.projectName = 'financial analysis';
```

Indexed nested-loop join Case 1: Scan foreign key table once and index to the primary key table once.

The basic strategy is to do a full scan of the table containing the foreign keys, and for each qualifying join attribute value, locate the corresponding unique row in the primary key table via a unique index. There will be a scan of the foreign key table and $(h + 1)$ block accesses to the primary key table via the unique index to each target row. Let the number of target rows, ntr = 100 qualifying rows for the foreign key table (assignedTo) matching one row in the primary key table (project) in Example Query 4.2. Assume height $h = 2$ for the B+tree index to table project.

join I/O time = scan the entire foreign key table (assignedTo) +
    index to the primary key table (project) qualifying row
    = (77 buffers + (h + 1) block (buffer) accesses) × 5.8 ms
    = (77 + 3) × 5.8 ms
    = .46 seconds.

Indexed nested-loop join Case 2: Index to the primary key table, and then index to the foreign key table.

Another indexed nested-loop join strategy is to use a B+tree or hash index to the primary key table once for the qualifying primary key value, then use a B+tree composite index to the foreign key table for the rows containing the qualifying foreign key values that match the primary key value. For this case, assume the composite index height, $h = 3$, one block required for the pointers to ntr = 100 target foreign key rows as given in Case 1.

join I/O time = index to the primary key table +
    index to the foreign key table
    = ((h + 1) + [h + 1 + ntr]) × 5.8 ms
    = (4 + 104) × 5.8 ms
    = .63 seconds.

Comparing the join times, we see that table scans have become very efficient, making Case 1 the better strategy here.

4.4.4 Sort-merge Join

The sort-merge join strategy, unlike the nested-loop strategy, takes advantage of row order in the same way that batch processing does. If the tables are both sorted on the join columns, then only a single sequential scan of each table is required to complete the join. If one or both tables are not sorted on the join column, then each unsorted table is sorted before the merge is executed. Even with the overhead of a sort operation, this algorithm is faster than nested-loop. We assume the complexity of the sort of *nb* blocks is approximately $2 \times nb \times \log_3 nb$ for a three-way sort, and that project has one buffer (250 rows) and assignedTo has 77 buffers (50,000 rows), as shown in Figure 4.2.

Sort-merge join Case 1: Both project and assignedTo are already ordered by projectName.

join I/O time = merge time (to scan both tables)
= (77 buffers + 1 buffer) × 5.8 ms
= .45 seconds.

Sort-merge join Case 2: Only project is ordered by projectName.

join I/O time = sort time for assignedTo +
merge time (to scan both sorted tables)
= $(2 \times 77 \times \log_3 77 + 77 + 1$ buffer accesses$) \times 5.8$ ms
= (2 × 77 × 3.954 + 78) × 5.8 ms
= 3.98 seconds.

Sort-merge join Case 3: Neither project nor assignedTo are ordered by project-Name.

join I/O time = sort time for both tables + merge time for both tables
= $(2 \times 77 \times \log_3 77 + 2 \times 1 \times \log_3 1 + 77 + 1) \times 5.8$ ms
= (608.9 + negligible + 77 + 1) × 5.8 ms
= 3.98 seconds.

We see that the sort phase of the sort-merge join strategy is the costliest component. If no sort is required (or the sorted tables are saved for future use), the sort-merge join is much more efficient than the block nested-loop join. However, if a sort is required, then the block nested-loop join tends to be more efficient.

4.4.5 Hash Join

The hash join strategy is also effective for low-selectivity joins. The basic strategy is to build a hash table in memory, if possible, or on disk if it won't fit into memory, by scanning each join table, and hashing the qualifying join column attribute values to partitions. An alternative algorithm has also been used that hashes the smaller of its two join inputs into memory and then reads the larger input to match with the in-memory hash table. We will assume the first algorithm here, where the two partitions are searched to confirm equal attributes (note that different attribute values could hash to the same location, thus necessitating a search to check them, but the same attribute values will never hash to different locations).

Once the hash table has been built, the second phase of the algorithm is to access the actual qualifying rows from each of the two tables (i.e., those rows from the two tables with matching attribute values in the hash file partitions). The complexity is $O(3m + 3n)$ because of the three phases of scanning: one to read the two tables, one to rewrite the two tables into partitions by hash value, and one to read the partitions for the actual join. We assume the time needed to check the two partitions is negligible. As we have assumed before, let ntr = 100 qualifying rows for the foreign key table.

Hash join Case 1: Hash table partitions stored on disk.

join I/O time = scan both tables (assignedTo and project) +
> write partitions + scan partitions to locate target rows
> = 3 × (77 + 1 buffers) × 5.8 ms
> = 1.36 seconds.

Hash join Case 2: Hash table partitions stored in memory (RAM).

In this case you only need to scan the tables once to put everything into memory and all access is then done directly from memory with no I/O costs.

join I/O time = scan both tables (assignedTo and project) into partitions in memory + scan partitions to locate target rows
> = (77 + 1) × 5.8 ms
> = .45 seconds.

In the hash join implementation, the table scans for partitioning may only have to be done infrequently as long as the hash file partitions in memory remain intact (with no updates) for a series of queries.

A summary of all the join strategies, including index selection, is given in Table 4.1. For high-selectivity queries, both the block nested-loop join and the sort-merge join perform very well. For low-selectivity joins, both the indexed nested-loop and the hash join perform well, with the hash join having a lower value for the upper bound for the given query.

Table 4.1   I/O Time Comparison for Example Queries 4.1 and 4.2

High-selectivitiy Query (4.1)		
Join Strategy	*Range of Performance*	*Best Performance*
Nested-loop join	112–290 seconds	Project is outer loop
Block nested-loop join	.45–.89 seconds	Project is outer loop
Sort-merge join	.45–3.98 seconds	No sorting required
Low-selectivity Query (4.2)		
Join Strategy	*Range of Performance*	*Best Performance*
Indexed nested-loop	.46–.63 seconds	Both tables indexed, ntr = 100
Hash join	.45–1.36 seconds	Hash partitions in memory

TIPS AND INSIGHTS FOR DATABASE PROFESSIONALS

- **Tip 1. The number and sizes of indexes varies.** However as a general rule indexes usually consume between 10% and 20% of the database disk storage. More than about 25% of disk being used for indexes should raise eyebrows and motivate a sober second look.

- **Tip 2. Indexes help queries and hurt write operations.** There-fore databases that are query heavy can err on slightly more in-dexes, and databases that either have a lot of insert/update/delete activity, or for whom performance of these write activities are very important, should be more conservative in the number of indexes they define for the system.

- **Tip 3. Review all the indexing rules of thumb listed in Section 4.2.** This section contains 12 practical rules for selecting indexes.

4.5 Summary

This chapter discusses the relationships between the different types of queries, indexing methods, and access methods. Knowledge of these relationships and what makes an index effective is very helpful in the decision-making process for index selection. There are seven critical index design decisions:

1. Whether or not an index is required, and if so which search key to use.
2. When to use a multi-attribute (composite) index and which search keys to use.

3. When to use a dense or sparse index.

4. When you can set up a covering index to avoid searching actual data rows.

5. When to use clustered indexes.

6. When an index choice will still be beneficial when table updates are considered.

7. When performance is bad and you need to revisit your other design decisions.

Several examples of index selection decisions are then given to illustrate the basic rules.

When joins are used, there are several choices among indexing, depending on whether the query is high selectivity (returns a large number of rows) or low selectivity (returns a small number of rows). Simple performance analysis illustrates the conditions when different indexing strategies are best.

4.6 Literature Summary

Burleson, D. *Physical Database Design Using Oracle*. Boca Raton, FL, Auerbach Publishers, 2005.

Date, C. J. *An Introduction to Database Systems*, vol. 1, 8th ed. Boston: Addison-Wesley, 2003.

Elmasri, R., and Navathe, S. B. *Fundamentals of Database Systems*, 4th ed. Boston: Addison-Wesley, and Redwood City, CA, 2004.

Garcia-Molina, H., Ullman, J., and Widom, J. *Database Systems: The Complete Book*. Englewood Cliffs, NJ: Prentice-Hall, 2001.

Hoffer, J. A., Prescott, M. B., and McFadden, F. R. *Modern Database Management*, 8th ed. Englewood Cliffs, NJ: Prentice-Hall, 2007.

Hubel, M. A Simple Approach to DB2 Index Redesign. *IDUG Solutions Journal,* 8(3), 2001.

Ramakrishnan, R., and Gehrke, J. *Database Management Systems*, 3rd ed. New York: McGraw-Hill, 2004.

Rees, S. Index Design for Performance. IDUG–North America, 2004.

Shasha, D., and Bonnet, P. *Database Tuning*. San Francisco: Morgan Kaufmann, 2003.

Shekhar, S., and Chawla, S. *Spatial Databases*. Englewood Cliffs, NJ: Prentice-Hall, 2003.

Silberschatz, A., Korth, H. F., and Sudarshan, S. *Database System Concepts*, 5th ed. Boston: McGraw-Hill, 2006.

Selecting Materialized Views

What is the answer to life, the universe, and everything? That is the question posed to Deep Thought in *The Hitchhiker's Guide to the Galaxy* by Douglas Adams. The question tied up Deep Thought for seven and a half million years. We tend not to ask such profound questions of our databases, but we do hope to find meaningful answers in a reasonable amount of time. If our query analyzer tells us a query will take seven and a half million years to run, we should probably look for a better solution. This chapter explores the use of materialized views to speed up query responses.

Make the common case fast. A large number of queries are posed against our database every day. There tend to be many queries that occur a few times, and a few queries that occur frequently. We have a database in third normal form (3NF). Some of the tables are rather large in terms of the number of disk blocks utilized. Accessing and joining these large tables can consume significant resources. We will focus on the queries that occur frequently, and also heavily consume disk input/output (I/O). If we have the result of such a query, then why not save the result to disk, and just read the answer the next time the query is posed? Materialized views are precalculated results stored on disk. Quick query response is the goal.

There are two ways that materialized views can be accessed. The first is the brute force method where the SQL is written to explictly access the view. This method limits the choices for the query optimizer in selecting other potentially superior query execution plans perhaps using some of the base tables on which the materialized view is based. Another issue is that it places a burden on the application designer to be aware of the available materialized views and exploit them. In fact for many enterprise scale databases the people designing the database application may not be the same people who perform the database design—making it hard or impossible for the application to explicitly access the materialized view. The second method for accessing materialized views is for the decision to be made by the query compiler during query optimizaton (when the query execution plan is selected). This method is known as "materialized view routing" or "automatic materialized view routing." In this case the query is written exclusively against the base tables (without reference to any materialzed views), and the query compiler makes a choice to access an available materialized view if it determines a superior query execution plan will result. Materialized view routing is far more usable than hand crafting access to each materialized view. However, automatic routing of this sort depends heavily on the sophistication of the query compiler to a) recognize a materialized view can be used in the query execution plan, and b) to determine correctly that such a substitution is beneficial. Both requirements turn out in practice to be highly complex choices for all but the most simple cases (such as the trivial case where the materialized view exactly matches an incoming query). As a result, materialized view routing is still an inexact science in modern database systems.

5.1   Simple View Materialization

The most straightforward type of materialized view contains data that exactly matches the result of a specific query. Reading from the materialized view gives the same result as calculating the result from the base tables. We illustrate with an example, and demonstrate the query I/O savings.

Figure 5.1 is a portion of a schema from a normalized database. We refer to these base tables throughout the chapter, as our examples build upon each other. The corresponding tables in the database instance contain data useful for the billing cycle, and job costing at a manufacturing plant.

Each invoice has an invoice date and an associated customer. The terms of the invoice track how many days the customer has to pay the invoice. The status indicates the current stage of the billing cycle for the given invoice. The notations can hold any

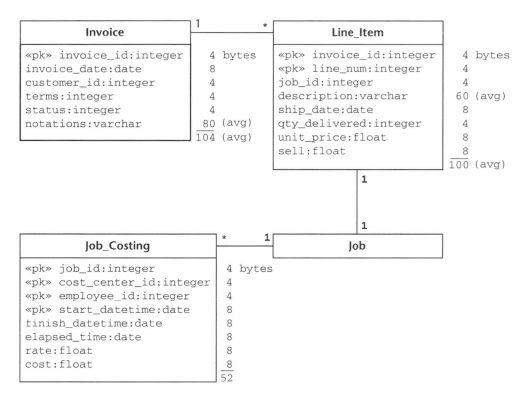

Figure 5.1   Schema snippet from an operational database.

general comments, such as notes on phone conversations with the customer regarding the invoice.

An invoice may list a variety of items, each on its own line. For example, you may have purchased blue widgets, which shipped on October 23, 2006, the quantity being 100 at a unit price of $2.50 each, for a sell value of $250. You may also have purchased red widgets, which appear on another line on the same invoice. This data is stored in the Line_Item table.

Each line item is associated with a job that was manufactured by the plant. The Job table contains the specifications for the job. The details of the Job table are not shown here, since those details do not enter into our discussion.

The Job_Costing table contains data tracking the time and costs expended in producing each job. When a job reaches a machine, the employee at that machine scans a job ID on the job ticket. The employee also scans a cost center bar code representing the operation to be performed, and a bar code containing their employee ID. The start and stop times for the operation are automatically recorded by the computer system. The data is stored in the Job_Costing table, along with the hourly rate for the cost center, and the cost calculated from the elapsed time and the hourly rate. This information is useful for comparing the actual cost versus the sell value of each job, which can lead to process improvement and better profits.

For the calculations that follow, let's assume the following statistics about our database:

- Average jobs per day = 10,000.
- Average invoices per day = 5,000.
- Average Job_Costing rows per job = 50.
- Days on record = 200.
- Customers = 5,000.
- The rows in all tables are clustered in primary key order.
- Anything 200 MB (i.e., 50,000 blocks) or less can be sorted in memory.

We continue to utilize the I/O time formulas introduced in Appendix A. Our calculations in this chapter are based on the IBM U320 146 GB hard drive.

- I/O time (4 KB block in a dedicated disk) = 2.0 ms.
- I/O time (64 KB buffer in a dedicated disk) = 2.2 ms.
- I/O time (4 KB block in a shared disk) = 5.6 ms.
- I/O time (64 KB block in a shared disk) = 5.8 ms.

Table scans should assume the use of prefetch buffers. Even though the individual I/O time is slightly longer for 64 KB than 4 KB I/O transfers, the 64 KB transfer only has to be executed 1/16 as many times, so the overall efficiency is almost 16 times better.

The management of the company likes to keep track of job profitability. Information Services has provided an excellent profit analysis application. Typically the application is run by 10 managers per day. The application requires the cost, sell, and profit for each job. The query to obtain the data from the existing database follows:

```
SELECT c.job_id, sum(c.cost) AS cost, sum(li.sell)
       AS sell,
    sum(li.sell) - sum(c.cost) AS profit
    FROM Job_Costing AS c, Line_Item AS li
    WHERE c.job_id = li.job_id
    GROUP BY c.job_id;
```

Let's calculate the time for this query, and then we'll improve the performance using a materialized view. The query involves the Line_Item and the Job_Costing tables. We need to calculate the row quantity, blocking factor, and number of blocks for each of the two tables. There are 10,000 jobs per day, with 200 days on record, for a total of 2,000,000 rows in the Line_Item table. Since we will be doing table scans, we will assume 64 KB prefetch buffers for the I/O read and write operations. The Line_Item calculations are:

Average rows per prefetch buffer
= floor((65,536 bytes/block)/(100 bytes/row)) = 655.
Number of buffers
= ceiling(2,000,000 rows/(655 rows/buffer)) = 3,054.

The Job_Costing table contains 50 rows average per job, for 10,000 jobs per day, with 200 days on record, for a total of 100,000,000 rows. The Job_Costing calculations are:

Average rows per buffer
= floor((65,536 bytes/block)/(52 bytes/row)) = 1,260.
Number of buffers = ceiling(100,000,000 rows/(1,260 rows/buffer))
– 79,366.

Since we are joining the two tables in full, a merge-join is efficient. The data in the Job_Costing table is ordered by job_id. The Line_Item table needs to be sorted by job_id in order to do a merge-join. The Line_Item table is small enough to sort in memory, so we only need one sequential scan to load the table into memory.

join cost (shared disk) = scan time (Line_Item and Job_Costing tables using 64 KB prefetch buffers)
= (3,054 + 79,366 buffers) × 5.8 ms
= 82,420 × 5.8 ms
= 478 seconds ≈ 8 minutes.

This is a bit long for a query, especially when you have to do several of them and the 10 managers decide to run your excellent profit analysis program to obtain information for their big meeting, which begins in five minutes. Soon there is a knocking at your door! What can we do? We can calculate the necessary results during off hours, and store the processed data in a materialized view. Then when the managers come in, they can obtain results blazingly fast! Figure 5.2 shows the schema of the materialized view.

First, let's calculate the time to create the view, and then we'll compute the time to obtain our results from the Profit_by_Job table. The view is created by running the original query and then writing the results to the Profit_by_Job table. The number of block (buffer) accesses for the join is the same, but the I/O time is now shorter because the environment is dedicated during off hours.

Join cost (dedicated disk) = 82,420 × 2.2 ms ≈ 181 seconds ≈ 3 minutes.

We need to calculate the blocking factor in order to calculate the time to write the results into the Profit_by_Job table. We have 10,000 jobs per day, with 200 days on record, so we have 2,000,000 rows in the Profit_by_Job table. The Profit_by_Job calculations are:

Average rows per buffer = floor((65,536 bytes/block)/(28 bytes/row))
    = 2,340.
Number of buffers = ceiling(2,000,000 rows/(2,340 rows/buffer))
    = 855.
Write cost (dedicated disk) = 855 × 2.2 ms ≈ 2 seconds.
Profit_by_Job creation cost = join cost + write cost = 181 + 2
    = 183 seconds.

The profitability-by-job query is very simple based on the new materialized view:

```
SELECT * FROM Profit_by_Job;
```

We've already calculated that there are 855 buffers for the Profit_by_Job table. The query is run in a shared disk (five minutes before the meeting).

Query I/O time (table scan, shared disk) = 855 × 5.8 ms ≈ 5 seconds.

The managers have their reports in hand with plenty of time for small talk before the meeting is called to order. Coffees are sipped, and the mood is mellow as someone mentions how your excellent profit analysis program really rocks!

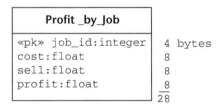

Figure 5.2   Profit_by_job materialized view.

Let's recap:

Disk I/O time before Profit_by_Job
    = query frequency × I/O time per query
    = (10 queries/day) × (478 sec/query)
    = 4,780 seconds (or about 1 hour, 20 min)

Disk I/O time with Profit_by_Job
    = creation cost + query frequency × I/O time per query
    = 183 sec creation cost + (10 queries/day) × (5 sec/query)
    = 233 seconds.

Utilizing materialized views can bring marked improvement in both total disk I/O and query response. Some gain derives from taking advantage of a dedicated disk to generate the view, but the lion's share comes from two factors. First, the materialized view may be much smaller than the base tables, leading to large gains in disk I/O performance per query. Second, frequent queries multiply the gain.

5.2 Exploiting Commonality

There are a number of frequent queries that look at profitability from different perspectives. Trends over time can yield valuable insights, triggering decisions that curtail problems and provide a brighter future. Another useful analysis is to track profitability by customer. For example, if we know who our most profitable customers are, we can solicit more jobs by offering bulk discounts if they agree to bring some minimum number of jobs within a fixed timeframe. We examine the possibility of materializing two more materialized views to quickly answer these queries. Then we look at an alternative materialized view that takes advantage of the commonality of our three profitability queries.

The trends in profitability by date are looked over briefly once a day by upper management and also the accounting manager. We determine that the query is typically run five times a day. The profitability by invoice date query when posed against the base tables is as follows:

```
SELECT i.invoice_date, sum(c.cost) AS cost, sum(li.sell)
AS sell,
    sum(li.sell) - sum(c.cost) AS profit
    FROM Invoice AS i, Job_Costing AS c, Line_Item AS li
    WHERE i.invoice_id = li.invoice_id
    AND c.job_id = li.job_id
    GROUP BY i.invoice_date;
```

This query reads from the Invoice, Job_Costing, and Line_Item tables. We've already calculated the number of blocks for the Job_Costing and the Line_Item tables. We still need to calculate the number of blocks for the Invoice table. We average 5,000 invoices per day, with 200 days on record, giving 1,000,000 rows in the Invoice table. The Invoice calculations are:

Average rows per block (buffer)
= floor((65,536 bytes/buffer)/(104 bytes/row)) = 630.
Number of blocks (buffers)
= ceiling(1,000,000 rows/(630 rows/buffer)) = 1,588.

There are two possible join orderings, leading to two alternative query plans.

Plan A:

Step 1: Merge-join Line_Item with Invoice (no sorting required)

Step 2: Merge-join step 1 result with Job_Costing (requires sorting step 1 result by job_id)

Plan B:

Step 1: Merge-join Line_Item with Job_Costing (requires sorting Line_Item by job_id)

Step 2: Merge-join step 1 result with Invoice (requires sorting step 1 result by invoice_id)

Both plans require the three base tables to be scanned in full. Plan A is superior since it requires much less sorting than plan B. After the merge-join of Line_Item with Invoice, the only columns to be kept are invoice_date, job_id, and sell. The result is 2,000,000 rows of 20 bytes each for less than 10,000 blocks. The result is small enough to sort in memory, so we only need to figure the time to scan the tables once.

Query I/O time (shared disk)
= scan Line_Item + scan Invoice + scan Job_Costing
= (3,054 blocks + 1,588 blocks + 79,366 buffers scanned) × 5.8 ms
= 84,008 × 5.8 ms
= 487 seconds.

The same results could be obtained from the materialized view specified in Figure 5.3.

We can generate the materialized view from scratch during off hours by running the same query, and then storing the results.

Query I/O time (dedicated disk) = 84,008 × 2.2 ms ≈ 185 seconds.

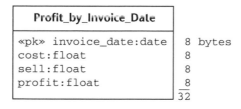

Figure 5.3   Profit_by_invoice_date snapshot.

We have 200 days on record, so the Profit_by_Invioce_Date table has 200 rows. The Profit_by_Invoice_Date calculations are:

Average rows per block (buffer)
  = floor((65,536 bytes/buffer)/(32 bytes/row)) = 2,048.
Number of blocks (buffers) = ceiling(200 rows/(2,048 rows/block))
  = 1.

Write cost (dedicated disk) = 1 × 2.2 ms = 2.2 ms.

Profit_by_Invoice_Date creation cost = query cost + write cost
  = 185 sec + .0022 sec
  ≈ 185 seconds.

The user query becomes as follows:

```
SELECT * FROM Profit_by_Invoice_Date;
```

The query I/O time calculations for this query in a shared disk follow:

Query I/O time (shared disk) = 1 × 5.8 ms = 5.8 ms.
Disk I/O time before Profit_by_Invoice_Date
  = query frequency × I/O time per query
  = (5 queries/day) × (487 sec/query)
  = 2,435 seconds (just over 40 min)
Disk I/O time with Profit_by_Invoice_Date
  = creation cost + query frequency × I/O time per query
  = 185 sec creation cost + (5 queries/day)
  × (5.8 ms/query) ≈ 185 seconds.

There is another approach to maintaining materialized views that can further improve the gain in many cases. Instead of computing the materialized views from scratch each night, they can be maintained incrementally. For example, in the case of the Profit_by_Invoice_Date table, we could keep the existing data, and just add a new row whenever a new invoice cycle completes. Let's finish up the current train of thought, and we'll return the idea of incremental updates in Section 5.4.

The profitability by customer query is very similar to the profitability by invoice date. This query is run primarily by the sales department. We determine that the query is run on average three times per day. Here's the query on the base tables:

```
SELECT i.customer_id, sum(c.cost) AS cost, sum(li.sell)
AS sell,
    sum(li.sell) - sum(c.cost) AS profit
    FROM Invoice AS i, Job_Costing AS c, Line_Item AS li
    WHERE i.invoice_id = li.invoice_id
    AND c.job_id = li.job_id
    GROUP BY i. customer_id;
```

Notice the tables and the joins are the same as those used in the profitability by invoice date query. Since the same tables are read, and the same joins are performed, the query I/O time is also unchanged.

Query I/O time (shared disk)
    = scan Line_Item + scan Invoice + scan Job_Costing
    = 84,008 × 5.8 ms = 487 seconds.

Profit_by_Customer	
«pk» customer_id:integer	4 bytes
cost:float	8
sell:float	8
profit:float	$\frac{8}{28}$

Figure 5.4   Profit_by_Customer materialized view.

Figure 5.4 shows the corresponding materialized view. The I/O cost to create the Profit_by_Customer table is equal to the cost to query the base tables plus the cost to write the result to disk.

Query I/O time (dedicated disk) = 84,008 × 2.2 ms ≈ 185 seconds.

We have 5,000 customers, so the Profit_by_Customer table has 5,000 rows. The Profit_by_Customer calculations are:

Average rows per block (buffer)
= floor((65,536 bytes/block)/(28 bytes/row)) = 2,340.
Number of blocks (buffers)
= ceiling(5,000 rows/(2,340 rows/block)) = 3.

Write cost (dedicated disk) = 3 × 2.2 ms = 6.6 ms.

Profit_by_Customer creation cost = query cost + write cost
≈ 185 sec + .0066 sec ≈ 185 seconds.

The user query becomes as follows:

```
SELECT * FROM Profit_by_Customer;
```

The query I/O time calculations for a shared disk follow.

Query I/O time (sequential scan of entire table, shared disk)
= 3 × 5.8 ms = 17.4 ms.

Disk I/O time before Profit_by_Customer
= query frequency × I/O time per query
= (3 queries/day) × (487 sec/query) = 1,461 seconds.
Disk I/O time with Profit_by_Customer
= creation cost + query frequency × I/O time per query
= 185 sec creation cost + (3 queries/day)
× (0.017 sec/query) ≈ 185 seconds.

Profit_Fact	
«pk» job_id:integer	4 bytes
invoice_date:date	8
customer_id:integer	4
cost:float	8
sell:float	8
profit:float	8
	40

Figure 5.5   Profit fact table.

Again, we see a savings in disk I/O resulting from utilizing a materialized view to answer repeated queries. At this point, one might think, "I'll just keep going, and create a materialized view for each of the common queries and make a huge net gain!" However, we do need to live within our resource constraints. There are a number of constraints discussed in Section 5.4. Suffice it to say here, we need to keep the number of materialized views under control. Let's examine the possibility of combining some materialized views.

If you'll look back at Figures 5.2, 5.3, and 5.4, you'll notice that they all have cost, sell, and profit in common. It is reasonable to consider combining these tables, since they are very similar. Figure 5.5 specifies the schema for the combined table. The job_id is the primary key, since we have this functional dependency: job_id → invoice_date, customer_id, cost, sell, and profit.

The query to generate the data for the Profit_Fact table is the following:

```
SELECT c.job_id, i.invoice_date, i.customer_id,
sum(c.cost) AS cost, sum(li.sell) AS sell, sum(li.sell)
- sum(c.cost) AS profit
    FROM Invoice AS i, Job_Costing AS c, Line_Item AS li
    WHERE i.invoice_id = li.invoice_id
    AND c.job_id = li.job_id
    GROUP BY i.customer_id;
```

The I/O cost to create the Profit_Fact table is equal to the cost to query the base tables plus the cost to write the result to disk. The query against the base tables leads to the same joins that we calculated for the Profit_by_Customer table.

Query I/O time (dedicated disk) = 84,008 × 2.2 ms ≈ 185 seconds.

The number of rows is equal to the number of jobs, since the job_id is the primary key. Thus, there are 2,000,000 rows in the Profit_Fact table. The Profit_Fact calculations are:

Average rows per block (buffer)
   = floor((65,536 bytes/buffer)/(40 bytes/row)) = 1,638.
Number of buffers = ceiling(2,000,000 rows/(1,638 rows/buffer))
   = 1,222.

Write cost (dedicated disk) = 1,222 × 2.2 ms ≈ 3 seconds.

Profit_Fact creation cost = query cost + write cost
   ≈ 185 sec + 3 sec ≈ 188 seconds.

Using the materialized view described by Figure 5.5, our three user queries are as follows:

```
SELECT job_id, cost, sell, profit
   FROM Profit_Fact;

SELECT invoice_date, sum(cost) AS cost, sum(sell) AS
sell, sum(profit) AS profit
FROM Profit_Fact
GROUP BY invoice_date;

SELECT customer_id, sum(cost) AS cost, sum(sell) AS
sell, sum(profit) AS profit
FROM Profit_Fact
GROUP BY customer_id;
```

All three of these queries scan the Profit_Fact_Table in full.

Query I/O time (sequential scan, shared disk)
= 1,222 × 5.8 ms ≈ 7 seconds.

Let's recap again. We'll total up the I/O times for our three queries: profitability by job, profitability by date, and profitability by customer. We'll figure the numbers for three different cases: using the base tables, using materialized views specific to the three queries, and using the common Profit_Fact table.

Disk I/O times using base tables
= (4,780 sec + 2,435 sec + 1,461 sec)/day = 8,676 seconds.

Disk I/O times using Profit_by_Job, Profit_by_Invoice_Date,
and Profit_by_Customer = (233 sec + 185 sec + 185 sec)/day
= 603 sec/day.

Disk I/O time using Profit_Fact table
= creation cost + query frequency × I/O time per query
= 188 sec creation cost + (10 profit by job queries/day)
   × (7 sec/query)
   + (5 profit by date queries/day) × (7 sec/query)
   + (3 profit by customer queries/day) × (7 sec/query)
≈ 314 seconds per day.

Look at this! Using one common materialized view gains more in terms of total disk I/O than having the three materialized views specifically designed for the given three queries. Sometimes, less is more. There is a small drawback, the user queries now take 7 seconds of disk I/O. If this is not acceptable in rare cases, then another possibility is to create the Profit_Fact table first and then create the other materialized views from the Profit_Fact table rather than from the base tables directly. Since the Profit_Fact table is much smaller than the base tables, the creation time for the other materialized views can be greatly reduced. We leave the I/O time calculations as an exercise.

5.3 Exploiting Grouping and Generalization

The health of the company depends on monitoring both short- and long-term trends. Daily snapshots are the pulse, but we also need monthly and yearly reports. Likewise, monitoring profitability by customer is very useful in focusing our efforts, but knowledge at the level of state or province and country is needed to make broader decisions. We can easily augment the fact table from Figure 5.5 to support these additional queries. Figure 5.6 shows the addition of two tables to facilitate the more general queries. The Calendar table contains month and year columns that can be used in "group by" clauses to obtain more general trends from the Profit_Fact table. The state_province and country columns of the Customer table can be used in "group by" clauses to gain strategic knowledge in geographical terms.

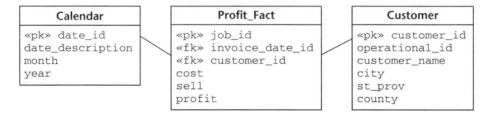

Figure 5.6   Profit fact table with Calendar and Customer dimension tables.

If you are familiar with data warehousing, then you will recognize Figure 5.6 as a simple star schema with two-dimension tables, namely the Calendar and the Customer tables. This chapter to this point is a progression leading up to the star schema. Hopefully the progression clarifies the reasoning behind star schemas, and why they can be efficient designs. Chapter 14 covers the star schema and the dimensional design approach in more depth. If you are unfamiliar with star schemas, it will help to keep in mind the discussion from this chapter when you reach Chapter 14.

We offer two example queries that illustrate how the dimension tables can be used to group data into more general results. Then we cover the product graph, which enumerates and relates the possible combinations of groupings along each dimension.

Here is the query to obtain profitability information at the monthly level for 2006:

```
SELECT month, sum(cost), sum(sell), sum(profit)
    FROM Calendar AS c, Profit_Fact AS p
    WHERE year = 2006
    AND c.date_id = p.date_id
    GROUP BY month
    ORDER BY month;
```

This is the query to obtain data at the state level by year:

```
SELECT country, st_prov, year, sum(cost), sum(sell),
sum(profit)
    FROM Calendar AS cal, Profit_Fact AS p, Customer AS
cust
    AND cal.date_id = p.date_id
    AND cust.customer_id = p.customer_id
    GROUP BY country, st_prov, year
    ORDER BY country, st_prov, year;
```

There are many combinations of levels possible. We can enumerate the combinations and illustrate the relationships in a product graph. Figure 5.7 is the product graph for the star schema in Figure 5.6. Actually, the product graph would be three dimensional, because there is also a Job dimension. However, to keep the diagram simple we are leaving off the level that includes the job_id, except for the Profit_Fact table, which is important as a data source. The Calendar and the Customer dimensions are orthogonal. The levels along each dimension are arranged in order from the most specific at the top to the most general at the bottom. Each node represents a view. For example, the Profit_Fact table corresponds to the node labeled "job, date, customer." Since the Profit_Fact table is materialized, we have shaded its node gray.

Following a path from specific to general signifies aggregation. For example, monthly customer data can be aggregated from the daily customer data. More generally, the view at any node can be computed by aggregating data from any materialized ancestor. If aggregation is complete along a dimension, the level is described by the word "all." For example, the Profit_by_Customer table corresponds to the node labeled "all, customer," and the Profit_by_Invoice_Date table corresponds to the node "date, all." Both of these can be materialized from the Profit_Fact table, since it is a materialized ancestor. The bottom node represents the grand totals of all the data in the Profit_Fact table. Let's say we've decided to materialize the Profit_by_Customer and the Profit_by_Invoice_Date views, as indicated in Figure 5.7. If we run a query for the grand totals, which of the three materialized ancestor views is the best to use as a data source? The smallest would be the best choice, since the smaller source leads to

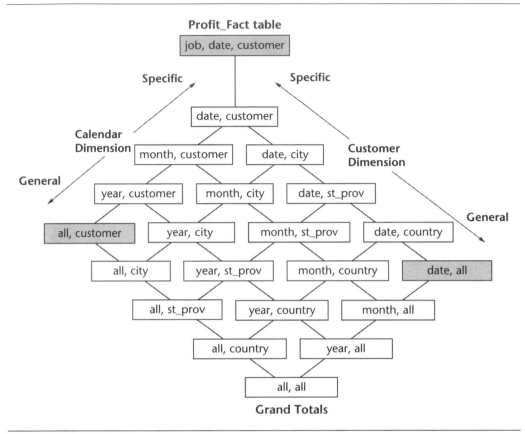

Figure 5.7   Product graph in Calendar and Customer dimensions.

reduced disk I/O and faster response. The Profit_by_Invoice_Date (i.e., the "date, all") node) is the best choice, requiring the reading of only one block.

5.4 Resource Considerations

There are a number of resource constraints to keep in mind as you design your materialized views. These include the number of materialized views, the extra disk space required, and the length of the available update window. We discuss each in turn.

The number of possible views in a typical database is tremendous. Given a set of dimensions, the number of views is the product of the number of levels in each dimension. The number of possible views for the example in Figure 5.7 is 4 Calendar levels × 5 Customer levels × 2 Job levels = 40 possible views. Remember, we left out a level of the Job dimension in order to make the graph readable. We have only examined the business process of profit analysis. There are typically many business processes to consider when designing a database. Obviously, it is not possible to materialize all the views, so we must pick a strategic subset of the views for materialization.

Early research on the problem of selecting materialized views utilized a constraint on the number of views materialized [Harinarayan, Rajaraman, and Ullman 1996]. Today, it is still useful to constrain the number of materialized views for at least two reasons: the time available for designing the database is a constraint and materializing more views requires more design time. Also, materializing more views requires more update processes. Not only does increasing the number of materialized views consume more computer resources, it also requires more database administration. As the base tables evolve with the company's needs, the materialized views and the update processes must be adjusted. Set a limit on the number of views you are willing to design and maintain.

Focusing on views that answer frequent queries is a heuristic that reduces the complexity of the design process to a more manageable level. Constructing a complete product graph is a problem with exponential complexity relative to the number of dimensions. However, a simplified lattice is easily constructed based on the frequent queries. The lattice in Figure 5.8 illustrates a simple lattice structure. The pertinent base tables are included at the top. The Profit_Fact view can be created from the base tables. The other three views can be calculated from the Profit_Fact view.

Basically, the lattice in Figure 5.8 is a reduced version of the product graph in Figure 5.7. The views that are queried infrequently are not included, leading to a much simpler diagram. We've added the base tables and the view schemas into the lattice, succinctly capturing the situation. Each node is tagged with the size in blocks, and the associated query frequency when appropriate. This metadata is important when calculating the relative benefits of various possible view materializations.

Notice the 4-byte invoice_date_id replaces the 8-byte invoice_date column used in Figure 5.5. The number of blocks is recalculated accordingly. The Profit_Fact table calculations are:

Average rows per block (buffer)
= floor((65,536 bytes/buffer)/(36 bytes/row)) = 1,820.

Number of buffers = ceiling(2,000,000 rows/(1,820 rows/buffer))
= 1,099.

The amount of disk space required to store the materialized views is an obvious constraint. Kimball et al. [1998, p. 544] mention that as a rule of thumb in the context of data warehousing, many database administrators (DBAs) limit the space increase needed for aggregated materialized views to a factor of two or less. This may vary depending on the purpose of the database, and the resources of the organization. If you are hoping to improve performance without implementing a full-fledged data warehouse, then you can set your disk space limit at a more modest level. If the views that

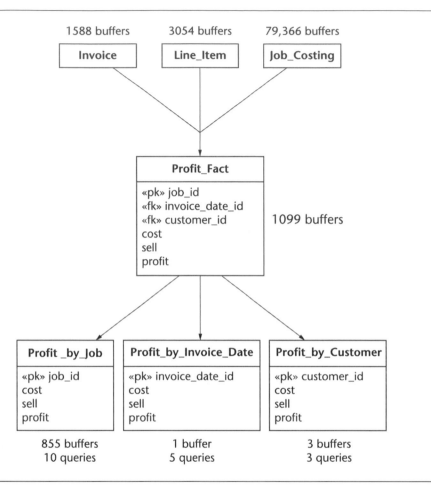

Figure 5.8   A simplified lattice.

bring the greatest gain are selected for materialization first, then in general, committing even modest levels of disk space can bring marked improvements to query responses. Committing larger amounts of disk space will in general bring quicker query response, but with diminishing returns. Decide on a limit for the amount of disk space.

If you find that growth is pushing the disk space limit, there are options to extend the usefulness, while remaining within your organization's means. For example, let's say that management decides they want to track summary data for five years. You can continue to purge data from the base tables after say half a year, and at the same time maintain five years of historical data in the materialized views. Likewise, if a materialized view containing fine-granularity data becomes too large, the details can be purged after some appropriate amount of time, while summary views can continue to hold extended history. For example, if the Profit_Fact table becomes too large, data older than two years could be purged, while the Profit_by_Invoice_Date table can hold five years' worth of data and still be very small. The purging of detailed data while holding on to summary data requires an incremental update strategy.

The time available for updates is another constraint to consider. Often, an update window is set aside during off hours, when the materialized views are updated in a dedicated disk. Determine the amount of time available for the update window, if applicable. You may determine that an update window is not possible. Perhaps your organization operates 24 hours a day, and the system cannot be made unavailable for any update window. Perhaps the users need real-time summary data, and can't use data that was computed last night. Incremental updates can often address these problems.

Instead of computing a view from scratch, incremental updates keep the majority of the rows of a materialized view intact, and add new results as appropriate. For example, consider the Profit_by_Invoice_Date table. Let's say the invoices are processed in a daily cycle. Information is gathered for the jobs that have shipped since the previous invoice cycle. Each customer that has jobs in the current cycle has an invoice assigned. The customer's jobs are placed on the invoice. After the invoices are verified, the invoices are printed and sent to the customers, and the status of each invoice is updated in the database. As the cycle completes, the sell value for each job is known. The costs for each job are also known, since the Job_Costing table is updated in real time and work completes on each job before it is invoiced. We can calculate the daily totals and add a single row to the Profit_by_Invoice_Date table. Updating the materialized views in real time is sometimes referred to as a *trickle feed*.

5.5 Examples: The Good, the Bad, and the Ugly

Materialized views and star schemas are good approaches for reducing disk I/O, resulting in quicker query responses. Figure 5.6 is an example of a star schema, illustrating the dimensional design approach. Typically, there are more dimensions in a star schema, but the example is sufficient for discussion. The fact table is a materialized view derived from the base tables. The materialized view amounts to stored calculations that reduce the amount of disk I/O. The dimension tables provide a means to group data by various levels along a variety of dimensions. The dimension tables add flexibility, multiplying the gains of the fact table over a larger family of queries. The star schema and the dimensional design approach can be good for improving query responses.

A question naturally arises. If precomputing saves time, then why not precompute the joins between the fact table and the dimension tables? Wouldn't this save even more time? The schema shown in Figure 5.9 is a possible consolidation of the fact table with the dimension tables from Figure 5.6. Now we can query just one table, and we still have the same ability to group by levels that we had with the dimension tables.

Let's rewrite the second query from Section 5.3. The query is now simpler:

Consolidated_Profit	
«pk» job_id	4 bytes
invoice_date_id	4
date_description	12 (avg)
month	4
year	4
customer_id	4
customer_name	12 (avg)
city	12 (avg)
st_prov	12 (avg)
country	12 (avg)
cost	8
sell	8
profit	8
	104

Figure 5.9   The bad: consolidating dimension tables into fact tables.

```
SELECT country, st_prov, year, sum(cost), sum(sell),
sum(profit)
    FROM Consolidated_Profit
    GROUP BY country, st_prov, year
    ORDER BY country, st_prov, year;
```

All we need to do is scan one table. Let's figure out how many blocks (buffers) that entails. There are 2,000,000 rows since there are 2,000,000 jobs. The Consolidated_Profit table calculations are:

Average rows per block (buffer)
   = floor((65,536 bytes/buffer)/(104 bytes/row)) = 630.

Number of buffers = ceiling(2,000,000 rows/(630 rows/buffer))
   = 3,175.

Let's figure the number of blocks scanned if the schema in Figure 5.6 is used instead. The Calendar table has 200 rows averaging 24 bytes each. The Profit_Fact table has 2,000,000 rows of 36 bytes each. The Customer table has 5,000 rows, averaging 64 bytes each. The Calendar table calculations are:

Average rows per block (buffer)
   = floor((65,536 bytes/buffer)/(24 bytes/row)) = 2,730.

Number of buffers = ceiling(200 rows/(2,730 rows/buffer)) = 1.

Profit_Fact table (calculated previously): 1,099 buffers.

The Customer table calculations are:

Average rows per block (buffer)
= floor((65,536 bytes/buffer)/(64 bytes/row)) = 1,024.

Number of buffers = ceiling(5,000 rows/(1,024 rows/buffer)) = 5.

Total blocks scanned using star schema
   = 1 + 1,099 + 5 = 1,105 blocks.

Consolidating the dimension tables with the fact table actually slows down the query by almost threefold. Consolidating the dimension tables with the fact table is a bad idea.

Why are the dimension tables denormalized in Figure 5.6? If consolidating the dimension tables with the fact table is a bad idea, perhaps if we normalize the dimension tables into smaller tables we can make further gains. Figure 5.10 shows the dimension tables normalized. This is referred to in the literature as a snowflake schema.

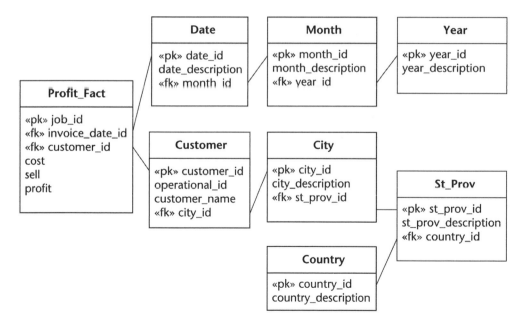

Figure 5.10   The ugly: normalizing the dimension tables.

Here is our query, rewritten for the schema shown in Figure 5.10:

```
SELECT country, st_prov, year, sum(cost), sum(sell),
sum(profit)
    FROM Profit_Fact, Customer, City, St_Prov, Country,
        Date, Month, Year
    WHERE Profit_Fact.customer_id = Customer.customer_id
    AND Customer.city_id = City.city_id
    AND City.st_prov_id = St_Prov.st_prov_id
    AND St_Prov.country_id = Country.country_id
    AND Profit_Fact.invoice_date_id = Date.date_id
    AND Date.month_id = Month.month_id
    AND Month.year_id = Year.year_id
    GROUP BY country, st_prov, year
    ORDER BY country, st_prov, year;
```

The query is now much more complex, requiring seven joins. Kimball and Ross [2002] site the join complexity as one reason to avoid the snowflake schema. The queries are more difficult to write, and the query optimizer may have difficulty finding a good plan. Furthermore, the star schema is more intuitive than the snowflake schema. Some may find the normalized form of the dimensions in the snowflake schema an elegant solution, but most find it an undesirable solution.

5.6 Usage Syntax and Examples

We illustrate some of the available update strategies, utilizing examples written in SQL. The SQL examples in this section are valid for Oracle 10g. If you are using another version of Oracle, check your documentation for possible variations.

SQL in Oracle includes constructs for creating materialized views and for specifying the update strategy. Let's say you want to create a materialized view for storing the profit by customer data, based on the schema shown in Figure 5.6. If you want the materialized view refreshed from scratch each morning at 3:00 A.M. starting with January 31, 2007, the SQL for this would be as follows:

```
CREATE MATERIALIZED VIEW Profit_by_Customer
REFRESH COMPLETE
START WITH TO_DATE('31-01-2007 03:00:00',
    'DD-MM-YYYY HH24:MI:SS')
NEXT SYSDATE + 1
AS SELECT customer_id, sum(cost) AS cost, sum(sell) AS
sell, sum(profit) AS profit
    FROM Profit_Fact
    GROUP BY customer_id;
```

Of course, a complete refresh would drain resources if the Profit_Fact table has many rows. When the source table is huge, as is often the case in a data warehouse, another more viable option is to use the fast refresh option. Fast refresh is an incremental update strategy. Basically the existing data in the materialized view is left intact, changes to the source table are tracked, and the update process summarizes the new data and then adjusts/creates the appropriate rows in the materialized view. If we want to use the fast refresh option, then we need to tell Oracle to track the changes to the source data table.

```
CREATE MATERIALIZED VIEW LOG ON Profit_Fact
WITH ROWID, SEQUENCE(job_id, invoice_date_id,
customer_id, cost, sell, profit)
INCLUDING NEW VALUES;
```

The definition for the profit by customer summary, taking advantage of the fast refresh strategy, is as follows.

```
CREATE MATERIALIZED VIEW Profit_by_Customer
REFRESH FAST
START WITH TO_DATE('31-01-2007 03:00:00',
  'DD-MM-YYYY HH24:MI:SS')
NEXT SYSDATE + 1
AS SELECT customer_id, sum(cost) AS cost, sum(sell) AS
sell, sum(profit) AS profit
    FROM Profit_Fact
    GROUP BY customer_id;
```

Other strategies are also possible. For example, the following definition keeps the materialized view updated in real time, whenever there is a commit on the Profit_Fact table.

```
CREATE MATERIALIZED VIEW Profit_by_Customer
REFRESH ON COMMIT
AS SELECT customer_id, sum(cost) AS cost, sum(sell) AS
sell, sum(profit) AS profit
    FROM Profit_Fact
    GROUP BY customer_id;
```

Typically, data warehouses contain huge fact tables, and the refresh processes run during designated update windows. The "fast" option supports this strategy. If you have a materialized view where a sizeable portion of the rows change each day, then a "complete" refresh may perform faster, since bulk operations are more efficient than a large number of incremental changes. The "on commit" option supports real-time updates. If you need real-time data, keep in mind that updating a materialized view whenever there is a commit on the source table(s) can be resource intensive. You may not be able to support as many materialized views as you would with a scheduled refresh strategy.

Oracle has a QUERY_REWRITE_ENABLED setting that should be set in the configuration parameter file to make fuller use of the materialized views you create. If query rewrite is turned on, then Oracle automatically recognizes when a small materialized view can be used to answer a query, instead of reading the larger underlying source tables.

TIPS AND INSIGHTS FOR DATABASE PROFESSIONALS

- **Tip 1. Utilizing materialized views can bring marked improvement in both total disk I/O and query response.** Focus on the queries that occur frequently and also heavily consume disk I/O. These queries are the greatest opportunities for performance gain through materialized views.

- **Tip 2. Good candidates to consider for materialization are the natural views of frequent queries, and also common ancestors of those views.**

- **Tip 3. Star schemas can make a materialized view applicable to a large family of queries, thereby multiplying the gain for the given resources.**

- **Tip 4. Lattice structure diagrams can facilitate the selection of materialized views and also the planning of data update paths through the lattice.**

- **Tip 5. Decide on the update strategy for each materialized view.** Incremental updates within a fixed update window during off hours are a common strategy. If a large portion of the rows in a materialized view change with each update, the complete refresh strategy takes advantage of bulk load operations. If real-time data is needed, the refresh on commit strategy is the way to go.

- **Tip 6. Set a limit on the number of views you are willing to design and maintain.** There are two reasons why this is so important. First because each materialized view consumes storage space on disk. Second, each materialized view adds compelxity to the search for the optimal query execution plan during query compilation. As a result, a large number of materialized views can have a profoundy negative consequence on the time required for query compilation. Queries that might otherwise compile in fractions of a second may expand to take minutes. In some extreme cases where a large number of materialized view have been defined the compilation time can significantly exceed the time for the query to execute.

- **Tip 7. Decide on a limit for the amount of disk space available for materialized views.** Committing larger amounts of disk space will in general bring quicker query response, but with diminishing returns. Generally, few data warehouses allocate more than 10 -20% of the total system storage for materialized views.

- **Tip 8. Materialized views need indexing too!** Materialized views, the best ones, are generally useful to multiple queries. That often means that the materialized view will not be a perfect match for a query, and may require indexing of its own.

- **Tip 9. Help the query compiler find matching materialized views.** Materialized view routing is complex enough. In order to help the query compiler find the materialized views you create give the compiler as much information as possible by doing the following:

    - Keep statistics up to date on the materialized views (some database do this automatically, not all)

    - Define refential integrity- Make FK columns NOT NULL

    - Include FK columns in the materialized view

    - Define functional dependencies (if the database supports it)

    - Consider using GROUPING SETS, ROLLUP or CUBE

    A few words on why RI is so helpful. RI can tell the database that a join to the dimension table in the materialized view does not add or delete rows. The aggregation is the same with or without the join to the dimension table so the materialized view can be used. If enforced RI is not possible consider informational constraints, if the database supports it.

- **Tip 10: Avoid problematic materialized view designs that make routing hard.** The following clauses are notoriously hard for a DBMS to match for materialzed view routng and should be avoided in materialized view design unless the materialized view is designed as an exact match for a query: EXISTS, NOT EXISTS, SELECT DISTINCT. For SELECT DISTINCT materialized view consider rewriting it to a GROUP BY materialized view.

    Secondly, avoid correlated predicates within materialized view design. Simple cases can usually be handled but generally these are challenging for materialized view routing.

5.7 Summary

Materialized views are the results of a query stored to disk. Effectively a materialized view caches calculations, permitting the reuse of the results, which leads to faster query responses. The number of possible views is typically extremely large, requiring the database designer to pursue the selection of a strategic set of materialized views. A good heuristic is to focus on frequent queries, which also consume large amounts of disk I/O. Each query naturally maps to a view. Product graphs and lattice structures can capture the relationships between views, facilitating the choice of views to materialize. Good candidates to consider for materialization are the natural views of frequent queries, and also common ancestors of those views. The star schema is often a good model to follow, multiplying the applicability of the fact table to a larger family of queries. The selection of materialized views typically follows a greedy approach, selecting the most advantageous view at each step, until a resource constraint is reached. Resource constraints can include the number of materialized views, the disk space consumed, and the time required to maintain the materialized views.

5.8 Literature Review

Harinarayan, V., Rajaraman, A., and Ullman, J. D. Implementing Data Cubes Efficiently. *Proceedings of the 1996 ACM-SIGMOD Conference*, 1996, pp. 205–216.

Kimball, R., Reeves L., Ross, M., and Thornthwaite, W. *The Data Warehouse Life Cycle Toolkit*, New York: John Wiley, 1998.

Kimball, R., and Ross, M. *The Data Warehouse Toolkit: The Complete Guide to Dimensional Modeling*, 2nd ed. New York: John Wiley, 2002.

Kotidis, Y., and Roussopoulos, N. DynaMat: A Dynamic View Management System for Data Warehouses. *Proceedings of SIGMOD 1999*, 1999, pp. 371–382.

Uchiyama, H., Runapongsa, K., and Teorey, T. J. Progressive View Materialization Algorithm. *Proceedings of DOLAP 1999*, 1999, pp. 36–41.

Shared-nothing Partitioning

Nothing is particularly hard if you divide it into small jobs
—Henry Ford (1863–1947)

In politics and sociology, divide and rule (also known as divide and conquer) is a strategy of gaining and maintaining power by breaking up larger concentrations of power into chunks that individually have less power than the one implementing the strategy.
—From Wikipedia, the free encyclopedia

Shared-nothing partitioning is a divide-and-conquer strategy for solving hard computationally complex problems over large data sets. The idea of breaking large, difficult problems into smaller ones is an ancient one that crosses many cultures. The expression "divide and conquer" is common is several languages: French "diviser pour régner," German "teile und herrsche," Latin "divide et impera," and Spanish "divide y vencerás." The term is most famously associated with Julius Caesar for his use of divide-and-conquer strategies in his military campaign against Gaul. More important, divide and conquer is a well-known technique in computer science. The technique is named divide and conquer because a problem is solved efficiently by dividing it into several smaller problems.

So when you have a truly large data set and a nasty looking query to resolve, why not divide up the data into little bits and exploit a team of computers to each solve the problem on just a fragment of the data, and on just a fragment of the data? In this way queries can be answered in a fraction of the time. That's the concept of shared-nothing partitioning, and we'll see it has distinct benefits and design challenges. Interestingly, shared-nothing partitioning is more like political divide and conquer than the usual computer science version because it is nonrecursive.

6.1 Understanding Shared-nothing Partitioning

6.1.1 Shared-nothing Architecture

The two extremes of parallel-processing architecture are shared everything and shared nothing (Figure 6.1). The terms mean pretty much what they imply. With shared everything, a single computer solves complex processing problems using shared memory, shared disk, and a shared bank of CPUs. This class of machine is typically called a symmetric multiprocessor (SMP) or nonuniform memory architecture (NUMA). NUMA systems are a special subset of SMP systems. On the other extreme, shared-nothing systems use a set of relatively independent servers to work cooperatively on subsets of a problem. Occasionally these servers will need to share data, which they will pass between them over a high-speed interconnect. Shared-nothing systems have become famous for their ability to scale out to a very large number of processors and servers, which has earned the high end of this domain the name massively parallel processing (MPP).

There are three major products that offer shared-nothing architecture today: DB2's Data Partitioning Facility, which allows users to purchase commercially available com-

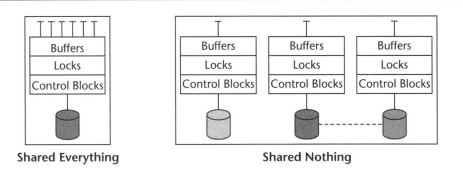

Shared Everything	**Shared Nothing**

Figure 6.1   Shared everything versus shared nothing.

ponents, servers, disks, and network interconnects to construct a shared-nothing system; Informix Extended Parallel Server (XPS)[1] is similarly based on commodity components; and NCR Teradata, which uses commodity disk servers with proprietary hardware interconnect to implement its shared-nothing architecture. Netezza is another company emerging that exploits shared-nothing architecture to produce a powerful business intelligence offering that includes specialized hardware. Product discussion in this chapter will focus on DB2 and Teradata, which are the dominant players today. Chapter 14 includes additional discusson of Netezza.

Shared-nothing databases continue to dominate the industry for large complex data sets, particularly where complex analysis of the data is required. Therefore, database management system (DBMS) parallelization has focused on domain-specific research such as data mining, decision support systems, geographical information systems (GIS), and life sciences genomic/proteomic systems.

Using a shared-nothing architecture, several servers collaborate to solve single problems. Each server owns a fragment of the data, and has no access to the on-disk data on any of the other servers (even database catalogs need to be transferred via communication interconnect). As a result, each server manages and operates on a distinct subset of the database, using its own system resource to perform analysis of that fragment. After each server has processed its fragment, the results from all of the servers are shipped across a high-speed network or switch and merged by a designated server on the system. Each server in this model is called a "node" or a "partition."[2] Throughout this chapter, to avoid confusion and bias, we will use the term "node" to represent a single server within an MPP. The model is called "shared nothing" because the data is private to each node, as are the caches, control block, and locks. The node performing the final coalescing of results from the other nodes is sometimes called the "coordinator" node.[3] The coordinator may itself have a fragment of data that it operates on, or it may simply be dedicated to the task of merging results and reporting them back to the client.

Each node operates as though it had a total world view of all the database data— only the "coordinator" node has special processing that understands a deeper view. The coordinator node, while aware of the other nodes, has no view of their activity or data except through network communications.

To see how this improves the performance and scalability of database processing consider the following simple aggregation query:

---

[1] Informix was bought by IBM in 2001. Informix products are still actively sold and supported by IBM.

[2] IBM's DB2 uses the term "partition" and NCR Teradata uses the term "access module process (AMP)."

[3] DB2 uses the terminology of "coordinator partition," which is defined as the node that the application connects to perform a query/transaction. Any partition on the MPP can be a coordinator at any moment in time if an application is connected to it. Teradata uses the term "parsing engine (PE)." Parsing engines are dedicated nodes on the MPP. These can be logical nodes, as described later.

```
Select SUM(SALES) from
MYSCHEMA.SALESDATA
where SALESDATE < '2006-11-17' and SALESDATE >
    '2004-01-01'
```

If there is an index on {YEAR, SALES} the database will likely scan the index and sum all the sales by year where the year equals 2006. For the sake of argument, let's assume there are 3 million entries in the database for that date range. In order to compute the result the database would need to access 3 million keys, and sum the sales for each. If the sales data were distributed across 10 nodes, each server would only need to access and sum 300,000 index keys. After each of the 10 nodes has computed a sum, the 10 summations are then passed back to the coordinator and collectively summed. The total sum is therefore calculated in nearly one-tenth of the time.

In real systems, shared-nothing MPP configurations with several hundred nodes are not uncommon. This impressive scale-out has not been achieved with other multiprocessor architectures to date.

6.1.2 Why Shared Nothing Scales So Well

A casual observer may reject this argument by pointing out the benefits achieved are simply the result of applying 10 times the processing power rather than anything specific to a shared-nothing server topology. Perhaps the use of a single server with 10 times the CPU capacity and memory might scale just as well. Indeed there are classes of problems where that would be the case, but there are multiple problems with trying to increase processing time linearly by simply buying larger and larger servers. These problems have kept shared-nothing architectures as the dominant topology for highly scalable decision support systems.

First, it may not be possible to purchase a server that has 10 times the CPU power and 10 times the memory, bus bandwidth, etc. Second, even the largest and most powerful NUMA systems are often constrained by their bus architectures. What if the number of nodes was 100 or 200 instead of 10, would it be reasonable to simply or even possibly purchase a single server that is 200 times faster and larger than the single server alternative that is available?

Second, it turns out to be quite difficult to design algorithms that can scale linearly to perform parallel processing on shared data. For example, considering the example above, if we could increase the system resources and number of CPUs by a factor of 10, what algorithm would we use to scan subsets of the index in parallel? Such algorithms exist, but they are harder to adaptively determine at runtime by a generic query processing engine and are prone to conflicts such as latch contention, cache coherency, and false sharing[4] across the L1 caches of the CPUs that affect scalability.

Third, there is the "N^2 effect," which will be discussed in more detail later. This effect is a natural consequence of how joins are processed on a shared-nothing system, which leads mathematically to an exponential gain in efficiency of join execution.

6.2 More Key Concepts and Terms

- *Shared-nothing architecture:* The ability for several processors to parallelize a single task by processing a subset of data where the data is partitioned and assigned to nonoverlapping subsets of processors.
- *Massively parallel processing (MPP):* A set of servers/nodes, communicating using high-speed network, on which runs a shared-nothing solution.
- *Massively parallel processor (MPP):* A generic term for a shared-nothing system, more frequently used when the number of nodes exceeds eight, though more casually used as a shorthand reference to any shared-nothing system.
- *Cluster:* A multicomputer configuration in which nodes share a common disk subsystem. When a node fails another node, having physical access to the disk of the failed node can take over processing responsibilities for the failed node.
- *Scalability:* The measure of the architecture to grow while still achieving positive processing gains:
  - Scale-up: grow by adding components to a single node.
  - Scale-out: grow by adding more nodes.
- *Linearity:* Linear scaling is the measure of efficiency. Are two nodes twice as effective as one? 1.9 times as effective as one?

6.3 Hash Partitioning

Both of the major products that support shared nothing distribute records to the database nodes using a hashing function. The hashing function performs a mathematical transform on one or more columns in each record, hashing them to a numeric value. Because the shared-nothing system can have different numbers of nodes, depending on the particular configuration, the hash value can't be directly converted to a node number. Instead a mapping is required, which is usually based on a table lookup (not a "relational table" lookup, but more likely a lookup into an array). The lookup table is usually referred to as a *hash map* or a *partition map*. It maps every possible hash value of a record to a destination node. As a result, each time a new node is added to the MPP the hash map will need to be recomputed. Vendors generally use a format for the hash map that

---

[4] Chapter 13 has a brief introduction to the topics "cache coherence" and "false sharing."

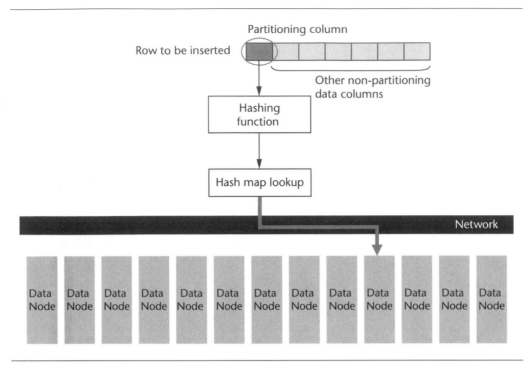

Figure 6.2   Hash partitioning records to data nodes.

has as many or more entries than the largest number of nodes supported by the product.[5]

Figure 6.2 illustrates the process for hashing a new record of data to the correct data node. In DB2 the partitioning columns are defined during the table creation processes and are an extension of the CREATE TABLE DDL. For Teradata, the partitioning is by primary index, which may or may not be the primary key of the table. These two can be different, and often are. If a user defines a table with a primary index and a primary key, the table will have a unique secondary index defined on the primary key columns to enforce uniqueness. If the primary key is the same as the primary index, then the primary index is defined as a unique primary index. Otherwise, the user has the choice of having either a unique primary index or a nonunique primary index.

The design goal for selecting good partitioning keys will be to minimize data skew across the nodes, while trying to maximize collocation between tables for joins. Choosing partitioning columns with a fairly large number of distinct values and relatively lim-

---

[5] Teradata uses a hash map of 64K entries and supports scale-out to 16,383 AMPs. DB2 uses a hash map of 4K entries and supports scale-out to 999 partitions.

ited data skew is a good design practice. There will be more discussion on best practices for partitioning selection when we discuss skew and collocation later in the chapter.

6.4 **Pros and Cons of Shared Nothing**

In his short paper on shared nothing, Michael Stonebraker [1986] compared the benefits and drawbacks of shared-nothing architectures, which he summarized in a table comparing attributes. The table is reproduced here as Table 6.1. In this table attributes are ranked 1, 2, or 3, where 1 is superior.

The main observations here are the improved bandwidth and scalability and the reduced susceptibility to critical sections. In fact, Stonebraker's observations have borne out in practice with the overwhelming majority of very large complex workload benchmarks being achieved on shared-nothing architectures over the past five years. The current industry standard for complex business intelligence processing is the TPC-H benchmark. A quick review of the leading benchmark results for large-scale, multiterabyte processing shows that databases using shared-nothing architecture are heavily used in this space.[6]

However, conversely, MPP shared-nothing systems have suffered from some of the other predictions that can largely be summarized as "complexity." Shared-nothing systems are harder to design and manage than single-node servers. Some would argue that the complexity is actually a critical limitation in the adoption potential of this architecture as a mainstream platform. However, the ability to outperform combined with rapid advances in self-managing systems (storage, servers, and databases) is shrinking these concerns rapidly and broader adoption is likely.

For all its concerns and performance benefits, what really sets shared-nothing architectures apart is their impressive linearity and scale-out for complex business-intelligence workloads. It's because of the impressive ability to scale well that shared-nothing systems have achieved such impressive performance results. In one experiment reported by Goddard [2005], users compared the performance of a single-server 24-way system with 0.5 TB to a two-node 1.0 TB system with identical hardware. The only difference between the two systems was that in one case a single server held 0.5 TB of data on a single server, and in the second case two identical servers each held 0.5 TB with data hash partitioned to each server in a shared-nothing architecture. What the experimental data showed was near-linear scalability for both the database build processing and the query execution performance (Figure 6.4).

At first glance it may not seem obvious why shared nothing should scale quite so well. While it's true that shared nothing doesn't suffer from the same physical inhibitors

---

[6] Teradata has not participated in TPCH benchmarks in recent years, though their benchmarking success with a shared-nothing architecture was very good during the years they published results.

Table 6.1   Comparison of Shared Resource Architectures

System Feature	Shared nothing	Shared memory	Shared disk
Difficulty of concurrency control	2	2	3
Difficulty of crash recovery	2	1	3
Difficulty of data base design	3	2	2
Difficulty of load balancing	3	1	2
Difficulty of high availability	1	3	2
Number of messages	3	1	2
Bandwidth required	1	3	2
Ability to scale to large number of machines	1	3	2
Ability to have large distances between machines	1	3	2
Susceptibility to critical sections	1	3	2
Number of system images	3	1	3
Susceptibility to hot spots	3	3	3

that SMP does (shared bus, false sharing, etc.), does that really explain the dramatic difference in scalability? There is another phenomenon occurring that is more subtle. It's loosely termed the "N^2 effect." Consider the computational complexity of a 30 × 30 join. The computational complexity is analyzed in Table 6.2. In the case of the uniprocessor, a single CPU performs the join of 30 × 30 elements. In the case of the SMP, with three CPUs working on the problem, the same 30 × 30 elements can be joined in one-third the time. Now watch carefully what happens with the shared-nothing architecture.

3,000 GB Results

Rank	Company	System	QphH	Price/QphH	System Availability	Database	Operating System	Date Submitted	Cluster
1	IBM	IBM eServer xSeries 346	54,465	32.34 US $	08/15/05	IBM DB2 UDB 8.2	Suse Linux Enterprise Server 9	05/18/05	Y
2	hp invent	HP BladeSystem ProLiant BL25p cluster 64p DC	110,576	37.80 US $	06/08/06	Oracle Database 10g R2 Enterprise Edt w/Partitioning	Red Hat Enterprise Linux 4 ES	06/08/06	Y
3	UNISYS	Unisys ES7000/one Enterprise Server (16P)	30,013	37.83 US $	09/08/06	Microsoft SQL Server 2005 Enterprise Itanium Ed	Microsoft Windows Server 2003 Datacenter Itanium Ed SP1	07/18/06	N

10,000 GB Results

Rank	Company	System	QphH	Price/QphH	System Availability	Database	Operating System	Date Submitted	Cluster
1	IBM	IBM System p5 575 with DB2 UDB 8.2	180,108	47.00 US $	08/30/06	IBM DB2 UDB 8.2	IBM AIX 5L V5.3	07/14/06	Y
2	Sun microsystems	Sun Fire[TM] E25K server	108,099	53.80 US $	01/23/06	Oracle 10g Enterprise Ed R2w / Partitioning	Sun Solaris 10	11/29/05	N

Figure 6.3   TPCH from October 2006 showing 3TB and 10TB price-performance results

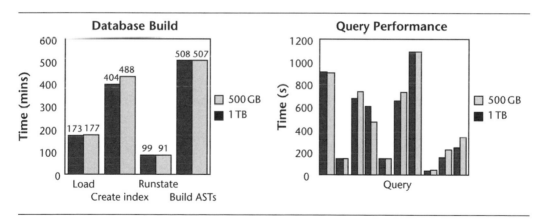

Figure 6.4   Nearly identical performance results for a 0.5 TB and 1.0 TB warehouse.

Each node in the three-node MPP holds one-third of the data. So each node processes a 10 × 10 join. Although each of the nodes processes this amount, the joins on each machine occur in parallel, so the execution time is gated by the speed of the slowest node, namely 10 × 10. Had the shared-nothing server been a 30-way complex, then the computation time would be only one–one-hundredth! This is an idealized scenario, of course. It assumes that data can be distributed perfectly across nodes, and that the join data is perfectly collocated. However, in practice even data distribution is common, and careful selection of the partitioning keys can give good collocation.

Table 6.2   The N^2 Effect by Processor Type

Processor type	Computational complexity	Total execution time in arbitrary units
Uniprocessor	$30 \cdot 30$	900
SMP (3-way)	$30 \cdot 30/3$	300
MPP (3-way)	$10 \cdot 10 \cdot 3/3$	100
MPP (30-way)	$1 \cdot 1 \cdot 30/30$	1

6.5 Use in OLTP Systems

Shared-nothing systems have been shown to produce tremendous scaling results when the online transaction processing (OLTP) applications can be partitioned. There's a very subtle change in the language "application partitioning." Earlier in this chapter we discussed partitioning data on the server, but said nothing about the application. In the case of OLTP transactions, the individual statement execution time is very short, and the system load comes from the very high volume of concurrent transactions on the server. In this case, the overhead of connecting to a given server and then broadcasting requests to multiple nodes in order to find the required records, then flowing these result sets back to a central node and so on, is far too much overhead per transaction. As a result, applications that run efficiently on a single server, typically run worse on a shared-nothing server if the application is moved to a shared-nothing server without further modifications. However, the solution to this problem is to modify the application so that the application connects to the node that holds the data required for the request. This can only be done if two of the following three requirements are met:

1. The data is partitioned by a column (or set of columns) that the application will have values for at query time.

2. If the application has access to the hashing function used by the database server to distribute data to the correct partition.

3. Data can be partitioned to provide excellent collocation, avoiding interserver communication during joins.

Table 6.3   Scale of the Firestorm Benchmark

Benchmark	Servers	CPUs	TPMC
Firestorm	32	128	440
Previous best	8	32	138

If all three conditions are met, then the client can invoke the hashing function to determine which node holds the required data. By directly accessing the node that holds the data for the transaction and by carefully designing the system so that joins do not generally result in data transfer, the shared-nothing architecture transforms the OLTP database into almost literally a set of nearly independent databases each working on a subset of the application space. There have been some high-profile industrial examples exploiting shared nothing in this way. One of the most famous was the joint IBM–Microsoft "Firestorm" benchmark published during the summer of 2000 (Table 6.3).

The Firestorm result was achieved and could only have been achieved using a shared-nothing partitioned OLTP application. This benchmark exploited a shared-nothing architecture and a partitioned application to achieve huge scalability results, far exceeding anything that had been achieved until then (Figure 6.5). The results achieved four times the scale-out in number of servers and number of CPUs. The result, while impressive, was only possible because the application was partitionable along the partitioning keys.

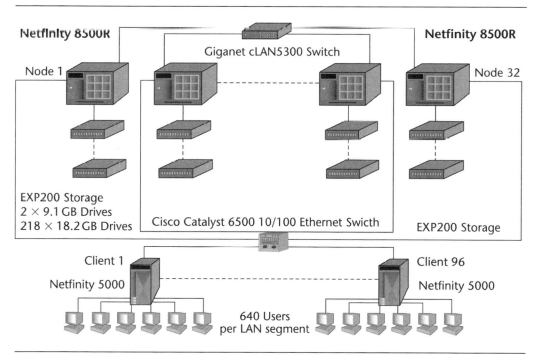

Figure 6.5   System topology example for partitioned OLTP result using shared-nothing architecture.

Very often this kind of application partitioning is not practical. OLTP applications tend to have workloads that have short queries and frequent updates. It is often not practical for the application code to determine which node of the cluster the data required for the SQL statement. Fortunately, the majority of OLTP applications does not need cluster scale-out and a single multiprocessor server (symmetric multiprocessor or NUMA) can handle the vast majority of OLTP workloads. Larger SMPs come out every year, with increasingly large RAM and number of CPUs (64- or 128-way systems), making it feasible in most cases to run most OLTP applications without multi-server support to achieve scale.

6.6 Design Challenges: Skew and Join Collocation

At first glance the shared-nothing model looks very impressive. Each node operates on a fragment of the data, and the results are merged in a trivial way, leading to amazing performance scalability. There are challenges in getting the design right, and in fact in practice the scalability is rarely perfectly linear with the number of nodes.

Both commercial shared-nothing systems (DB2, Teradata) partition data across the nodes using hashing techniques. Columns are selected by the database designer as the "partitioning key" or "partitioning columns." Hash partitioning is where the data is assigned to a node by a hash function over the partitioning columns on each record.

With shared-nothing architecture the ultimate goal is to keep all the nodes busy working in a linear fashion on the larger database problems, and also to minimize the degree to which data must be shared between the nodes. Two serious problems pose a major challenge for the database designer. These are data skew and poor collocation. Each problem will be discussed below, describing why it is a problem and what to do about it.

6.6.1 Data Skew

In order for shared-nothing partitioning to be effective, the data needs to be distributed evenly across the nodes. If one of the nodes has significantly more data than the others, it will certainly take the longest to complete the processing, and the entire computation time becomes limited by the slowest node in the system. Selecting the partitioning columns such that the data is distributed evenly across all nodes is very difficult. In the case of range partitioning, the process is nearly impossible, since each data range will have a different number of records associated with it. For example, consider a sales table that is range partitioned by date. You can expect December to have considerably more sales data for retail products than most other months. Even with a very fair hash function, a large density of data at a few data points can seriously skew the data. For example, hash partitioning retail sales data by "week-of-year" would likely result in a lot of data for the week before December 25 as people rush to finish last-minute holiday shopping. Therefore, the nodes that these dates hash to would have a disproportionate volume of data.

The solution to this is not to improve the hashing function (which in most cases is internal to the relational database management system [RDBMS]) but rather to be careful what columns you select as the partitioning columns. If you are partitioning retail sales data, the date-of-sale column may be a poor choice to partition on. Similarly, partitioning by product ID is likely to seriously skew the data distribution, since some products will be more popular than others. For an even distribution of data across the nodes look for columns that:

1. Have several times more unique values than the number of nodes in the system.
2. Have a reasonable even distribution of data to the partitioning column values.

6.6.2 Collocation

In order for shared-nothing architectures to scale well with good linearity, communication between the nodes should be kept to a minimum. A common problem occurs when tables need to join and the join columns are not collocated on the same node. When this happens data for one table will need to be shipped from remote nodes to join with data at the local node. This is a very expensive process that can cripple the benefits of shared-nothing processing.

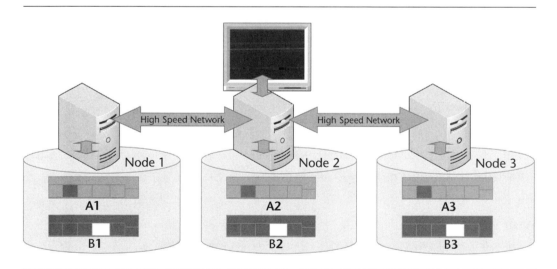

Figure 6.6   Collocation between two tables.

Collocation is the placement of rows from different tables that contain related data in the same database node. In Figure 6.6 you can see two tables A and B that are hashed across three nodes. The shaded sections show the join data. If the tables are perfectly collocated, the shaded section of data for table A on each node will join with the shaded section of data in table B. However, in a worst-case scenario the entire join data for one of the tables will need to be transferred to the other's nodes for joining.

This represents a very interesting and challenging design goal of trying to find partitioning keys that achieve good collocation while still providing even data distribution across the nodes.

You can be certain that tables are collocated if they have the same number of columns in the partitioning key, and if the data types of the corresponding columns are node compatible. Rows in collocated tables with the same partitioning key value are always placed on the same database partition.

6.7 Database Design Tips for Reducing Cross-node Data Shipping

The first set of techniques is based on careful selection of the partitioning columns. The second set is based on various forms of duplicated partitioning of subsets of data.

6.7.1 Careful Partitioning

The following guidelines can help. Fortunately, there are some other practices that help ensure collocation of join tables and reducing the amount of cross-node data shipping and cross-node activity that occur during workload processing.

- In an OLTP environment, when the partitioning columns are equivalent to equality predicates using constants or host variables then the database can determine before query execution exactly which node holds the required data simply by hashing the predicate's operand. For example, consider a table Employees with an employee identifier "*emp_id*" often used in transactions such as:

  ```
  UPDATE EMLPOYEES SET <... etc...>
      WHERE emp_id = <host-variable>
  ```

  In this case, partitioning on the emp_id column would allow the database to determine before execution exactly which nodes need to process the UPDATE command.

- Join columns are a classic choice for partitioning columns, provided they don't result in massive data skew across the nodes.

6.7.2 Materialized View Replication and Other Duplication Techniques

Because an individual table can only be partitioned one way, there will be times when a column used in a join with one table is a poor partitioning choice when joining with another table. Similarly, there will be times when columns used in equality predicates are not ideal to satisfy join collocation. At first glance this appears to be a case of picking the lesser of several evils. There are, however, techniques that can be used to create alternative partitioning of data. These come in the following forms:

1. *Replicated tables.* The ability to locate an entire table on all nodes, so that every node contains 100% of the table data.

2. *Repartitioned materialized views.* Using materialized views to create an alternate partitioning of data stored in base tables.

3. *Replicated materialized views.* The ability to locate an entire materialized view on all nodes, so that every node contains 100% of the materialized view. The view itself may include only a subset of the columns from the base table, as well as possible aggregation.

4. *Repartitioned indexes.* The ability to create indexes that have distinct partitioning from their parent table.

5. *Global join indexes.* A special class of repartitioned indexes that includes record identifier (RID) access back to the records in the base tables from which it is derived.

Each of these techniques has benefits and detriments, which will be introduced here. In the following sections, let's consider an employee table with columns:

```
EMP_ID, SIN, DIVISION, DEPARTMENT, JOB_ID,
SALARY, REGION
```

The base table may be partitioned perhaps on EMP_ID, which is useful for several joins. However, there may be some joins on JOB_ID as well, and the database designer is trying to exploit alternative techniques to achieve good collocation for the joins on JOB_ID without disruption of the excellent collocation that exists for joins on EMP_ID.

Replicated Tables

Replicated tables are a powerful technique for avoiding collocation problems. Using this technique all records for a given table are stored on every node in the MPP that the table is defined on. As a result, if there are *n* nodes in the MPP, then approximately *n*-

times the storage is required for the table because every node must store 100% of the table data instead of $1/n$. However, since all of the table data is included on every node, all joins with this table are guaranteed to be collocated. In our example Employee table, clearly once all the records are replicated to every node, the MPP joins will be perfectly collocated on both EMP_ID and JOB_ID.

Naturally, in order to limit the storage overhead, this strategy is best suited to small tables. Due to the duplication of records on every node, insert, update, and delete on replicated tables must be processed on every node, not just on a single node where the records hash to. The best practices for using replicated tables are therefore to use them sparingly, with smaller tables, and in particular with tables that are mostly read access.

This technique is supported by DB2 using its replicated table feature.

Repartitioned Materialized Views

Materialized views can be created that mirror a parent table, or a subset of a parent table's columns, which have a different partitioning strategy than the parent table. This allows for the repartitioning of data (or a subset of it) so that collocation can be achieved. This offers powerful design flexibility, since a materialized view can be defined as an exact replica of an existing table, as a subset of columns from existing tables, or as aggregations, etc. The downside to this strategy is the additional storage required for the data duplication, though this is mitigated by partitioning and by including only the minimally required subset of columns in the materialized view.

Using the Employee table example, the database designer can choose to partition the Employee table by EMP_ID and create a materialized view that includes and is partitioned by JOB_ID. The materialized view can also include other columns from the Employee table that need to be accessed by the queries that join on JOB_ID.

This technique is supported by both DB2 and Teradata through materialized query tables and join indexes, respectively.

Replicated Materialized Views

Just as tables can be replicated on each node, similarly so can materialized views. This technique combines the idea of replicated tables, and the idea of repartitioned materialized views to provide the ability to replicate only a subset of the data columns required for the join processing.

Using the Employee table example, the database designer can chose to partition the Employee table by EMP_ID and create a replicated materialized view that includes a small subset of the columns of the Employee table, perhaps only the JOB_ID column. Provided the resulting table is relatively small and changes infrequently, this can be a useful design strategy.

Using replicated materialized views will frequently yield performance advantages from improved collocation when the table you replicate data from:

1. Is very frequently joined with.
2. Needs to be partitioned in multiple ways due to different join requirements in the SQL workload.
3. Is rarely updated.
4. Is relatively small.

Unlike repartitioned materialized views, replicated materialized views have much higher storage requirements since their contents are replicated not partitioned. However, careful selection of the minimal required subset of columns can help reduce this overhead.

This feature is supported by DB2 using its replicated table feature in combination with its materialized view feature.

Repartitioned Indexes

The techniques above using materialized views suffer from an additional drawback, which is that just as the base table requires indexing, and associated index maintenance, similarly materialized views generally require indexing. A technique to avoid this pitfall is based on repartitioned indexes. These indexes are regular indexes based on normally partitioned data, but the keys of the index are themselves hashed to nodes on the MPP. As a result, the index keys are not collocated with the records they reference. While this is clearly bad for index maintenance and index-table lookups, it can be a very powerful technique for repartitioning data to exploit an alternate partitioning scheme.

For example, considering our Employee example, by creating a repartitioned index that is partitioned on JOB_ID, one or more columns in the base table can effectively be repartitioned as an index. The storage is somewhat more efficient than using a repartitioned materialized view since the materialized view would require storage for the view and the indexes on the view, while the repartitioned index is all inclusive.

This technique is superior to replicated table strategies because the storage overhead is better since data is partitioned not fully reproduced on every node as occurs with replicated tables.

Teradata supports this technique through repartitioned join indexes and repartitioned hash indexes.

Global Join Indexes

Teradata offers structures called join indexes and global join indexes. To describe the concepts we need to clarify some Teradata terminology:

- *Unique secondary indexes.* A unique index that is not the primary index that defines the table.
- *Nonunique secondary indexes.* A secondary index that supports duplicate values.

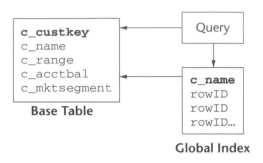

Figure 6.7   Use of global join index.

Join indexes, as described before, allow data to be joined between tables that otherwise would not be collocated. Global join indexes are really the same as join indexes (repartitioned indexes) except the index keys also include the RID access back to the base table from which they are derived, as illustrated in Figure 6.7.

Global join indexes are similar to repartitioned indexes and similar to materialized views in Oracle and DB2 (materialized view and materialized query table, respectively) except they include pointers to the base table from which they are derived, which makes them another method for doing lookups into the base table from remote nodes. Using a repartitioned index for base table access is referred to as partial covering because the index only partially covers the query. A global index offers the advantages of a nonunique secondary index (which supports duplicate rows per value) combined with the advantages of a unique secondary index (its index rows are hash distributed on the indexed value), and is often able to result in query execution plans that access a subset of the database nodes. The following description from the Teradata Database Design Release [2005] describes the process:

> The Optimizer looks for opportunities to transform what would otherwise be an all-AMP query plan into a few-AMP plan. This few-AMPs approach is called Group AMP. The Group AMP approach not only reduces the number of AMPs active in supporting a query, it also reduces the locking level from a table-level lock to several row-level locks. Removing the need for table-level locks eliminates two all-AMP steps from the query plan:
>
> • A step to place the table-level lock on all AMPs.
>
> • A step to remove the table-level lock from all AMPs when the query completes.

The use of global join indexes can therefore often lead to query execution plans that require access to a reduced number of nodes (few-AMP query execution plans). The result is a significant decrease in the amount of data that needs to be transferred between nodes to complete the join.

Using the Employee table example, the database designer can choose to partition the Employee table by EMP_ID and create a global join index that is partitioned by

JOB_ID. The global join index may reduce the amount of cross-node traffic even when collocation is not perfect. This index type will require additional storage for the RIDs that point back to the base table. Generally speaking, the storage requirements for the RIDs are a relatively small overhead when the index keys are more than 8 bytes wide. The wider the index key, the less concern the designer needs to have over the overhead of the RIDs in the global join index.

6.7.3 The Internode Interconnect

There will always be some degree of communication between shared-nothing partitions. Even when data is perfectly collocated, results from each data node will need to be merged into a result set to be returned to the calling application. Three major points are worth mentioning in this respect:

- Fast interconnects, such as Fibre Chanel or InfiniBand.
- Teradata ByNET.
- Logical partitioning.

The first and most obvious strategy is to make sure your MPP database uses a high-performance interconnect such as a high-speed Fibre Channel interconnect. The four major generic interconnect alternatives are Fibre Channel, InfiniBand, Gigabit Ethernet, and ATM. Table 6.4 reproduces a summary comparing the technologies courtesy of the Fibre Channel Industry Association (www.fibrechannel.org). Fibre channel has gained adoption in recent years for applications that require high-bandwidth, reliable solutions that scale from small to very large.

Teradata AMPs use a specialized interconnect called the ByNET that has properties that are well suited to data warehousing. The ByNET can create dynamic groups, messaging, and sorting directly within the interconnection network. The following is a paraphrased tech note from the Teradata's web pages that summarizes the capabilities and advantages of the ByNET.

The BYNET works like a phone switch, quite different from the typical network. Its switched "folded banyan" architecture delivers additional network bandwidth for each node added to the configuration. Each connection to a node delivers 120 MB/sec. A 2-node system has a 240 MB/sec. interconnect; 4 nodes, 480 MB/sec.; 8 nodes, 960 MB/sec.; 100 nodes, 12 GB/sec. The current BYNET implementation can support up to 512 nodes (1 to 4 PB) but the design is capable of 4,096 nodes (8 to 32 PB) if a customer is ready to solve a problem of that magnitude.

In addition to delivering fully scalable point-to-point bandwidth, the BYNET implements specialized functions not offered by other networking solutions. It can broadcast-deliver a single message to some or all of the nodes in the MPP configuration. There are many database functions that need to be performed on all nodes at once. With broadcast,

Table 6.4   Summary of Three Major Interconnect Technologies

	Fibre Channel	**Gigabit Ethernet**	**ATM**
Technology application	Storage, network, video, clusters	Network	Network, video
Topologies	Point-to-point loop hub, switched	Point-to-point hub, switched	Switched
Baud rate	1.06 Gbps	1.25 Gbps	622 Mbps
Scalability to higher data rates	2.12 Gbps, 4.24 Gbps	Not defined	1.24 Gbps
Guaranteed delivery	Yes	No	No
Congestion data loss	None	Yes	Yes
Frame size	Variable, 0–2 KB	Variable, 0–1.5 KB	Fixed, 53 B
Flow control	Credit Based	Rate Based	Rate Based
Physical media	Copper and Fiber	Copper and Fiber	Copper and Fiber
Protocols supported	Network, SCSI, Video	Network	Network, video

the database has to send and manage only one message and one response, lowering the cost and increasing the performance.

When it is time to return results to a user or application, the BYNET supplies the merge function. Unlike other parallel databases that pull the result set together in one node to deliver the appropriately sorted result, Teradata leaves each portion of the result set on the node where it was created, sorted locally. The merge function collates just enough of the result to fill the user's buffer with result records, then waits for the user to request more rows. Merge makes returning results a scalable operation regardless of their size.

Finally the third and most effective way to avoid communication costs between nodes is to avoid internode communication completely by using logical nodes rather than physical data nodes. Logical nodes will be described in more detail below in Section 6.8. Using logical nodes, a single larger multiprocessor system is used to house several data nodes. Since multiple data nodes reside on the same physical server, the internode communication between them does not require the use of an external network (or switch) and data can be transferred between them using shared memory.

6.8 **Topology Design**

6.8.1 **Using Subsets of Nodes**

To achieve an optimal topology in table storage and data access it may be preferable not to use all nodes for tables that are moderately small in size. Similarly it may be optimal to keep tiny tables on a single node. Some database designers like to use dedicated nodes for ETL processing, another reason to have dedicated nodes for specific subtasks. These are generally referred to as partition groups (or, alternatively, node groups). Partition groups are subsets of nodes. Tables can be created in partition groups so that their data is spread across only a subset of nodes.

In Figure 6.8 you can see an example of a six-node MPP shared-nothing system with three different partition groups and three tables named T1, T2, and T3. T1 is stored in partition group 3, which includes all nodes. T2 is stored in partition group 2, which includes only nodes 1, 2, and 3. Finally, T3 is stored in partition group 1, which includes only node 1. What is clear from the illustration is that when tables are in different partition groups collocation is impossible regardless of the choice of partitioning columns when join tables are not in the same partition group.

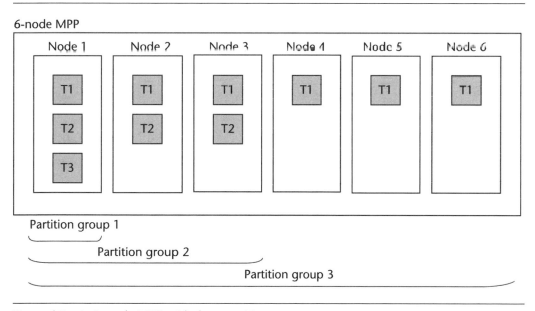

Figure 6.8   A six-node MPP with three partition groups.

The partition groups could also be designed so that the nodes are not overlapping. For example, partition group 2 could be designed to include only nodes 2 and 3, and partition group 3 could be designed to include only nodes 4, 5, and 6, as illustrated in

Figure 6.9. At first glance this seems like a strange strategy. Why limit access to table T1 by the processing resources of nodes 4, 5, and 6 when the table could be partitioned across all six nodes? However, strangely, access to T1 may be faster when partitioned across only nodes 4, 5, and 6 because access will be limited to the access efficiency of the slowest node in the partition group. When the partition groups overlap as they do in Figure 6.8, access to data in table T1 on node 1 is limited by competition for node 1 resources (disk bandwidth, CPU, memory, etc.) due to activity on tables T2 and T3 on the same node. If tables T2 and T3 are hot, access to T1 on node 1 may be quite slow. As a result, the coordinator will be limited in returning return results from T1 by the speed of T1 on node 1. The chain is as strong as its weakest link. By designing the partition groups with nonoverlapping topologies the problem is resolved at the cost of overall reduced resources for table T1.

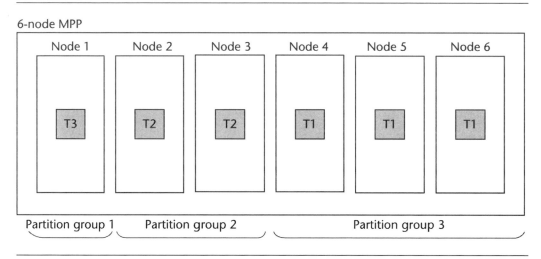

Figure 6.9   A six-node MPP with three nonoverlapping partition groups.

DB2 supports the notion of partition groups. With NCR Teradata all tables are spread across all AMPs. This ensures that all AMPs are working on behalf of all tables, and leads to a conceptually simple design, but does not allow the exploitation of subsets of nodes. In general, overlapping topologies, such as the one illustrated in Figure 6.8, are prone to skew, applying more work to some nodes than others. A best practice when multiple partition groups are needed is to use a nonoverlapping model as shown in Figure 6.9.

6.8.2 Logical Nodes versus Physical Nodes

Logical nodes refer to the separation of data into shared-nothing nodes, independent of the underlying hardware. This means that the concept of a database node is an abstraction that is somewhat independent of the number of physical servers where the number of logical nodes can be equal to or greater than the number of actual servers. This is a powerful concept in particular on NUMA systems, where subsets of CPUs (called quads) can be segregated for use by a logical node (i.e., DB2 partition or Teradata AMP). Figure 6.10 shows our previous example of a six-node system with three tables and three partition groups. In this example, T1 has been assigned a partition group with nodes 3, 4, 5, and 6 so that it has exclusive access to the memory, CPU, and disk of two physical servers.

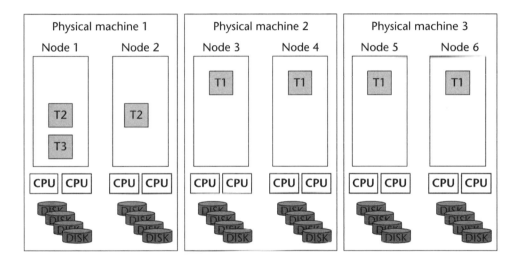

Figure 6.10   Six logical nodes on three physical machines.

Both Teradata and DB2 support the notion of logical nodes. The terms used by both products to describe database nodes (the DB2 terminology of "partitions" and the Teradata terminology of "AMPs") are actually logical constructs. From a database design perspective logical nodes offer some important advantages:

- Data sharing/shipping between nodes (e.g., when processing joins) can be performed within shared memory, without the need to flow data across an external network, which would have dramatically higher latency.

- Multiprocessor systems can be exploited for their high-performance components, without the usual limitations of scale-up caused by bus contention and false sharing,[7] because each data node will use its CPUs independently of the others.

6.9 Where the Money Goes

Shared-nothing partitioning remains most useful for complex query processing, which is a hallmark of data warehousing and decision support systems. These systems are usually expensive. After reading this chapter you may think the reason for the expense is the cost of all the components. In fact the dominant expense in most warehousing systems is storage, which is always the most expensive component in a warehouse. In fact the cost of storage is itself very cheap. In Fall 2006 multiple companies began selling terabyte-sized drives for only $500 U.S. However, these high-volume inexpensive drives are slow and not suitable for data warehousing applications. While raw storage is cheap, performance and reliability are expensive. High-performing parallel access RAID storage remains expensive per GB, which drives the cost of storage for enterprise database systems. Chapter 13 discusses storage requirements, striping, RAID, SAN, and NAS in more detail.

6.10 Grid Computing

Another form of shared-nothing architecture focuses on a widely distributed model for data analysis, known as Grid computing. Advances in Grid computing are offering alternatives for specific classes of problems. Grid computing is emerging as another model for massive computational processing. It is not yet a well-established industrial platform. Grid computing exploits "function shipping," whereby distinct problems are shipped to any number of participating computers on a network. Each node on the Grid (a participating computer) computes a solution for the problem it receives. This allows a massive number of computers to collectively solve pieces of a problem with little communication between the systems. The most well-known example of Grid computing is the Internet-connected computers in the Search for Extraterrestrial Intelligence (SETI).

With SETI, Internet users can participate by running a program that downloads and analyzes radio telescope data. While participants are not using their computer for personal use the computer's available processing cycles can be used to help in the search for otherworldly life. While shared-nothing architectures scale to hundreds of nodes, Grid computing can scale to tens of thousands if not millions of nodes. Industrial Grid-based solutions are starting to emerge. IBM reported that the Institute of Plant Genetics

---

[7] False sharing is described in Chapter 13.

and Crop Plant Research was able to exploit Grid-based solutions to sequence the barley genome. This resulted in dramatic improvements in the time to make single comparisons of 400,000 barley ESTs with the rice genome from 200 days to 30 hours. A deeper discussion of distributed processing is presented in Chapter 16.

TIPS AND INSIGHTS FOR DATABASE PROFESSIONALS

- **Tip 1. Choose partitioning keys that evenly distribute data across the partitions.** An uneven distribution will result in a poor system design due to some nodes having a much larger proportion of the data than others. An even distribution reaps the benefits of dividing the work. Therefore, use a column for the partitioning key that has much larger column cardinality (number of unique values) than the number of database partitions.

- **Tip 2. Focus on collocation of join data.** If data is not well collocated the internode traffic will be high, resulting in machine-machine data shipping. When table A must join with table B the ideal situation is for the join data in A and B to both reside on the same node so the join can be processed without having to retrieve data for A or B from other partitions. Where possible, use join columns as the first part of the partitioning key. This will maximize collocation during the join and also give you the benefits of the "N^2 effect." If this results in poor data distribution across nodes, consider adding additional columns to the partitioning key, or using another column that correlates well with the join columns (even if not perfectly) to reduce internode communication.

- **Tip 3. Use replicated tables to minimize the problems associated with poor collocation if the database supports it.** This should be limited to small tables (i.e., don't replicate large tables to all partitions). This is particularly useful with smaller tables that are infrequently updated, and materialized views. Since any updates to a replicated table must occur on all nodes where the table is replicated, there is substantial system overhead (looking at the system as a whole) in processing updates. However, since the updates can occur in parallel, the response time is not necessarily dramatically impacted provided the system is not resource constrained (disk, CPU, or network).

- **Tip 4. Use repartitioned indexes and global join indexes with Teradata to minimize the problems associated with poor collocation.** This is particularly useful with narrow indexes. Note that any update to the columns referenced in the unique secondary index and nonunique secondary index will add additional overhead, so it's important not to go overboard on these.

- **Tip 5. Use application partitioning for OLTP systems.** For large-scale OLTP systems to achieve optimal price performance you will need to partition your application so that the client knows in advance exactly which server to connect to. In most cases you can achieve the required scale and performance for OLTP systems without using a shared-nothing architecture.

- **Tip 6. Don't try to save money on the server interconnect.** Internode data shipping can be a killer. In most shared-nothing systems for business intelligence it is impossible to completely eliminate the cross-server data shipping. As a result, when planning the system make sure you invest in high-speed interconnects between the nodes (partitions) so that when data does need to move between nodes it can move quickly. You can have good success using commercially-available interconnects with DB2 and by using NCR's ByNET interconnect with Teradata. In most cases today the interconnect speeds are high enough that the interconnect speed is rarely an issue, though prior to 2000 that was often not the case. If you experience performance bottlenecks over the system interconnect, in most cases (not all) this is caused primarily by collocation problems rather than interconnect problems. As of fall 2006 InfniBand switched fabric communications links offer bandwdth of 6Gb/s. Despite all that, using a substandard interconnect will cripple the MPP.

- **Tip 7. Avoid using multiple partition groups if possible.** Access skew is a major danger, and the design becomes very complex quickly. If you need to use multiple partition groups it's usually best to make these nonoverlapping with other data nodes.

6.11 Summary

Shared-nothing computing has a leadership role in the processing of large-scale data systems, particularly for processing vast data for OLAP and decision support. The effectiveness of shared nothing comes from its ability to scale almost linearly when data is collocated and its ability to scale-out so that vast processing power can be applied to database problems. Special care is required in the design of MPP systems to ensure even data distribution and good collocation of join data. Tricks such as repartitioning and view replication can help obviate some of the collocation problems, at the expense of some additional storage.

6.12 Literature Summary

Baru, C. K., Fecteau, G., Goyal, A., Hsiao, H., Jhingran, A., Padmanabhan, S., and Wilson, W. G. An Overview of DB2 Parallel Edition. *SIGMOD Conference,* 1995, pp. 460–462.

Baru, C. K., Fecteau, G., Goyal, A., Hsiao, H., Jhingran, A., Padmanabhan, S., Copeland, G. P., and Wilson, W. G. DB2 Parallel Edition. *IBM Systems Journal*, 34(2), 1995: 292–322.

DeWitt, D. J., and Gray, J. Parallel Database Systems: The Future of High-Performance Database Systems. *Commun. ACM,* 35(6), 1992: 85–98.

Furtado, P. Physical Design: Experimental Evidence on Partitioning in Parallel Data Warehouses. *Proceedings of the 7th ACM International Workshop on Data Warehousing and OLAP,* Nov. 2004.

Goddard, O. L. 17 Laws of Building Terabyte Class DB Systems. *IBM DB2 Information Management Technical Conference*, Orlando, FL, 2005.

Gottemukkala, V., Jhingran, A., and Padmanabhan, S. Interfacing Parallel Applications and Parallel Databases. *ICDE,* 1997, pp. 355–364.

Hitz, M., and Mück, T. A. Interconnection Topologies for Shared Nothing DBMS Architectures. *Australian Database Conference,* 1993, pp. 228–249.

Jhingran, A., Malkemus, T., and Padmanabhan, S. Query Optimization in DB2 Parallel Edition. *IEEE Data Eng. Bull.,* 20(2), 1997: 27–34.

Kudlur, M., and Govindarajan, R. Performance Analysis of Methods That Overcome False Sharing Effects in Software DSMs. *Journal of Parallel and Distributed Computing* 64(8), 2004: 887–907.

Kuznetsov, A. Using Materialized Query Tables to Speed up Queries in DB2 UDB, IBM developerWorks, at http://www.128.ibm.com/developerworks/db2/library/techarticle/0208kuznetsov/0208kuznetsov.html.

Laing, W. A. Shared Nothing Will Ultimately Prevail, *HPTS,* 1993.

Mehta, M., and DeWitt, D. J. Data Placement in Shared-Nothing Parallel Database Systems. *VLDB Journal*, 6(1), 1997, pp. 53–72.

Padmanabhan, S. Extracting Large Data Sets Using DB2 Parallel Edition. *VLDB,* 1996: 582.

Stonebraker, M. The Case for Shared Nothing. *IEEE Database Eng. Bull.,* 9(1), 1986: 4–9.

Weikum, G. Tutorial on Parallel Database Systems. *ICDT,* 1995: 33–37.

Talwadker, A. S. Survey of Performance Issues in Parallel Database Systems. *Journal of Computing Sciences in Colleges Archive*, 18(6), June 2003: 5–9.

Teradata Database Design Release V2R6.1, NCR Corp., Nov. 2005.

Range Partitioning

The best armor is to keep out of range.
—Italian proverb

The idea is simple and powerful: divide data into ranges so that the database can make intelligent decisions at processing time on what segments of the data to completely ignore or completely focus on. For example, by dividing data by date ranges (January data over here, February data over there, etc.) the database can completely focus on the ranges that are specific to incoming queries. This is another clear variant of a nonrecursive divide-and-conquer strategy, and the operational details will be discussed below.

Range partitioning has become such a ubiquitous notion in database design that we had a hard time tracing back its origins—a bit like trying to discover who invented the sailboat. To find out where the idea came from we contacted one of the world's leading database researchers, David DeWitt. DeWitt is the John P. Morgridge Professor of Computer Science at the University of Madison at Wisconsin, author of over 100 technical papers, a member of the National Academy of Engineering, and was named a Fellow of the AC in 1995. According to DeWitt, a graduate student named Bob Epstein as part of his thesis proposed the idea of range partitioning for distributing tuples of tables among different nodes of a distributed database system (distributed Ingres). DeWitt was the first to apply this idea to parallel database systems as part of the Gamma project. The paper on Gammma [DeWitt 1986] published at the 1986 VLDB conference discusses the three forms of horizontal partitioning that

Gamma provided (range, hash, round-robin). Interestingly, Bob Epstein went on to get his Ph.D. from the University of California at Berkeley. In 1984 he was a leading architect and proponent for client/server computing with the creation of Sybase and the development of SQL Server that eventually grew into a billion dollar business with the inclusion of middleware and development tools. So was the humble origins of range partitioning!

Despite its academic origins, relatively little appears within the academic literature on the topic of range partitioning that is relevant for database designers (though there is a huge body of literature on theoretical aspects of horizontal partitioning). Most of the practical ideas appear in the user manuals and administration guides of commercial products that support range partitioning as a product feature. Sometimes simple ideas are the best. The fact that virtually every major database vendor has implemented range partitioning speaks volumes to its practical value.

7.1 Range Partitioning Basics

The essential concept of range partitioning is to divide a single table into multiple little tables, so that each little table holds a specific range of the data (Figure 7.1). Each "little table" is called a fragment, or a table partition, depending on the product. From an application perspective the collection of partitions is accessed as a single table, and the application need not be programmed to be aware of the partitioning design. However, what is important for the database designer to know is that range partitioning is, by its nature, implemented at the disk level by creating multiple table objects. Unlike shared-nothing partitioning described in Chapter 6, range partitioning is almost always used to partition a table within a server, not across multiple servers. Although range partitioning could in theory be used to split data across shared-nothing nodes (as discussed in Chapter 6), in practice the requirements of shared-nothing systems for evenly distributed data are much better served by hashing than by range.

There are several important reasons why range partitioning has become a ubiquitous feature for major database products worldwide.

Many database architectures limit the size of a table, often due to the addressability of records that are constrained by the record identifier (RID) architecture being used (see discussion on RIDs in Chapter 2). Range partitioning divides a large table into several smaller ones. Even though the table remains a single table from the application perspective, the database kernel will store each partition in its own table object. As a result, each partition has the supported capacity of a single table. Therefore, a table with 10 range partitions can grow 10 times larger than a table without range partitioning. The major factor limiting the size of a table is usually the addressability of the records within the tables, which is an attribute of the RID architecture. Some RID architectures support a huge addressability domain, which removes the need to exploit range partitioning for purely increased table size.

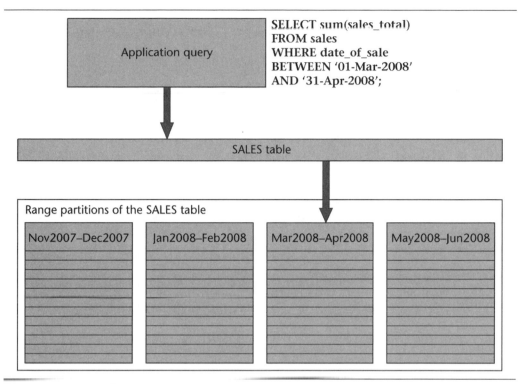

Figure 7.1   Essential range partitioning.

Very briefly, the benefits of range partitioning include:

1. Increased addressability allowing databases to store larger tables.
2. Partition elimination, allowing the query compiler to select more efficient query execution plans.
3. Improved administration, allowing database administrators (DBAs) to perform administration tasks on a subset of table data, including tasks like BACKUP, LOAD, defragmentation, and reclustering.
4. Fast roll-in and roll-out.
5. Implicit data (input/ouput [I/O]) clustering

7.2 List Partitioning

7.2.1 Essentials of List Partitioning

Although users normally think of range partitioning as a technique that groups a range of data together, such as a range of dates or a range of numbers, the same technique can be used to group point values, such as regions (e.g., New York, Ohio, Florida). A single value or a set of distinct values can form the "range." Some vendors refer to this as *list partitioning* (e.g., Oracle), because each range of data is defined by a list of one or more values. Other vendors don't bother with the distinctions, and simply include this capability as part of their range partitioning abilities (e.g., IDS, DB2).[1]

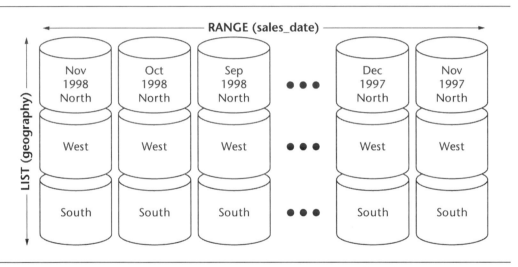

Figure 7.2   Composite range and list partitioning. (Picture courtesy of Oracle Corp.)

7.2.2 Composite Range and List Partitioning

List partitioning can be combined with normal range partitioning to produce a grid of multi-attribute nonoverlapping ranges.

The following section, "Syntax Examples," illustrates a typical combination of range and list partitioning over both date and geographies.

---

[1] List partitioning was introduced in Oracle in Oracle 9i, and in DB2 9 as part of its partitioned tables capability. Informix IDS has supported this concept for several releases as part of its Fragment clause.

7.3 **Syntax Examples**

The following examples from DB2, Informix, and Oracle illustrate the syntax used by the different vendors.

```
DB2 9
CREATE TABLE sales(sale_date DATE, customer INT, …)
PARTITION BY RANGE(sale_date)
(STARTING '1/1/2006' ENDING '3/31/2008',
STARTING '4/1/2006' ENDING '6/30/2008',
STARTING '7/1/2006' ENDING '9/30/2008',
STARTING '10/1/2006' ENDING '12/31/2012');
```

Example showing MINVALUE and excluding ENDING in each clause.

```
CREATE TABLE sales(sale_date DATE, customer INT, … )
PARTITION BY RANGE(sale_date)
(PART rem STARTING MINVALUE ENDING '1/1/2000' EXCLUSIVE,
PARTITION q1 STARTING '1/1/2006',
PARTITION q2 STARTING '4/1/2006',
PARTITION q3 STARTING '7/1/2006',
PARTITION q4 STARTING '10/1/2006'
                ENDING '12/31/2012');
```

With Informix Data Server (IDS), the following examples use two variable nonoverlapping ranges and list partitioning (see Figure 7.3). In Informix you'll see the keyword "FRAGMENT" used, which is a synonym of "PARTITION." Informix actually allows both KEYWORDS as synonyms in their DDL syntax.

```
...
FRAGMENT BY EXPRESSION
0<sales_price AND sales_price <=10 AND region IN ('E', 'F', 'G')
IN dbsp1,
0<sales_price AND sales_price <=10 AND region IN ('H', 'I', 'J')
IN dbsp2,
10< sales_price AND sales_price <=20 AND region IN ('E', 'F',
'G') IN dbsp3,
10< sales_price AND sales_price <=20 AND region IN ('H', 'I',
'J') IN dbsp4,
20< sales_price AND sales_price <=30 AND region IN ('E', 'F',
'G') IN dbsp5,
20< sales_price AND sales_price <=30 AND region IN ('H', 'I',
'J') IN dbsp6;
```

Oracle simple range partitioning:

```
create table sales (sales_date DATE, customer int, …,
 partition by range(sales_date)
 (partition d1 values less than (10) tablespace sales1,
  partition d2 valuesless than (20) tablespace sales2,
  partition d3 values less than (maxvalue) tablespace sales3);
```

Microsoft SQL Server introduced range partitioning in SQL Server 2005. The syntax is rather different than what is used by other vendors. The steps for creating a partitioned table include:

1. Creating a partition function that specifies how a table or index that uses the function can be range partitioned.
2. Creating a partition scheme to specify the placement of the range partitions onto file groups.
3. Creating tables using the partition scheme.

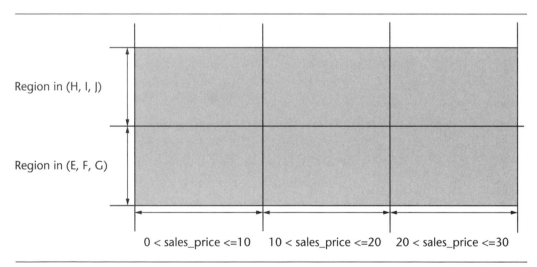

Figure 7.3   Nonoverlapping ranges. (Courtesy of IBM.)

An example of the SQL Server process follows.
Following is an example of a partition function:

```
CREATE PARTITION FUNCTION myRangePartFunc (int) AS RANGE
LEFT FOR VALUES (1, 50, 100);
```

The keyword "LEFT" implies that each range is defined to the left of the value specified, such that each value represents the right most (or largest) value in the range. In this example, four ranges are created: Values <=1, Values <=50, Values <=100, and values greater than 100.

Following is an example of a partition scheme:

```
CREATE PARTITION SCHEME myRangePartScheme
AS PARTITION myRangePartFunc
TO (FileGp1, FileGp2, FileGp3, FileGp4);
```

Finally the range partitioned table is created:

```
CREATE TABLE Sales (sale_price int, date_of_sale date)
ON myRangePS1 (sale_price) ;
```

7.4 Administration and Fast Roll-in and Roll-out

Despite the healthy and impressive discussion above about range partitioning and partition elimination, the dominant use of range partitioning within the industry is actually to improve system administration, not query performance. This simplification occurs in three ways: utility isolation, data roll-in, and data roll-out.

7.4.1 Utility Isolation

Consider the implementation of running utilities, such as reorganization (clustering and defragmentation) and backup, on tables that are range partitioned versus those that are not.

With a nonpartitioned table, reorganization and backup must occur on the entire table. Reorganization in particular can be very expensive due to the examination and movement of every record in the table. Some vendors allow this movement to occur online, but even so the process remains daunting. Most vendors support reorganization of data for reclustering and defragmentation as an offline process. Therefore, the more inefficient the process is, the longer it takes and the longer the entire table is offline. Backup similarly is usually performed on a per-object basis. Some vendors provide an incremental backup capability. However, incremental backup must still evaluate metadata across the entire table, and is often not desirable for customers due to their business policies for backup and recovery.

Range partitioning helps tremendously. Let's examine the reorganization case first. With a range partitioned table an individual range can be reorganized to improve clustering and defragmentation. Because reclustering in particular involves a sorting operation followed by data placement, the cost is typically measured as

$$O(C_1 M \log N + D_1 N),$$

where N is the number of records being reorganized, C_1 is a constant for CPU time, and D_1 is a constant for I/O time. A table with 20 range partitions can therefore have a single partition reorganized in roughly time:

$$O(C_1 (N/20)\log(N/20) + D_1 N/20).$$

For a million-row table, the savings are roughly:

$$C_1 6,000,000 + D_1 \times 1,000,000$$
$$C_1 234,948.5 + D_1 \times 200,000.$$

Choosing 0.1 for C_1 and 0.3 for D_1, we have ended up with a speedup of roughly 96%. Of course this analysis depends heavily on the speed of the CPU and the disks. The important observation is that the benefits can be superlinear because sorting is typically nonlinear.

In the case of backups, range partitioning by date fits neatly with the normal operational practices of organizations. A table can be range partitioned by date, and then subsequently backed up by partition. In many cases this means that only the newest partition needs backup (i.e., where there is no data change on the old partitions, as in the case of many data warehousing environments). Because backup time tends to scale linearly with the data volume, backup of a single data range partition can improve performance of the nonpartitioned case in proportion to the number of range partitions in the table. For example, if a table contains five years of data range partitioned by month, a backup of the latest range partition alone will probably execute in 1.7% the time required to perform a full table backup that included all the table rows.

In addition to the performance savings, utility operations on a single or subset of range partitions incur contention and risk exclusively on the ranges they operate on. As a result, the remaining partitions are unfettered for normal operations, aside from the resource bandwidth consumed by the utility that naturally affects the system as a whole.

Finally, utility isolation is viewed by many as a risk-aversion strategy. Utility processing, and particularly utilities that manipulate data, is viewed by DBAs as having some associated risk. In the unlikely event that a utility fails due to a processing defect or device failure, it can leave the objects in an indeterminate state, possibly even corrupted. Performing utility operations on a per-range basis limits the potential risk to the range that is under the scope of the utility.

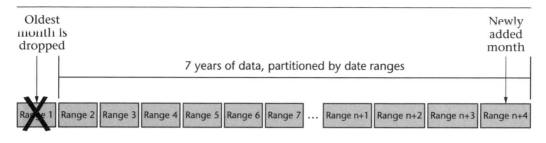

Figure 7.4   Database with a sliding seven-year history.

7.4.2 Roll-in and Roll-out

Consider the implementation of maintaining a database with a sliding window of data, for example, the most recent seven years of data (see Figure 7.4). This is an extremely popular model for database administration, particularly with data marts and data warehouses. In these sliding-window cases, data is often added to the database from an OLTP source on a weekly or monthly basis.

Adding the new range of data is referred to as "roll-in," while dropping the oldest range of data is referred to as "roll-out." The roll-in process faces several challenges in a data that is not range partitioned. For example, as new data is added to the existing table, the table indexes require row-by-row maintenance, which is costly in terms of resource consumption and impact on concurrency as object and key locks are obtained.

Similarly with roll-out, dropping the oldest range of data on a nonpartitioned table requires an index scan to retrieve the qualifying rows, key-by-key access of every index and row-by-row access to the table. Moreover, every row that is dropped will require logging to ensure the process is atomic, recoverable, and undoable.

Using a range partitioned table with ranges defined along the roll-in and roll-out boundaries, the database can be much more efficient when rolling-in data. For example, local indexes can be fully rebuilt rather than incrementally extended, which is much more efficient per key. No index key locking is required when an index is fully rebuilt, since there are no other users of the index aside from the building process. The entire roll-in can be performed in isolation, without impacting any of the queries and transactions examining other range partitions. Once the new partition is fully constructed it can be merged (attached) into the existing table by means of simple catalog manipulations. If a global index exists, this process slows down dramatically, for the reasons discussed before.

With roll-out the efficiencies are even more profound. The oldest partition can be dropped from the system catalogs, and a single event logged to indicate the range was dropped. To actually achieve the physical deletion of the data, the table objects and indexes storing data for the range are dropped. For file-based storage systems, for example, this would means that the database is simply deleting the files associated with the range. Once again we see this situation become murkier when global indexes are introduced, since keys in the global index can't easily be dropped in a single operation. Some databases solve the handling of global indexes for roll-out by removing the keys for the deleted ranges asynchronously (i.e., perhaps minutes or hours after the range has otherwise been deleted). Metadata is stored regarding the index to ensure that index-only access to the deleted ranges will not access the keys pending deletion.

7.5 Increased Addressability

There are two major reasons why range partitioning is valuable as an addressability aid. Using a classic 4-byte RID[2], with row addressability defined by page number and record (or slot) number, RIDs can only address into a 3-byte space for pages (1 byte of the 4 being needed for the record or slot number). This restricts the addressability of pages to $0 \times 00FFFFFF$, or roughly 16.5 million pages per table. Again, depending on the architecture this limit may apply to a single table or possibly a higher-level abstraction such as a storage group. Regardless of whether the page size is 4 KB or 32 KB the restriction can pose serious capacity limitations for databases measured in tens of terabytes (TB). Using page sizes larger than 32 KB is not practical for most applications, and few if any commercial database products support it. Range partitioning helps reduce the capacity problem by splitting a table into multiple tables (internally, though not exposed to the application) so that each range can be independently addressed. For example, a table with 10 balanced ranges will have 10 times the capacity (addressability) of a single unpartitioned table.

Another strategy for resolving the storage capacity constraint is to support larger RIDs, possibly even variable-length RIDs. For example, an 8-byte RID with 7 bytes used for page addressing could support over 72 zillion (7×10^{16}) pages! However, while larger RIDs resolve the addressability constraint, they incur a storage constraint of their own. RIDs are stored on disk as part of index structures to provide pointers from the index keys back into the data pages. Using a wider format for RIDs will significantly increase the storage required for indexes, and similarly increase the memory required for index operations. Similarly, RID-based operations that occur through index ANDing and index ORing become more computationally complex, largely a linear increase that is proportional to the width of the RID structure. Various techniques have been devised to try and counter the overhead of wider RIDs, including variable-length RIDs. However, suffice it to say that short RIDs provide computation and storage efficiency. Range

---

[2] 4-byte RID is the classic RID structure described in C.J. Date, *An Introduction to Database Systems*, Vol. 1, 8th Ed., Addison-Wesley, 2003. Many other formats for RIDs are commonly in use, with several having larger size and addressability.

partitioning can provide the needed release to gain this efficiency and still avoid the addressability constraints.

7.6 Partition Elimination

The major performance advantage of range partitioning comes through a technique known through most of the industry as "partition elimination." Partition elimination occurs during SQL compilation time when the query compiler searches for the optimal query execution plan for a query. The presence of range partitioning based on columns used in query predicates provides the query optimizer a much clearer view on which ranges are likely to be accessed as part of the query. This allows the compiler to select a query execution plan that limits the execution to the ranges that are relevant, and can exploit the indexing and RID architectures unique to range partitioned tables. The following example, courtesy of Kevin Beck at IBM, illustrates partition elimination showing the impact on plan selection. The following query assumes the schema for the industry standard TPC-H benchmark, selecting attributes from the LINEITEM table.

```
select l_shipdate, l_partkey, l_returnflag
 from lineitem
 where l_shipdate between
 '01/01/1993' and '03/31/1993' and l_partkey=49981
```

Several query execution plans are possible for this query. Without range partitioning, one likely plan would exploit index ANDing, as follows:

- Read all relevant index entries from each index.
- Save both sets of RIDs.
- Match them up to find which occurred in both indexes.
- Use those to fetch the rows.

The DB2 RID architecture for range partitioned tables is that each RID in the index contains a small identifier that indicates the specific range partition that the record belongs to. The database can examine the range partition ID to discover if the row might be in the desired date range, instead of reading from the l_shipdate index. This strategy will result in half the I/O for indexes, lower memory requirements, and no index ANDing, which will yield CPU savings as well. Figure 7.5 illustrates the differences in the query execution plans that can result from the two different physical table designs. In this notation the triangles represent index access. Notice how the query execution plan on the left, without range partitioning, requires access to two indexes, followed by index ANDing, while the query execution plan on the right, which assumes

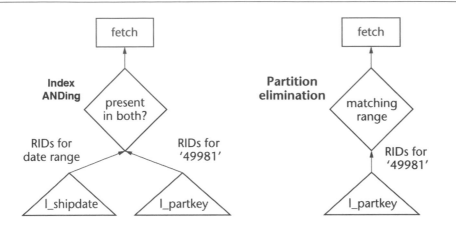

Figure 7.5   Partition elimination impact on query execution plan selection.

range partitioning, accesses a single index, without any ANDing. While the index ANDing plan on the left passes RIDs back up for ANDing prior to the fetch, in contrast, partition elimination skips irrelevant RIDs.

Here's another example, using a stock table:

```
CREATE TABLE STORE_ITEM_STOCK
( product_num INT, product_type INT, stock_num INT,
location INT, item_name VARCHAR(50))
PARTITION BY RANGE(location)
   (STARTING FROM (1) ENDING AT (200) IN partitionA,
    STARTING FROM (201) ENDING AT (400) IN partitionB,
    STARTING FROM (401) ENDING AT (600) IN partitionC,
    STARTING FROM (601) ENDING AT (800) IN partitionD)
```

Now consider a simple range query over this table with predicates on the location column:

```
SELECT * FROM PRODUCT_STOCK WHERE location >= 250 and
location <= 382
```

The SQL query compiler can detect immediately that the result set includes exclusively data within partition B, and only data in that partition needs to be accessed for this query.

Similarly, partition elimination can lead to dramatic improvements in join efficiency in the case of missing indexes on the join columns. Consider the following example in Figure 7.6, joining a table of customer orders with a table of orderable products.

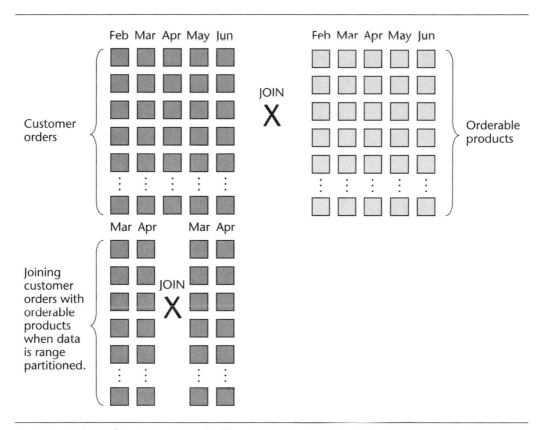

Figure 7.6   Join of range partitioned tables.

In the first case, shown at the top of the figure all dates in the customer orders table are joined with all dates in the products table. However, if the tables are range partitioned by date, the compiler can immediately detect that only some months are interesting for the join based on the predicates in the query (i.e., we assume a date predicate for orders in March and April in this example), dramatically reducing the number of rows that needs to be joined. In most cases this is not a big savings because the join columns should be indexes. However, another extremely important observation here is the impact of explicit clustering. By storing each range in its own internal tables, the data is indirectly clustered by range. Therefore, in this join example, the March and April data is guaranteed to be clustered (i.e., not intermingled with other data on the same storage pages), resulting in a minimum amount of I/O for the query. This benefit is valuable even when the join columns are properly indexed.

7.7 Indexing Range Partitioned Data

Commercial databases have two strategies for indexing range partitioned data, namely global indexes and local indexes. Global indexes index over all ranges in the table. They provide the same service and functionality that an index would serve on a non-partitioned table, holding keys and RIDs for all records in the table. Local indexes are quite similar but index only the records stored in a single range partition. With local indexes every range partition in the table has its own physical instance of the indexes defined on the table. In a local index, all keys within the index refer exclusively to the records of data stored in the table for that range partition. The index itself is partitioned on the same columns as the partition columns of the ranged partitioned table that is being indexed.

Local indexes are often more efficient because if they are stored as B+trees they may reduce the height of the tree, improving search time, and they can be operated on independently, providing huge efficiencies for roll-in and roll-out and utility operations, which will be discussed later.

When using a global index, the index may need to be fully rebuilt when some table maintenance operations are performed, even when those operations only impact specific (or one) range partition. Removal of keys from the global index by range is clearly far less efficient as well, as discussed below. However, global indexes are the natural way to enforce uniqueness for secondary indexes that are not defined along the range partition columns. Not all commercial database products currently support both index types.[3]

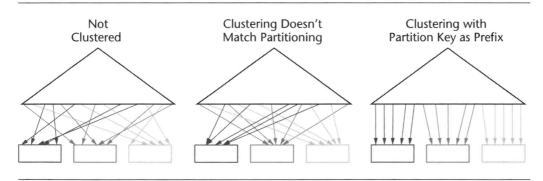

| Not Clustered | Clustering Doesn't Match Partitioning | Clustering with Partition Key as Prefix |

Figure 7.7   Matching range partitioning with index clustering.

[3] DB2 for Linux Unix and Windows only supports global indexes over range partitioned tables as of v9.1. If you are using a more recent version, please check the latest product documentation.

7.8 Range Partitioning and Clustering Indexes

Clustering indexes dramatically improve the efficiency of scans by reducing the I/O required on the base table by ensuring that records with similar key data are located near each other within the table storage. As described earlier, range partitioning implicitly clusters data according to the range partition. However, the design of range partitioning is often driven predominantly by administration needs (utility isolation, roll-in, and roll-out), while clustering design is often driven by performance goals. The goals can therefore conflict. Optimal scans are achieved when clustering index design matches the partitioning key, as shown in the right-hand picture in Figure 7.7.

However, even when the clustering design and the range partition design do not coincide, the system can still perform well, with a number of advantages (middle image):

- Within each partition, rows are in key order. Since each range partition represents its own storage object in the physical implementation within the database, access to the storage object remains clustered, and good I/O characteristics are achieved.

- During the scan operation, rows will be retrieved from a set of n pages in the buffer pool (or disk) where n is the number of partitions. Contrast this with a scan of a clustered index in a nonpartitioned table, where all reads come from the same page until it is consumed and clearly the range partitioned design is not as attractive. However, contrasting with the unclustered case, the I/O savings are enormous. To summarize this, consider a scan with 200 qualifying rows, over 10 range partitions (for simplicity we'll assume an even distribution), and we'll assume 50 records per page, as shown in Table 7.1.

Notice in Table 7.1 that while mismatched range partitioning and clustering is clearly not as efficient as matched range partitioning and clustering, the I/O benefit is still very significant, twice as efficient with I/O compared to range partitioning on the scan column, and 20 times more efficient than the baseline.

7.9 The Full Gestalt: Composite Range and Hash Partitioning with Multidimensional Clustering

Figure 7.8 illustrates the combination of the various slicing and dicing techniques we have discussed in the book. A table T1 is hash partitioned across three servers–server 1, server 2, and server 3—providing the scale-out benefits of shared-nothing partitioning as described in Chapter 6. The data for the table is then range partitioned by date according to month, at each partition on the shared-nothing architecture (i.e., at each

Table 7.1   Impact of Range Partitioning on Clustering Efficiency

Design	Pages	I/O savings versus baseline
Basline, no clustering, no partitioning	200	0%
Range partitioning only, not on the scan column	200	0%
Range partitioning on the scan column	20	90%
Mismatched range and clustering	10	95%
Clustering only	4	98%
Matching range and clustering	4	98%

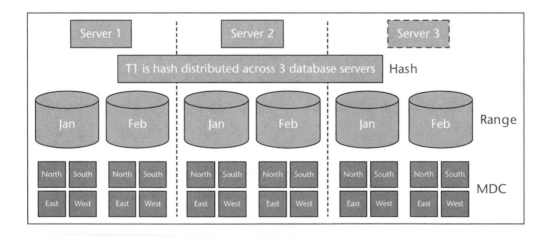

Figure 7.8   Range partitioning combined with hashing and MDC. (Picture courtesy of IBM.)

server). Within each range partition data is clustered using multidimensional clustering (MDC) according to a regional geography. In the large this hierarchy is the most reasonable one for the various ways of slicing and dicing data, with shared-nothing partitioning being the coarsest level of partitioning and MDC being used as the finest. A detailed discussion of what MDC is and its benefits follows in Chapter 8.

TIPS AND INSIGHTS FOR DATABASE PROFESSIONALS

- **Tip 1. When to use range partitioning:**
  a. Large tables, to ease the addressability concerns, will still use shorter RIDs. Some vendors offer larger addressing using large (wider) RID formats, but this consumes significantly more space in the indexes, where RIDs are stored.
  b. Roll-in/roll-out. If you need to add or drop ranges of data, especially by date, you have a classic need for range partitioning.
  c. Business intelligence—style queries, where partition elimination can offer significant improvement in query execution plan selection.

- **Tip 2. Which column(s) to partition on:** The practical observation is that range partitioning is used predominantly for date columns. Roll-in and roll-out scenarios are almost always based on dates. The second major use of range partitioning is for improved query execution plan selection exploiting partition elimination, and a significant set of those opportunities are also based on date predicates. However, look for range queries not based on date predicates to find other column candidates.

- **Tip 3. Selecting the granularity of ranges:** When you are using range partitioning for roll-in/roll-out, the most important design point is that the range partitioning match the roll-in and roll-out ranges. For example, if you need to roll-in and roll-out data by month, then range partitioning by month is a reasonable strategy.

- **Tip 4. Use range partitioning to improve the granularity of administration tasks like backup and data load.**

- **Tip 5. Use range partitioning to enable rapid deletion of ranges of data (roll-out).** This is particularly useful when your database is composed of a sliding window of data, such as a weekly, monthly, or quarterly updated database, where you want to keep a fixed history of data in the database. A typical example is a five-year data mart that is updated monthly. Every month a new month's worth of data is added, and the oldest month is rolled-out.

- **Tip 6. Use range partitioning to improve your SQL workload performance by exploiting "partition elimination."** To do this, examine your workload for range, quality, and inequality predicates, and design range partitioning around those.

- **Tip 7. Remember that range partitioning is implemented by most vendors using multiple tables.** As a result, it is not advisable to design a range partitioned table with thousands or millions of partitions. When you plan to exploit range partitioning, design your ranges with two rules of thumb in mind: at least 50 MB of data in each range (several gigabytes of data per range is best) and no more than 500 ranges per table.

- **Tip 8. Take care when combining range partitioning, list partitioning, MDC, and hash partitioning.** Combinations are possible, but remember that as you increase the number of ways you slice and dice the data, you are creating an increasingly complex system to make sense of. Only the most expert and brave DBAs will consider combining more than two of these for a single table.

7.10 Summary

Range partitioning is one of the surprising techniques of physical database design, doing so much with a fairly simple idea. While relatively little academic literature has been published on the theme, the feature's ubiquitous presence in all major commercially available database products is a clear indicator of its value. Range partitioning is used both to improve the performance and ease of administrative tasks like roll-in and roll-out, and to improve query execution plan selection (and therefore workload performance) for decision support queries by means of partition elimination.

7.11 Literature Summary

Ceri, S., Negri, M., and Pelagatti, G. Horizontal Data Partitioning in Database Design. SIGMOD Conference, 1982, pp. 128–136.

DeWitt, D. J., Gerber, R. H., Graefe, G., Heytens, M. L., Kumar, K. B., and Muralikrishna, M. GAMMA—A High-Performance Dataflow Database Machine. *VLDB,* 1986: 228–237.

Ganesan, P., Bawa, M., and Garcia-Molina, H. Online Balancing of Range Partitioned Data with Applications to Peer-to-Peer Systems. *VLDB,* 2004: 444–455.

Nguyen, K. Q., Thompson, T., and Bryan, G. An Enhanced Hybrid Range Partitioning Strategy for Parallel Database Systems. DEXA Workshop, 1997, pp. 289–294.

Tripp, K. L. SQL Server 2005 Partitioned Tables and Indexes, at http://www.sqlskills.com/resources/Whitepapers/Partitioning %20in%20SQL%20Server%202005%20Beta%20II.htm#_Toc79339950.

Multidimensional Clustering

Man's mind, once stretched by a new idea, never regains its original
dimensions.
—Oliver Wendell Holmes (1809–1894)

Can data be clustered different ways simultaneously without duplicating the data? There are times for all of us where we want to "play it both ways," and times when we probably would like to play things much more than two ways. Live in the quiet of the country, or live in the action of the city. Enjoy the decadence of tasty foods, or enjoy the benefits of a healthy diet. Unfortunately, many of these situations are mutually exclusive. In the space of database design, data clustering long appeared to be one of these situations; a data set can be clustered (or grouped on disk) along a set of dimensions one way and one way only, unless the designer is willing to incur the overhead of duplicating the data for each unique clustering model. At least this has appeared to be the case for the past few decades before the introduction of multidimensional clustering (MDC) into industrial database systems. MDC enables a database system to cluster data along multiple dimensions at the same time. So, for example, data can be kept clustered by region of sale and by date of sale simultaneously. The essence of MDC is fundamentally to do the impossible: the clustering of data in different ways simultaneously without duplicating the data.

The author's first exposure to MDC was in the year 2000. About 15 people crammed into a small meeting room to listen to Dr. Sriram Padmanabhan from the TJ Watson

Research Laboratory in New York present the idea of MDC describing the technical benefits and merits. I confess that my first reaction was: *I don't get it. That's impossible.*

Fortunately, it is possible, under the right conditions. In this chapter we'll discuss what MDC is, how it works, and how to design a database to exploit it. In addition to its clustering benefits, MDC also produces dramatic improvements in indexing efficiency. The combination of clustering and indexing benefits allows the database designer to index large volumes of data using three orders of magnitude less storage than traditional indexes, and the ability to cluster across multiple dimensions simultaneously can often achieve performance gains of an order of magnitude.

MDC has been motivated to a large extent by the spectacular growth of relational data, which has spurred the continual research and development of improved techniques for handling large data sets and complex queries. In particular, online analytical processing (OLAP) and decision support systems (DSS) have become popular for data mining and business analysis. OLAP and DSS systems are characterized by multidimensional analysis of compiled enterprise data, and typically include transactional queries including group-by, aggregation, (multidimensional) range queries, cube, roll-up, and drill-down.

The performance of multidimensional and single-dimensional queries (especially those using group-by and range queries) is often dramatically improved through data clustering, which can significantly reduce input/ouput (I/O) costs, and modestly reduce CPU costs. Yet the choice of clustering dimensions and the granularity of the clustering are nontrivial choices and can be difficult to design even for experienced database designers and industry experts.

MDC techniques have been shown to have very significant performance benefits for complex workloads. The only current industrial implementation of MDC is in IBM's DB2 UDB for Linux, UNIX, and Windows. Prior to the IBM implementation most of the research literature on MDC had focused on how to better design database storage structures, rather than on how to select the clustering dimensions. In other words, it has focused on what the database vendors need to create under the covers within the database management system (DBMS), and not on what the database administrator (DBA) needs to design. However, for any given storage structure used for MDC, there are complex design tradeoffs in the selection of the clustering dimensions. To perform the physical design of MDC tables, it's quite important to understand how MDC works, why it works, and what pitfalls to watch out for.

8.1 Understanding MDC

8.1.1 Why Clustering Helps So Much

To understand the huge benefit that clustering offers, there are two simple ideas to first come to terms with:

1. Only a fraction of the database data can be cached in system memory. While the exact ratio of cache size to storage size varies widely from system to system, ratios of 1:10 or 1:5 are common.

2. The unit of I/O and similarly the unit of caching within the database is a "page" that represents some number of records. Page sizes are usually in the range 2 K to 1 MB (with 4–16 K being typical), and record width is usually in the range of 20–1,000 bytes, with ~150 bytes being a prototypical table design. Therefore, one database storage page will typically store several dozen records.

The characteristics used for clustering depend on the data use. For example, pixels in an image may be clustered by color density or by object boundaries. Data in a relational database is often intended to be clustered by significant query use. For example, in a database where range queries on data are common it may be useful to cluster data by date ranges. January records may be in one physical cluster, while February records may be in another cluster. Figure 8.1 shows the same data as it might appear in either clustered or unclustered form. The following three significant observations can be made from this figure:

1. A query on a given month of data would only need to access a single storage block to obtain all of the query result data if the table data are clustered by month. The same query on this example data, when the data is unclustered, would need to access all four storage blocks. Thus, a query on January data in the clustered case performs one-quarter of the I/O that the same query on unclustered data might. Perhaps more importantly, if the pages are randomly distributed on disk, the unclustered data is likely to incur four times as many disk seeks.

2. Within a cluster, data are not sequenced. The cluster for January contains only January data, but the records for each day of the month appear in an arbitrary order within the storage block.

3. A query over all data will access all four storage blocks in both the clustered and unclustered data cases. In this example, the I/O overhead for table scans is not affected by the cluster strategy for the data. However, later in this section we will see important examples where this is not the case.

8.1.2 MDC

The performance of multidimensional queries (group-bys, range queries, etc.) is often improved through data clustering, which can reduce I/O costs enormously and reduce CPU costs. Clustering groups of records physically in storage is based on one or more specified clustering dimensions. Yet the scheme for clustering, the definition of the clustering keys, and the granularity of the clustering are nontrivial choices and can be

Storage block #1	Storage block #2
Record for January 3	Record for February 3
Record for January 23	Record for February 23
Record for January 12	Record for February 12
Record for January 20	Record for February 20
Record for January 19	Record for February 19
Record for January 17	Record for February 17
Record for January 9	Record for February 9
Record for January 7	Record for February 7

Storage block #3	Storage block #4
Record for March 3	Record for April 3
Record for March 23	Record for April 23
Record for March 12	Record for April 12
Record for March 20	Record for April 20
Record for March 19	Record for April 19
Record for March 17	Record for April 17
Record for March 9	Record for April 9
Record for March 7	Record for April 7

(a)

Storage block #1	Storage block #2
Record for January 3	Record for February 3
Record for February 23	Record for March 23
Record for March 12	Record for April 12
Record for April 20	Record for January 20
Record for January 19	Record for February 19
Record for February 17	Record for March 17
Record for March 9	Record for April 9
Record for April 7	Record for January 7

Storage block #3	Storage block #4
Record for March 3	Record for April 3
Record for April 23	Record for January 23
Record for January 12	Record for February 12
Record for February 20	Record for March 20
Record for March 19	Record for April 19
Record for April 17	Record for January 17
Record for January 9	Record for February 9
Record for February 7	Record for March 7

(b)

Figure 8.1 Physical clustering of data: (a) data blocks clustered by date of month, and (b) data blocks unclustered.

difficult to design even for experienced database designers and industry experts. As noted by Jagadish, Lakshmanan, and Srivastava [1999], the design of optimal clustering in this context has combinatorial complexity, having an extremely large search space. For hierarchical dimensions (such as City → State → Country) the search space is typically doubly exponential in the number of dimension hierarchy levels! Range dimensions (dimensions that are typically queried by range, such as salary or date) more often have a continuous domain, and further exacerbate the problem since there is a near infinite set of ways in which they can be clustered since the range can be subdivided by various degrees of granularity. For example, looking at a date dimension, the data could be clustered by day, or by week, or by month, etc. Similarly, a salary dimension could be clustered by dollar, or by every ten thousand dollars, and of course by any granularity in between.

The same concept of data clustering can similarly be applied to multiple dimensions (columns or column attributes) of a table. In order to preserve the clustering as new, data elements are added to the table; without incurring massive reorganization, the standard approach is to divide the table into logical cells. Each cell represents a unique value of the clustering key. For each cell in the table, a number of storage blocks will be allocated on disk to hold the data. To conserve space and reduce complexity, most implementations of MDC ignore cells that have no data associated with them. Fast selection of data from this multidimensional cell–based model is enabled by indexing over cells or blocks instead of indexing over individual records. For example, if we wished to cluster by month, logical cells would include January, February, March, etc. Each month would have storage blocks associated with it to hold the data associated with the cell.

DB2 uses the classical B+tree as the storage structure for indexing over a set of MCD storage blocks. This is a powerful technique for industrial databases that typically serve many functions because it allows the storage data to reside in flat storage pages accessible to non-multidimensional queries and operators in a familiar way, while indexing over these blocks using powerful multidimensional techniques. As a result, the MDC storage structure coexists with the non-MDC access structures. This scheme is, however, subject to storage constraints caused by sparsely populated cells, which will be discussed in detail below. More details on DB2's storage model for MDC can be found in papers by Padmanabhan and by Bhattacharjee.

In the DB2 implementation each unique combination of dimension values is represented as a logical cell. Data for each cell is stored in blocks, where each block is a contiguous fixed number of pages on disk (blocks sizes of 2, 4, 8, 16, 32, etc. would be typical). Cells without data require no storage at all (zero blocks), while cells with data consume as many blocks as required to hold the records for the cell. Blocks containing a single value of one dimension are known as a *slice*, as in Figure 8.2(b, c, and e). The clustering dimensions are individually indexed by B+tree indexes known as *dimension block indexes*. These indexes contain dimension values in the intermediate nodes of the tree, and block identifiers in the leaf nodes. Since a single block includes multiple storage pages, and each storage page may contain multiple data records, dimension block indexes contain a small fraction of the data in their leaf nodes that a traditional row-based index would require. The resulting indexes are typically two or even three orders of magnitude smaller than row-based indexes.

Figure 8.2(a) shows the entire table with each cell represented by a single cube. Figure 8.2(b, c, d, and e) shows various queries on the data, selecting data by one or more dimensions, with the shaded cells representing the cells in the query result set.

You may still be wondering how this works, and how this really makes it possible to cluster data in different ways at the same time. The classic confusion comes from thinking of clustering as a sorted sequence on disk, like a string of number-letter pairs like 1a, 2c, 3b, 4g, 5d, 6f, 7e. These are sorted (clustered) by numeric rank. They could also be

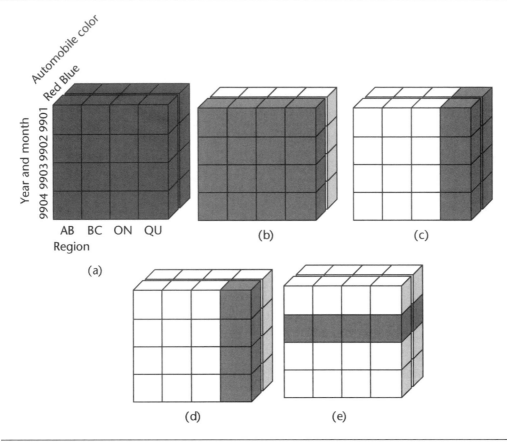

Figure 8.2   Examples of three-dimensional MDC. Car sales by color, date of sale, and region: (a) all data cells, (b) all sales of red cars, (c) all car sales in the province of Quebec, (d) sales of all red cars in the province of Quebec, and (e) all cars sold during February 1999.

sorted by alphabetic rank as 1a, 3b, 2c, 5d, 7e, 6f, 4g. How does MDC make it possible to cluster both numerically and alphabetically at the same time? By using two tricks. First, by requiring high data density within the MDC cells. Consider how things would change if we had a million 1a's and 1.5 million 2c's. With that kind of volume one could put all the 1a's together in their own blocks, without worrying at all if the 1a's were anywhere near the 2c's on disk. Secondly, by not worrying too much about the physical location of storage blocks on disk. The assumption with MDC is that provided the storage blocks are large enough, the savings obtained from reading a single large block of clustered data will achieve more benefit than the seek time caused by blocks not always being adjacent on disk.

The following example illustrates an MDC table with two dimensions: region and year. Each row below is a cell. For example, East, 1993 is a cell and North, 1997 is another cell. You can see how the data does not need to be duplicated in order to achieve MDC because each unique combination of region and year has its own "cell." Because the database indexes over blocks instead of indexing over individual records the block indexes will have a small fraction of the number of entries.

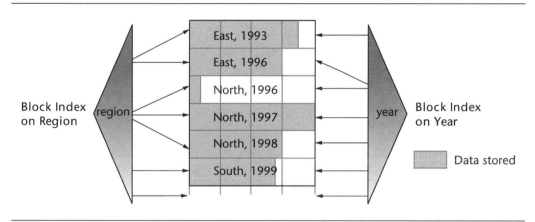

Figure 8.3   Blocks making up an MDC table with dimensions region and year.

The following examples illustrate how MDC with block indexing leads to elegant access patterns that mesh well with classical relational database management system (RDBMS) storage structures.

Example 1: Assume an MDC Table with Dimensions on Color and Nation

```
SELECT * FROM mdctable WHERE Color='Blue' AND
Nation='USA'
```

Sequence:

1. Dimension block index lookup.
2. Block ID ANDing (Figure 8.4).
3. Minirelation scan of only the resulting blocks in the table.

The DB2 implementation was chosen by its designers for its ability to coexist with other database features such as row-based indexes, table constraints, materialized views, and high-speed loading. The benefit of these coexistence properties, for example, allows

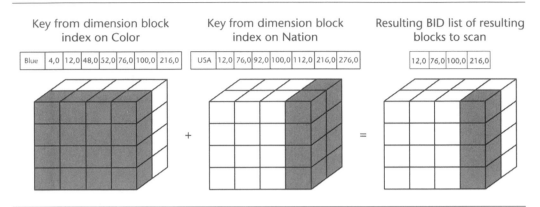

Figure 8.4 Example of block ID ANDing.

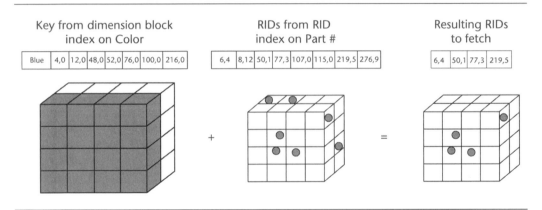

Figure 8.5 Example of block ID and RID ANDing.

the database to perform index ANDing and index ORing between MDC dimension block indexes and traditional row-based (RID) indexes within the same database.

Example 2: Assume an MDC Table with Dimensions on Color and a Traditional Non-MDC Row-based Index on PartNo

```
SELECT * FROM mdctable WHERE Color='Blue'
    AND PartNo < 1000
```

Sequence:

1. Dimension block index lookup on color.

2. RID index lookup to find qualifying rows on PartNo.
3. Block ID and RID ANDing (Figure 8.5).
4. The result is only those RIDs belonging to qualifying blocks.

8.1.3 Syntax for Creating MDC Tables

There is not a formal standard for the DDL defining MDC tables. The following examples highlight the syntax for defining MDC in the DB2 implementation. The main thing to notice is the ORGANIZE BY clause that defines the clustering dimensions.

```
CREATE TABLE mdctable (
    Year        INT,
    Nation      CHAR(25),
    Color       VARCHAR(10),
    ... )
    ORGANIZE BY( Year, Nation, Color )
```

Following is syntax for creating an MDC table with coarsification on the Dateofsale column, converting it to a year.

```
CREATE TABLE mdctable (
Dateofsale      DATE,
Year            generate always as
INT(Dateofsale)/10000,
Nation    CHAR(25),
Color     VARCHAR(10),
... )
ORGANIZE BY( Year, Nation, Color )
```

8.2 Performance Benefits of MDC

MDC is predominantly about improving performance by reducing I/O. However, it can offer some moderate improvements in CPU time because of the increased indexing efficiency, which reduces the number of index items that needs to be processed by the RDBMS in order to resolve a query. The following list summarizes the major performance advantages of MDC, based on a summary from Kennedy [2005]:

- Dramatic reduction in I/O requirements due to clustering.
- The ability to cluster along multiple dimensions independently.
- Clustering that is guaranteed, not just approximately enforced.

- Using MDC data is never placed in the wrong cell.
- Scans on any dimension index provide clustered data access.
  - Each block ID identifies a storage block guaranteed to contain data having that dimension value.
- Dimensions/slices can be accessed independently using their block indexes.
  - One block index does not impact the cluster factor of another block index.
- Block index scans can be combined (ANDed, ORed).
  - The resulting list of blocks also provides clustered data access.
- Access to the clustered data is much faster.
  - More efficient scan using a block ID to access blocks versus multiple RIDs for each row.
- Enabled MDC-specific 'block lookahead prefetching'.
  - Read ahead in the index and prefetch the extents using big-block I/O.

Bhattacharjee et al. [2003] report significant performance benefits using MDC on a star schema database named "POPS," which included a 36 GB fact table and five dimension tables as shown in Figure 8.6.

Another example, cited by Kennedy et al. [2005], describes a real customer experience for a customer who converted a 60-million-row fact table to MDC (Figure 8.7). This system experienced an 11 times performance improvement on some queries, with an average of 3 to 4 times improvement.

Kennedy reports that in a survey of users who were exploiting MDC, dramatic performance increases were reported by almost all users (Figure 8.8). Most of these systems averaged around or just above 3 times query performance improvement with much more dramatic improvements in the maximum speedup of the most improved queries. Maximum speedup included 10 times, 30 times, 100 times, and > 2,000 times.

8.3 Not Just Query Performance: Designing for Roll-in and Roll-out

For fast load, deletion and constraint checking the DB2 implementation also include a block map bit mask that defines the state of each block in a table as being used or unused. Data for a cell or slice can be deleted en masse by simply marking entries in the block map as unused (cleanup of entries for the slice in the dimension block indexes is also required). This process of mass delete is often referred to as "roll-out." It's particularly common in warehousing environments where a rolling window is maintained, such as a seven-year warehouse, having a new month of data rolled-in each month, and the oldest month "rolled-out." The following example illustrates how MDC helps improve the efficiency of data roll-out (Figure 8.9).

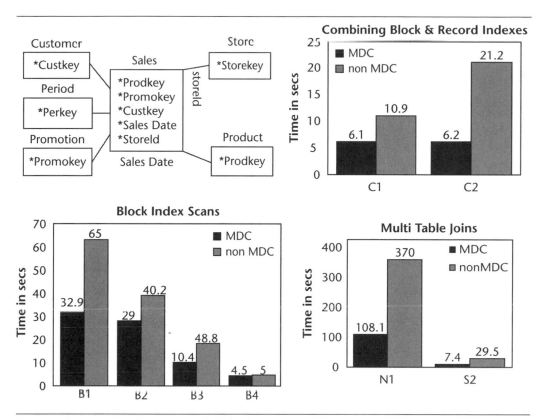

Figure 8.6   MDC performance on POPS schema.

Example 3: MDC Table with Three Dimensions (Nation, Year, Product ID)

```
DELETE FROM table WHERE year = 1992 and product_id = 1
```

- MDC will enable faster delete along cell or slice boundaries.
- The query compiler determines if the DELETE statement qualifies for roll-out.
- There is no need for a specialized statement or command.

8.4 Examples of Queries Benefiting from MDC

The following examples describe SQL queries that can take advantage of MDC. In these examples we have a multidimensionally clustered table MY_TABLE with clustering dimensions DATEOFSALE, COLOR, and REGION. Nonclustering columns in the tables include the "sales" column, a numeric field. In these scenarios, consider

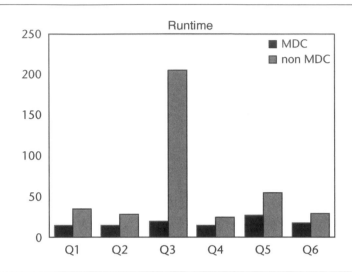

Figure 8.7   Customer experience with MDC.

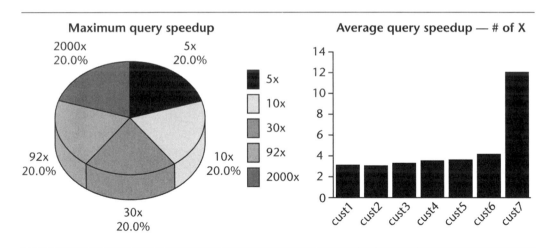

Figure 8.8   Performance improvements reported by customers using MDC.

MY_TABLE to be the sales history table. Examples 2 through 6 are variations of examples that were originally provided by Leslie Cranston[1] and modified to match our

---

[1] Personal correspondence with the author. Ms. Cranston is development manager of the MDC Development department at IBM Canada.

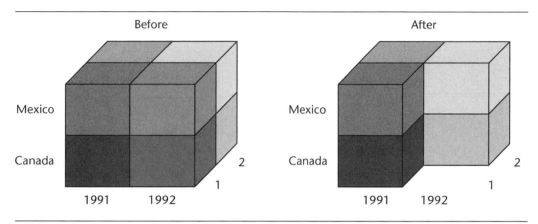

Figure 8.9   Data roll-out with MDC.

MY_TABLE example. These serve to illustrate the runtime exploitation of MDC with various kinds of SQL queries, predicates, and operators.

1.  ```
    SELECT  year(DATEOFSALE), avg(SALES), COLOR FROM MY_TABLE
    WHERE REGION = 'ON'
    GROUP BY (COLOR, YEAR(DATEOFSALE));
    ```

In this case we are grouping by COLOR and the year of the DATEOFSALE, and filtering by REGION. The GROUP BY feature will require the RDBMS to evaluate the select result per unique instance of COLOR value and year. Clustering by all of (or any of) COLOR, REGION, or DATE means that the data in each row of the result set can be fetched by the RDBMS without filtering on COLOR or REGION and the minimum I/O will be performed for each row.

2.  ```
    SELECT * FROM MY_TABLE
    WHERE DATEOFSALE < '12/30/1999';
    ```

This involves a range predicate on a single dimension, so it can be internally rewritten to access the table using the dimension index on DATEOFSALE. The index will be scanned for the locations of all cells/blocks with values less than '12/30/1999', and a minirelational scan will be applied to the resulting set of blocks to retrieve the actual records.

3.  ```
    SELECT  * FROM MY_TABLE
    WHERE REGION  IN ('NY', 'CA');
    ```
    ```

This involves an IN predicate on a single dimension, and can trigger dimension index–based scans. This query can be internally rewritten to access the table using the dimension index on REGION. The index will be scanned for the locations of keys with values of 'NY' and 'CA', and a minirelational scan will be applied to the resulting set of blocks to retrieve the actual records.

```
4.  SELECT SUM(SALES) FROM MY_TABLE
    WHERE DATEOFSALE > '01/01/1998'
    AND COLOR = 'BLUE'
    AND REGION IN ('NY', 'CA');
```

This involves a range predicate on DATEOFSALE, an equality predicate on COLOR, an IN predicate on REGION, along with an AND operation. This can be internally rewritten to access the table on each of the dimension block indexes. A scan of the DATEOFSALE dimension index will be done to find the locations of keys with values greater than '01/01/1998', of the COLOR dimension index to find those with value BLUE, and of the REGION dimension index to find those whose values are either 'NY' or 'CA'. Index ANDing will then be done on the resulting locations from each block scan to find their intersection, and a minirelational scan will be applied to the resulting set of blocks to find the actual records.

```
5.  SELECT ...... FROM MY_TABLE
    WHERE DATEOFSALE <'01/01/1997' OR REGION IN ('NV', 'WA' );
```

This involves a range predicate on the DATEOFSALE dimension and an IN predicate on the REGION dimension, as well as an OR operation. This can be internally rewritten to access the table on the dimension block indexes DATEOFSALE and REGION. A scan of the DATEOFSALE dimension index will be done to find values less than '01/01/1997' and another scan of the REGION dimension index will be done to find values 'NV' and 'WA'. Index ORing will be done on the resulting locations from each index scan, then a minirelational scan will be applied to the resulting set of blocks to find the actual records.

```
6.  SELECT ...... FROM MY_TABLE,d1,d2,d3
        WHERE MY_TABLE.REGION = d1.c1 and d1.region = 'CA'
        AND MY_TABLE.DATEOFSALE = d2.c3 and d2.year='1994'
        AND MY_TABLE.PRODUCT_CLASS = d3.c3 and
        d3.product_COLOR  = 'BLUE';
```

This involves a star join. In this example, MY_TABLE is the fact table and it has foreign keys REGION, DATEOFSALE, and PRODUCT_CLASS corresponding to the primary keys of d1, d2, and d3, the dimension tables. The dimension tables do not have to be multidimensionally clustered, though they may be. Region, year, and product are columns of the respective dimension tables, which can be indexed using regular or dimension indexes (if the dimension tables are multidimensionally clustered tables). When we access the fact table on REGION, DATEOFSALE, and PRODUCT_CLASS values, dimension index scans of the dimension indexes on these columns can be done, and then index ANDing of the resulting location identifiers is performed. Again, once we have a list of blocks, a minirelational scan can be done on each block to get the records.

8.5 Storage Considerations

Figure 8.10 illustrates several MDC cells, each containing a number of storage blocks. Usually, except by pure chance, the number of rows in the cell will not exactly fill a whole number of storage blocks. As a result, in most cases each cell will contain one partially filled storage block. The greater the number of cells there are, the more partially filled blocks, and therefore, the more space wasted.

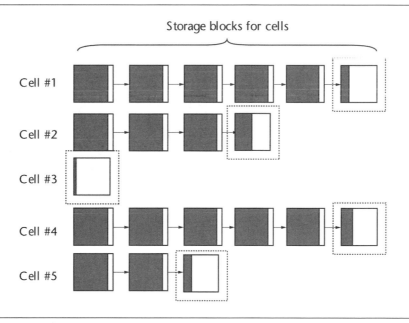

Figure 8.10   Partially filled blocks within cells.

Having a large number of partially filled blocks will result in a large amount of wasted storage and significantly larger table sizes. The large table sizes counteract the benefits of data clustering. Clustering reduces the I/O required to resolve a query while table expansion increases the amount of pages and therefore the I/O associated with a table. Of course, aside from the performance concerns, the extra storage requirements require additional disk, which means increased capital expenditure. Therefore, a key design goal when designing an MDC table is to select the clustering dimensions such that the ratio of the number of unique cells to the number of required storage blocks is kept relatively low. No exact formula currently exists to model an "ideal" storage expansion, though most of the empirical data suggests that keeping the storage expansion to a minimum is an important design goal. In the expert MDC designs that have been published, in most cases the MDC dimensions were selected so as to deliberately limit table expansion to 3–10%.

Estimates of the space waste can be made by assuming each cell contains a single partially filled block at the end of its block list. The space waste is then:

$$W = \eta_{cells} \cdot P_\% \cdot \beta$$

8.1

where η_{cells} is the number of unique cells in the resulting MDC table, $P_\%$ is the average percentage of each storage block left empty per cell, and is the blocking size. On average, the last block in each cell will be 50% filled, except in cases of largely empty cells (very few tuples in the cell). In the presence of either data skew, or very high cell cardinality, the number of cells with very few rows may increase, resulting in a high vacancy rate in the final block of some cells. In fact, from a practical point of view when designing MDC tables, a design should always be chosen that is very conservative on storage expansion, constraining the expansion within the range of 5–10%. With that goal in mind the choice of $P_\%$ is not critical, provided it is larger than 50%, since the goal is to observe gross expansion of space rather than to estimate space use accurately. We recommend using 65% as a fairly conservative value for $P_\%$.

To complete the design examination, it is necessary to know the number of cells in the candidate table design under consideration, namely η_{cells}. There are two ways that η_{cells} can be determined:

1. Estimating the value using available table statistics.
2. Counting the number of cells using an SQL query.

For example, consider the candidate MDC design in Figure 8.3, using COLOR, YEAR, and REGION. Using table statistics available in the database catalogs, we can find the number of unique values in each of these three columns. The number of cells in the MDC design will be, at most, the product of these numbers.

Using an SQL query we can improve on this by actually querying the number of unique combinations of COLOR, YEAR, and REGION, which will almost always be most accurate and a smaller number than the simple product of unique values of each column. Why will the result be different? Correlation. The simple estimation method based on individual column cardinality assumes dimension independence, namely that there is no correlation between any of the dimensions, which is a worst-case scenario. In more real-world systems, some degree of correlation is found between dimensions, reducing the number of unique combinations. A discussion on counting and sampling for MDC storage estimation can be found in Chapter 10.

8.6 Designing MDC Tables

8.6.1 Constraining the Storage Expansion Using Coarsification

In many cases a base column alone may have an unsuitably large cardinality of distinct column values to make it useful as a candidate for defining cells in a cell-block MDC storage structure, since each cell requires at least one storage block. A high cardinality of cells can lead to a large number of partially filled blocks, resulting in storage expansion and poor I/O characteristics. Salary is a typical example, where even in a large corporation most employees are likely to have slightly different salaries, and clustering by similar salaries may not be effective. By using expression-based columns we can derive mathematical and logical models that are based on the base columns of a table, but which have superior clustering potential across one or more dimensions. Again, using salary as an example, INT(SALARY/1000) is likely to be superior in terms of clustering potential to clustering directly on SALARY. Expression-based columns offer a mechanism to express a mathematical model for defining clustering cells so that the domain of cells in the cell-block model for MDC can be specified as an expression, rather than specifying the domain of each cell explicitly.

Some popular RDBMS products available today provide the ability to define expression-based columns as part of a relational table definition. These columns are mathematical functions of columns within their record tuple. Currently, two of the leading RDBMS vendors, IBM and Microsoft, support expression-based columns in their product. IBM's DB2 supports this by a feature known as "Generated Columns," while Microsoft's SQL Server supports it through a feature known as "Computed Columns." For example, using the DB2 syntax one might define an expression-based column on an employee table that is a function of each employees' salary as follows:

```
CREATE TABLE EMPLOYEES (EMPLOYEE_ID INT,
    SALARY DECIMAL(10,4),
    SALARY_RANGE
    GENERATED ALWAYS AS (SALARY/1000))
```

An expression-based column is defined in a base table where the column value is computed using an expression. The expression is an SQL expression based on the physical columns in a table. When creating a table where it is known that certain expressions or predicates will be used all the time, one can add one or more generated columns to that table. Using an expression-based column makes it possible for tables to contain precomputed results, thus reducing the computation time during query processing. However, our use of these special columns is a bit different, and readers interested in other uses of expression-based columns are encouraged to read the sidebar. For MDC, the advantage of expression-based columns will be their ability to coarsify (i.e., reduce the granularity) of clustering dimensions.

In the context of MDC we are interested in the potential new use of expression-based columns in facilitating the definition of clustering keys. We hope first to derive SQL expressions that are useful as clustering models, and second to define expression-based columns that are based on these expressions. Once such virtual clustering keys have been created, they can be used directly to cluster data through any one of a variety of clustering techniques (grid/cell clustering, range partitioning, clustering indexes, etc). A simple example follows.

Consider an employee table, which includes a SALARY field, stored as a 4-byte signed integer. A range query may be interested in employees with salaries in a specific range:

```
SELECT * FROM EMPLOYEES WHERE SALARY > 50000
    AND Salary < 75000;
```

Clustering on SALARY may be a good choice when using a simple clustering index scheme. However, when using a cell/block model where each unique key value resides in its own cell, the range of 50,000 through 75,000 may contain far too many cells to be of practical value in clustering (since most cells will be largely empty in such a case). However, using an expression-based column a good solution can be found for both the clustering index scheme, and the cell/block clustering scheme as follows:

```
CREATE TABLE EMPLOYEES (Name VARCHAR(50),
            Salary INTEGER,
            MyClusterKey INTEGER
             GENERATED ALWAYS AS (Salary / 5000))
```

With this table definition we are free to cluster on MYCLUSTERKEY, which is likely to provide far-superior cell density when clustering than would have been achieved using SALARY as the clustering key.

A very common use of expression-based columns with MDC is with use on DATE fields. Dates are commonly used as predicated in business intelligence applications. Clustering on a day of year directly often does not provide excellent data density, but

---
OTHER USES OF EXPRESSION-BASED COLUMNS

The following example illustrates the specification of an expression-based column on the CREATE TABLE statement, taken verbatim from the DB2 Universal Database Version 7.1 Administration Guide:

```
CREATE TABLE MY_TABLE (c1 INT, c2 DOUBLE, c3 DOUBLE GENERATED
  ALWAYS AS (c1 + c2)
  c4 GENERATED ALWAYS AS (CASE WHEN c1 > c2 THEN 1 ELSE NULL
  END))
```

After creating this table, indexes can be created using the generated columns. For example,

```
CREATE INDEX I1 ON MY_TABLE(c4)
```

Queries can take advantage of the generated columns. For example,

```
SELECT COUNT(*) FROM MY_TABLE WHERE c1 > c2
```

can be written as

```
SELECT COUNT(*) FROM MY_TABLE WHERE c4 IS NOT NULL
```

Another example:

```
SELECT c1 + c2 FROM MY_TABLE WHERE (c1 + c2) * c1 > 100
```

can be written as

```
SELECT c3 FROM MY_TABLE WHERE c3 * c1 > 100
```

There are a number of potential benefits that flow from expression-based columns. First, the reduction of SQL complexity as a single column name can be substituted for an expression. Second, if the computed value is actually stored inside the database (not all vendors do this, but rather compute the expression at runtime), then the cycle time for the computation is removed. Further, the ability to index on expression-based columns means that sorted results can be obtained immediately, rather than incurring an expensive sorting phase on every query.

---

clustering on a week of year or month of year is usually more appropriate. Assume an MDC table with dimensions on generated column month, where a "month" column has been generated as an expression-based column using the expression 'INTEGER(date)/100':

- For queries on the dimension (month), block index range scans can be used.
- For queries on the base column (date), block index range scans can also be used to narrow down which blocks to scan.

To accomplish this, the compiler internally generates the additional dimension predicates.

For example, given this query:

```
SELECT * FROM mdctable WHERE date > "1999/03/03" AND
date < "2000/01/15"
```

the compiler generates the following additional predicates:

```
month >= 199903 AND month <= 200001
```

that can be used as range predicates for a block index scan. This allows the RDBMS to determine the list of blocks to be scanned, and the original predicates are applied to the rows in those blocks.

8.6.2 Monotonicity for MDC Exploitation

Using expression-based columns clearly helps improve the density of data within the MDC cells by reducing the number of cells in the table. How does the database's query compiler actually manage to perform search operations using these expression-based columns when the queries themselves do not reference them, and the expressions may be quite complex? The query compiler performs this magical mapping for MDC by exploiting qualities of monotonicity and the ability to detect a monotonic relationship between the base column and the expression-based column. In the next few paragraphs we'll describe what this means, and how it works.

Simply put, monotonic functions are ones that do not oscillate. For example, for a function $f(x)$, as x is increased the value of $f(x)$ will not increase then decrease or decrease then increase. This is stated more formally in the following two definitions:

- **Definition 1:** A function $f(x)$ is monotonic increasing if, and only if, for any two values $x1$ and $x2$, where $x1 < x2$, it is always true that $f(x1) < f(x2)$.

- **Definition 2:** A function $f(x)$ is monotonic nonincreasing if, and only if, for any two values $x1$ and $x2$, where $x1 < x2$, it is always true that $f(x1) \geq f(x2)$.

The test for monotonicity is performed if needed during the query rewrite phase of an SQL statement while the query compiler is processing predicate expressions. When a range predicate expression includes a column that has a corresponding expression-based column, the monotonicity algorithm tests to see if a substitution is possible. A substitution is only possible when the expression-based column is monotonic compared to the base column. Without the ability to test for monotonicity of an expression, expression-based columns would not really be useful for MDC. While they would certainly succeed in improving cell density, it would be impossible for the query compiler to map predicates on the base columns to the block indexes on the expression-based columns.

A clever scheme to detect monotonicity is described in the ICDE paper by Malkemus et al. [2005]. The technique parses the expression that is used in the expression-based column and does a quick analysis of the operand types and sequence to determine if the expression can be reliably asserted as monotonic.

Malkemus et al. cite the following examples of real-world data uses where coarsification has been used to help improve the creation of dense and effective MDC dimensions:

- Time attribute used in 30-minute intervals. The timestamp attribute can be made into a large integer and then divided to obtain this generated column.
- Latitude divided by 15 (i.e., intervals of 15 degrees).
- Longitude divided by 30.
- Year and month of a date (i.e., INT(date) = 100).
- Mathematical functions to compute rank, error value, range, etc.

Once the generated column is detected as monotonic, the query rewrite engine of the SQL compiler will rewrite the SQL statement to use the expression-based column instead of the base column.

8.6.3 Picking the Right Dimensions

Many factors affect the choice of clustering design, including the database schema, workload, relative importance of cluster-based roll-out and utility maintenance by the enterprise, impact of multidimensional clustering on storage requirements, and so on. MDC benefits come mostly from reducing the I/O performed during query and roll-out operations. To select MDC dimensions to help query performance, begin by determining the most expensive (long running) queries in the workload or application. Once the longest-running queries have been identified, examine each statement for the predicates that use equality, range, or general inequality conditions. Equality predicates are specified by '=' or 'IN' conditions. Range predicates are specified by '>', '<', '>=', '<=', or 'BETWEEN' clauses in SQL. The columns used in these clauses will provide the key candidates for clustering. This is not very different than what might be done when selecting indexes. What is slightly different here is the following:

- You rarely need to be concerned about multipart dimensions. Each dimension can usually be defined as a single column. To achieve multidimensional qualities, simply create *n* single-part clustering dimensions.

- You need to be very concerned about table storage expansion due to partially filled blocks. This is not a concern with index selection.

You can improve your selection by looking at the query execution plan for each query (all relational database products allow you to view the query execution plan).[2] The query execution plan can show you how much I/O is projected to happen at each stage of the plan execution. You can focus your dimension selection on the columns that are used in operators incuring high I/O cost. This will focus your design efforts where they matter most allowing you to gain a better sense of which clustering dimensions are more likely than others to help reduce disk I/O.

Additionally, because MDC is very helpful for roll-out, if your system has roll-out requirements, consider creating an MDC dimension on the roll-out predicate. This is almost always a DATE field. In most cases it is advisable to coarsify the date to WEEK or MONTH before using it as an MDC dimension.

Finally, consider using MDC even when there is only a single interesting dimension for clustering within a given table. MDC has the advantage over most other single-dimensional clustering indexes that:

- The clustering is guaranteed to be enforced.
- The block indexes will be orders of magnitude smaller than RID-based indexes.

Once you have a set of candidate dimensions you must test the number of cells to see if the table expansion for each table on which you wish to apply MDC is going to be reasonable (~10% or less, ideally less than 5%). If not, then you have a choice of reducing the number of dimensions or coarsifying one or more dimensions in order to reduce the number of cells.

TIPS AND INSIGHTS FOR DATABASE PROFESSIONALS

- **Tip 1. Start your selection for MDC candidates using the same initial set of columns you would use for index selection,** by looking for columns that are used in your SQL workload as predicates for equality, inequality, range, and sorting.
- **Tip 2. Focus on keeping the number of cells reasonably low.** Keeping the table expansion low is critical so that storage requirements don't expand unreasonably beyond roughly 5–10% for any single table. You can use the MDC storage approximation equation to estimate the expansion.

---

[2] In DB2 this is done through the EXPLAIN facility.

- **Tip 3. You can get a conservative estimate on the number of cells by assuming dimension independence and simply multiplying their individual column cardinalities (five unique A's and five unique B's, yields at most 25 unique AB's).** In fact, however, you can get better and more aggressive designs by watching carefully for dimensions that are correlated with each other (if A and B are perfectly correlated then five unique A's and five unique B's yield still five unique AB's).

- **Tip 4. Coarsify some dimensions to improve data density.** Use expression-based columns to create "coarsifications" of a table column that have much lower column cardinality and may be excellent choices for clustering (e.g., create a column on "month of year" from a date column). This will result in better data density within the MDC cells.

- **Tip 5. Don't go overboard on the number of dimensions.** In practice, it is very rare to find useful solutions that have more than three MDC dimensions that still constrain storage expansion to a reasonable degree. In most cases, when these circumstances exist, they are detectable through automated data mining systems, and not easily detected by a human designer. (See Chapter 16 for a discussion on automated design tooling for MDC.) In practice look for MDC designs that have three or less MDC dimensions.

- **Tip 6. Consider one-dimensional MDC.** Single-dimensional MDC can still provide massive benefits over traditional single-dimensional clustered indexes. Why? Because the clustering is 100% guaranteed, and because the data is indexed by "block" and not by "row" resulting in indexes that are roughly 1/1,000 the size. As a result, many index operations on block indexes are dramatically faster and more efficient than operations on traditional row-based indexes.

- **Tip 7. Be prepared to tinker.** It may take some trial and error to find an MDC design that works really well. But the investment in tinkering is often worth it. In many cases you can achieve huge gains with MDC that simply are not possible any other way.

8.7 Summary

MDC has emerged as a powerful new physical database design technique. Although it has been discussed in the research literature for several decades, it has emerged onto the industrial scene with a full implementation in DB2. It offers potentially huge performance improvement for query processing and roll-out by dramatically reducing the I/O processing performed. Special care needs to be taken in designing MDC tables, in particular to achieve data density in the storage blocks, so that table storage requirements do not expand unreasonably. A design constraint of 5–15% expansion is recommended.

8.8 Literature Summary

Bhattacharjee, B., Padmanabhan, S., Malkemus, T., Lai, T., Cranston, L., and Huras, M. Efficient Query Processing for Multi-Dimensionally Clustered Tables in DB2. *Proceedings of VLDB,* 2003, Berlin, Germany, 2003.

Jagadish, H. V., Lakshmanan, L. V. S., and Srivastava, D. Snakes and Sandwiches: Optimal Clustering Strategies for a Data Warehouse. Proceedings of the 1999 International Conference on Management of Data, 1999, pp. 37–48.

Kennedy, J. P. Introduction to MDC with DB2 UDB LUW. IBM DB2 Information Management Technical Conference, Orlando FL, 2005.

Lightstone, S., and Bhattacharjee, B. Automating the Design of Multi-dimensional Clustering Tables in Relational Databases. *VLDB,* 2004, Toronto, Canada.

Liou, J. H., and Yao, S. B. Multi-dimensional Clustering for Database Organizations. *Information Systems*, 2, 1977: 187–198.

Malkemus, T., Padmanabhan, S., Bhattacharjee, B., and Cranston, L. Predicate Derivation and Monotonicity Detection in DB2 UDB. *ICDE,* 2005: 939–947.

Markl, V., Ramsak, F., and Bayer, R. Improving OLAP Performance by Multi-dimensional Hierarchical Clustering. *Proceedings of IDEAS,* 1999, Montreal, Canada.

The OLAP Report, at http://www.olapreport.com/.

Padmanabhan, S., Bhattacharjee, B., Malkemus, T., Cranston, L., and Huras, M. Multi-Dimensional Clustering: A New Data Layout Scheme in DB2. *SIGMOD,* 2003, San Diego, CA.

Pendse, N., and Creeth, R. Benchmarking an Extremely Large Decision Support Requirement: Proof Point of Scalability with IBM and DB2, Winter Corporation (www.wintercorp.com) DB2 9 Technical Library, at http://publib.boulder.ibm.com/infocenter/db2luw/v9/index.jsp?topic=/com.ibm.db2.udb.doc/doc/r0008264.htm.

Stöhr, T., Märtens, H., and Rahm, E. Multi-Dimensional Database Allocation for Parallel Data Warehouses. *Proceedings of VLDB*, 2000, Cairo, Egypt.

The Interdependence Problem

The challenge of database design, more than anything else, is the challenge of the interconnectedness of all things. The interdependence issues are in principle so central to database design that perhaps this book should have been titled *Zen and the Art of Database* or *Buddhism for Databases*. As if designing indexes, materialized views, partitioning, and other design qualities were not each individually complex enough, the nasty little secret is that these design problems are woefully and massively interconnected. The choice of a single index may remove the need for a materialized view or vice versa. Choice of partitioning can affect join efficiency so dramatically that index design may need a complete rethink. Multidimensional clustering (MDC) can obviate the need for B+ indexes. So we have a problem upon a problem: each of the design choices is exponentially complex pushing the limits of human designers to cope. When taken in combination, the possible combinations and considerations are so explosively large it appears far beyond the ability of mere mortals to manage.

In truth, tackled in a direct and comprehensive manner this is not a problem that human beings can grapple with, leading us to the possible conclusion that we should probably just give up. Close this book, turn on the TV, and leave database design for someone else. But databases do get designed by human beings, and designed well. To do this people use a number of strategies we will discuss. Very little has been formally published on this topic until now, though there have been some loose reflections in various articles in recent years. Automated design utilities, discussed in Chapter 12, have had to grapple with this problem as well. However, these automated utilities have the computational power of the database query engine and the full computational power of the computer to explore combinations in ways impractical for human designers. Fortunately database practices are not defined by published literature alone, and for years practitioners have been getting by despite the interdependence problem using practical strategies. Practical strategies are not always steeped in scientific analysis but much like chicken soup for a bad cold, they have over time demonstrated effectiveness and gained broad acceptance.

9.1 Strong and Weak Dependency Analysis

In a technical paper, Zilio et al. [2004] discuss automated database design in which they distinguish between strong and weak design relationships. Zilio et al.'s assumption is that although all design attributes are related to each other, some are more related than others. They define a matrix of strong and weak relationships, shown below in Table 9.1. Weak relationships are those where the design choices can be made in sequence. This does not mean that the choices are independent, but rather that designing the attributes one after another will not lead to a grossly suboptimal design. An example of a weak relationship is the design of B+tree indexes followed by the design of MDC (block indexes). Although the design of MDC will result in block indexes that can obviate the use of an existing B+tree index, it is unlikely to result in the need for different B+tree indexes. Therefore, it is generally reasonable to design B+tree indexes, followed by MDC, and subsequently determine which B+tree indexes are no longer required.

An example of a strong relationship is one where the design attributes are so tightly coupled that sequential modeling and design will often lead to significantly suboptimal database designs. An example of this is the design of materialized views and indexes. Materialized views are often large enough to require indexes themselves. Designing materialized views without the corresponding indexes at the same time will often lead to design choices that appear to be useless by every normal analysis (examining object access, plan selection, resource modeling, etc.).

Notice in Table 9.1 that partitioning appears to be weakly related to other design attributes. This is extremely fortunate since it allows the database designer to select partitioning for shared-nothing databases after most of the other attributes have been designed using a default (basic) partitioning scheme in the interim. Recall from the discussion in

Table 9.1   Zilio et al.'s Dependancy Analysis

	Index	Materialized View	Shared-nothing Partitioning	Multi-dimensional Clustering
Index	–	S	W	W
Materialized View	S	–	W	S
S.N. Partitioning	W	S	–	W
MDC	W	S	W	–

Chapter 6 that partitioning design depends predominantly on join collocation and even distribution of data across the MPP (massively parallel processors). However, one would expect the design of materialized views to very significantly affect joins in the query execution plans of many statements, even entirely eliminating many joins that would otherwise be required. This suggests that the design of partitioning is indeed tightly coupled with the design of materialized views. Which is it—weak or strong dependency? If you examine the dependency table closely you'll notice that the dependency is strong when viewed from the perspective of partitioning (i.e., materialized views impact partitioning choices very strongly). However, the dependency is weak when viewed from the perspective of materialized views, meaning that materialized views can be designed reasonably well using a suboptimal partitioning design.

Table 9.2   Dependncy Analysis Extended to Include Range Partitioning

	Index	Materialized View	Shared-nothing Partitioning	MDC	Range Partitioning
Index	–	S	W	W	W
Materialized View	S	–	W	S	S
S.N. Partitioning	W	S	–	W	W
MDC	W	S	W	–	W
Range Partitioning	W	S	W	W	–

This analysis leads one to conclude that the selection can have the following order:

1. Materialized views and index design.
2. Shared-nothing partitioning design.
3. MDC design.

This analysis does not include range partitioning, an important design attribute discussed in Chapter 7. Extending the work of Zilio et al. to include range partitioning might give a dependency table, such as Table 9.2.

Judging between range partitioning and MDC the generally accepted practice is that range partitioning is a coarser higher-level granularity of partitioning. This suggests the following order for design exploration:

1. Materialized views and indexes need to be designed together and probably should be designed first.
2. Shared-nothing partitioning design.
3. Range partitioning design.
4. MDC design.

9.2 Pain-first Waterfall Strategy

In practice the consequences of changing the physical database design for some attributes are much more challenging than others. For example, creating a new secondary B+tree index is a moderately costly effort, requiring (typically) a scan through the entire table to extract keys, a full sort of these keys, and input/output (I/O) for the pages for the index, which will include I/O for all the keys plus additional I/O for the intermediate nodes of the tree. However, conversion of a table to MDC is dramatically more expensive since it requires full reconstruction of the base table (with either sorting or hashing of every record), reconstruction of all secondary indexes, and the creation of additional new block indexes. It is not unlikely that conversion of a table to MDC will require an order of magnitude more time and storage than the creation of a new secondary index. Similar comparisons can be made for shared-nothing partitioning, range partitioning, and materialized views. In general the hierarchy of "pain" looks something like the following from most to least painful to redesign:

1. Shared-nothing partitioning.
2. MDC.
3. Range partitioning.

4. Materialized views.

5. Indexes.

This ranking suggests that shared-nothing partitioning and MDC should be designed first, and index design last with the goal of minimizing the inconvenience of database redesign. In practice, few database designers design new databases in this sequence. However, understanding the relative pain of changing design choices does seriously impact the design planning process. Understanding the relative inconvenience usually means that database designers are loathe to design shared-nothing partitioning and MDC casually because the overhead of redesign is quite high. Decisions for shared-nothing partitioning and MDC are usually made carefully, slowly, and applied with the assumption that the design will not be tinkered with for a long time. In contrast, database designers often try out new indexes and materialized views with relative freedom, knowing that if the attempting index was not significantly worthwhile, it can be easily dropped without much disruption.

9.3 **Impact-first Waterfall Strategy**

Another strategy in designing databases is to focus on the dominant design point first and work toward refinement of the design by adding the features that are likely to have less impact. This is extremely difficult to assess a priori because the impact of a design choice depends dramatically on the definition of the workload and data in the database (as well as many other factors such as system resources and topology). There are many documented cases where any of the design choices discussed in this book have improved system performance by an order of magnitude or more.

However, most practitioners will agree that indexes are the first and most dominant design requirement for databases because without them the query execution plans are doomed to include table scans for many lookups and joins even in the presence of a rich set of materialized views, for any sizable table will prove extremely inefficient. It is almost impossible for real-world systems to avoid the need for indexes by other means (such as purely through the use of materialized views) since indexes tend to be generic in their utility, providing value to a wide range of queries that use the leading key of the index, which other design features tend to be more specific-to-specific query fragments.

Following index design, the relative impact is less obvious. In environments where materialized views are usable, they can reduce the cost of individual queries by orders of magnitude, and are therefore the next most important design choice. However, as discussed above, indexes on the materialized views need to be considered during the design of the materialized views and not as an afterthought.

Shared-nothing partitioning is usually the next most important design choice, usually impacting system performance in the range of 10 to 30%.

The expected impact of MDC and range partitioning varies between workloads, but again anecdotal information from benchmarks and user experiences suggests that MDC is the more critical design feature being more likely to contribute significant performance gains.

These leave range partitioning as the final design attribute. As discussed in Chapter 6, the design of range partitioning is often driven by factors beyond performance related to data availability and utility processing.

This leaves us with the following suggested design sequence:

1. Indexes.
2. Materialized views and their indexes.
3. Shared-nothing partitioning.
4. MDC.
5. Range partitioning.

9.4 Greedy Algorithm for Change Management

After developing an initial design almost all real-world databases will undergo some design change in response to new usage requirements caused by application changes (new features or enhancements) or shifts in workload pressures (new users or changing user patterns).

As the use of the database changes the optimal design may change as well. In an idealized world the database designer would redesign the database from scratch using one of the strategies above. However, this is usually impractical due to the time required for the analysis and the time requirement for fully implementing the changes on a database containing a large volume of production data. In these cases it is almost universal to exploit a greedy algorithm.[1]

The greedy algorithm for incremental database design starts with the assumption that preexisting database design is fundamentally sound and that only incremental changes are required to satisfy the new requirements. This assumption is often not true, particularly where legacy databases are involved, but it's a reasonable starting point. The performance of the new statements and old statements is examined to find the most

---

[1] Many readers will be familiar with the notion of "greedy algorithms." For those who are unfamiliar with the term, a reasonable definition appearing on Wikipedia (http://en.wikipedia.org/wiki/Greedy_algorithm) follows: *A greedy algorithm is an algorithm that follows the problem-solving metaheuristic of making the locally optimum choice at each stage with the hope of finding the global optimum. For instance, applying the greedy strategy to the traveling salesman problem yields the following algorithm: At each stage visit the unvisited city nearest to the current city.*

serious performance problems. These statements and utilities are then ranked in terms of urgency and each one is reviewed to determine what database design changes will help alleviate the problem.

9.5 The Popular Strategy (the Chicken Soup Algorithm)

It's worth noting what most database designers opt to do, however suboptimal this strategy is. The typical database administrator (DBA) operates on the assumption that it is possible to achieve a reasonably performing system using careful selection of indexes and then applies advanced physical design capabilities to the remaining query hotspots. This assumption is true as a general rule, but is also common wisdom that is based on 30 years of database design, much of which evolved before the advent of advanced physical design features like MDC and materialized views. As a result, the designer will begin with a careful and exhaustive selection of indexes. Shared-nothing partitioning is chosen next if the system uses a shared-nothing architecture, simply because an operational system can't be created on the MPP without choosing the partitioning. Using a default partitioning is possible but not usually adequate. This will be followed by range partitioning, where the design choice is based almost purely on administrative requirements for partition isolation to help with the manageability of the database during utility operations, such as roll-out, backup, and the like (rather than query performance based on partition elimination). Materialized views are chosen next usually for the highest cost queries, followed by MDC, which is typically viewed as an emerging technology and is therefore seen as somewhat optional. This leads to the following selection sequence:

1. Indexes.
2. Shared-nothing partitioning.
3. Range partitioning.
4. Materialized views.
5. MDC.

This process isn't scientific, but it is the one most commonly used by the bulk of DBAs today worldwide. It's used not because it is scientific or efficient, but because DBAs have become accustomed to it and it seems to work in the large. Much like chicken soup for a cold this selection strategy has a following because it has played itself out over years of experience and gained a following. For these reasons we affectionately refer to it as the "chicken soup algorithm for database design."

Pure online transaction processing (OLTP) systems rarely use shared-nothing architectures, materialized views, or MDC, which reduced the complexity design for those systems.

TIPS AND INSIGHTS FOR DATABASE PROFESSIONALS

- **Tip 1. Use a strategy.** Many very intelligent database designers don't come close to maximizing the potential of their systems simply because they developed the database design in an ad hoc manner. Using a strategy for exploring the possible database design choices will definitely help the practitioner develop a better design than a database developed using ad hoc planning (i.e., nonplanning).

- **Tip 2. Start with indexes.** Chicken soup is good for a cold and the chicken soup approach to database design is used by most database designers most of the time. It's reasonable, and you can achieve "near optimal" result that are more than adequate. Indexes are the most important feature and as a general rule are the most broadly applicable. A database with only indexes can still be perfectly functional. A database with all the bells and whistles, but that lacks a reasonable set of indexes, will usually be unusable.

- **Tip 3. Think about the strategy that is most appropriate for you.** Dependency analysis is very hard for most human designers to use effectively. Pain first is a good strategy to use if you have a complex environment with a lot of data and feel you really need to design with a significant amount of data to get a good feeling for how the system will behave. Large volumes of data will mean large pain (i.e., time and waiting) when you want to explore each new design attribute. If you are dealing with a smaller volume of data during the design process, you may want to start with the impact-first strategy. (Strategies for dealing with the problem of exploring design changes on a fully populated database are discussed in Chapter 11.)

- **Tip 4. Use design automation technology.** Many vendors provide design automation utilities. This emerging technology is not yet able to provide recommendations that are as high quality and reliable as the very best database designers. However, they often can come quite close, and can form an excellent basis for a database design that the human designer can refine. A detailed discussion of these utilities can be found in Chapter 12. Oracle provides the Oracle SQL Access advisor, Microsoft SQL Server provides the Database Tuning Advisor, and IBM DB2 has the DB2 Design Advisor. All of these vendors provide these utilities as part of the basic database product, and no additional purchase or installation is required.

- **Tip 5. Iterate.** Database design is as much an art as a science. The complex interactions do make this process very difficult. Don't be afraid to tinker and to go back and reconsider previous decisions, especially after making changes in other areas of the system. As long as you don't let your iterations become a habitual unstructured ad hoc design antiprocess, you'll end up with a better design than you would achieve using a single-pass strategy. Force yourself to make the first pass a very structured process and that will allow you to use more freedom and flexibility in the iterations that follow.

9.6 **Summary**

We've presented a few different strategies for the order of selecting design attributes. Some are better than others depending on your environment and the size and complexity of the system you are designing. The complex interactions between the design features mean that human designers will not be able to consider them in combination in a single design step. As a result, whatever design a human expert develops has a high probability of not being the absolute best theoretical design possible—and that's completely fine. The goal of the database designer should be to ensure that the database is running well, that the resources are well used, and that applications are not suffering from deleterious performance issue. If your database design is a good one, it can achieve better than 95% of the theoretical maximum and that is more than enough to achieve the primary objectives. In reality, end users won't notice the difference from the final 5%, and nobody will be expecting it. Automation tooling, discussed in Chapter 12, can be used to help bootstrap this process, giving you an initial design to start fine tuning. It can also be used to fine tune a design you've crafted by hand. Bear in mind that the more complex your workload and the more your workload includes analysis and reporting functions, the more likely you can achieve large performance gains by exploiting multiple design features.

9.7 **Literature Summary**

Agrawal, Sanjay, Surajit Chaudhuri, and Vivek R. Narasayya Automated Selection of Materialized Views and Indexes in SQL Databases. *VLDB*, 2000: 496–505

Zilio, D. C., Rao, J., Lightstone, S., Lohman, G. M., Storm, A. J., Garcia-Arellano, C., and Fadden, S. DB2 Design Advisor: Integrated Automatic Physical Database Design. *VLDB,* 2004: 1087–1097.

Counting and Data Sampling in Physical Design Exploration

Get your facts first, and then you can distort them as much as you please.
Facts are stubborn, but statistics are more pliable.
—Mark Twain (1835–1910)

There are three kinds of lies: lies, damned lies, and statistics.
—Benjamin Disraeli (1804–1881)

Counting and sampling are critical to effective database design. There is perhaps nothing more natural than wanting to explore something to see what it is really like before plunging in and committing. Most of us use counting and sampling strategies every day for various things we do. We nibble on food that we are cooking to see how it tastes or we read a few lines from a book before we buy it. Sampling is one of the oldest and most common strategies for getting a good sense of a large system quickly. It has marvelous applications to physical database design, particularly using SQL capabilities for counting and sampling that are being added by database vendors.

Some of the most important design problems that can be helped through sampling include materialized view size estimation, index size and key duplication (or cardinality) projections, multidimensional clustering storage, and shared-nothing partitioning skew. In some ways data sampling is so important it can be hard to develop a truly top-notch database design without it. In all of these cases understanding the data is the goal, and sampling is a tool that can help speed the analysis.

The need for sampling in database design is actually growing. Why? Because data volumes are growing and doing so at a rate that is larger than the exponential growth in power of CPUs. In short, data growth is outstripping Moore's Law! As data volumes grow from gigabyte to terabyte to exabyte levels and beyond, they become prohibitively difficult to analyze in their entirety, and the cost of changing the physical database design becomes increasingly more expensive. However, as we'll soon see, sampling has pitfalls of its own, and must be used carefully to avoid seriously misleading results. As the old adage goes: "Lies, damn lies, and statistics!"

In the sections that follow we first introduce techniques to improve database design by "counting," using common SQL techniques. Secondly, we discuss sampling, sampling techniques, and support for data sampling in the SQL language to show how this can speed the process, but not without some risks.

10.1   **Application to Physical Database Design**

The power of SQL, and even parallel processing, can be brought to bear to count the number of distinct values of a column or a group of columns. This counting is extremely important for most aspects of physical database design. To perform the counting, you can use the COUNT and DISTINCT operators in SQL. Here is an example of the syntax that can be used to count the number of distinct values on a column named "COL1":

```
SELECT COUNT(*) FROM (SELECT DISTINCT COL1, FROM
MY_FAV_TABLE) AS NUM_DISTINCT;
```

Similarly, the number of distinct combinations of a few columns can be determined this way. For example, the following syntax shows how this can be counted for three columns named COL1, COL2, and COL3.

```
SELECT COUNT(*) FROM (SELECT DISTINCT COL1, COL2, COL3
FROM MY_FAV_TABLE) AS NUM_DISTINCT;
```

Consider a table named MY_FAV_TABLE (Table 10.1).

Table 10.1 has 14 rows of data. Issuing our query to determine the number of distinct values in COL1 will return the following:

```
NUM_DISTINCT
--------------------
9
```

Table 10.1   Data for MY_FAV_TABLE

COL0	COL1	COL2	COL3	COL4
John	12	3	2	4
George	13	4	3	5
Gene	13	5	4	21
Jonah	12	3	2	3
Giuseppe	3	5	6	7
Jillian	4	3	2	8
Jack	5	7	4	8
Jane	6	8	3	9
Jim	7	9	5	7
Janet	8	7	6	9
Jeff	9	9	5	4
Jesse	9	9	5	5
Jeremiah	6	7	3	6
Joseph	4	4	12	3

There are only nine distinct values used in COL1. (Note that the largest number used is 13 and values 1, 2, 10, and 11 do not appear.) Issuing the same query for the combination of COL1, COL2, and COL3 produces:

```
NUM_DISTINCT
---------------------
12
```

This is because row 1 and row 4 have the same values for columns COL1, COL2, and COL3, and so do rows 11 and 12.

Also important to us will be the count of the number of rows in a table. This data is often available in the database system catalogs. However, it can be counted explicitly with SQL using:

```
SELECT COUNT(*) FROM MY_FAV_TABLE AS MY_COUNT;
```

which in Table 10.1 would return 14:

```
MY_COUNT
-----------------
14
```

10.1.1 Counting for Index Design

In general, indexes are valuable because only a small percentage of the index data needs to be accessed to find qualifying rows, as compared to scanning the entire table. However, there are other considerations. Specifically, scanning an entire table, though input/ouput (I/O) intensive, is a reasonably efficient process per page of data because of the efficiencies of large block I/O, I/O prefetching, and sequential I/O. All three of these will generally make a table scan much more efficient per page than lookups into indexes. Indexes are much more prone to fragmentation and random I/O on disk.

It is critical, therefore, that the index data being accessed is not only a fraction of the table data, but is also a rather small fraction because the cost per page of index access will be higher than the cost per page of table access during a brute-force scan. If the index data includes a very high number of duplicates, then the number of distinct values in the index drops, and the number of row identifiers returned by an index scan increases, as does the number of index pages that needs to be accessed. As a general rule you should design indexes so that the number of distinct elements in the index is at least 30% of the table cardinality. For example, if the table has 1,000,000 rows, the index should usually have at least 300,000 distinct values, otherwise it may not be a generally useful index to a broad class of queries. There are exceptions, of course, but this is a reasonable rule of thumb.

10.1.2 Counting for Materialized View Design

One of the biggest challenges with materialized view design is estimating the ultimate size of the materialized view, which can be large. When the view is the result of one or more joins, it's possible for the view size to become extremely large. Because the view is materialized, it will require real storage, which is expensive, and if the view is very large, the maintenance overhead of maintaining the view can also be prohibitive. The brute-force strategy is of course to try to create the view and see how big it gets! However, for complex large views it's more than worthwhile to spend a few minutes to run a count rather than spend hours to find out the hard way the view is unreasonably large. To determine the approximate size of a view you can do the following.

First, count the number of rows in the view as follows:

```
SELECT COUNT(*) FROM (<view definition> ) AS
NUM_ROWS_IN_VIEW;
```

For example, here's an example of an MQT created for an employee database:

```
ALTER TABLE EMPLOYEE ADD UNIQUE (EMPNO);
ALTER TABLE DEPARTMENT ADD UNIQUE (DEPTNO);

CREATE TABLE EMP AS (SELECT E.EMPNO, E.FIRSTNME, E.LASTNAME,
E.PHONENO, D.DEPTNO, SUBSTR(D.DEPTNAME, 1, 12) AS DEPARTMENT, D.MGRNO FROM
EMPLOYEE E, DEPARTMENT D
WHERE E.WORKDEPT = D.DEPTNO)
   DATA INITIALLY DEFERRED REFRESH IMMEDIATE;

SET INTEGRITY FOR EMP IMMEDIATE CHECKED NOT INCREMENTAL;

SELECT * FROM EMP;
```

EMPNO	FIRSTNAME	LASTNAME	PHONENO	DEPTNO	DEPARTMENT	MGRNO
000010	CHRISTINE	HAAS	3978	A00	SPIFFY COMPU	000010
000020	MICHAEL	THOMPSON	3476	B01	PLANNING	000020
000030	SALLY	KWAN	4738	C01	INFORMATION	000030
000050	JOHN	GEYER	6789	E01	SUPPORT SERV	000050
000060	IRVING	STERN	6423	D11	MANUFACTURIN	000060
000070	EVA	PULASKI	7831	D21	ADMINISTRATI	000070
000090	EILEEN	HENDERSON	5498	E11	OPERATIONS	000090
000100	THEODORE	SPENSER	0972	E21	SOFTWARE SUP	000100
000110	VINCENZO	LUCCHESSI	3490	A00	SPIFFY COMPU	000010
000120	SEAN	O'CONNELL	2167	A00	SPIFFY COMPU	000010
000130	DOLORES	QUINTANA	4578	C01	INFORMATION	000030
...						
000340	JASON	GOUNOT	5698	E21	SOFTWARE SUP	000100

32 record(s) selected.

Instead of creating the EMP materialized view to determine the number of records it contains you could count the number of records using the SQL described above as follows:

```
SELECT COUNT(*) FROM (SELECT E.EMPNO, E.FIRSTNME,
e.lastname, e.phoneno, d.deptno, substr(d.deptname, 1,
12) as department, d.mgrno from employee e, department d
WHERE E.WORKDEPT = D.DEPTNO) AS NUM_ROWS_IN_VIEW;
```

which would return:

```
NUM_ROWS_IN_VIEW
----------------
32
```

Once the number of rows in the view is known or estimated, the total storage requirement for the view is usually pretty obvious within a factor of 2 by multiplying by the average row width, which is easy to estimate by looking at the table definition. If the count is small, like 32 in our example, it's somewhat irrelevant, but view sizes can get very large, running into many gigabytes of storage and millions of rows. A good database design should never spend more than 10 to 20% of total storage on materialized views.

10.1.3 Counting for Multidimensional Clustering Design

In Chapter 8 we discussed the fact that space waste in a multidimensional clustering (MDC) table can be estimated by assuming each cell contains a single partially filled block at the end of its block list. The space waste is then:

$$W = \eta_{cells} \cdot P_{\%} \cdot \beta$$

10.1

where η_{cells} is the number of unique cells in the resulting MDC table, $P_{\%}$ is the average percentage of each storage block left empty per cell, and is the block size. We recommend using 65% as a fairly conservative value for $P_{\%}$. The block size is typically a number of pages, 32 × 4 KB pages being a typical block size. However, the space waste is going to be driven heavily by the number of cells η_{cells}, which grows exponentially with the number of columns in the MDC if the columns are poorly correlated. As space waste grows, many of the benefits of clustering can be undone because too much I/O ends up being done on largely empty pages. A good rule of thumb is to constrain the space waste to less than 10% of the total non-MDC table size. Most expert MDC designers pick MDC designs with less than 5% growth. η_{cells} can be counted using methods similar to the index counting. For example, to count the number of distinct MDC cells for an MDC table clustered on COL1, COL2, and COL3, use the following:

```
SELECT COUNT(*) FROM (SELECT DISTINCT COL1, COL2, COL3
FROM MY_FAV_TABLE) AS NUM_MDC_CELLS;
```

The size of the table and the block size for the table are usually readily available in the system catalogs, making it possible to complete the calculation and determine the MDC growth without going through a very expensive trial-and-error process to actually materialize the MDC table to evaluate its size.

10.1.4 Counting for Shared-nothing Partitioning Design

As a reminder, shared-nothing partitioning is usually based on a hashing scheme that hashes records to data nodes (see Figure 10.1). Real-world systems exist with as little as two data nodes and as many as several hundred.

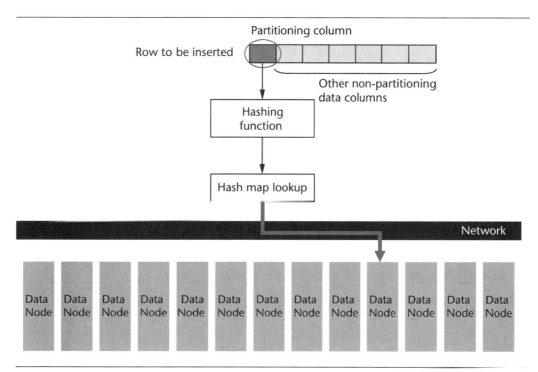

Figure 10.1   Hashing of records into a shared-nothing database.

For the database to perform well, it is critical that data be distributed across the data nodes fairly evenly. Having a data node with less data than others isn't going to cause massive problems, but having a partition with a disproportionately large amount of data will usually mean that partition will become the slowest partition in the processing. In a decision support (business intelligence) workload where multiple data nodes collaborate to each solve a portion of the query and then merge results, a partition with a disproportionately large volume of data will significantly slow the processing, becoming a bottleneck. For a partitioned OLTP shared-nothing system, the partition with the most data will receive a disproportionate amount of requests, becoming the slowest node in the system and impacting the service level achievement for transactions being processed by that data node. In short, data skew on a shared-nothing architecture is bad news for any kind of workload. To avoid this it's important that the columns used to partition the data have sufficiently high cardinality of distinct values so that skew across the data nodes is unlikely.

Another factor in avoiding skew is the fairness of the hash algorithm, which is usually not a problem, except in very rare scenarios. The database designer can generally assume with confidence that the database's hashing function has been chosen carefully and is fair. The major cause of skew is a poor ratio of distinct values in the partitioning columns versus the number of partitions in the system. In general the number of distinct values in the partitioning column should be at least 20 to 100 times the number of partitions in the database system. If the count of distinct values is too low consider adding additional column(s) to the partitioning columns (partitioning key) so that the hashing function can balance data more evenly. As before, the count of distinct values of the partitioning key can be determined through the SQL.

```
SELECT COUNT(*) FROM (SELECT DISTINCT COL1, COL2 FROM
MY_FAV_TABLE) AS PARTITIONING_VALUES;
```

Another loose indicator in the selection of the partitioning key is the ratio of distinct values in the key to total rows. If the ratio is low there are many duplicates in the data and the partitioning is subject to skew. As a rule of thumb, a ratio of better than 7:10 should be a design point. However, this rule is very approximate. If there is heavy skew in the 30% of nonunique values (e.g., consider the pathological case where 70% of the partitioning key values were unique and all of the remaining partitioning values had a single common value, then 30% of the data would hash to the same data node!), then even the 7:10 rule may not be adequate. Conversely if the data is evenly distributed so that every distinct value has roughly the same number of duplicates then a very low ratio of distinct value may be perfectly fine.

10.2 The Power of Sampling

10.2.1 The Benefits of Sampling with SQL

The act of counting can itself be time consuming over very large data sets. In many cases the performance of the count can be dramatically improved and the accuracy little changed if the data is sampled.

Certainly, in terms of counting the relative numbers of values, sampling has been shown to be highly effective with little loss in accuracy over many varied data sets. SQL offers sampling syntax, supported by a number of vendors.

Figures 10.2 and 10.3 illustrate the effectiveness of sampling in determining relative amounts of data with very good accuracy and dramatic performance benefits.

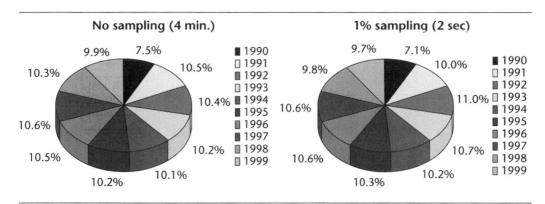

Figure 10.2   Effect of sampling on an aggregation query. (Image courtesy of IBM.)

Figure 10.2 [Haas 2003] shows how sampling was used to determine a distribution of data by year in 2 seconds versus 4 minutes with very little loss in accuracy, while producing the result 100 times faster.

Similarly, Figure 10.3 [Haas 2003] illustrates sampling a million-row data set and performing linear regression. Notice how a 0.01% sample produced almost exactly the same results as a full table scan, though it has the potential of running ten thousand times faster.

A variety of alternatives to "pure" sampling are based on various synopses of the data that are computed during a complete scan. See, for example, Acharya et al. [1999], Chaudhuri et al. [1999], and Ganguly [1996]. Although such methods can yield very accurate estimates, the synopses are expensive to compute, impose continual storage space requirements, must be incrementally maintained over time, and allow relatively little user control over estimation accuracy. These synopses are therefore not currently supported by commercial database systems.

10.2.2 Sampling for Database Design

Sampling is supported in SQL via the TABLESAMPLE clause, which allows Bernoulli sampling or system sampling choices, and a sampling rate. These types of sampling will be described below in the next section. An example of the SQL syntax follows, illustrating a 5% sample of the EMP table:

```
SELECT SUM(BONUS) FROM EMP TABLESAMPLE BERNOULLI (5)
WHERE DEPTNAME = 'H917'
```

Sampling works extremely well when the objective of sampling is to determine a distribution. When sampling is used to determine a count, however, serious problems arise, because the sample may include all of the distinct values or only very few. Unfor-

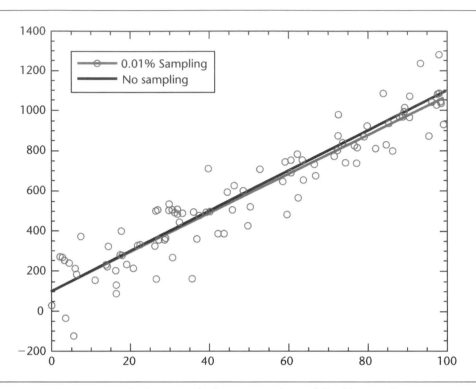

Figure 10.3   A 0.01% sample shows nearly the same result as a full table scan. (Image courtesy of IBM.)

tunately extrapolating the number of distinct values in a set from a sample is nontrivial because much depends on the degree of skew and scarcity of the data. Many advanced mathematical techniques have been developed, a survey of which can be found in Haas [1995] and Haas [1998].

Fortunately, high accuracy in counting is not required for most database design problems. It suffices to figure out whether the number of distinct values is large or small, rather than exactly how large or small. Still, simply multiplying by the inverse of the sampling rate is not wise, because the impact of skew and sparseness has nonlinear effects. Several algorithms exist, and can be divided into two main categories: (1) algorithms that evaluate cardinality of distinct values by examining the frequency data in the sample, and (2) those that generate a result without considering the frequency distribution of the values in the sample. We focus on the latter type of estimator because estimators of this type can be calculated easily from a small set of input variables that summarize the sample, such as sample frequency, sample size, and the cardinality of distinct values in the sample.

The best of these latter estimators is the First-order Jackknife estimator [Haas 1995], which can be described as follows: When the data set contains no skew, the scale-up factor, defined as *Scale = D/E[d]*, is given by

$$Scale = D/E[d] = 1/(1-(1-q)^{(N/d)}),\qquad 10.2$$

where D is the number of distinct values in the set and d is the number of distinct values in the sample. Also, $E[d]$ is the expected number of distinct values in the sample under Bernoulli sampling with rate $q = n/N$, where n is the target[1] sample size and N is the set size. $E[d]$ is the theoretical expected value of d (i.e., the average value of d over many repeated samples). The idea behind the "method of moments" estimator is to derive an equation relating $E[d]$ to D, based on theoretical considerations. We solve for D to get a relation of the form:

$$D = f(E[d]),$$

for some function f. Our estimator $\hat{D}$ is then obtained by substituting d for $E[d]$ in the above relation:

$$\hat{D} = f(d).\qquad 10.3$$

Such a substitution is reasonable if the sample is not too small. $E[d]$ is the "first moment" of d, so we are replacing a moment by an observed value.

Importantly, the First-order Jackknife estimator is an inferior cousin to the more advanced estimators that factor in data skew more carefully by including value frequency in their estimation models. The best of the more advanced estimators is the Hybrid estimator described in Haas [1998]. However, the experimental results comparing the two estimators show that both estimators are quite reasonable. Their relative correctness at various sampling rates is summarized in Table 10.2 [Haas 1998], according to root mean squared error (RMSE).[2]

---

[1] As discussed later, the size of a sample produced by Bernoulli sampling is random, although with high probability it is close to the target size.

[2] The mean squared error for an estimator is simply the average value of the quantity (estimate − true value)^2 over many trials. The root mean squared error (RMSE) is the square root of this quantity, and has the advantage of having the same units at the quantity being estimated. The RMSE measures the average distance of the estimator from the value that it is trying to estimate.

While the Hybrid estimator clearly provides superior estimates, the First-order Jackknife estimator does a relatively good job while being much easier to compute. Also, although the First-order Jackknife estimator has worse average-case behavior than the Hybrid estimator, experiments in Haas [1998] show that the former estimator is more robust in the presence of data skew, in the sense that it has better worst-case performance. The First-order Jackknife can therefore be a useful tool for database design problems, provided the database designer keeps in mind that this estimator often has up to double-digit RMSE, and can be highly error prone at low sampling rates.

Table 10.2   Qualitative Comparison of the Hybrid and First-order Jackknife Estimators

	1% sample	5% sample	10% sample
Hybrid estimator, average RMS error	35.74	20.37	14.33
First order Jackknife estimator, average RMS error	40.87	32.00	27.07

One of the places where sampling can be very powerful in database design is in the area of materialized-view size estimation where, as in our previous example, the view definition does not have any aggregation functions (such as SUM or COUNT) in the SELECT clause. In this case, estimation of the number of distinct values is not required. For a materialized view that is defined on a single base table, the size can usually be predicted with good accuracy using sampling, by multiplying the number of rows returned from the sample by the inverse of the sampling rate. When the materialized view comprises a select-join query on two or more base tables, the size can again be predicted by multiplying the number of rows in the sample by the inverse of the "effective" sampling rate, where the effective sampling rate is defined as the product of the sampling rates over all sampled tables [Haas 1996]. The difficulty here is that the accuracy of the estimate is very sensitive to the choice of sampling rates, and it is very hard to determine a good allocation of the overall sampling effort a priori. The most effective sampling techniques learn the optimal sampling rates as they go and adapt their behavior accordingly [Haas 1996, Haas 1999]. Current database systems do not yet support such complex sampling schemes.

The situation becomes even more complicated when the view definition starts to invoke the full power of SQL, with correlated subqueries and other advanced features. View-size estimation in these complex scenarios remains an open problem. Fortunately, there exists a very important and common multitable scenario where sampling can be applied in a straightforward way. An example is given by the EMP table defined previously. In this case, the Department table is most likely a small table with a short list of departments and the bulk of the data is coming from the Employee table. Because the

Department table is small, it's possible in this case to sample only on the Employee table, and extrapolate by the inverse of the sampling rate. In many cases this is not possible or is nontrivial to detect. Even if the Department table is large, such sampling is still feasible provided that there is an index available on DEPARTMENT.DEPTNO. This example is a special case of a star join, where a large "fact" table is joined to one or more "dimension" tables. In this very common setting, it is often possible to simply sample from the fact table and scale-up the number of rows by the inverse of the sampling rate.

Unlike the foregoing setting, estimates of the number of distinct values are required when a materialized view has aggregation operators in the SELECT clause of the view definition, as is typical in online analytical processing (OLAP) settings. This problem is a more complex version of the distinct-value counting problem for a single table, and there has been relatively little work on sampling-based estimators. Nadeau and Teorey [2003] explored the use of parametric sampling-based distinct-value estimators to determine the size of materialized views in an OLAP environment. Unlike nonparametric estimators, such as the First-order Jackknife estimator, a parametric estimator makes an a priori assumption that the frequency distribution of the values in the set has a specific form (Pareto, in the case of Nadeau and Teorey [2003]). The sample is then used to estimate the parameters of the distribution, and the fitted distribution implies a count for the number of distinct values. Such an approach works well when the actual frequency distribution for the data has (at least approximately) the postulated form. Nadeau's tests showed the Pareto model algorithm performed well against three published algorithms. However, these kinds of strategies are mathematically and algorithmically complex, and are best suited for incorporation into CASE tools, rather than for direct use by database designers.

10.2.3 Types of Sampling

There are four basic kinds of sampling that are important to be aware of for database processing:

- Simple random sampling of size k
- Bernoulli sampling
- System sampling
- Stratified sampling

Simple random sampling is the best known kind of sampling, in which a fixed number k of items are selected uniformly and randomly from a sample. The number to be chosen is selected in advance. However, this can be done with and without replacement. Replacement refers to how items are handled after they are selected: Are they removed from the set or are they kept in the set and possibly reselected? The former type of sample is called a "simple random sample of size k without replacement," whereas the latter type of sample is called a "simple random sample of size k with replacement." Because duplicates are ruled out, a without-replacement sample contains (in a statistical sense) more information than a with-replacement sample, and hence is usually preferred. Indeed, the phrase "simple random sample" usually refers implicitly to the without-replacement version, and we adopt this usage here. Simple random sampling of size k is a uniform scheme in that it produces any two samples of size k with equal probability; no samples are favored over others. The main drawbacks to simple random sampling are that (1) efficient implementation requires a priori knowledge of the size of the table to be sampled, and (2) it is hard to parallelize the sampling operation when the sampled table is horizontally partitioned. For these reasons, most database management systems do not support simple random sampling directly. It is possible to simulate simple random sampling by appending a column of random FLOATs to a table, and then returning rows sorted according to this column. This approach is very cumbersome in practice, however.

Bernoulli sampling is much easier to implement than simple random sampling, and hence is supported by all the major database vendors and is part of the SQL standard. Row-level Bernoulli sampling (denoted as BERNOULLI in the SQL standard) gets a sample of P percent of the table rows by means of a SARGable predicate that includes each row in the sample with a probability of $P/100$ and excludes it with a probability of $1 - P/100$. Each record is sampled independently of the others. Unlike simple random samples, which have a fixed size specified a priori, the size of a Bernoulli sample is itself random (it has a binomial distribution). For example, a 5% Bernoulli sample of 200 items would evaluate each of the 100 items in turn and accept each item with a 5% probability. Because each item is individually assessed independent of all others, the number of items that are ultimately selected in the sample will be close to 10 items, but will have some random variation around that size. Specifically if we define N to be the number of items in the data and p is the inclusion probability, the actual size of a Bernoulli sample will, with high probability, be within $\pm q$ of expected size where:

$$q = 2(Np(1 - p))^{\int}$$
                                                                 10.4

For example, if $N = 1,000,000$ and $p = \int$, then the actual size is within 0.2% of expected size with high probability.

Row-level Bernoulli sampling always gets a valid, random sample regardless of data clustering. However, the performance of this type of sampling is very poor if no index is available because every row must be retrieved and the sampling predicate applied to it. If there is no index then there are no I/O savings over executing a query without sampling. If an index is available, then performance using this type of sampling is improved because the sampling predicate is applied on the record identifiers (RIDs) inside the index leaf pages. In the usual case, this requires one I/O per selected RID, and one I/O per index leaf page.

System sampling is defined in the SQL standard to be a vendor-dependent sampling method. In practice, system sampling is implemented by virtually all vendors as similar to Bernoulli sampling, except that it samples database data at the level of I/O units (e.g., storage pages) instead of sampling at the record level. For example, a 5% system sample of a table would sample 5% of the storage pages. Sampling pages instead of records dramatically improved the performance of the sampling process, as shown in Figure 10.4. A page is included in the sample with a probability of $P/100$. If a page is included, all of the rows in that page are included. However, if the data has any significant clustering in the table a system sample can lead to seriously erroneous results.

Performance of system (page-level) sampling is excellent because only one I/O is required for each page that is included in the sample. Compared with no sampling, system page-level sampling can improve performance by orders of magnitude.

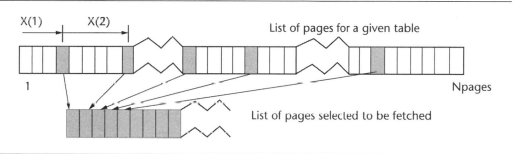

Figure 10.4   System level sampling in SQL. (Image courtesy of IBM.)

However, the accuracy of aggregate estimates tends to be worse under system page-level sampling than row-level sampling. This disparity in accuracy is most pronounced when there are many rows per block or when the columns referenced in the query exhibit a high degree of clustering within the pages. I/O sampling on a table with significant clustering (i.e., having a good cluster ratio and therefore storing similar data together on the same or nearby pages on disk) can lead to dramatic inaccuracies. For example, Haas [2003] used the following example to show the massive inaccuracies that can result from using system sampling on clustered data. Haas defined a table with one million rows, with 100 records per page. He performed experiments to take a 1% sample on a numeric column in the table using both row-level sampling and system sampling and for each. The sum of the data in the column was then estimated by multiplying the sum of the sample data by 100 (because a 1% sample was used). The estimate based on applying system sampling to clustered data was an order of magnitude too large. See Table 10.3 and Haas [2004] for a further discussion of these issues.

Table 10.3   Failure of System (Page-level) Sampling for Clustered Data

	Estimated sum using row level Bernoulli sampling	Estimated sum using system (page-level) sampling
Data is unclustered	995	995
Data is clustered	995	9950

Stratification is the process of grouping the data to be sampled into subgroups before sampling. Stratified sampling can reduce the chances of poor results caused by possible bad luck of the "random" choices being poorly distributed. Because random sampling is truly random it's possible that a random selection could (in theory) disproportionately choose records from a given range of the table—however improbable that is. This is similar to rolling a die five times and landing on the same number each time. Unlikely, but possible. With random sampling (Bernoulli or simple), the final choice may not be well distributed even though the selection probabilities are fair. To solve this problem, stratified sampling divides the table into ranges of pages and performs random sampling within each range as shown in Figure 10.5. This ensures that records are chosen from each range. Some database vendors support stratified sampling, although it is not normally part of the SQL standard.

10.2.4 Repeatability with Sampling

The SQL standard supports the REPEATABLE keyword for use with the TABLESAMPLE clause, which allows the caller to specify a seed for the sampling process. This makes it possible to perform sampling repeatedly, so that the same sample will be chosen over the same data set every time, provided that the seed, data, sampling type, and sampling rate are all held fixed. The REPEATABLE clause is very useful for debugging and testing when using sampling. Sample syntax follows:

```
SELECT SUM(BONUS) FROM EMP TABLESAMPLE BERNOULLI (5)
REPEATABLE (Y) WHERE DEPTNAME = 'H917'
```

10.3 An Obvious Limitation

We've presented a fairly positive perspective on the use of SQL to count and sample data in order to make effective database design choices. However, there is a chicken and egg problem. All of the techniques above do require a database to exist that is populated with data in order for SQL to be executed. In the early stages of database development a

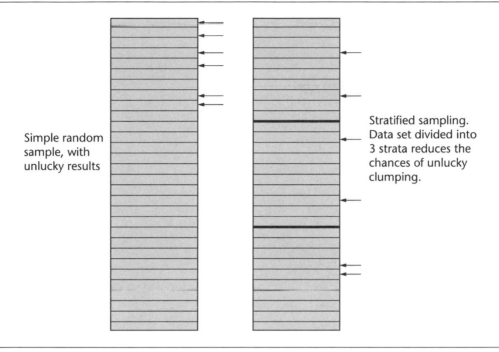

Figure 10.5   Random sampling versus stratified sampling.

full complement of data is often not available and the database may be populated (if at all) with synthetic data that does not have the same skew and sparseness qualities as the real user data that will eventually populate the production database. Despite this serious limitation, these methods are broadly applicable where data is available.

TIPS AND INSIGHTS FOR DATABASE PROFESSIONALS

- **Tip 1. If you have data, count it.** Counting will help you significantly improve your database design, for index selection, materialized views, multidimensional clustering, and hash partitioning. It is one of the most basic things to do, and in many ways decisions that are made about physical database design without counting are unreasonably risky.

- **Tip 2. Remember the rules of thumb when counting for database design:**
  a. *Indexes:* The number of distinct elements in the index is at least 30% of the table cardinality.
  b. *Materialized views:* A good database design should never spend more than 10 to 20% of total storage on materialized views.

TIPS AND INSIGHTS FOR DATABASE PROFESSIONALS

c. *MDC* should never expand table size by more than 10%; 5% is even better.

d. *Hash partitioning:* Select the partitioning so that the ratio of distinct values in the key to total rows is at least 7:10.

- **Tip 3. Sample where possible.** Sampling can dramatically improve the efficiency of design exploration. But as we described above, sampled data can't be directly used to determine the number of distinct values, and requires some extrapolation. Careful attention is required to make sure the counts are extrapolated reasonably. Fine accuracy is *not* required. Reasonable accuracy is still needed.

- **Tip 4. Sampling and counting distinct values.** Skew and sparseness in the data can unwittingly cause massively misleading results in the appearance of the number of distinct values in a data set when sampling is used. Even the more advanced extrapolation algorithms are error prone. We recommend using a simple extrapolation routine, such as the First-order Jackknife estimator. However, even more important than choosing a particular estimator is to be careful with the sampling rate. Using sample rates below 5% is probably unwise when your goal is to count the number of distinct values.

- **Tip 5. Sampling is hard with joins.** Joins complicate the art of sampling, because good sampling rates are hard to choose when multiple tables are involved that have different table cardinalities. If you have a star join situation, you can often sample from the fact table. There is no magic bullet, however, and very little has been published. When in doubt, don't sample! You are better off waiting a little longer for a good number than getting a number that is way off. Lies, damn lies, and statistics!

10.4 Summary

Counting is a key aspect of physical database design in terms of understanding

- The number of distinct values of a column or a set of columns to be used as a design attribute, such as index keys, partitioning columns, MDC columns, etc.
- The absolute number of rows in a table or materialized view.
- The ratio of unique values to total rows.

The SQL language supports counting naturally through the COUNT and DISTINCT keywords, making it possible to exploit the power of SQL to help design the database. Exploration can be dramatically sped up by the use of sampling. Care should be taken with system-level sampling since it is prone to giving skewed results when used on clustered data. Extrapolating the number of distinct values in a set from a sample is nontrivial and even the best mathematical models for this have double-digit RMS error. However, there are simple estimators that can be used to give a reasonable result and these are appropriate for rapid exploration of database design possibilities. The best database designs are almost always developed with the aid of counting.

10.5 Literature Summary

Acharya, S., Gibbons, P., Poosala, V., and Ramaswamy, S. Join Synopses for Approximate Query Answering. In *Proceedings of 1999 SIGMOD*. New York: ACM Press, 1999, pp. 275–286.

Chan, T. F., Golub, G. H., and LeVeque, R. J. Algorithms for Computing the Sample Variance: Analysis and Recommendation. *Amer. Statist.*, 37, 1983: 242–247.

Chaudhuri, S., Motwani, R., and Narasayya, V. R. On Random Sampling over Joins. In *Proceedings of 1999 SIGMOD*. New York: ACM Press, 1999, pp. 263–274.

Chaudhuri, S., Motwani, R., and Narasayya, V. R. Random Sampling for Histogram Construction: How Much Is Enough? SIGMOD Conference, 1998, pp. 436–447.

Devroye, L. *Non-Uniform Random Variate Generation*. New York: Springer-Verlag, 1986.

Flajolet, P., and Martin, G. N. Probabilistic Counting Algorithms for Database Applications. *Journal of Computer and System Sciences,* 31, 1985: 182–209.

Ganguly, S. Gibbons, P. B., Matias, Y., and Silberschatz, A. Bifocal Sampling for Skew-resistant Join Size Estimation. In *Proceedings of 1996 SIGMOD*. New York: ACM Press, 1996, pp. 271–281.

Haas, P. J., and K^nig, C. A Bi-level Bernoulli Scheme for Database Sampling. In *Proceedings of 2004 SIGMOD*. New York: ACM Press, 2004, pp. 275–286.

Haas, P. J. The Need for Speed: Speeding Up DB2 Using Sampling. *IDUG Solutions Journal*, 10, 2003: 32–34.

Haas, P. J., and Hellerstein, J. M.. Ripple Joins for Online Aggregation. In *Proceedings of 1999 SIGMOD*. New York: ACM Press, 1999, pp. 287–298.

Haas, P. J., and Stokes, L. Estimating the Number of Classes in a Finite Population. *J. American Statistical Association* 93, Dec. 1998: 1475–1487.

Haas, P. J., Naughton, J. F., Seshadri, S., and Swami, A. N. Selectivity and Cost Estimation for Joins Based on Random Sampling. *J. Comput. Sys. Sci.*, 52, 1996: 550–569.

Haas, P. J., Naughton, J. F., Seshadri, S., and Stokes, L. Sampling-based Estimation of the Number of Distinct Values of an Attribute. *Proceedings of the 21st International Conference on Very Large Databases*, Zurich, Switzerland, 1995.

Haas, P. J., Naughton, J. F., and Swami, A. N. On the Relative Cost of Sampling for Join Selectivity Estimation. *PODS, 1994*: 14–24.

Hellerstein, J. M., Haas, P. J., and Wang, H. J. Online Aggregation. In *Proceedings of 1997 SIGMOD*. New York: ACM Press, 1997, pp. 171–182.

Hou, W., Ozsoyoglu, G., and Taneja, B. Statistical Estimators for Relational Algebra Expressions. In *Proceedings of Seventh ACM SIGACT-SIGMOD-SIGART Symp. Principles of Database Sys*. New York: ACM Press, 1988, pp. 176–287.

König, A. C., and Nabar, S. U. Scalable Exploration of Physical Database Design. *ICDE*, 2006: 37.

Nadeau, T. P., and Teorey, T. J. A Pareto Model for OLAP View Size Estimation. *Information Systems Frontiers*, 5(2), 2003: 137–147.

Olken, F. Random Sampling from Databases. Ph.D. Dissertation, University of California, Berkeley, CA, 1993.

Runapongsa, K., Nadeau, T. P., and Teorey, T. J. Storage Estimation for Multidimensional Aggregates in OLAP. *Proceedings of 10th CASCON Conference*, Toronto, Canada, 1999, pp. 40–54.

Shukla, A., Deshpande, P. M., Naughton, J. F., and Ramasamy, K. Storage Estimation for Multidimensional Aggregates in the Presence of Hierarchies. *Proceedings of 22nd VLDB Conference*, Mumbai, 1996, pp. 522–531.

Query Execution Plans and Physical Design

It is a bad plan that admits of no modification.
—Publilius Syrus (~100 B.C.), Maxims

Make a new plan Stan … and get yourself free.
—Paul Simon

Throughout this book we've presented the major attributes of physical database design, and how they are used and why. How can you determine if a specific database design attribute is really helping or hurting your database? Or even more fundamentally, how can you determine if a design feature is being used by the database? There's a brute-force method of course: Run experiments with your application workload to evaluate the contributions of every single physical design change to determine the impact. This kind of brute-force strategy is probably inefficient since it means actually creating and testing each design possibility with a real database packed with a lot of data. There's another way to evaluate the benefit of design choices, and interestingly it's the same method that the database itself uses; namely, to examine the impact of design choices on the query execution plans of your workload. This technique is in fact the dominant technique used by database administrators (DBAs) and database designers for every major database product, and as a result every major database product provides tooling to allow users to examine the query execution plans chosen by the database for each query. By viewing the query execution plan one can observe whether the database itself thinks that design choices, such as materialized views and indexes, are likely to be useful. How so? Because if the database thinks the design feature is useful, it will exploit it in the query execution plan. For example, if an index A is beneficial to a query at runtime we should expect to see access to index A in the query execution plan for the query. In this chapter we'll show examples of the different ways that query execution plans are presented both in text and graphically by the major database vendors, and illustrate how they can help improve physical database design.

11.1 Getting from Query Text to Result Set

How does a query submitted to a database get transformed into an answer set? Figure 11.1 shows the basic order of operations that occurs for incoming SQL statements. When a query is submitted to a database, the first thing the database will do is parse the statement text to catch errors and then construct an internal representation of the query that is usually stored in a graph model that the user cannot see.

The query is then examined for semantic correctness to ensure the query makes sense. For example, do all the object's references in the query exist, and can the query even conceptually be executed (even with a NULL answer set)? During this phase the database may also extend the query graph by adding logic for constraint checking and triggers.

Following semantic checking, the query is then rewritten by the database to improve the efficiency of the text. Here's an example using query 1 from the industry standard TPC-R benchmark.

```
select l_returnflag, l_linestatus, sum(l_quantity) as
sum_qty,
sum(l_extendedprice) as sum_base_price,
sum(l_extendedprice * (1 - l_discount)) as
sum_disc_price, sum(l_extendedprice * (1 - l_discount) *
(1 + l_tax)) as sum_charge, avg(l_quantity)as avg_qty,
avg(l_extendedprice) as avg_price,
avg(l_discount) as avg_disc,
count(*) as count_order
from tpcd.lineitem
where l_shipdate <= date ('1998-12-01') - 90 day
group by l_returnflag, l_linestatus
order by l_returnflag, l_linestatus
```

Here is the same text after it has been rewritten by a database:

```
SELECT Q3.$C7 AS "L_RETURNFLAG",
 Q3.$C6 AS "L_LINESTATUS",
 Q3.$C5 AS "SUM_QTY",
```

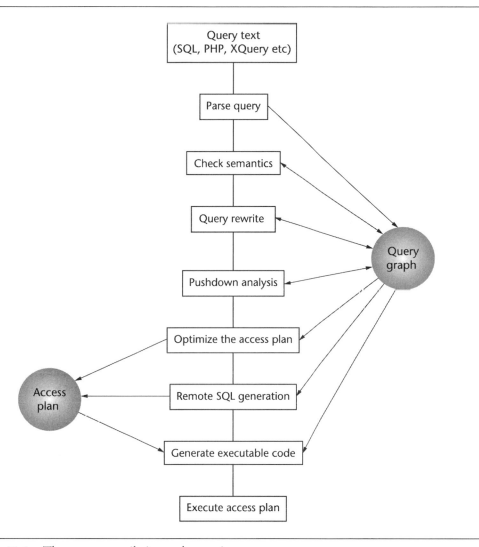

Figure 11.1   The query compilation and execution process.

```
Q3.$C4 AS "SUM_BASE_PRICE",
Q3.$C3 AS "SUM_DISC_PRICE",
Q3.$C2 AS "SUM_CHARGE",
(Q3.$C5 / Q3.$C0) AS "AVG_QTY",
(Q3.$C4 /Q3.$C0) AS "AVG_PRICE",
(Q3.$C1 / Q3.$C0) AS "AVG_DISC",
INTEGER(Q3.$C0) AS "COUNT_ORDER"
FROM
    (SELECT SUM(Q2.$C2), SUM(Q2.$C3), SUM(Q2.$C4),
```

```
      SUM(Q2.$C5),SUM(Q2.$C6),SUM(Q2.$C7), Q2.$C0, Q2.$C1
  FROM
      (SELECT Q1.L_LINESTATUS, Q1.L_RETURNFLAG, Q1.COUNT,
       Q1.S5, Q1.S4, Q1.S3, Q1.S2, Q1.S1
       FROM TPCD.L_SUMMARY AS Q1
        WHERE (Q1.L_SHIPDATE <= '09/02/1998')) AS Q2
     GROUP BY Q2.$C1, Q2.$C0) AS Q3
  ORDER BY Q3.$C7, Q3.$C6
```

The rewritten query is a little difficult to read, because it uses internal representations of tables and columns instead of the normal user-defined names that the database designer has specified in the DDL. That's okay, because the rewritten version of the query is just a steppingstone during the internal processing of the query, prior to query execution plan selection. It's not essentially designed for human beings to read. However, many database vendors allow users to view the rewritten query through the query execution plan visualization tooling. This can be helpful in determining if a performance problem has been caused by the database during this rewrite phase.

It's possible that during query rewrite the database query compiler may find such a good match for a materialized view that one is selected and substituted into the rewritten query, though most vendors leave the final selection of materialized views for the query optimization step the majority of the time.

Finally, a query execution plan can be selected based on the combined data within the query graph. This will include not only the rewritten query text, the list of objects, columns accessed, available indexes, and materialized views and other physical design attributes, but also existing statistics on the object (table, materialized view, and index statistics) and information about the physical resources of the database server, such as CPU speed, storage device access speeds, and network speed and latency. As discussed in Chapter 3, the process of query execution plan selection is complex and can involve varying degrees of search complexity. There are almost always multiple ways the result set for a query can be determined, and the database will attempt during query optimization to select the query execution plan that can retrieve the result set most efficiently. Different databases have different goals for determining "most efficient," though selecting the query execution plan with the lowest resource consumption appears to be a common strategy.

However, the query execution plan itself is still an abstraction. A final step is required prior to retrieving the answer set, called *code generation*. This process generates the executable code required to perform the tasks recommended by the query execution plan identified by the query optimization process. Code generation will convert the abstract notation of the query execution plan into compiled object code that the database can understand and execute.

Finally, the object code produced by the code-generation phase is executed, including the operations for index access, joins, sorts, etc., and the query result is produced and communicated back to the calling application through a communication process, such as TCP/IP. Unbelievably, for short online transaction processing (OLTP) transactions this entire process can execute in fractions of a second.

11.2 What Do Query Execution Plans Look Like?

Each vendor has its own proprietary format for visualizing query execution plans and the specific information these include. However, although the details vary, the basic theme is the same. The query execution plan for a query is shown as a directed graph, with both the database objects and the operators of the query execution plans shown as nodes with the graph. Objects will include tables, indexes, materialized views, catalogs, temporary tables, etc. Operators will include joins (and their type, such as hash join, nested-loop join, semi-join, and merge join), sort, etc. The Oracle utility is called Explain Plan (Figure 11.2) and Graphical Explain Plan. The Microsoft SQL Server utility is called Query Analyzer, and the DB2 utility is called Explain and Visual Explain (Figure 11.3).

11.3 Nongraphical Explain

Oracle also provides a text-based Explain that allows administrators to view access paths for queries without using the graphical user interface (GUI). Their usage is quite simple, using the EXPLAIN PLAN FOR text followed by the SQL statement, as follows:

```
EXPLAIN PLAN FOR
    <SQL statement text>
```

This generates the Explain output and stores it in the PLAN_TABLE table. Administrators can then select the execution plan from PLAN_TABLE to view the access path.

If you want to explain multiple SQL statements and store the access paths for all of them (or some of them), you can specify a statement identifier on the EXPLAIN PLAN FOR syntax to uniquely identify the specific execution plan for each statement. For example:

```
EXPLAIN PLAN
    SET STATEMENT_ID = <identifier> FOR
    <SQL Statement>
```

The following example illustrates Oracle's text-based Explain, and shows how Oracle formats the output.

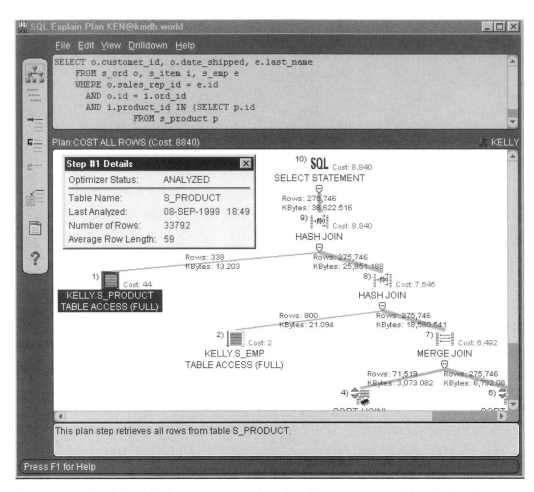

Figure 11.2   Oracle Explain for a query execution plan. (Image courtesy of Oracle Corp.)

```
EXPLAIN PLAN SET statement_id = 'Oracle-example1' FOR
SELECT arrival_date, name, description, inventory_id
  FROM product_stock
 WHERE arrival_date = :b1
   AND name LIKE '%-COM'
AND NVL(end_date_active,sysdate+1) > SYSDATE ;

Plan
------------------------------------------------------
SELECT STATEMENT
 TABLE ACCESS BY INDEX ROWID PRODUCT_STOCK
  INDEX RANGE SCAN STOCK_ITEMS
```

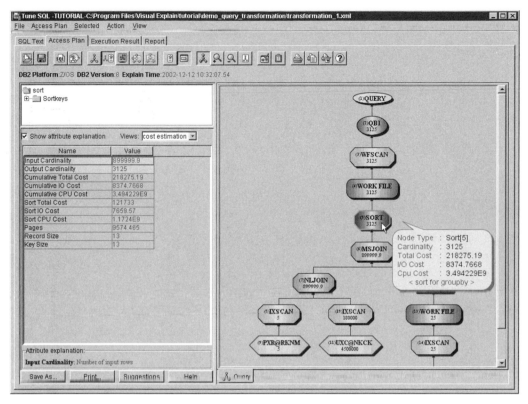

Figure 11.3   DB2 Visual Explain, zOS version. (Image courtesy of IBM Corp.)

```
    EXPLAIN PLAN SELECTION SET QUERYTAG = 'DB2-example1'
FOR
SELECT arrival_date, name, description, inventory_id
  FROM product_stock
 WHERE arrival_date = :b1
    AND name LIKE '%-COM'
AND NVL(end_date_active,sysdate+1) > SYSDATE ;
```

The syntax is very similar; where Oracle uses statement_id DB2 uses QUERYTAG, and DB2 includes the keyword SELECTION following EXPLAIN PLAN.

Alternatively, both Oracle and DB2 can be configured to explain every new query incoming for the current session. For DB2 this is done by placing the session into EXPLAIN MODE ON, as follows:

```
SET CURRENT EXPLAIN MODE YES
```

or

```
SET CURRENT EXPLAIN MODE EXPLAIN
```

The former generates Explain data while statements are executing, while the latter generates Explain data for incoming statements, but otherwise instructs the database not to execute the statements. As a result, after plan selection the query execution plan information is written to the Explain database control tables and processing for the statement stops (without executable code generation or execution).

For Oracle a similar process is enabled using the AUTOTRACE feature:

```
SET AUTOTRACE ON
```

Oracle SET AUTOTRACE ON is similar to DB2's SET CURRENT EXPLAIN MODE YES.

Following plan capture in DB2 the db2exfmt command can be used to format the Explain data to text, generating text output with a tree structure similar to the structure shown through the graphical interfaces of most products. Here's an example for the following query:

```
SELECT year(dateofsale), avg(sales), color
FROM LIGHT.MyTable
WHERE REGION = 'NY'
GROUP BY (COLOR, YEAR(DATEOFSALE))
```

The Explain output for this query is shown in Figure 11.4. You'll notice the use of keywords to describe the operators in the plan. They are, for the most part, fairly intuitive. For example, GRPBY is used to indicate a group-by, TBSCAN is used for table scan, etc. The number appearing in brackets is an identifier for each operator, and the detailed report produced by Explain provides more information for each operator, which is numbered accordingly. The two numbers appearing below each operator are the total cost and the input/output (I/O) cost, respectively.

There are some obvious differences between the text-based output of the two products. The DB2 scheme yields a tree structure very similar to the tree structure used in the graphical interfaces of most products. Oracle's output is more tabular, using a nest next structure to show the hierarchical relationships. The DB2 presentation is easier to follow, provided the access path is narrow enough to fit within a text-based editor (usually 80–120 characters wide). However, for very wide plans the Oracle format stays compact while the DB2 format wraps and can be more difficult to view in text. Clearly, each format has its benefits.

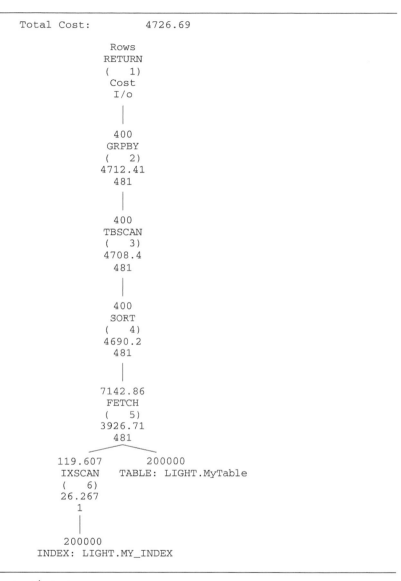

```
              Total Cost:        4726.69

                         Rows
                        RETURN
                        (    1)
                         Cost
                         I/o
                           |

                         400
                        GRPBY
                        (    2)
                       4712.41
                         481
                           |

                         400
                        TBSCAN
                        (    3)
                       4708.4
                         481
                           |

                         400
                        3ORT
                        (    4)
                       4690.2
                         481
                           |

                       7142.86
                        FETCH
                        (    5)
                       3926.71
                         481
                    _____
                   /           \
          119.607              200000
          IXSCAN      TABLE: LIGHT.MyTable
          (    6)
          26.267
             1
             |
          200000
      INDEX: LIGHT.MY_INDEX
```

Figure 11.4   Explain output in text.

11.4 Exploring Query Execution Plans to Improve Database Design

The following example highlights some of the typical attributes of a query execution plan, and although this example uses DB2 similar to a query execution plan, insights are typical of the major vendors with their respective tooling. In this example we will look at a fragment of a query execution plan for a complex query. The full query is query #20 from the TPC-H industry-standard benchmark (see www.tpc.org). The full query is as follows:

```
select
    s_name,
    s_address
from
    tpcd.supplier,
    tpcd.nation
where
    s_suppkey in (
        select
            ps_suppkey
        from
            tpcd.partsupp
        where
            ps_partkey in (
                select
                    p_partkey
                from
                    tpcd.part
                where
                    p_name like ':1%'
            )
            and ps_availqty > (
                select
                    0.5 * sum(l_quantity)
                from
                    tpcd.lineitem
                where
                    l_partkey = ps_partkey
                    and l_suppkey = ps_suppkey
                    and l_shipdate >= date (':2')
                    and l_shipdate < date (':2') + 1 year
            )
    )
    and s_nationkey = n_nationkey
    and n_name = ':3'
order by
    s_name;
```

The full query execution plan for this statement will be very involved, but we can use a fragment of the query execution plan to highlight the main ideas. Figure 11.5 shows a fragment of the query execution plan that performs a nested-loop join between the PARTS table and the PARTSUPP (part supplier) table. The query execution plan

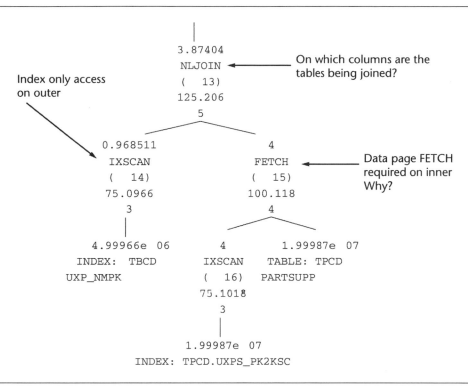

Figure 11.5   Query execution plan in text format for join of parts table with a supplier table. (Image courtesy of IBM.)

graph should be read from the bottom up and from left to right. The leafs of the graph show the objects that are being accessed. The first unusual thing you'll notice is that the PARTS table does not appear anywhere in this plan. Instead, an index on the PARTS table called TPCD.UXP_NMPK is used! Brilliant—this is a great indicator that this index not only works, but saves the database the need to access the PARTS table! Next, you'll see the keyword IXSCAN, which is the DB2 symbol for an index scan. This tells us that the index TPCD.UXP_NMPK is being scanned for qualifying keys, which are passed to NLJN(13). You may have guessed that NLJN stands for nested-loop join. The number (13) in parentheses is an identifier. As we'll show, elsewhere in the Explain output there is more information about each numbered node in the graph.

The query execution plan clearly shows that the information for PARTSUPP requires access to both the index TPCD.UXPS_PK2KSC and the PARTSUPP table itself. Can we determine why? Looking at the additional information for operator (15) that appears in the Explain output, and is reproduced here in Figure 11.6, we can see that the FETCH requires access to the PARTSUPP table because the index includes PS_PARTKEY and PS_SUPPKEY columns, but does not include the

```
15) FETCH : (Fetch)
        Arguments:
        ---------
  ...
        Input Streams:
        -------------
            7) From Operator #16
                Column Names:
                ------------
                +PS_PARTKEY(A)+PS_SUPPKEY(A)+$RID$
            8) From Object TPCD.PARTSUPP
                Column Names:
                ------------
                +PS_AVAILQTY
```

Figure 11.6   Details for Explain on operator #15. (Image courtesy of IBM.)

PS_AVAILQTY column. This suggests strongly that by adding the PS_AVAILQTY column to this index we can avoid access to the PARTSUPP table in this subplan, thereby improving performance.

Next, we'll examine the use of a materialized view (see Chapter 5) to demonstrate how that changes the access path and how we can use the access path to confirm that the new materialized view is both used by the database at runtime and provides value.

```
select * from department where 10 in (select count(*)
from employee where admrdept = workdept and salary >
1000 group by job);
```

A materialized view is designed for this query as follows (using DB2 syntax):

- Create a materialized view named MQT3; create table MQT3 as (select workdept, job, count(*) as ct from employee where salary > 1000 group by job, workdept) data refresh immediate in userspace1.

- Create an index on this materialized view, on the workdept column; create index IDX3 on MQT3(workdept).

- Update the statistics for this materialized view in the system catalogs; runstats on table MYSCHEMA.MQT3 and indexes all; commit.

Figure 11.7 shows the access paths before and after creating the materialized view. In this example we are using the DB2 Visual Explain tooling. In this format each node in the access path is assigned a number in brackets that identified the operator for further detail. The second number beside each operator is an approximate cost for the operator and all its suboperators within its branch of the access path. The figure on the left shows the access path before the materialized view was created, showing table scans on both the department table and employee table. Following the creation of the materialized view, the database selects the access path shown on the right, which accesses both the materialized view and its index, avoiding the costly table scan on the employee table. The approximated cost for each plan is 24,305,758 versus 2,866.53 units, suggesting the benefit from creating the materialized view and its index reduced the resource consumption of this query by 99.99%.

If that resource consumption translates to execution time savings (a rough approximation, not always true) the query could now run 8.5 thousand times faster! However, we aren't done with the design refinement. Even this new and dramatically improved

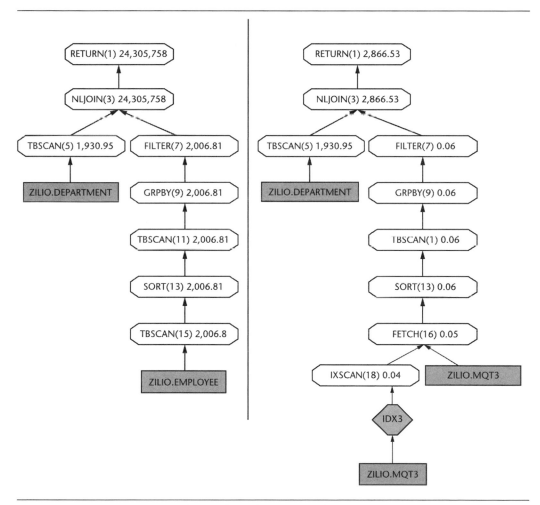

Figure 11.7   Query execution plan (*right*) and without (*left*) the materialized view.

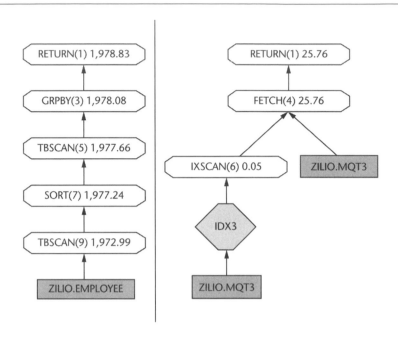

Figure 11.8   Query execution plans before (*left*) and after (*right*) MQT3 for the second query.

plan shows a table scan on the DEPARTMENT table that appears to consume a significant percentage of the total resource consumption for the query. If the qualifying rows from DEPARTMENT are a small percentage of the total table size (much less than 50%), an index on DEPARTMENT can further reduce the cost of access.

The great value of materialized views is that a single view can provide benefits to multiple query statements. Consider the same materialized view MQT3 above with a new query:

```
select workdept, job, count(*) as ct from employee where
salary > 1000 group by job, workdept;
```

The before and after query execution plans are shown in Figure 11.8. Again, we see a huge performance difference between the before and after resource consumption: 1,979 versus 26 units, suggesting a 76 times resource consumption reduction and a potential corresponding speedup of query execution. Two very important points are worth noting: first, that the same materialized view was useful to two rather different queries, and second, that in both cases the text of the queries made no reference to the materialized view MQT3. In both cases the detection that MQT3 was useful and the decision to exploit the materialized view in the access path were made entirely by the database query compiler without the involvement of the application designer who authored the query text.

In this final example let's look at a full query execution plan for a single query with and without multidimensional clustering (MDC). This example looks at a very simple range query over the salary column within an EMPLOYEE table. The caller may be looking for the highest or the lowest paid employees, for example, or perhaps looking for employees paid within a certain range, such as $50,000–$60,000 per year. Two query execution plans are shown in Figure 11.9.

The first query execution plan is selected when the database is not using MDC, but does have an index on the SALARY column of the EMPLOYEE table. The query execution plan is fairly straightforward. This is a list prefetch plan, first obtaining the record identifiers (RIDs) of the qualifying rows from the index. The RIDs are then sorted (in data page order) and the sorted list of RIDs is sent to prefetchers, who should get all those pages into the buffer pool (hopefully) by the time we start processing the FETCH operations. The total resource consumption is estimated by the query optimizer as 387.527 units, which is a blend of the I/O, CPU, and network consumption the query execution plan will require. In the second example the database has been modified with the multidimensional clustering on the SALARY dimension of the EMPLOYEE table. A generated column was added defined as INT(SALARY/1000) so that salary ranges would be grouped together in MDC blocks (see Chapter 8, where these terms are explained).

The most obvious difference in the resulting query execution plan for the same range query on the database with MDC is that the resulting plan is clearly simpler, with fewer steps and operators. The query execution plan selects blocks from an internally generated block index called SQL0110171419248, and the qualifying rows are fetched and returned, already having been sorted by cells. The optimizer estimates the resource consumption for the new plan to be 325.172 units, roughly 15% less resource consumption than the first plan. This shows us that the design choice for MDC appears to be beneficial to this query, quantifiably how much, and also gives us assurance that the design attribute will be used by the query at runtime.

11.5 Query Execution Plan Indicators for Improved Physical Database Designs

There are definite indicators within a query execution plan that can signal a problem with (or perhaps an opportunity for improvement of) the physical database design. Here are some examples of situations to watch out for the following:

1. *Table scans.* It is almost never ideal for a database to perform a scan of an entire table. There are two major exceptions to this rule: brute-force queries that explic-

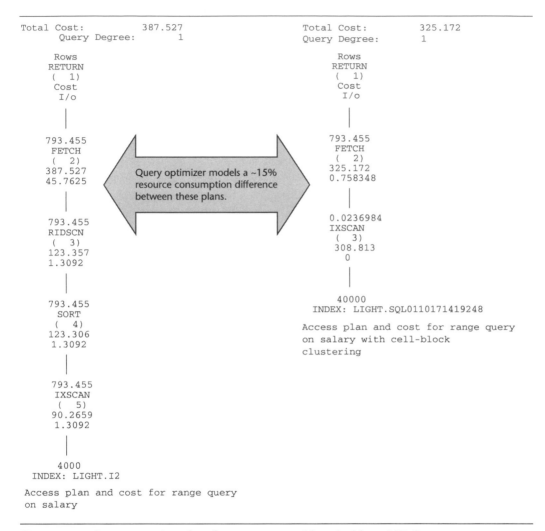

```
Total Cost:         387.527          Total Cost:         325.172
    Query Degree:       1                Query Degree:       1

      Rows                                Rows
     RETURN                              RETURN
     (   1)                              (   1)
      Cost                                Cost
      I/o                                 I/o
        |                                   |
        |                                   |
    793.455                             793.455
     FETCH                               FETCH
     (   2)                              (   2)
    387.527                             325.172
    45.7625                             0.758348
        |                                   |
        |                                   |
    793.455                           0.0236984
     RIDSCN                             IXSCAN
     (   3)                              (   3)
    123.357                             308.813
    1.3092                                 0
        |                                   |
        |                                   |
    793.455                              40000
      SORT                     INDEX: LIGHT.SQL0110171419248
     (   4)
    123.306              Access plan and cost for range query
    1.3092               on salary with cell-block
        |                clustering
        |
    793.455
     IXSCAN
     (   5)
    90.2659
    1.3092
        |
        |
     4000
 INDEX: LIGHT.I2
Access plan and cost for range query
on salary
```

Query optimizer models a ~15% resource consumption difference between these plans.

Figure 11.9   Query execution plans for range query with and without MDC.

itly request it, such as SELECT * FROM MYTABLE, and tiny tables that are stored in their entirety within a single storage block on disk (i.e., typically less than a few pages of data). Save for these two exceptions, a table scan is often an indicator that the physical database design can be improved dramatically by adding an index or some other physical design attribute.

2. *Large sorts.* Sorts can be expensive when they are large. Sorts that cannot fit entirely in memory spill to disk (temporarily), incurring not only significant CPU resources to perform the sorting but also extensive I/O to manage the temporarily spilled portions of the data. Large sort can be an indicator that an

index is missing or that a materialized view or MDC design can be used to remove the need for the sort. If the sort is used for a group-by operation, it may form an excellent portion of a materialized view.

3. *Small sorts.* Small sorts are not usually a problem if they occur rarely. But a small sort on thousands of short-running concurrent queries can be a disaster. Again, an index, MDC, or materialized view will usually correct the problem.

4. *High interpartition communication on shared-nothing systems.* If the query execution plan suggests very high interpartition communication, it may be an indicator that the tables involved in many joins are poorly collocated. A new partitioning design for the tables (or use of replicated materialized views) can help resolve this issue.

5. *Very high execution cost (resource consumption).* If the execution cost of a query is very high, it's probably going to be one of the slowest queries and will consume a lot of system resources (possibly CPU, I/O, network; the query execution plan should tell you which). This may not be a problem—the query may indeed be an expensive one to execute because of its complexity. But the high cost can help lead you to the queries that need your attention.

6. *Frequently occurring predicates.* Commonly recurring predicates can form potential start/stop keys for an index. Consider the columns used in frequently occurring predicates as candidates for leading columns of a new index.

7. *Design attributes not used.* If attributes you have added to your database design (indexes, materialized views, MDC, etc.) are not being used, you may have incorrect assumptions about the database and the workload, or perhaps the query optimizer has erred and selected a suboptimal query execution plan that fails to use the design attributes you have built into the system. Either way, it's a problem that needs attention. If some design attributes turn out not to be useful, you should examine the maintenance cost of keeping them around and consider removing them.

There are some broader reasons why being able to see the query execution plans selected by the query optimization process can be very beneficial for database design:

1. Capturing the query execution plans allows the user to maintain a history of the most expensive, and therefore usually the most problematic, query execution plans across transition periods.

2. New index additions and other design attributes, such as range and list partitioning, MDC, materialized views, and partitioning choices can be examined for their impact on the query execution plans of the queries typically issued against the database.

3. Large data updates and/or additions will significantly change the statistics of the database objects. These statistics are used by the query compiler during optimization and changes to them often result in new query execution plans. It is common that performance problems can occur in a database system following such large data changes for two reasons:

   • The data has changed and the old query execution plan is suboptimal for the new data within the system.

   • The data has changed and the object statistics for one or more objects referenced in the query were updated, resulting in the selection of a new query execution plan that happens to be suboptimal due to poor choices by the query compiler (i.e., during optimization).

4. During product upgrade, the latest version of any relational database product may include updates to the mathematical models used for query optimization. Changes in modeling can result in changes in the selected query execution plans. If the new plans perform worse than the old ones, it can be very beneficial to debug the root cause of the problem if the before and after upgrade query execution plans are available to compare and contrast. This is true for both the database designer and the vendor customer service group should they need to be called upon for assistance.

5. Finally, there are database configuration settings that are used as part of query execution plan selection. For example, the amount of memory available for data caching is often used in a stochastic model to determine the likelihood of a data page being cached at the time of the query execution (as opposed to requiring I/O from disk). If the configuration changes result in performance reduction, contrasting the query execution plans before and after the configuration change can determine if a query execution plan change occurred that may be the root cause of the performance change, and, if so, what specific changes have led to the choice of a new query execution plan.

11.6   Exploring without Changing the Database

Many vendors allow users to perform what-if physical database design analysis without actually making full-scale changes to their database. There are multiple ways this is done.

First, users are able to extract a replica of the database design for creation in a new, but data-free, database. The lack of data makes design exploration easy, since design changes can be made without the actual expensive and time-consuming process of creating indexes or materialized views, converting tables to MDC, range or list partitioning, or changing shared-nothing partitioning choices. All of these design changes are very time consuming when large amounts of data are involved, but are relatively quick within a data-free environment.

We mentioned earlier that query execution plans depend on the size and distribution of data in the database. Thus, one might wonder how a valid simulation of the database can be set up that is data free, but still provides a fair simulation of the query execution plans. The answer lies in the fact that the query optimizer uses statistics that are stored in the system catalogs and these cataloged statistics can be copied over to the data-free database. As a result, even though the database has no data in it, the query compiler (and optimizer) sees a database full of data with associated statistics. The query compiler's optimizing component is, in essence, a mathematical model and as such it is completely unaware whether data exists within the objects referenced by an incoming query. The model consumes statistics found within the system catalogs and assumes they are representative.

The second strategy is to carry out the what-if analysis within the database that holds the data. This can be done by several vendors through the support of "virtual" objects. Virtual objects are objects that the user defines as though they were real, but instructs the database to create them purely as definitions for the purpose of what-if analysis. Several databases support the creation of user-defined virtual objects for indexes and materialized views. As we'll see in Chapter 12, most vendors use virtual objects to perform automated design assistance for databases, covering a broader range than just indexes and materialized views. As a result, it is likely that in the coming years the support for user-defined virtual objects will expand, giving database designers more range to explore design choices within the primary database they use to store data.

11.7 Forcing the Issue When the Query Optimizer Chooses Wrong

11.7.1 Three Essential Strategies

Despite 30 years of advanced research into system modeling and query optimization, at the end of the day the query optimizer uses mathematical models, and these models are not perfect. Without going into a detailed laundry list of why it is so difficult to create a flawless query optimizer, we ask our readers to accept this as reality and focus on the more important question—what to do about it. There are essentially three major techniques for working around the problem of the query optimizer selecting a poor query execution plan, perhaps one that does not exploit the physical design attributes you have designed into the database. These are the following:

1. Change the query optimization search depth.
2. Modify some of the statistics for objects accessed.

3. Force certain plan choices using "query hints."

As we have seen, the process of query optimization is very complex and can involve very deep and exhaustive searching to find an ideal plan. The more complex the query and the more design attributes to choose from, the more choices and complexity the query optimizer faces. In fact, the time required for the query optimization process can be significant. Most database engines try to automatically determine the depth of the optimization search (or use a default search depth that is reasonable for most queries, most of the time). However, there are often overrides. When the query optimizer appears to be making wrong choices and selecting a suboptimal query execution plan, one strategy is to modify the search depth by either increasing or decreasing it, hoping a different and superior plan will be selected.

Another strategy to bias plan selection is to modify the statistics that the optimizer relies upon when selecting the query execution plans. Many database vendors provide user-updatable views for these statistics. By default, these user-modifiable views show the same values for the object statistics as the primary catalogs storing the actual statistics. When these views are updated, the new values supercede the actual statistics. In this way the database designer can bias the access of an object. For example, you can make an index appear more desirable by increasing its clustering statistics or by decreasing its size (number of tree levels or number of pages).

Finally, the most explicit way of biasing query execution plans is through query hints. SQL Server, Oracle, and DB2 all provide a facility for query hints, though the interfaces vary significantly. Hints should be used with caution and only if the query optimizer appears to have serious trouble finding a reasonable query execution plan for a query. Hints are most commonly used to force index access or a specific join method, or to essentially freeze a volatile query execution plan for a complex query, in order to reduce runtime risk of a sudden poor plan choice on a production system.

11.7.2 Introduction to Query Hints

What follows are some quick syntax insights on using query hints for the major vendors, without any attempt at being comprehensive.

SQL Server query hints can be added directly to the SQL text by adding the OPTION clause. This has the following format:

```
OPTION (hint1 [, ...hintn])
```

The following example uses the OPTION clause to force the query optimizer to use a hash join method when joining two tables.

```
SELECT *
FROM receipts.supplier AS t1
INNER JOIN receipts.address AS t2
ON t1.supplier_id = t2.supplier_id
WHERE Territory_id = 12 OPTION (HASH JOIN);
```

The following example uses the OPTION (OPTIMIZE FOR...) clause to select the query execution plan that would be best for the city_name 'New York' even though the actual city_name predicate is 'Toronto'.

```
DECLARE city_name nvarchar(50)
SET city_name = 'Toronto'
SELECT * FROM employee.Address
WHERE City = city_name
OPTION (OPTIMIZE FOR (city_name = 'New York'))
```

Other SQL Server hint options include the following, and a description of these can be found online at the Microsoft SQL Server web pages:

```
EXPAND VIEWS, FAST n, FORCE ORDER, { HASH | ORDER }
GROUP, KEEPFIXED PLAN, KEEP PLAN, { LOOP | MERGE | HASH }
JOIN, MAXDOP number, { MERGE | HASH | CONCAT } UNION,
OPTIMIZE FOR, ROBUST PLAN
```

Oracle supports a wide array of hints. Advocates suggest this attests to the richness of Oracle optimizer features, while opponents have been vocal that it may suggest a weakness in Oracle optimization modeling, requiring the heavy use of hint technology to avoid bad query execution plans. Regardless of where you stand in this debate, there is little doubt the list of hints supported by Oracle is very comprehensive. Unlike SQL Server, which includes hints using a keyword, Oracle hints are added as a comment on the SQL text. Here are a few examples. The first example shows how Oracle hints can be used to accomplish exactly the same, as in the SQL Server example above: force a hash join using the USE_HASH hint.

```
SELECT *
/*+ USE_HASH (supplier, address) */
FROM receipts.supplier AS t1
INNER JOIN receipts.address AS t2
ON t1.supplier_id = t2.supplier_id
WHERE Territory_id = 12;
```

The following example shows how an Oracle hint is used to force the use of an index using the INDEX hint:

```
SELECT
/*+ INDEX (employees employee_dept_inx)*/
employee_id, department_id
FROM employees
WHERE department_id < 35;
```

The following list shows the range of supported Oracle hints and the undocumented hints as well.

```
ALL_ROWS, AND_EQUAL, ANTIJOIN, APPEND, BITMAP, BUFFER,
CACHE, CARDINALITY, CHOOSE, CLUSTER FULL, CPU_COSTING,
DRIVING_SITE, FACT, FIRST_ROWS, HASH, ROWID, HASH_AJ,
HASH_SJ, INDEX, INDEX_ASC, INDEX_COMBINE, INDEX_DESC,
INDEX_FFS, INDEX_JOIN, INLINE, LEADING,
MATERIALIZE, MERGE, MERGE_AJ, MERGE_SJ, NL_AJ, NL_SJ,
NO_ACCESS, NO_BUFFER, NO_EXPAND,
NO_EXPAND_GSET_TO_UNION, NO_FACT, NO_INDEX, NO_MERGE,
NO_MONITORING, NO_PUSH_PRED, NO_PUSH_SUBQ, NO_QKN_BUFF,
NO_SEMIJOIN, NOAPPEND, NOCACHE, NOPARALLEL,
NOPARALLEL_INDEX, NOREWRITE, OR_EXPAND, ORDERED,
ORDERED_PREDICATES, PARALLEL, PARALLEL_INDEX,
PQ_DISTRIBUTE, PUSH_PRED, PUSH_SUBQ, REWRITE ,RULE,
SELECTIVITY, SEMIJOIN, SEMIJOIN_DRIVER, STAR,
STAR_TRANSFORMATION, SWAP_JOIN_INPUTS, USE_ANTI,
USE_CONCAT, USE_HASH, USE_MERGE, USE_NL, USE_SEMI.
```

Undocumented hints:

```
BYPASS_RECURSIVE_CHECK, BYPASS_UJVC, CACHE_CB,
CACHE_TEMP_TABLE, CIV_GB, COLLECTIONS_GET_REFS, CUBE_GB,
CURSOR_SHARING_EXACT, DEREF_NO_REWRITE, DML_UPDATE,
DOMAIN_INDEX_NO_SORT, DOMAIN_INDEX_SORT,
DYNAMIC_SAMPLING, DYNAMIC_SAMPLING_EST_CDN,
EXPAND_GSET_TO_UNION, FORCE_SAMPLE_BLOCK,
GBY_CONC_ROLLUP, GLOBAL_TABLE_HINTS,
HWM_BROKERED, IGNORE_ON_CLAUSE, IGNORE_WHERE_CLAUSE,
INDEX_RRS, INDEX_SS, INDEX_SS_ASC, INDEX_SS_DESC,
LIKE EXPAND, LOCAL_INDEXES, MV_MERGE,
NESTED_TABLE_GET_REFS, NESTED_TABLE_SET_REFS,
NESTED_TABLE_SET_SETID, NO_FILTERING, NO_ORDER_ROLLUPS,
NO_PRUNE_GSETS, NO_STATS_GSETS, NO_UNNEST,
NOCPU_COSTING, OVERFLOW_NOMOVE, PIV_GB, PIV_SSF, PQ_MAP,
PQ_NOMAP, REMOTE_MAPPED, RESTORE_AS_INTERVALS,
SAVE_AS_INTERVALS, SCN_ASCENDING, SKIP_EXT_OPTIMIZER,
```

SQLLDR, SYS_DL_CURSOR, SYS_PARALLEL_TXN, SYS_RID_ORDER, TIV_GB, TIV_SSF, UNNEST, USE_TTT_FOR_GSETS.

11.7.3 Query Hints When the SQL Is Not Available to Modify

In the majority of cases the database designer is not the same person as the application designer and he or she does not usually have access to the application code in order to add the hints. Because of this, a more powerful strategy for hints is one that allows database administrators to add the hints without modifying the SQL text of the incoming queries. The basic strategy that database vendors use to accomplish this is to allow an administrator to define a template for queries with an associated hint. When a query enters the system, it is briefly examined to see if it matches one of these templates and, if there is a match, the rules for that template are applied to the incoming query. Oracle calls this Stored Outlines and DB2 calls this Optimization Profiles. Stored Outlines and Optimization Profiles provided via a table allow prepackaged applications to be "hinted" without opening them up to modify the SQL. A disadvantage is that the external guideline must be matched to the SQL statement fairly closely. Products like DB2 and Oracle try to normalize the statement as much as possible by squeezing white space and uppercasing, but if the statement text gets rearranged at all, it will often no longer match.

TIPS AND INSIGHTS FOR DATABASE PROFESSIONALS

- **Tip 1. Alarm bells.** Table scans and large sorts that appear in the query execution plans are alarm bells. These should immediately grab your attention and prompt exploration for design features to add or remove.

- **Tip 2. Determine where the bulk of the query execution time is spent.** Use query execution plans heavily during database design to detect major resource consumption points. These points in the query execution plan are the areas where you should focus your design efforts to improve query performance and therefore system efficiency.

- **Tip 3. Ensure your design features are being used.** Use query execution plan analysis to see if indexes, MDC, materialized views, and range partitioning are actually being appropriately used by the query compiler the way you expect.

- **Tip 4. Index cardinality.** Use query execution plan analysis to determine the selectivity of predicates applied on base table accesses; this can be a good indicator for whether an index can help reduce table access time. If the selectivity is very high (i.e., not many rows get filtered out), more than 40% or so, it is unlikely an index will help reduce I/O, unless the index is designed to include all the columns required by the operator on the table.

- **Tip 5. Cheat if needed.** You can force the issue by changing the optimizer's search depth, modifying statistics, or by adding hints. You should consider these last-ditch efforts in precisely that order. Before resorting to hints, you may be able to get a better query execution plan without forcing the compiler down a specific access path simply by changing its aggressiveness or its view of the data by adjusting the statistics on the database objects. Why not just jump straight to hints? The optimizer may still be able to find a much better plan than the one you would force with the query hint.

- **Tip 6. Remember the cost of write operations.** Adding design features like materialized views and indexes can dramatically improve performance of queries, but they can have a detrimental impact on insert, update, and delete (IUD) operations. Every write operation will require work to be performed to keep these objects up to date. In the case of materialized views, most vendors support the ability to update materialized views only periodically (e.g., weekly, monthly, etc.), which can reduce the overhead that materialized views cause for IUDs, but as a result query execution plans that access these materialized views will return old data!

- **Tip 7. Shared-nothing specifics.** If your database server uses a shared-nothing architecture (see Chapter 6), a common concern to watch out for is the communication resource projected in the query execution plans. High communication costs can be an indicator of poorly collocated data causing inefficient joins and a high volume of data shipping. If you have a running system, there is usually monitor data available that can show you the actual (not just optimizer projected) rates, which you can contrast with the optimizer's estimates to check if there might be a problem with the plan.

11.8 Summary

The ability to view query execution plans and some of the associated resource and selectivity for operators within the plan is a major tool in the process of physical database design. So much so that no modern database is effectively designed today without exploring access paths. The access path analysis can help the database designer see where the resource hot spots are, and whether the designs attributed that they have created in the database are being exploited. When the database design seems good, but the query optimizer is not selecting the available design feature, some adjustments may be needed by the administrator to set things right. The possibilities include: adjusting the optimization search depth, modifying the statistics for objects used in the offending query, or adding query hints (or profiles) to force the query execution plan choices for specific queries.

11.9 Literature Summary

DB2 database, at http://www-306.ibm.com/software/data/db2/udb/.

Deigin, Y. DB2 UDB Query Execution Plans: Up Close and Personal. DB2 Information Management Technical Conference Agenda, Orlando, FL, September 12–16, 2005.

Microsoft SQL Server Home, at http://www.microsoft.com/sql/default.mspx.

Oracle Database, at http://www.oracle.com/database/index.html.

Ramakrishnan, R., and Gehrke, J. *Database Management Systems*, 3rd ed. New York: McGraw-Hill, 2004.

Selinger, P. G., Astrahan, M. M., Chamberlin, D. D. Lorie, R. A., and Price, T. G. Access Path Selection in a Relational Database Management System. ACM SIGMOD Conference, 1979, pp. 23–34.

Automated Physical Database Design

Any intelligent fool can make things bigger and more complex . . .
It takes a touch of genius—and a lot of courage to move
in the opposite direction.
—Albert Einstein

Civilization advances by extending the number of important operations
which we can perform without thinking about them.
—Alfred North Whitehead

The year 1997 was a turning point in the popular understanding of the capability of modern computers to solve complex problems that we normally associated with human intellect and wisdom. The turning point had little to do with the design of database systems. In 1997 a supercomputer produced by IBM, named "Deep Blue II," became the first ever computer to beat a reigning world chess champion: grandmaster Gary Kasparov. What changed on that day in 1997 was the realization that computers could actual compete successfully against the best human experts in an important domain that we normally associate with creative problem solving. Similarly, leading corporations have begun to produce advanced technology for the automated physical design of database systems.

The contest was the second between the two, Kasparov having beaten Deep Blue's earlier version in 1996. However, the 1997 confrontation was significantly more challenging. Deep Blue was significantly upgraded for the second confrontation. It boasted a 30-node massively parallel computer with 480 special-purpose (CPUs). Deep Blue was able to search to a depth of 12 moves (ply) ahead,[1] evaluating 200,000,000 positions per second, twice as fast as the system Kasparov had beaten in 1996. It contained an extensive database of opening moves and endgames, including every possible endgame with five pieces or less. Furthermore, Deep Blue's chess database was refined by grandmasters Joel Benjamin, Miguel Illescas, John Fedorovich, and Nick De Firmian. In retrospect it was amazing that Kasparov faired as well as he did. After the match, Kasparov made a public statement that he was unfairly disadvantaged by not being able to study a history of the machine's play the way he would normally have studied an opponent. He felt that despite its awesome computational power and extensive database of potential moves, Deep Blue was beatable by the very best human players.

In truth Deep Blue's accomplishments were achieved to a large extent by brute-force calculations and massive databases of alternatives. At the end of the day it doesn't matter that Deep Blue doesn't really understand what a king or a knight really is. It has no understanding of the game of chess; it feels no joy or tension or excitement. It's simply a computer executing a program that evaluates a dramatic number of alternatives. This process is not dramatically different from the database design process, which includes a massive scale of possibilities from which to select a near-optimal solution.

Computers like Deep Blue have proven successful at chess because chess has qualities that make it suitable for computer play: the game does not require a physical understanding; everything can be abstracted and encoded. Second, the game does not require a complex understanding of language—simply the ability to express where the current pieces are and where the next piece should be moved. Finally, as a game of strategy, even before the final checkmate, the strength of a position and the value of a move can be estimated. This ability to evaluate some positions as better than others lends itself to an "evaluation function" which forms the basis of most Artificial Intelligence systems. Compare the qualities of gaming programs to the problem of physical database design. Databases can be abstracted and modeled; in fact as described earlier during the discussion of query optimizers most query optimizers model physical resource consumption and have been doing so in the database industry for more than a decade. Secondly, physical database design does not require understanding of a complex language, but rather the ability to parse SQL statements and generate DDL. Database servers already include the former—a basic ability required to process SQL as part of day-to-day processing. Finally, there is the all-important notion of an "evaluation function," which we will see can be constructed by exploiting variations of existing database components. In short, just as Deep Blue conquered the domain of chess, high-quality technologies are emerging to perform automated physical database design. These technologies can be

---

[1] The best human players evaluate roughly 10 moves ahead.

successful at providing solutions in an otherwise extremely complex space largely because the domain they are exploring has many of the same attributes that lend themselves to automated computer design. As we will see below, products exist today that already provide automated design of indexes, clustering, multidimensional clustering, shared-nothing partitioning, and materialized views.

Database design does not have the benefit of hundreds of years of competition and documented wisdom that the game of chess benefits from. As a result, automated systems that perform physical database design are not as expert as programs that play chess. Even so, the quality of these features is improving at a rapid rate in richness of function, scalability, and quality of their recommendations. The increased need to simplify database systems has been a major focus of all database vendors in recent years, and the development of utilities that provide semi-automated physical database design recommendations has been a pillar of these research and development initiatives. Not-for-profit industrial initiatives have also emerged[2] under the auspices of the IEEE, ACM, and others, focused on the important goal of reducing the complexity of database administration. For database systems, whenever the topic of simplified management arises, automated physical database design always plays a prominent role due to the massive impact that it can play on system performance and ease of administration. This chapter will provide examples from the automated design utilities for DB2, SQL Server, and Oracle. This will include an overview of the features as well as a review of strategies and research they use.

12.1 What-if Analysis, Indexes, and Beyond

Chapter 3 discussed how many modern query compilers perform a process of resource modeling to perform the most optimal query execution plan for a query. The cost model will typically include estimates for resource consumption for the different plan possibilities such as CPU, memory, network bandwidth, and input/output (I/O). The cost model will also determine, based on the physical design of the database, whether an index should be exploited, such as which indexes to access or what join method to use (e.g., hash join versus nested-loop join). Much of the literature on automated physical design has focused on the possibility of "what-if analysis" using the database's existing query optimizer. "What-if analysis" is the art of carefully lying to the query optimizer and observing the impact. For example, what if a new index

---

[2] Examples include numerous workshops on self-managing and autonomic computing for database systems at conferences like VLDB, ICDE, and CASCON between 2000 and 2006, and the establishment by the IEEE of a workgroup under the Technical Committee on Data Engineering called the IEEE Workgroup on Self-Managing Database Systems. See http://db.uwaterloo.ca/tcde-smdb/.

were created for the table, would it be used and would it improve the performance of the workload? To discover where additional indexing will be beneficial the definition of a new index is added to the physical design of the table within the memory of the system strictly for exploration purposes.

The index is not actually created, but rather the definition of the index along with associated statistics is simulated within system memory, without any associated data. When a query is processed the query optimizer will treat the virtual index as though it were a real index, and include it as query execution plans are considered and evaluated. From the point of view of the query compiler's cost-based optimization it does not matter at all that the index does not really exist. The compiler requires information about the index (such as its key definitions and statistics) but does not require that the index actually exists on disk. If the resulting estimated cost (calculated by the query compiler) of the overall workload is lower than the estimated cost without the virtual index, then the assumption is that the index has been beneficial to the workload. Naturally this requires a special mode of execution for the query compiler where such virtual objects can be attached and evaluated without queries actually being executed (i.e., where query execution plans are evaluated, but data is not accessed and retrieved) similar to the Explain processing described in Chapter 11.

In 1997 Chaudhuri and Narasayya published a landmark paper where they suggested the use of the database's query optimizer to help automatically select indexes. They proposed that the value of candidate indexes to the system workload could be estimated by evaluating their impact on the access path cost, as simulated by the query optimizer. The candidate indexes need not be fully materialized, but simply created in a virtual sense with enough detail that the query optimizer would perceive as real within its modeling of the cost and access path selection. Although their paper does not use the terminology, in essence they suggested that the query optimizer be used as an "evaluation function" for an optimization search.

The notion of an evaluation function is standard terminology in the artificial intelligence (AI) community, and is used to evaluate the relative virtue of points considered during the search.[3] The idea of reusing the database optimizer's cost estimations for evaluating the cost benefit of physical design changes is based on the observation that the query optimizer's cost modeling is sensitive to both the logical and physical design of a database. Having a model for workload resource consumption allows us to exploit

---

[3] Very commonly used in AI search schemes such as genetic algorithms, simulated annealing, hill climbing, etc. In many optimization search algorithms the algorithm must have some way of evaluating the benefit to attribute to a current possible solution. This process is commonly referred to as an "evaluation function." In hill climbing this can be a measure of the slope between the current position in the search and each of the candidate next steps. In genetic algorithms the evaluation function measures relative "fitness" of member elements of the population, etc.

this model for "what-if" analysis. Chaudhuri's initial approach as described in the 1997 paper is summarized in the following list, paraphrased directly from the paper:

1. Run the query-specific-best-configuration algorithm for identifying candidate indexes. This requires splitting the given workload of n queries into n workloads of one query each, and finding the best configuration for each query. The union of these configurations is the candidate index set for step 2. This step is restricted to single-column indexes only.

2. Run the greedy (m, k) algorithm, where m is the initial seed set of virtual indexes, and k is a target recommendation size, to enumerate configurations subject to the single-join atomic configuration pruning technique and select a set of indexes until the required number of indexes has been picked or total cost can be reduced no further. We found that $m = 2$ produced very good solutions. The single-join atomic configuration considers at most two indexes per table and at most two tables per query.

3. Select a set of admissible multicolumn indexes using the assumption that leading columns of all multicolumn indexes must have appeared in the single-column solutions found in steps 1 and 2, based on single-column indexes picked in step 2.

4. Repeat steps 1 and 2 starting with the admissible index set consisting of single-column indexes that were chosen in step 2, and multicolumn indexes selected in step 3.

In 1999 and 2000 IBM published papers on the same topic [Schiefer 1999, Valentin 2000], suggesting a similar approach but with three very significant changes:s:

1. The selection and ordering of columns within an index can be biased not only by the columns used in predicates and joins within the statements of the workload, but also by considering the order in which the query optimizer evaluated these predicates, which can give rise to a preferred ordering scheme. In a sense, almost like running the optimizer rules in reverse, candidates columns can be recommended in a more useful sequence.

2. Instead of limiting the number of indexes to consider in a very highly constrained way, IBM proposed to add a much larger set of virtual indexes to be evaluated on the first pass through the optimizer. This enables a much broader search through the possible useful indexes. In general only a few of these indexes will be selected for any given SQL statement. When more than one index is selected the benefit of each index to the query improvement is hard to distinguish without recompiling the entire workload, however, this confusion is amortized over many statements and is not usually a major inhibitor. The bene-

fit of exploring a much larger set of indexes was found to outweigh the minor confusion on the relative contribution of benefit of the given indexes to queries where more than one virtual index was selected by the optimizer.

3. A time-constrained random variation algorithm was inserted as a postprocessing phase to allow the system to evaluate variations in the solution, if the user-specified longer evaluation time was acceptable.

Both the Microsoft and IBM papers suggested using cost estimates provided by the database optimizer as part of the evaluation engine of an index advisor that recommends table indexes. The database management system (DBMS) is taught to consider "virtual" indexes within its query compiler, resulting in an effective costing of query performance.

The empirical results for this technique were found to be quite good for index selection leading to production of the features and continued research in expanding the methods. Just as virtual indexes can be attached, similarly most other physical design attributes can be simulated and evaluated based on the query compiler's costing estimations. Materialized views, clustering, multidimensional clustering, and partitioning are all good examples.

The process is far from perfect. It suffers from a number of issues that researchers have been working to minimize or solve in recent years, including:

1. Like any model of a physical system, the model used by query compilers for cost-based query execution plan selection is necessarily incomplete and imperfect. Just these gaps can lead to suboptimal query execution plan selection during normal operational processing of queries, similarly they can lead to suboptimal designs when used for what-if analysis in physical database design.

2. Physical database design choices can impact the performance of write operation very significantly (e.g. secondary indexes have a negative impact on INSERT performance). The challenge here is trading off the benefit of physical design choices for SELECT queries in the workload against its negative impact for write operations. This trade-off can be difficult in particular because the relative priority of query performance versus INSERT, UPDATE, and DELETE performance is not easily known or discovered by the automated design utility.

3. Query compilers evaluate the cost for query execution plans for one query at a time. Physical design choices must be made on a global basis, discovering not what is good or bad for a single query, but rather what is best overall. Often the best design choice is suboptimal for any single SQL statement, making it extremely difficult for an optimization process focused on "best" to detect.

4. Query optimization is not generally a time-consuming process, but if the what-if analysis were performed for every query in a large workload for every possible

combination of potential design attributes, the execution time for the what-if analysis would be prohibitive. Reducing the analysis time requires the careful design of a search algorithm.

5. Most physical design attributes require additional storage. Indexes, materialized views, clustering, and multidimensional clustering are all examples. As a result, an infinite allowance for additional design attributes is unreasonable. Most automated physical database design utilities solve this by defining an arbitrary limit on the additional storage that can be used for new design attributes, and by allowing the user to specify a storage limit if they choose.

6. Query compilers are designed to model the processing time of queries for various query execution plans given an existing physical design. They are not well designed to model the increased storage requirements for specific physical design attributes being potentially added to a system. The problem is not overly hard, but requires logic outside of the query compiler. The compiler is a powerful tool for what-if analysis, but it is not sufficient.

12.2 Automated Design Features from Oracle, DB2, and SQL Server

What's most notable about the technology offered by all three vendors is what they have in common. All three vendors use the query optimizer to help select physical design choices. From a set of candidates chosen in part by the query optimizer the advisors then select the best candidates that provide the most benefit to the entire workload with the least creation, maintenance, and storage costs. The advantage of integrating directly with the optimizer compared to building a rule-based candidate generator is that the recommendations are always guaranteed to be in sync with the query optimizer and therefore have an extremely high probability of being used at runtime.

One of the most dangerous aspects of these features is the high dependency on a reliable and complete definition of a workload. These advisors do a superb job at making recommendations for a single query or a well-defined set of queries. However, from a software engineering perspective, the objective is really not just to improve the performance for the specified workload, but to also define a durable database design that gives reasonable performance for a changing workload. It is not always helpful to overoptimize a database. The advisors attempt to deal with this by generalizing statements and recommendations where possible, but much like a computer playing chess, they are currently limited in their thinking to what they see before them. Table 12.1 shows a high-level functional list of the capabilities in three of the major automated design utilities today for DB2, SQL Server, and Oracle.

Worth noting is that no single product has a superset of capabilities. This table is just a checklist and what the table does not illustrate is the quality of the recommendations that is naturally one of the most important factors. Since no formal benchmark exists for this, the only real way to assess the quality of these features is to run experiments using the freely available downloads all of the vendors offer (often a 60- or 90-day free trial, though many companies have started making free versions of their products available with reduced feature sets and no time limitation). Publishing a benchmark of the products would violate licensing agreements, which makes it impossible to comment within this text. All three products have had positive results with real production systems.

Notice that all three vendors offer a sophisticated utility that recommends indexes, materialized views, and modeling the impact (cost) on INSERT, UPDATE, and DELETE resulting from the new structures.

Table 12.1   Features for Popular Design Utilities

	DB2 Design Advisor	SQL Server Database Tuning Advisor	Oracle Access Advisor
Indexes	✓	✓	✓
Clustering indexes	✓[1]	✓	
Hash indexes	N/A*	N/A*	✓
Multi-dimensional clustering	✓	N/A*	N/A*
Shared-nothing part.	✓	N/A*	N/A*
Materialized views	✓	✓	✓
Combined attribute selection	✓	✓	✓
Range partitioning		✓	
Considers impact on insert update and delete	✓	✓	✓
Automated workload compression	✓	✓	
Automatic sampling (for MDC and/or materialized views)	✓		
What-if impact analysis for user suggested indexes and views	✓	✓	✓

*N/A: The design feature is not supported by the database server product, making "recommendation" impossible/meaningless.
1. Only in conjunction with MDC search.

Combined attribute selection is the ability of the advisor to make a combined decision about several design features that may be codependant—such as indexes and materialized views. One of the interesting problems in physical database design is the "interdependnace problem" discussed in Chapter 9. The choice of one design feature impact the choice of others. Superficially, it is easy to claim combined selection by staging the selection process, such as indexes followed by materialized views followed by range partitioning etc. But this is not truly what combined attribute selection is and simply stageding the slection is known to generate suboptimal database designs. In fact all three vendors claim to have developed sophisticated true combined attribute selection algorithms that allow indexes, materialized view and other features to be evaluated in combination.

The following examples were provided directly by Oracle, IBM, and Microsoft for inclusion in this book.[4] The examples show some of the interfaces to the design utilities, and illustrate the graphical interfaces of the different utilities from IBM, Microsoft, and Oracle, respectively.

What follows are some screenshots of the advisors from IBM (DB2 Design Advisor), Microsoft (SQL Server Database Tuning Advisor), and Oracle (Oracle SQL Access Advisor).

12.2.1 IBM DB2 Design Advisor

Figure 12.1 shows the selection screen for the DB2 Design Advisor where the user can select which performance attributes to search for. Notice that shared-nothing partitioning does not appear in the list. This is because the advisor was able to detect that the underlying hardware platform was not shared-nothing enabled, otherwise a selections choice for shared-nothing hash partitioning would appear as well.

The Design Advisor allows users to specify a set of statements for analysis that can come from several sources (Figure 12.2). These include a text file, a table, recently used statements from the query cache (package cache), or from DB2's workload management features, such as Query Patroller.

DB2 Design Advisor allows users to specify a time constraint for the search time, disk space constraint, how aggressive the workload compression should be, whether the advisor should sample the database data to obtain better data for analysis, and several other constraints. Figures 12.3 and 12.4 illustrate these capabilities.

The Design Advisor reports recommendations (Figure 12.5) for new design choices and also provides an estimate on the expected benefit of the changes and the expected disk consumption.

---

[4] Images of DB2 Design Advisor provided courtesy of IBM Corporation, images of SQL Server SQL DTA provided courtesy of Microsoft Corporation, and images of Oracle SQL Access Advisor provided courtesy of Oracle Corporation.

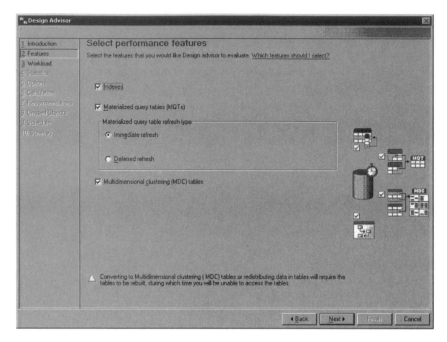

Figure 12.1   DB2 Design Advisor attribute choices.

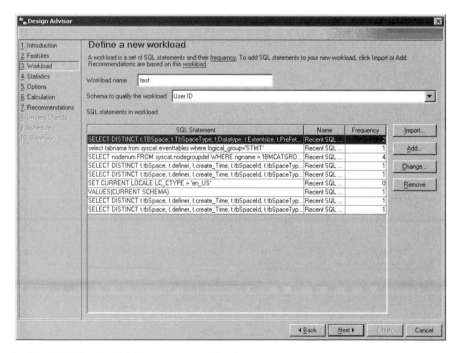

Figure 12.2   DB2 Design Advisor input workload.

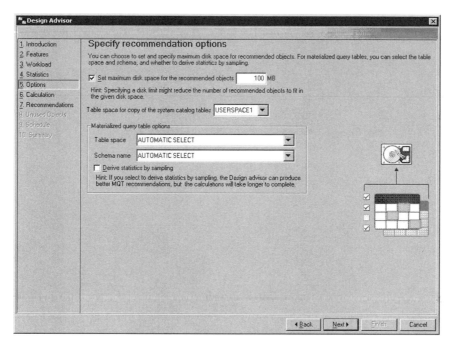

Figure 12.3   DB2 Design Advisor specifying storage constraints.

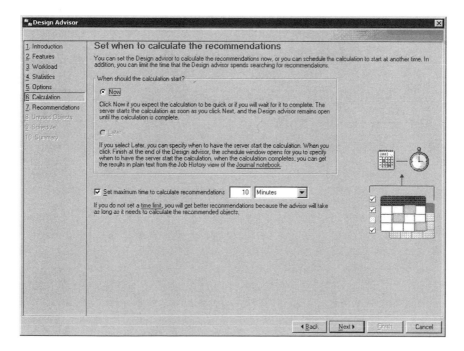

Figure 12.4   DB2 Design Advisor search time constraint.

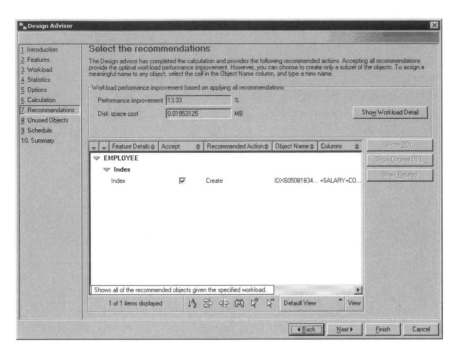

Figure 12.5   DB2 Design Advisor recommendations.

The Advisor also provides a list of unused objects to the user, which can then be reviewed and either left or dropped (Figure 12.6). Since the supplied workload for analysis may not have been comprehensive, it's possible that the unused objects are indeed used by other statements that were simply not explored in the more recent analysis of the Advisor. Because of this uncertainty a human decision maker is required to make a judgment call.

Finally, after optional review and modification by the user, the Advisor can apply the recommendations, modifying the database design and adding the new design attributes (Figure 12.7).

12.2.2 Microsoft SQL Server Database Tuning Advisor

The following examples showcase the Microsoft SQL Server utility called Database Tuning Advisor or DTA for short. Figure 12.8 highlights the following aspects of DTA:

- DTA enables *session-based tuning* where the input and output of each DTA invocation, including reports, tuning log, and recommendations, persist as named sessions. Figure 12.8 shows three different tuning sessions (shown as tabbed sessions), a currently initiated tuning session, and two tuning sessions that have been performed previously.

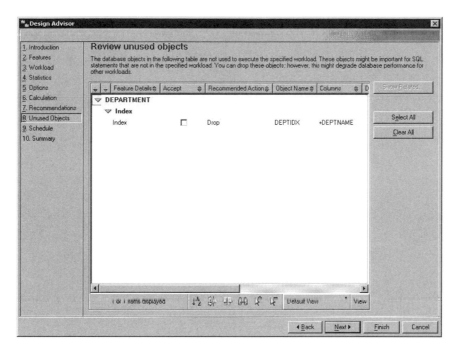

Figure 12.6   DB2 Design Advisor unused objects.

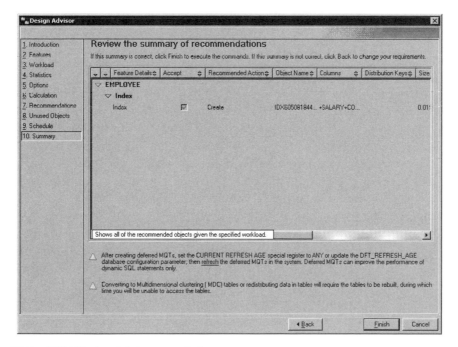

Figure 12.7   DB2 Design Advisor completion.

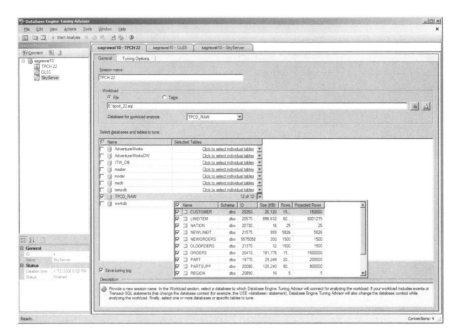

Figure 12.8   DTA session-based tuning.

- Users have the ability to select *multiple databases* as part of a single session. The users also have the ability to *restrict tuning to specific tables* or perform analysis for a *projected data size* (e.g., find a recommendation if the number of rows in a fact table in a data warehouse increases by a factor of 10) at the granularity of individual tables.

Figure 12.9 shows a session where the user has selected unlimited tuning time. The recommendation can have both indexes and indexed views (materialized views) and all existing structures can be dropped while optimizing for performance. DTA can (re)partition existing tables and indexes; the restriction is that the indexes and underlying tables be aligned (i.e., partitioned identically for manageability reasons).

DTA returns the expected improvement as a percentage of the current workload cost (as estimated by the query optimizer) as shown in Figure 12.10. The recommendation consists of indexes, indexed views, and statistics along with whether it was recommended to be created or dropped. The respective table and index partitions are also presented to the user. The tool allows a user to highlight a specific recommended structure and generate the script.

DTA generates a set of reports to supplement its recommendation. A tuning summary that includes total tuning time taken by DTA, expected percentage improvement, storage requirements of the recommendation, how many structures

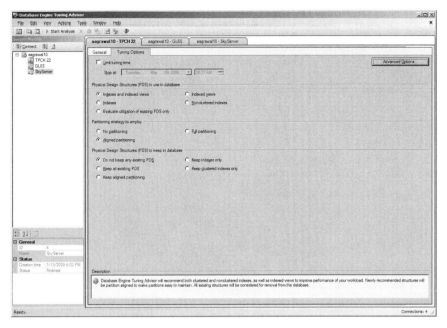

Figure 12.9   DTA selecting options and tuning time.

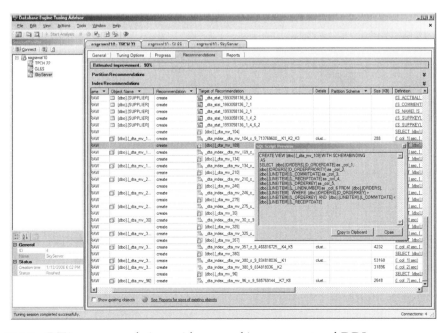

Figure 12.10   DTA recommendations with expected improvement and DDL.

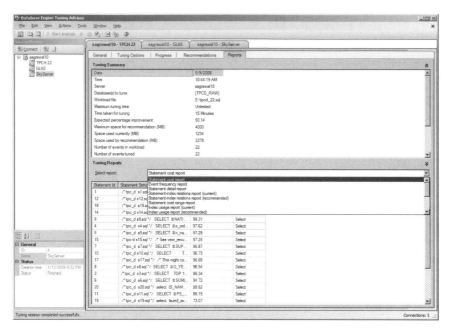

Figure 12.11   DTA summary report.

were proposed, etc. is presented to the user (Figure 12.11). Detailed reports include expected percentage improvement and usage of individual structures at the granularity of a statement.

12.2.3 Oracle SQL Access Advisor

Figure 12.12 shows the starting screen for the SQL Access Advisor, which begins with selecting an SQL tuning set, which is a set of SQL to be analyzed for performance improvements through physical database design. Although in this view the SQL Access Advisor is confirming the source of the workload to be analyzed, in fact the advisor can also be launched from the SQL tuning set interfaces as well, as shown in Figure 12.13. Oracle offers several methods to obtain a workload as input to the advisor. The advisor can go grab the current contents of the SQL cache, provide a set of SQL statements in a user-defined workload or get it to make a hypothetical workload based on your schema. These are very useful capabilities.

Figure 12.14 shows how SQL Access Advisor allows the user to select the attributes to be searched, and also has a workload compression choice on the same panel (Limited Mode and Comprehensive Mode).

SQL Access Advisor Results page shows improvements in SQL workload performance that can be realized by implementing its recommendations. The summary page

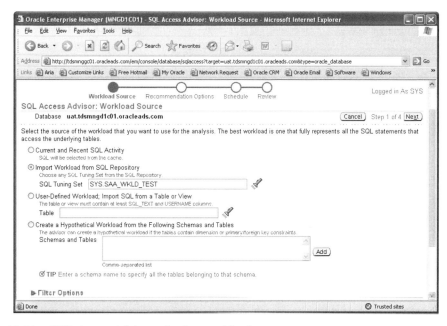

Figure 12.12   SQL Access Advisor selecting workload source.

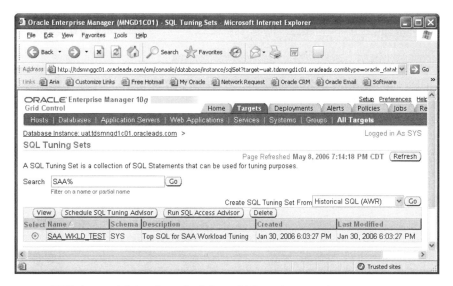

Figure 12.13   SQL Access Advisor launched from SQL tuning sets view.

Figure 12.14   SQL Access Advisor selection options.

shown in Figure 12.15 shows the expected savings in I/O and in projected total workload execution time. Like DB2's Design Advisor, Oracle's advisor has the ability to
determine what indexes and materialized views are not used by the supplied workload.
This can be useful in detecting obsolete objects. Within the Oracle SQL Access Advisor
this is called the "evaluation mode."

The Recommendations page, shown in Figure 12.16, lists the recommendations
reported by the advisor along with estimates on the relative benefit of each. This allows
the user to select only the more valuable recommendations if either the storage requirement is high, or the benefit to some of the recommendations seems marginal.

12.3 Data Sampling for Improved Statistics during Analysis

Although databases do keep statistics on the database they store, the statistics are not
comprehensive and they do get out of date. They can't be comprehensive; the combinations, permutations, and variants of possible statistics that can potentially be kept are
unfathomably large. As a result databases usually keep a reasonably complete set of statistics on each column of every table and each key of every index. Increasingly, the collection of statistics is an automated task, which reduces the need for manual administrative commands and reduces the chances of the statistics becoming stale over time. How-

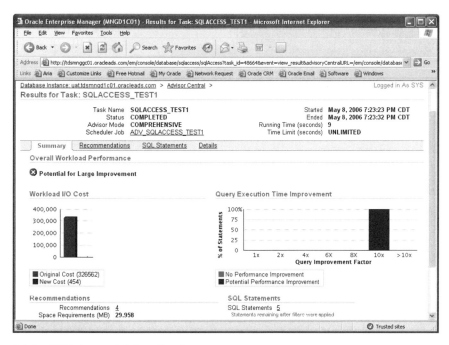

Figure 12.15   SQL Access Advisor Results page.

ever, the level of detail that is normally kept by default is often not enough to accurately project storage requirements for materialized views and multidimensional clustering.

It's true that query optimizers model the I/O and selectivity of many complex situations that can occur within SQL, but those models are often compromised because they were designed to be adequate for selecting optimal query execution plans and therefore are approximate, only needing to be accurate enough to select stable high-quality query execution plans for queries, not accurate enough to always predict runtime requirements with precision. You can be sure that these models are always designed to be as close to reality as possible, but the fact that the system continues to operate and function if the model is slightly inaccurate (or even significantly inaccurate) limits the need for perfection. However, when designing the physical structure of a database features like indexes, materialized views and multidimensional clustering can require significant additional storage, which translates into additional capital cost for the server. To solve this vendors have introduced the notion of data sampling to the problem of automated physical database design. Sampling was discussed earlier in Chapter 10.

Many of the sampling ideas introduced there are replicated in automated form in the utilities that recommend physical database design. Of these, the size of MDC and materialized views are the most important to model with improved accuracy, because the query optimizer is inadequate in these. Some products have advisors that automatically sample data to better calculate index statistics, though in the opinion of the

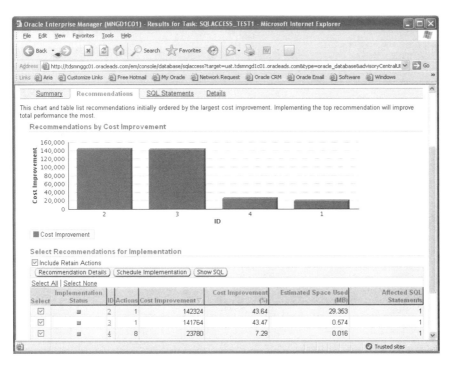

Figure 12.16   SQL Access Advisor Recommendations page.

authors this is a relatively minor enhancement since index statistics can be sufficiently estimated for the purposes of physical design advisors from relatively straightforward calculations based on the table and columns statistics of the underlying table that the virtual index will be based on. This is much less true for materialized views and MDC, where sampling becomes dramatically more important. In DB2 Design Advisor sampling is also used to help avoid data distribution skew when the advisor selects shared nothing hash partitioning.

12.4 Scalability and Workload Compression

One of the biggest misuses of utilities that perform automated physical database design is the attempted use of these powerful tools to help solve point problems with a single or small set of ill-performing queries. Although these intelligent tools can be quite helpful in resolving serious performance problems with one or more problem queries, the interdependence problems described in Chapter 9 are really countered when the tools are used in this way. For example, by using an index wizard to recommend indexes for a single problem query you may end up with three new indexes that really make the problem query run 100 times faster, but cause all of your insert operations to run three times more slowly! If the wizard was given both the queries and the inserts to analyze it may have recommended only one or two indexes, perhaps solving the bulk of the issues, for example, 80 times faster, and incurring a much smaller penalty for the insert processing. In fact the best tools are designed precisely to evaluate these tradeoffs, but they can only do so if given a broad view of the workload that the system will encounter.

The need to provide design utilities with a broad view of the workload has some serious issues of its own. Many real-world workloads include thousands if not hundreds of thousands of statements executed per day. Some may differ only slightly in their syntax while others may be radically different. This poses a serious problem for the utilities since the analysis of the workload and the time required to provide recommendations grow proportionately and sometimes exponentially with the size of the workload, the number of tables, and the number of predicates and joins, etc. The impact can be dramatic, causing the analysis to consume several days of execution time for even a very modest workload of a few dozen statements.

In an internal test using two different database products,[5] physical design utilities were compared against the same database data and the same workloads to test the reaction to workload size. The utilities searched for both indexes and materialized views. The tests used a synthetic workload against a classic MOLAP schema. The fact table had 8 measures and 16 hierarchical dimensions. In this experiment the design utilities were initially given 40 statements to analyze, and the workload size was subsequently increased to 60, 80, 100, and 150 statements. Each time the workload was increased the design utilities were rerun and the time to generate a recommendation was recorded. As shown in Figure 12.17 the utility with workload compression showed a linear increase in recommendation time, scaling from roughly 20 minutes with 40 statements in the workload, to over an hour of execution with a workload of 150 statements. In contrast the utility without workload compression had similar performance for providing a recommendation with the initial 40-statement workload, but as the workload size was increased, the recommendation time grew exponentially. With 150 statements, the utility without workload compression required over four days of analysis before returning a result!

There are a number of techniques that vendors use to avoid the explosive growth in execution time of the wizards. The first is to use an intelligent search algorithm that will traverse the domain of possible solutions trying to find an optimal or near-optimal solution without evaluating every possible alternative. Various techniques are used for this, including random sampling, genetic algorithms, Z-order evaluation, etc. Another key strategy is to reduce the complexity of the workload being analyzed in a way that will not significantly reduce the results of the analysis and recommendation. Doing so is called

---

[5] Due to licensing agreements the names of the database products are deliberately omitted. The tests were courtesy of Scott J. Fadden, IBM Systems & Technology Group, Development GPFS Performance Engineer.

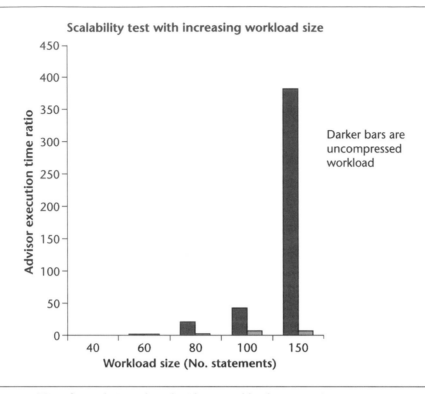

Figure 12.17   Time for analysis with and without workload compression.

"workload compression." None of the existing techniques today actually modify the input queries/statements. Rather, they choose a subset of the given workload for tuning.

Chaudhuri et al. [2002] propose a different strategy based on analyzing the workload to detect classes of statements, where a statement can be removed from the workload if another statement exists in the workload that is considered sufficiently similar based on a "distance" function. Statements are first partitioned by the tables that are accessed and the join columns. Statements with different tables and join columns are considered to be infinitely distant and reside in different classes. Within a class, the joint selectivity of the predicates is compared to estimate how similar queries within the same are to one another. A predetermined loss constraint is defined (e.g., 10%) and statements are dropped from the classes with the aim of removing the maximum number of statements while respecting the loss constraint. This description is only a summary, and the reader is referred to the original paper for the details.

Two major techniques for workload compression are used by modern physical database design utilities and published in the literature. One technique [Zilio et al. 2004] uses an approach based on focusing on the most complex and costly statements in a workload and ignoring the others. The rationale of this approach is that the gains that will be achieved from improved physical database design will manifest most as improvement on the most costly statements. Moreover, the costly statements typically represent the "problem" issues that database administrators (DBAs) will be most interested in improving. For example, improving a simple retail transaction from 0.1 sec to 0.01 sec may not be very meaningful for either a retail clerk or the consumer purchasing an item. However, an improvement from 45.0 sec to 4.5 sec will be very significant even though the *relative* improvement is the same—a difference of 40 seconds is much more important to humans than a difference of 0.09 seconds. Zilio et al. [2004] therefore compress the input workload by performing an initial evaluation of every statement and extracting only the most costly queries for analysis. The technique of picking the subset of queries with highest cost could have a significant weakness if applied naively. Consider a case where the workload has 10 queries, 2 queries of the same template A with a cost of 100 each, and 8 queries B with a cost of 50 each. Suppose our compression goal was to pick exactly 2 queries to tune. The above strategy would pick two instances from template A and completely ignore all 8 queries of template B even though the 8 queries have cumulative higher cost to the system. To solve this problem Zilio first matches like queries and multiplies the cost of each template by its frequency. In this example even before removing any queries based on cost, the compression algorithm would reduce the 10 statements in the workload to 2 statements, one for each of A and B. Then the cost of each query is multiplied by its frequency in the workload, so that A is assigned cost of 200 and B is assigned cost of 400. With a compression goal of 2 statements both queries end up being represented, and template B is given the higher weighting as desired.

The essential difference between these techniques is that the approach by Zilio et al. compresses the workload by focusing on the "most important subset" of the workload, while the approach by Chaudhuri et al. compresses the workload by finding the "most representative subset" of the workload. The initial experimental results by both teams of researchers appear to show very similar effectiveness when compared on the same workload, though the published experimental results have been admittedly limited.

In addition to compressing the workload, design utilities can improve the time it takes to find a solution by simply searching less carefully (less exhaustively!). Many vendors provide a mechanism to control the aggressiveness and completeness of the search. In DB2 Design Advisor the user can specify a maximum search time (clock time). In SQL Server DTA the utility can be executed in various modes—thorough, medium, fast, etc. In a 2000 white paper Agrawal et al. [2000] described the impact of controlling the thoroughness of the search on the time required to return a result and resulting impact on the quality of the recommendations.

> For large workload files and large databases, tuning may require a significant amount of time and resources. This option allows the user to trade off the running time of the Index Tuning Wizard with the thoroughness of the analysis. The Fast mode consumes the least amount of time and resources and produces a quick recommenda-

tion that is based on query analysis and limited interaction with the query processor. (Indexed views are not proposed in the Fast mode.) The Medium mode, which is the default, proposes indexes and indexed views and is significantly faster than the Thorough mode for large workloads. Although the Medium mode of operation searches fewer possibilities, in many cases it is able to provide a respectable set of recommendations. The Thorough mode consumes the maximum amount of time and resources, but it also gives the highest quality recommendation for the workload. Below is a comparison of the running times and expected improvements of the [Database Tuning Advisor (DTA)] in different tuning modes for a sample workload on a 1.2 GB database [Table 12.2].

In SQL Server 2005 a time limitation was added to the search options, extending the Thorough, Medium, and Fast options to an explicit clock time constraint, very similar to the DB2 approach.

Table 12.2   SQL Server DTA Characteristics

Server Version	Features Tuned	Tuning Mode	DTA Running Time	Expected Improvement
SQL Server 7.0	Indexes Only	Thorough	40 min 46 sec	49%
SQL Server 2000	Indexes Only	Fast	1 min 10 sec	37%
SQL Server 2000	Indexes Only	Medium	3 min 52 sec	39%
SQL Server 2000	Indexes and Indexed Views	Medium	4 min 54 sec	41%
SQL Server 2000	Indexes Only	Thorough	16 min 5 sec	62%
SQL Server 2000	Indexes and Indexed Views	Thorough	19 min 21 sec	79%

12.5 Design Exploration between Test and Production Systems

It's quite common for database designers and application developers to develop on a test system, and use a distinct system for production. Usually the test system differs significantly from the production system in many ways, including the following:

1. The production system usually stores a full complement of real data while the test system usually has a sample.

2. The production system has real data, while the test system usually has either a sample of old data or entirely synthetic data.

3. The production system is intended to support higher volumes of data and concurrency and there is often a larger physical system than the test system used for development.

4. The production system services real customers of the application and database and therefore cannot be experimented on lightly, while the test system exists largely for the purpose of tinkering and experimentation.

However, physical database design depends significantly on the schema, data, statistics, and resources of the server where the database will be run in production database designs developed on a test server with all these differences, which can result in database designs that are suboptimal for the production environment. Conversely, running database design utilities on the production server may introduce disturbance and risk to the production server that is not acceptable in highly available 24-7 environments. For example, the advisor may consume too many resources to perform the evaluation, or cause locking contention. To solve this problem many automated design utilities allow the following modes of operation:

1. Execute the utility on a test server, resulting in an initial though possibly suboptimal database design.

2. Export the schema and statistics of the production server to the test server so that the test server can be used to explore database designs that are meaningful on the production server.

3. Execute the automated design utility on the production server, perhaps during off-peak hours.

Figure 12.18 illustrates these possibilities. All of the modes of operation are commonly used in industry today. In fact the idea of exporting schema and statistics to a test server is also used by database vendors as a customer-service aid, so that problems detected at

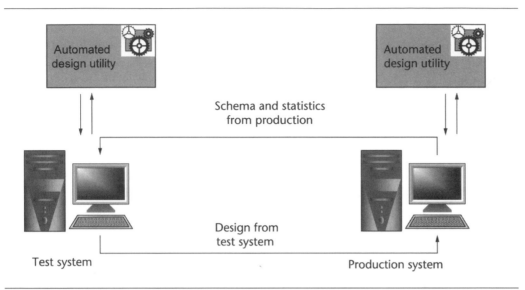

Figure 12.18　Options for executing automated design utilities with both test and production servers available.

customer sites can be reproduced by the vendor on local machines to help analyze reported problems. An important invariant to maintain is that the recommendation that is produced when tuning on the test server is identical to the recommendation that would be produced had the tuning been done directly against the production server. If this invariant is not maintained arbitrary degradation in quality may result. This requires that all statistics that would have been used on the production server be available on the test server as well. Products like DB2 and SQL Server provide services to easily enforce that statistics on the test system match those on the production system.

12.6 Experimental Results from Published Literature

Zilio et al. [2004] tested automated physical design technology against an industry-standard decision support workload (Table 12.3). They compared their advisor against a baseline TPC-H database that had a "reasonable" but not optimal design (Figure 12.19). The baseline database had all the major indexes defined and a reasonable partitioning scheme. The database was a relatively small 1 GB TPC-H database stored on an 8 CPU AIX 5.2 system with four logical partitions. The workload contained all the 22 TPC-H queries. In these experiments the Design Advisor was able to finish the design of all features in about 10 minutes. Most significantly the resulting design improved the performance of the TPC-H workload by 6.5 times (85% reduction in execution time).

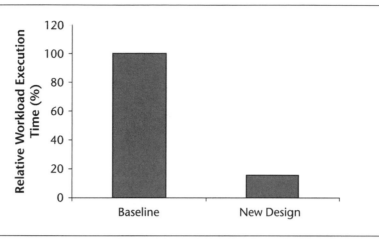

Figure 12.19   Zilio et al. TPC-H result.

IBM also published an experimental result on combined materialized view and index selection [Zilio et al. 2004]. The experiments used an OLAP-type (star) schema. The originating system was a shared-nothing database system with 10 processing partitions. There were more than 15 tables in the database, comprising roughly 400 GB of data. The workload contained 12 OLAP-like business queries to the star schema, each of which had an equal frequency of execution. In these experiments the DB2 Design

Table 12.3   Number and Type of Attributes Recommended in Zilio et al. Experiment

Design Feature	Number Recommended
Indexes	20
MDC dimensions	6
Partitioning changes	4
Materialized views	2

Advisor was tested using both multiquery optimization alone and a combination of multiquery optimization and whole queries as input to the candidate set of possible materialized views.

These results include the total workload estimated times with no materialized views, the total workload estimated times when materialized views are recommended by the advisor, the percentage improvement in the estimated run time gained by exploiting the recommended materialized views, and the number of materialized views recommended by the Advisor. The DB2 Design Advisor recommended a small set of high-quality materialized views that improve performance by 28.5%. The results also suggest that materialized views derived by the multiquery optimization algorithm provided the majority of the benefit. See Table 12.4.

Next they tested the DB2 Design Advisor for a search of materialized views and indexes together. In this experiment, the projected time improvement reduced the expected workload execution time from 493.7 seconds to only 51.4 seconds, representing a whopping 89% improvement. The Design Advisor recommended 7 materialized views and 18 new indexes, 8 of which were on the recommended materialized views. The ability of the design process to recommend indexes on base tables as well as candidate materialized views indicated that the Design Advisor algorithm correctly handled the interaction of indexes and materialized views.

Table 12.4   Performance of Materialized Views

Type of materialized view selection	Execution time without materialized views	Execution time with materialized views	Percentage improvement	Num. of materialized views
Materialized views from Multi Query Optimization and queries	493.7 seconds	353.0 seconds	28.5%	7
Materialized views from Multi Query Optimization only	493.7 seconds	352.0 seconds	28.4%	4

Lightstone and Bhattacharjee [2004] reported tests to compare the quality of the automated MDC design compared to expert human recommendations against a well-known schema and workload. The industry-standard TPC-H benchmark was used for the tests. The metric used for comparison is called the TPC-H Composite Query-per-Hour (QphH@Size). For the experiments, a 10 GB TPC-H database running on DB2 UDB V8.1 on a pSeries® server with AIX® 5.1, 4 × 375 MHz CPUs, and 8 GB RAM was used. Six experimental tests were performed:

1. *Baseline:* The performance of the benchmark without MDC. Table 12.1 describes those traditional RID (row) indexes used for the baseline experiment, which had a cluster ratio quality of 5% or better, a measure of percentage of data that is well clustered along one dimension.

2. *Advisor 1:* The performance of the benchmark using the topmost MDC design of the Advisor.

3. *Advisor 2:* The performance of the benchmark using the second best MDC design for the Advisor. This is a second best design for MDC that the advisor discovered in its search through thousands of possible designs.

4. *Expert 1:* The MDC design used during IBM's most recent 2003 TPC-H publication. According to TPC-H guidelines, the MDC design was constrained to clustering exclusively on base columns (coarsification was not permitted).

5. *Expert 2:* The top MDC design provided by the research and development scientists who developed MDC at IBM.

6. *Expert 3:* An alternative MDC design provided by the DB2 MDC development team.

In these experiments, all of the MDC designs showed significant benefit over the baseline throughput. The rank ordering of the five MDC designs according to their performance benefit (Figure 12.20) was Advisor 2 with 11.12%, Expert 1 with 13.35%, Expert 3 with 14.20%, Advisor 1 with 14.54%, and Expert 2 with 18.08%. Significantly, Advisor 1, which represents the DB2 Design Advisor's best recommendation, was measurably superior to DB2 Design Advisor 2 and both Expert 1 and Expert 3.

Agrawal et al [2004] published experimental results with SQL Server DTA showing the quality and performance of the advisor against internal users of SQL Server. "Internal users" are users of the product within the Microsoft corporation. No statement was made about the tuning skill of the internal users (i.e. they may or may not be experts). In this experiment four database systems that were hand tuned for physical database design by users. These hand-tuned designs were compared against designs recommended by DTA and against the default database design (which includes no indexes or materialized views except for those required for RI and uniqueness). The hand tuned workload performance and the DTA tuned workload performance are both compared against the default design. Table 12.5 lists the four customer workloads that were used.

The database sizes range from 60MB to 106GB. Similarly the size of the schema varied dramatically across these workloads from 11 tables in the smallest case, to 4374 in the largest. The results of these tests are shown in Table 12.6. In all cases the tuning advisor outperformed the human designers. Also worth noting is that the tuning time ranged from roughly half an hour to over 15 hours. This illustrates that physical database design, even when performed at the speed of a computer, is a very complex task.

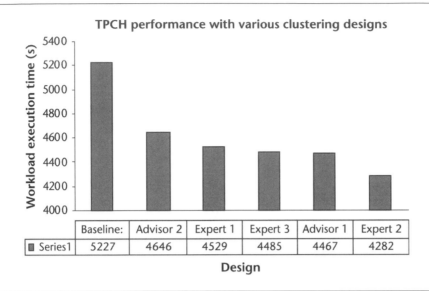

Figure 12.20   Experimental results for automated MDC design.

CUST3 has an unusual result where the hand-tuned design was actually worse than the default design and the DTA design offers no improvement. This was due to the presence of a large amount of UPDATE activity in the workload. DTA correctly recognized that the benefit of indexes and materialized views would be offset by a negative impact on UPDATE performance, and therefore recommended no design changes over the default. The hand-tuned design which included some additional indexes suffered overall because every UPDATE become slightly slower due to the additional index maintenance.

Table 12.5   Overview of Internal Customer Databases and Workloads

Database	Total size (GB)	#DBs	#Tables	#SQL statements tuned
CUST1	10.7	31	4374	15K
CUST2	1.4	6	48	252K
CUST3	105.9	23	1624	176K
CUST4	0.06	2	11	9K

Chaudhuri et al. [2002] published results on the effectiveness of workload compression in speeding up the search time for design utilities while having a relatively small impact on the quality of the results. Figure 12.21 is a reproduction of their

Table 12.6 Quality of DTA vs. Hand-tuned Design on Internal Customer Workloads

Workload	Improvement of hand-tuned design over default	Improvement of DTA design over default	Tuning time (hr:min)
CUST1	82%	87%	0:35
CUST2	6%	41%	8:21
CUST3	-5%	0%	15:14
CUST4	0%	50%	1:07

results. Chaudhuri et al. studied two different workloads: an industry standard workload and a synthetic workload. They found the compression strategy was effective in removing a large percentage of the statements in the input workload, between 60% and 80% reduction, while the quality loss in the recommendations was less than 18%. They also found that the processing time of the advisor reduced in approximately the same proportion as the reduction in workload size.

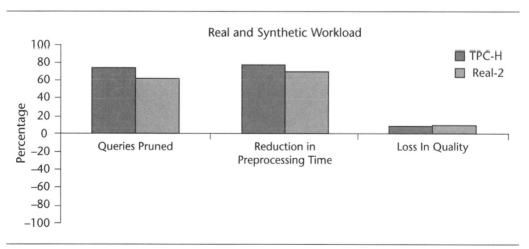

Figure 12.21   Impact of workload compression.

Outside of the published literature there have been scores of results reported by users of these technologies (from all vendors) attesting to the value these features have provided for production databases. Huge benefits have been reported often improving performance by 70% or more, while dramatically reducing CPU consumption and other system resources.

12.7   Index Selection

Virtually all of the utilities for automated physical database design evaluate candidate indexes using the technique mentioned above to determine the potential benefit of adding a new index to a system. However, comprehensive evaluation of every possible new index is never practical, since the permutation and combinations are too large. Therefore, what differs between the various products on the market is the degree of sophistication used in the search for new indexes. The most obvious first-order efficiency is to explore indexes on the column used in predicates and possibly in result sets, and exclude other columns. This reduces the scope of the search immensely and is a fairly obvious strategy.

However, the evaluation of virtual indexes (i.e., new candidates) is performed by the optimizer per statement, which makes it difficult to find indexes that have global benefit. Instead, most products begin with a local search, finding the indexes that are best for each statement, and then proceeding with an evaluation and merging process where similar indexes are merged or dropped in order to reduce the total number of indexes recommended. The idea of "merging" was first introduced in Chaudhuri et al [1999]. Merging attempts to avoid the problem of finding only the locally ideal indexes (which are best for each individual SQL statements, but which may not be optimal for the workload collectively) by introducing new candidates that are more widely useful for the workload. Valentin et al. [2000] use a merge process followed by a knapsack algorithm to first merge similar indexes, and then select the most valuable ones based on a value-to-size ratio, until a specified storage constraint is reached. This technique is used in DB2.

Research by Bruno et al. [2005] introduced the notion of "relaxation" in automated database design. Relaxation attempts to avoid the problem of finding only the locally ideal indexes (which are best for each individual SQL statement, but which may not be optimal for the group collectively) instead of the systemwide globally ideal solution.

12.8   Materialized View Selection

All three of DB2, Oracle, and SQL Server recommend materialized views using a similar high-level strategy. The submitted workload (SQL statements) is analyzed to detect common or similar elements, such as joins or aggregations, and from these a set of candidate materialized views are defined (internally) for evaluation by the query optimizer to assess the impact of workload cost if any of these virtualized materialized views are used. These candidates can range from exact replicas of the submitted statements to merged fragments of multiple statements. The advisors "generalize" the predicates, where a literal may be used in the actual submitted statement. The advisors tend to prefer generalized arguments, such as group-by. The reason for the generalization is simply that the specific literal is usually a sample, not a consistent constraint. For example, if a query includes a predicate on region where REGION = 'NEW YORK', it is likely that 'NEW YORK' is merely incidental, and that other locations are going to be submitted for this predicate. So grouping by region is a reasonable strategy.

The common technique used for generating candidate materialized views is to exploit the query graph that the query compiler generates for each query during compilation. The query compiler's optimizer runs its query optimization rules in reverse to generate a small set of candidate access structures that would ideally benefit a given query. In addition to that technique, an additional technique called "multiquery optimization" (or mass query optimization) was also published that does an excellent job of looking for materialized view candidates based on a simultaneous analysis of groups of queries.

The Oracle SQL Access Advisor also generally includes a COUNT(x) column matching every SUM(x) column, which they have found to be a useful strategy. For example, using Oracle SQL Access Advisor, if a query contains SUM(x), a recommendation for a materialized view containing SUM(x) will also contain COUNT(x). This idealization enables the computation of AVG(x) from SUM(x)/COUNT(x), which is a common occurrence.

For all three products it is possible to see a recommended materialized view that is an exact copy of the request query. This usually occurs with the most costly and complex queries where a materialized view devoted to just that one complex query is justified.

In principle a materialized view can be created for every distinct query on the system, but the storage and maintenance requirements would be completely unreasonable for most systems. Finding a good selection of materialized views that has the most benefit often requires finding complex materialized views that provide full or partial benefit to multiple queries, rather than selecting the materialized views that satisfy a smaller set of queries more completely. The goal is to build generally applicable materialized views rather than very specific ones. This is particularly important in the business intelligence world, which is often characterized by ad hoc (unpredictable) queries.

The idea of "merging" for materialized views was first published in Agrawal et al [2000]. This technique introduces new candidate materialized views that may not be optimal for any individual statement in the workload, but may be optimal for the workload as a whole. A powerful technique to detect similarities between fragments of different queries was described by Lehner et al. [2001], called mass query optimization or more commonly multi-query optimizaton. In this paper the authors describe a technique to detect query execution plans that are beneficial to sets of queries, rather than single statements. The combined query execution plans indirectly detect the commonalities that are useful for materialized view candidates. Though Lehner et al. planned to initially use this method for improving the performance of materialized view refresh, the same techniques were then reused by them and their colleagues [Zilio et al. 2005] to use the detected commonalities as suggestions for materialized views within the what-if analysis of the DB2 Design Advisor.

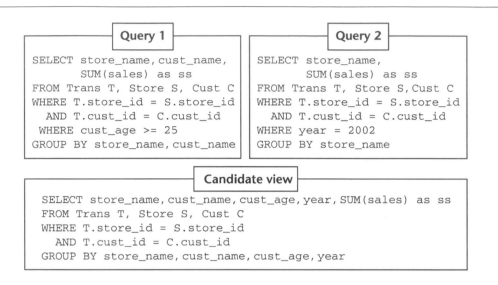

Figure 12.22   Multiquery optimization and materialized view selection.

Figure 12.22 shows an example of a workload with two different statements that have some commonalities. Both query 1 and query 2 select store_name and SUM(sales) and group by store_name. Even so the queries are quite different. A materialized view based on the definition of either one of these queries would likely not be generic enough to be useful by the other. Using multiquery optimization a candidate materialized view can be detected and suggested for what-if analysis, described below as "candidate view." Notice how the select operands are now a superset of the original two queries, and the GROUP BY clause includes both a superset of the original GROUP BY expressions in both queries 1 and 2 but also includes generalization of the WHERE predicate columns, cust_age and year. Multiquery optimization is used by DB2 Design Advisor. The technique is powerful and offers so many advantages it is likely that other vendors will begin using variants of the techniques in the near future.

12.9 **Multidimensional Clustering Selection**

In the area of automating MDC dimension selection, there are implementations such as WARLOCK that were limited to parallel warehouses for shared-everything or shared-disk architectures. It used its own cost model instead of using the database engines.

The search space for selecting clustering dimensions is huge. The basic problem of selecting clustering dimensions from a finite set can be modeled easily as a simple combination problem. However, since each dimension has some number of degrees of coarsification, the search space expands exponentially. Coarsification refers to the granularity of clustering along a dimension. For example, one can cluster by day of year, week of year, month, or quarter, etc. Assuming an equal number of degrees of coarseness for each dimension, the following equation shows the combinations of n dimensions each with c degrees of coarsification:

$$(\sum_{r=1}^{n-1}((n!)/(r!(n-r)!))c^r)+c^n. \qquad 12.1$$

This equation takes a standard formula for the combination of n items, and expands based on the fact that, for each iteration of the sum, each tuple has its combinations expanded by a factor of c^r because each part of the tuple has c degrees of coarsification (i.e., c ways in which it can be selected). Similarly, the formula concludes with c^n since the selection space for a selection that includes every dimension, each being selected at one of c degrees, is c^n. In general, not all dimensions have the same number of degrees of coarsification. Even so, the equation suggests the complexity of the space.

One of the key issues is to understand the likely effect of coarsification on the expected benefit in clustering on any given dimension. A brute-force approach to solving this problem would be to reevaluate (simulate) the workload cost with each individual coarsification of each dimension, or perhaps all possible combinations. Unfortunately this would be impractical because the number of combinations of dimensions at all possible coarsifications is frequently extremely large. Instead Lightstone and Bhattacharjee [2004] use a simple model sufficient for the MDC selection process, based on the following two observations:

1. When a database table has only one cell, MDC provides no value.
2. As dimensions become more fine grained (less coarse) the number of cells in the MDC table increases, which also increases the space waste (see Chapter 8). For any candidate dimension there exists a finest useful dimension granularity (FUDG) that represents the most granular coarsification of a dimension that does not result in space waste beyond a predefined limit (say 10% growth). This FUDG coarsification can be estimated deterministically. The expected benefit at the FUDG coarsification was determined through simulation within the SQL optimizer.

Knowing the benefit of MDC at two known extremes allows the design software to construct a model of what may happen in between those two points. How will the benefit to the workload change if a table is clustered by month of year instead of by week of year?

Although the exact shape of the monotonic curve cannot be easily determined, it has been modeled as a smooth logarithmic relationship, such that the penalty for coarsi-

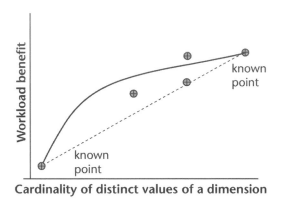

Figure 12.23   Curve-fitted benefit coarsification function.

fying (decreasing granularity of) a dimension is initially minor, but increases dramatically at higher coarsification levels. A curve-fitting process is used to plot a concave polynomial between the two well-known points to derive a benefit-coarsification function, as per Figure 12.23. From this relationship function, we can model the performance benefit of any coarsification level of a dimension given its cardinality of cells at the FUDG coarsification level.

The model is only approximate, but the insight is that even this very approximate model is far more accurate than what most human database designers can do, or perhaps more accurately, more than what humans are willing to do.

12.10 Shared-nothing Partitioning

Only one commercial utility provides automated design of shared-nothing partitioning; the IBM DB2 product uses the technique described in Rao et al. [2002]. Once again the explosive number of possible solutions makes comprehensive evaluation of the possible designs for shared-nothing partitioning practically impossible. The number of possible combinations is roughly:

$$\prod_{t=1}^{t}\left(2^{n}\times k\right)$$

12.2

where n is the average number of columns per table, k is the number of partition groups, and t is the number of tables. For example, assuming a fairly small database schema with 20 columns per table, 10 tables, and 3 partition groups, the number of

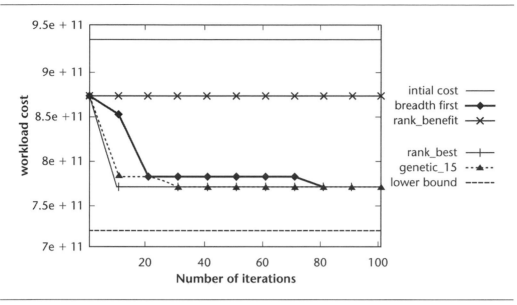

Figure 12.24   Rao et al. comparison of search schemes for shared-nothing partitioning.

possible ways to design partitioning for the database would be: $9.48e + 74$, roughly the number of atoms in the universe![6]

Another major problem in the design of shared-nothing databases is skew, as discussed in Chapter 6. The main concept behind shared-nothing systems is to divide the data relatively evenly across multiple servers. If the partitioning design is skewed, a lot of the data may end up on a small subset of servers completely defeating the main objective of shared-nothing designs.

To solve the skew issue, Rao et al. rely on the hash function and hash mapping to be fair, and focus on identifying columns that are very susceptible to skew because of low column cardinality (small number of unique values in the column data). Their automated design work automatically detects these columns and excludes them as candidates for partitioning columns. Additionally for the higher cardinality columns that remain sampling is used to determine whether the results of hashing will lead to a skewed distribution of data across nodes.

After selecting a set of possible partitioning designs for each table the remaining combinations remained extremely large since collocation requires that the partitioning designs for tables not be determined independently. To explore this space effectively Rao et al. tested several search algorithms, including genetic algorithms, to determine a reasonable strategy for converging quickly (Figure 12.24). Surprisingly, the best perform-

[6] Currently estimated to be between 10^{69} and 10^{81} atoms.

ing search appeared to be based on a simple *z*-order search over the partitioning designs ranked by individual benefit.

12.11 Range Partitioning Design

The Microsoft Database Tuning Advisor provides design automation for range partitioning. Again, the implementation is based on what-if analysis using the query optimizer. Predicates on range expressions provide clues for the boundaries of the horizontal partitioning that the DTA will recommend. The candidate partitioning is detected by the DTA detecting range and inequality predicates for table access as specified within the incoming SQL text. For example, queries with predicates on date can imply a reasonable strategy for range partitioning. For example, consider the following two predicates that could easily appear within a database workload:

```
Ship_date < 01-01-1997
Ship_date < 02-01-1998
```

Clearly these expressions suggest that range partitioning by month may be reasonable. The DTA parses inequality and range predicates from the workload to detect reasonable range partitioning schemes, and evaluates these through the query optimizer using what-if analysis. A novel aspect of DTA's range partitioning recommendations is that is able to also incorporate manageability requirements in its analysis. For example, a DBA can require that all tables and indexes must be "aligned", i.e., partitioned identically. Such a constraint is useful since it makes managing the database (e.g., backup/restore, loading new partitions etc.) easier. DTA searches the space subject to this manageability constraint. More details are available in [Agrawal 2004]. The ability to consider administrative within the automated design analysis is a very important because, as discussed in Chapter 7, range partitioning is heavily used to improve database administration.

Oracle's ILM Assistant recommends partitioning based on a lifecycle definition. This is not workload based or cost based analysis.

TIPS AND INSIGHTS FOR DATABASE PROFESSIONALS

- **Tip 1. Provide a complete workload as input to the advising utility.** The wizards/advisors for physical database design selection work best because they can make tradeoffs about physical database design. While they are quite useful to helping resolve problems with individual slow-running queries, they are really designed best to make choices over sets of queries, inserts, updates, and deletes.

- **Tip 2. Is workload compression required?** Depending on the utility you are using, it may or may not offer workload compression. Products that offer compression allow you to submit massive workloads with thousands of statements without any filtering on your part. Without compression most physical database design utilities (especially when searching for materialized views) will spend too much time during analysis to be useful. In those cases you would be best to filter the queries yourself and supply no more than a few dozen statements as input to the utility. Yes, this does conflict with Tip 1, and it's a practical reality.

- **Tip 3. Don't limit yourself to indexes.** Many vendors now offer combined support for materialized views as well as indexes, and the DB2 Design Advisor even offers MDC and shared-nothing partitioning. Many DBAs and database designers limit their use of design features to indexes, and it's a great shame. There are orders of magnitude in benefits to be had by exploiting the richness of the additional features, especially when the selection problem is simplified by the aid of automation tools, so why not try them?

- **Tip 4. Apply judgment and testing.** The physical design problem is extremely complex, and while automation tools can evaluate thousands of alternatives, they are not flawless. Treat the recommendations from these tools as "really great advice to be considered and tested" rather than absolute infallible truth.

- **Tip 5. Remember that your database is a moving target.** It is futile to optimize to perfection at a point in time because data and applications evolve. Near optimal is usually plenty sufficient in practice. Many industrial systems are deeply flawed (conceptual models, software engineering practices, db tuning, etc.) and far from optimal in practice. As a result take "comprehensive" optimization with a heavy dose of reality, and avoid the changes that offer only the most temporary and incremental gains.

- **Tip 6: Remember to include INSERT, UPDATE and DELETE statements.** Automated design tools, like most things in compter science, are only as good as the input they get. Like the saying goes "garbage in, garbage out". While query performance is often the primary motivator for invoking an automated design advisor, it's important for the advisor to see the write activity in the workload (INSERT, UPDATE and DELETEs) so it won't recommend database designs that have extremely negative impact on them. All the major vendors have taken steps to include technology in their advisors to factor in the impact on write operations, but that technology is only effective if the write operations are part of the input.

- **Tip 7. Constrain the advisors as you would yourself.** In previous chapters we recommended setting reasonable limits on the amount of disk space used for auxiliary structures like indexes, MDC, and materialized views. For example, storage space for indexes should rarely be more than 20-25% of total database storage. Use automated design advisors wisely by applying the same kind of common sense. Don't let an automated utility convince you to double or triple the size of your database so that dozens of indexes and materialized views can be created.

12.12 Summary

Utilities for automated physical database design are based on advanced technology with considerable sophistication. Even so, these technologies are maturing, and for the moment, most recommendations from these utilities should be reviewed before being directly applied to a system. If you are the Gary Kasparov of physical database design chances are you don't need to use these advisors. However, if you're mortal then you may just find these tools have something to offer because of their ability to evaluate thousands of alternatives and complex combinations that human designers will not. Even for the experienced database designers these utilities have been found to be useful, particularly as a starting point for new ideas.

12.13 Literature Summary

Agrawal, S., Chaudhuri, S., Kollar, L., and Narasayya, V. Index Tuning Wizard for Microsoft SQL Server 2000, white paper, at http://msdn.microsoft.com/library/techart/itwforsql.htm.

Agrawal, S., Chaudhuri, S., and Narasayya, V. Automated Selection of Materialized Views and Indexes for SQL Databases. *Proceedings of VLDB*, 2000: 496-505.

Agrawal, S., Narasayya, V., and Yang, B. Integrating Vertical and Horizontal Partitioning into Automated Physical Database Design. *Proceedings of ACM SIGMOD*, 2004.

Agrawal, S., Chaudhuri, S., Kollár, L., Marathe, A., Narasayya, V., Syamala, M.: Database Tuning Advisor for Microsoft SQL Server 2005. *VLDB 2004*, Toronto, Canada, pp: 1110-1121

BMC Index Advisor, at http://www.bmc.com.

Bruno, N., and Chaudhuri, S. Automatic Physical Design Tuning: A Relaxation-based Approach. *Proceedings of the ACM SIGMOD*, Baltimore, MD, 2005.

Bruno, N., and Chaudhuri, S. Physical Design Refinement. The Merge-Reduce Approach. *Proceedings of EDBT Conference*, 2006.

Chaudhuri, S., Gupta, A., and Narasayya, V. Workload Compression. *Proceedings of ACM SIGMOD*, 2002.

Chaudhuri, S., Dageville, B., and Lohman, G. M. Self-managing Technology in Database Management Systems. *VLDB*, 2004: 1243.

Chaudhuri, S., and Narasayya, V. An Efficient Cost-driven Index Selection Tool for Microsoft SQL Server. *VLDB*, 1997: 146-155.

Chaudhuri, S., and Narasayya, V. AutoAdmin "What-If" Index Analysis Utility. Proceedings of ACM SIGMOD, 1998.

Chaudhuri S. and Narasayya V., "Index Merging," *Proceedings of 15th International Conference on Data Engineering*, Sydney, Australia 1999.

Dageville, B., Das, D., Dias, K., Yagoub, K., Zaït, M., and Ziauddin, M. Automatic SQL Tuning in Oracle 10g. *VLDB*, 2004: 1098–1109.

Dias, K., Ramacher, M., Shaft, U., Venkataramani, V., and Wood, G. Automatic Performance Diagnosis and Tuning in Oracle. *CIDR*, 2005: 84–94.

Finkelstein, S., Schikolnick, M., and Tiberio, P. Physical Database Design for Relational Databases. *ACM Transactions of Database Systems*, 13(1), 1988: 91–128.

König, A., and Nabar, S. Scalable Exploration of Physical Database Design. *Proceedings of 22nd International Conference on Data Engineering*, Atlanta, GA, 2006.

Lehner, W., Cochrane, R., Pirahesh, H., and Zaharioudakis, M. Fast Refresh Using Mass Query Optimization. *ICDE*, 2001: 391–398.

Li, W. S., Zilio, D. C., Batra, V. S., Subramanian, M., Zuzarte, C., and Narang, I. Load Balancing for Multitiered Database Systems through Autonomic Placement of Materialized Views. *ICDE*, 2006: 102.

Lightstone, S., and Bhattacharjee, B. Automating the Design of Multidimensional Clustering Tables in Relational Databases. *VLDB*, 2004: 1170–1181.

Lightstone, S., Schiefer, B., Zilio, D., Kleewein, J. "Autonomic Computing for Relational Databases: the ten year vision," *Proceedings. IEEE International Conference on Industrial Informatics, 2003*. INDIN 2003. 21-24 Aug. 2003 pp: 419- 424

Rao, J., Zhang, C., Lohman, G., and Megiddo, N. Automating Physical Database Design in a Parallel Database. *Proceedings of the ACM SIGMOD*, 2002.

K. Bernhard Schiefer, Gary Valentin: DB2 Universal Database Performance Tuning. *IEEE Data Eng. Bull.* 22(2): 12-19 (1999)

Stohr T., Martens H., and Rahm, E. Multidimensional Aware Database Allocation for Parallel Data Warehouses. *Proceedings of VLDB*, 2000.

Valentin, G., Zuliani, M., Zilio, D., Lohman, G. DB2 Advisor: An Optimizer That Is Smart Enough to Recommend Its Own Indexes. *Proceedings of ICDE*, 2000.

Zilio, D. C. Rao, J., Lightstone, S., Lohman, G. M., Storm, A. J., Garcia-Arellano, C., and Fadden, S. DB2 Design Advisor: Integrated Automatic Physical Database Design. *VLDB*, 2004: 1087–1097.

Zilio, D. C., Zuzarte, C., Lightstone, S., Ma, W., Lohman, G. M., Cochrane, R., Pirahesh, H., Colby, L. S., Gryz, J., Alton, E., Liang, D., and Valentin, G. Recommending Materialized Views and Indexes with IBM DB2 Design Advisor. *ICAC,* 2004: 180–188.

Zilio, D. C., Lightstone, S., Lohman, G. "Trends in automating physical database design", *Proceedings IEEE International Conference on Industrial Informatics,* 2003. INDIN 2003. 21–24 Aug. 2003 pp: 441–445

Down to the Metal: Server Resources and Topology

*We must beat the iron while it is hot, but we may
polish it at leisure.*
—John Dryden (1631–1700)

*The real problem is not whether machines think
but whether men do.*
—B. F. Skinner (1904–1990)

Databases are intended to perform an abstraction from the application space to the data. However, despite the abstraction, as an industry we have yet to completely shield the database designer from the nuances of system design. It remains the case that to build a high-quality database system with good performance, longevity, and availability, the designers need a reasonable understanding of systems architecture and recovery strategies. In fact the range of systems issues that database designers need to understand is profound: multiprocessor servers, disk systems, network topologies, disaster-recovery techniques, performance models, and memory management. This is a broad space that realistically deserves a few books of its own. However, a book on database design would be incomplete without at least a summary discussion of the issues. The good news is that instead of buying another book, you'll now get a crash course on the issues here in a single chapter. The bad news is that this treatment can't possibly be sufficient. What follows is an attempt to strike the right balance between the need of the database designer to understand the systems issues relating to database design, and a careful balancing act to manage this information into a single condensed chapter. If you were hoping to read this chapter and become a guru in systems design issues for database servers, you will probably be disappointed. What we do hope, however, is that this chapter will present a summary review of the major systems issues, after which you'll feel comfortable to follow what the gurus constantly rave about.

In essence there is a core set of systems attributes that database designers need to understand:

- Performance modeling for CPU processing power
- CPU architecture basics
- Client server architectures
- Multiprocessors and nonuniform memory access (NUMA)
- Balancing resources correctly for database servers
- Operating system choices
- Storage area networks (SANs) and network attached storage (NAS)
- Storage reliability and availability using a reliable array of inexpensive disks (RAID)
- Database availability strategies, such as Real Application Clusters (RAC) and High Availability Disaster Recovery (HADR)
- Database memory management

Through the remainder of this chapter we will discuss each of these with the goal of providing the reader with a little more than conversational understanding of each.

13.1 What You Need to Know about CPU Architecture and Trends

13.1.1 CPU Performance

The most widely known measure of CPU performance is the CPU clock rate. CPUs operate by performing instructions. Each instruction requires some number of clock cycles to execute. Clock speed is generally measured today in giga-Hertz (GHz) or billions of cycles per second. The faster the clock cycles the faster the CPU can perform instructions. At least that's the crude theory. In practice the analysis is weak but still provides a rough guideline.

For a given CPU architecture, it is indeed possible to compare CPUs according to their clock rates. However, across different CPU architectures the same instruction (such as ADD) may require more instructions on one chip than another. As a result, a CPU with a slower clock rate may actually process faster because it requires fewer clock cycles to do the same work. Instruction sets differ across architectures and as a result some CPUs require multiple instructions to perform tasks that another CPU can perform in a single instruction. These combined effects result in CPUs in different architectures being comparable by clock speed within a factor of two to four times—not very telling.

Another major consideration in CPU performance is the size and efficiency of the CPU cache, which can dramatically reduce the time lag (latency) of accessing memory that is in RAM. RAM memory is relatively slow to access compared to memory on the CPU, usually by a few orders of magnitude.

With all the variables, how can the performance of CPUs be evaluated? In fact the only reasonable way is through direct comparison, and an industry standard has grown up around this. The Standard Performance Evaluation Corporation (SPEC) is a consortium of companies that defines benchmarking guidelines for CPUs. Their website publishes the latest official performance data on the newest CPUs (see www.spec.org).

Modern CPUs are generally much faster than the main memory (RAM) they access (Figure 13.1). As a result every time a CPU has to access memory from RAM it typically needs to wait (stall) while the memory is being retrieved. This delay is referred to as "memory access latency," or memory latency for short. Because database servers are both instruction and data intensive, the cache architecture used by the CPU is very important to the performance of the database (Figure 13.2). A fast CPU with a relatively small cache will result in a database that performs much more poorly

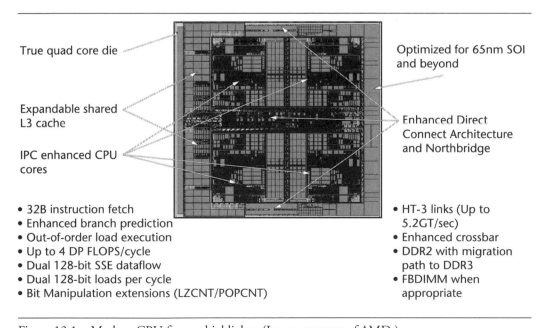

True quad core die

Optimized for 65nm SOI and beyond

Expandable shared L3 cache

Enhanced Direct Connect Architecture and Northbridge

IPC enhanced CPU cores

- 32B instruction fetch
- Enhanced branch prediction
- Out-of-order load execution
- Up to 4 DP FLOPS/cycle
- Dual 128-bit SSE dataflow
- Dual 128-bit loads per cycle
- Bit Manipulation extensions (LZCNT/POPCNT)

- HT-3 links (Up to 5.2GT/sec)
- Enhanced crossbar
- DDR2 with migration path to DDR3
- FBDIMM when appropriate

Figure 13.1   Modern CPU feature highlights. (Image courtesy of AMD.)

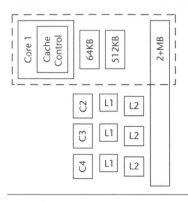

Figure 13.2   Modern CPU architecture. (Image courtesy of AMD.)

than a slower CPU with larger caches. Unfortunately, in a textbook authors are not always able to emphasize the major points easily through repetition. This point, regarding CPU cache sizes, is a major one. If space and reader patience permitted we would repeat this several times.

CPU caches are typically designed as a hierarchy of three tiers: level 1, level 2, and level 3. After the level 3 cache the next access is directly to RAM. Each tier is roughly 10 times faster to access than the next tier. Therefore, if accessing memory in the level 1 cache requires 1 unit of time, accessing the same data in the level 2 cache may take 10 units; level 3, 100 units; and RAM, 1,000 units. The caches closer to the CPU are faster but also smaller. One of the goals of database kernel vendors and the compilers who generate the object code for the database kernel is to try to optimize the instruction flow such that data and instruction access can occur with a high cache hit rate in the level 1 and level 2 caches. For CPUs that have a level 3 cache (not all do) it is usually a shared cache across multiple cores, while the level 1 and level 2 caches are usually dedicated to a single core.

Since the mid-1970s the performance of CPUs has continued to double roughly every 18 months, fueled by a phenomenon known as Moore's Law.[1] Moore's Law is a general observation noted by famed Intel scientist Gordon E. Moore, which noted the

[1] Gordon E. Moore cofounded Intel in 1968, serving initially as executive vice president. He became president and chief executive officer in 1975 and held that post until elected chairman and CEO in 1979. He was CEO until 1987 and named chairman emeritus in 1997.

In 1965 Moore predicted that the number of transistors the industry would be able to place on a computer chip would double every year. In 1975 he updated his prediction to once every two years. "Moore's Law" became one of the most well-known and predictable trends in the computing industry. Though the growth of transistor density will eventually drop off, the growth of computing power every two years may continue for decades to come because of other advancements.

trend that every 24 months the number of transistors that could be packed into a very large scale integration (VLSI) wafer per unit surface area was doubling due to improvements in lithographic and manufacturing techniques. Although Moore predicted a doubling every 24 months, the industry came to believe the rate was closer to 18 months, although Moore himself never said it.

The increased density resulted in shorter path length for electrons in the circuits, smaller design attributes, and better pipelining, all of which added to the improved performance of the CPU in a roughly linear way. However, in recent years several scientists have predicted the demise of Moore's Law as the VLSI attributes are approaching theoretical minimums that will prevent the exponential growth in transistor density to continue. Even so, a broader look at processing technology suggests that the performance trend actually predates VLSI, and is likely to continue into the future through other advances, such as improved pipelining, multicore CPUs, and alternative fabrication substrates like Gallium Arsenide and CMOS technology, and other emerging improvements (electro-optic, quantum, etc.). If the rate of performance growth remains roughly constant, one can expect a single $1,000 home computer by the year 2020 to have the processing power of the human mind. By the year 2060 a $1,000 home computer

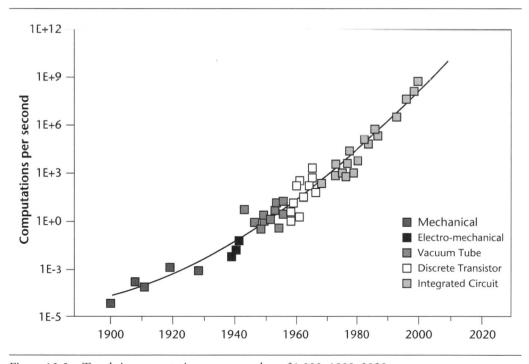

Figure 13.3   Trends in computations per second per $1,000, 1900–2020.

would include the processing power of all human minds on the planet. The consequence for database designers (and most scientific computing and processing intense applications) is that the processing power you purchase for your server at any moment in time will usually be supplanted in less than two years by technology that is approximately twice as fast. See Figure 13.3.

13.1.2 Amdahl's Law for System Speedup with Parallel Processing

In principle more processors should mean more processing capability, and therefore faster execution time. In practice several factors conspire—in logistics, physics, and economics—to prevent this from being possible. The most obvious is the simple observation that not all tasks are well suited to parallel processing. Three women cannot make a baby in three months. Owning three cars still does not make it possible to drive from Boston to San Jose in one-third of the time.

A simple expression of the maximum potential benefit from parallel processing was defined by Amdahl's Law.[2] Amdahl's Law considers the optimal potential processing gain assuming overhead processing is nil. To do this the model separates the tasks that can be performed in parallel from the tasks that need to be serialized. The speedup time on N processing, $S(N)$, is defined as the ratio of execution time on a single processor $T(1)$ to the execution time on N processors $T(N)$. Amdahl subdivides the time T into serial processing time Ts and parallel processing time Tp, and then expresses the optimal speedup as:

$$S(N) = \frac{T(1)}{T(N)} = \frac{Ts + Tp}{Ts + Tp / N}.$$

13.1

However, even tasks that are well suited to parallel processing often do not improve in performance with additional CPUs. The major limitation is generally called "overhead," and includes factors such as context switching, setup time (stack operators, thread or process initialization), bus contention, etc. When the overhead time is large compared to the processing time one can expect parallel processing to perform poorly and in some cases even cause performance to get worse. This overhead is often nonlinear, for example, the cost of bus contention, and context switching can increase in non-

---

[2] Gene Myron Amdahl is best known for his work in mainframe computers at IBM in the 1950s and 1960s. He founded Amdahl Corporation in 1970; manufactured "plug-compatible" mainframes, shipping its first machine in 1975. The 1975 the Amdahl 470 V6 was a less-expensive, more reliable, and faster computer than IBM's System 370/165. By 1979 Amdahl had more than 6,000 employees and had sold more than $1 billion U.S. in mainframe equipment. Gene left Amdahl in 1979 and went on to found and consult for numerous other technology firms.

linear ways as the system resource becomes saturated. If we model the overhead as *To(N)*, then the speedup becomes approximately:

$$S(N) = \frac{T(1)}{T(N)} = \frac{Ts + To(1) + Tp}{Ts + To(N) + Tp/N}.$$

13.2

13.1.3 Multicore CPUs

One of the major advances in CPU fabrication in the mid-2000s is the development of multicore CPUs. These CPUs are a single CPU in appearance and are purchased as such but internally have multiple CPUs within the chip. This allows parallel processing to occur within a single CPU fabrication and greatly reduces some of the processing overhead associated with parallel processing, such as cache coherence across cache lines (see section 13.3.2, where cache coherence and false sharing are discussed). The following is from Intel Corp., *Multicore Processing*, 2006:

> Have you ever waited impatiently for your PC to complete a compute-intensive task? Well those long waits are now a thing of the past. In April 2005, Intel ushered in a new era of processor architecture by releasing our first dual-core processor. Dual-core processors are the first step in the transition to multicore computing. Intel is already conducting research on architectures that could hold dozens or even hundreds of processors on a single die. So what exactly is multicore?
>
> Intel multicore architecture has a single Intel processor package that contains two or more processor "execution cores," or computational engines, and delivers—with appropriate software—fully parallel execution of multiple software threads. The operating system (OS) perceives each of its execution cores as a discrete processor, with all the associated execution resources. . . .
>
> We forecast that more than 85 percent of our server processors and more than 70 percent of our mobile and desktop Pentium family processor shipments will be multicore–based by the end of 2006.

13.2 Client Server Architectures

The term client server was introduced in the 1980s to describe the relationship between computers on a network. The term gained broad adoption in the 1990s and is widely used to refer to processing performed between a series of remote computers with a larger, more powerful central computer, usually through a message-based communication protocol, such as TCP/IP. The server provides services to one or more clients, such as access to database data.

A special case of client server processing occurs when the client runs on the same machine as the server. This is known as "local client" processing.

In general, the client server model is known as a two-tier architecture, where the client resides on the first tier, and the server is the second heavier tier. Two-tier models tend to scale well up to roughly 100 clients. Beyond that contention issues typically require expansion of the server to a shared-nothing architecture of some sort, or the introduction of a third tier.

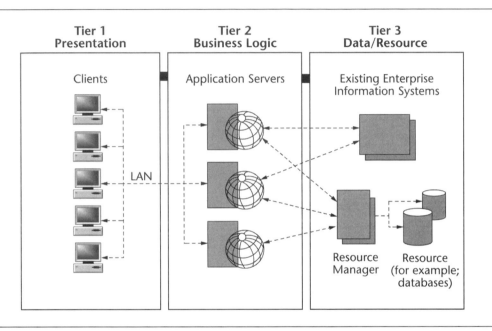

Figure 13.4   Three-tier database architecture. (Image courtesy of IBM.)

To resolve the limitations of two-tier architectures the industry began to adopt a number of three-tier architectures, as shown in Figure 13.4. These architectures separate the workload balancing and transaction flow from the database layer. The client tier and the database tier remain, but between them a new tier is inserted. The middle tier, often called the application server, includes the bulk of the application processing logic as well as transaction routing and queuing technology. The transaction handling usually also supports an asynchronous mode.

One of the key values of the application server concept is that it lends itself to load balancing, so that the middle tier may contain several physical servers that each assumes part of the load of the middle tier. The application server does not drive the graphical user interface (GUI) at the client, and similarly because the bulk of the business logic is executed at the application server, the client tier becomes predominantly a GUI with a small degree of business logic (the degree varies widely by application) and coupling with the application servers. One of the well-known architectures used for three-tier client server processing is CORBA, or Common Object Request Broker Architecture.

13.3 Symmetric Multiprocessors and NUMA

13.3.1 Symmetric Multiprocessors and NUMA

The mid-1990s saw the rise of servers with multiple CPUs, known as multiprocessors or symmetric multiprocessors (SMP). These servers included between two and eight CPUs. Typically only one of these CPUs can access memory at the same time. To avoid the serialization of memory access, the CPU caches become increasingly important for multiprocessors and increasingly sophisticated algorithms are used to avoid caches misses on the CPU caches as access to local RAM (memory not in the CPU cache), because the weak link in the performance characteristic becomes increasingly the access to RAM. The serialization of memory access on a symmetric multiprocessor increases this problem significantly. As a result, SMPs rarely have more than eight CPUs. As a result the next generation of multiprocessors was developed in the mid- to late 1990s called nonuniform memory access (NUMA).

NUMA processors divide CPUs into groups called "quads," each with their own local bus and RAM. Because each quad has its own local RAM and bus, the memory access and bus traffic are no longer necessarily balanced, hence the term "nonuniform memory access." NUMA architectures can scale to much larger numbers of CPUs, often 32 or 64 units. However, maintaining memory consistency (cache coherence) between the quads becomes complex, and NUMA systems remain an expensive option. While NUMA systems can scale to a larger number of CPUs than regular SMPs, they cannot scale as large as shared-nothing or Grid systems (discussed in Chapter 6). Even so, there is one tremendous advantage of SMP and NUMA system-based databases not offered by Grid and shared-nothing database architectures: lower administrative costs. While the capital expense to purchase a large NUMA system is significantly higher than purchasing multiple smaller single CPU systems and connecting them in a Grid or shared-nothing MPP, the result of Grid and MPP architectures is a network with multiple physical systems that each need to be administered and attended to. In contrast, a large NUMA system is usually more expensive to purchase, but the multiple CPUs it contains are housed within a single server—one box to manage.

Dmitri Besedin published a study of SMP and NUMA memory access bandwidth for a few different architectures and concurrency models on his website. His results from his August 9, 2005, study are repeated here in Table 13.1.

Table 13.1   SMP and NUMA Memory Access Bandwidths

Platform	Peak memory bandwidth, GB/s (dual channel DDR-400)			
	Single-threaded application	Several single-threaded applications	Multi-threaded application	NUMA-aware multi-threaded application
SMP	6.4	6.4	6.4	6.4
Asymmetric NUMA	4.2 (6.4)	6.4	6.4	6.4
Symmetric NUMA	4.2 (6.4)	8.4 (12.8)	6.4	6.4
Symmetric NUMA, Node Interleave	4.2	8.4	6.4	8.4

13.3.2 Cache Coherence and False Sharing

The terms "cache coherence" and "false sharing" refer to the consistency of memory in a server with multiple CPUs. Cache coherency is required to ensure that a data change in memory performed by one CPU is known by other CPUs, and to ensure that a CPU modifying a data value in memory cannot do so if the operand is currently being used by another CPU on the system. Within the CPU, data in the level 1 cache is stored in rows of data called *cachelines*. Each cacheline is either valid or invalid at a point in time. If the cacheline is invalid it will need to be reloaded from a higher-level cache or from RAM. Data is stored in cachelines based on its address in RAM. Therefore, the allocation of RAM data to specific cachelines is deterministic. Cachelines are typically 128–512 bytes wide.

False sharing is a related phenomenon where multiple CPUs modify totally different data points (i.e., at different addresses in real memory) that happen to lie on the same cache line in the level 1 cache of the processor CPU. Because the atomic unit of cache coherency in modern microprocessors is the cacheline, once the cacheline of one CPU is invalidated due to an update, the same cacheline on other CPUs on the server needs to be updated. The synchronization process is terribly inefficient. The process is called "false sharing" because in fact the memory addresses between an updater on one CPU and a reader on another CPU were not common—only the cacheline was common. As parallelism increases on a multiprocessor shared-memory server, the overhead of cache coherency and the frequency of false sharing also tend to increase. These phenomena limit the scalability of shared-memory systems under high concurrency situations.

13.4 Server Clusters

Another topology for multiprocessor exploitation is to use multiple servers in a cluster. This was described in Chapter 6 in some detail, though the terminology is somewhat vague until now as we mix systems language with database language. Let's try now to distinguish the concepts and clarify. Chapter 6 describes a database concept known as shared-nothing partitioning in which multiple servers (distinct physically or perhaps only logically) are used to each hold and process a fragment of the database. Shared-nothing partitioning refers to how data is divided and handled, and it is a database term. However, in the systems community (nondatabase world) the use of multiple servers working as a group is called "server clustering" or "machine clustering." In the systems world databases are just one possible way that machine clustering can be used. Machine clusters are often used for scale-out (additional performance) but also to provide failover, which will be discussed shortly in this chapter. Machine clustering does not typically include Grid computing since Grid generally assumes a distributed computing model where the servers are geographically spread out—possibly throughout a building or a city, and possibly even across international and continental borders.

13.5 A Little about Operating Systems

Operating systems (OS) are the software that connects the database processing code to the hardware. We assume a working knowledge of operating systems, so little will be described here about what operating systems are and how OS kernels are architected. However, the interesting question for database designers is generally which operating system to use for their database application. The answer to this question often depends as much on history as technology since a company with a large deployment of several applications on a particular operating system may be unwilling to introduce a radically different operating system for a new application. There are good reasons for the hesitancy: the people who administer the systems and databases on the operating system that is heavily used will have less skill on the proposed operating system, which will introduce short-term expense in skills development and administration costs for the new system. As well, there is risk, legitimate risk of the unknown. However, barring these uncertainties, there are reasons to choose one operating system over another.

The dominant operating systems used in the database market today include Windows, AIX, HP UNIX, Solaris, and LINUX. All of these operating systems have transitioned to support 64-bit processing in recent years. 64-bit addressability is hugely important for database systems, since 32-bit addressability limits the address space of a database to under 4 GB of real memory (usually closer to 2 GB). The larger addressability of 64-bit systems is massively important for data-intensive processing, allowing larger volumes of data to be cached in memory.

Of the operating systems in our list LINUX is the only open-source operating system. LINUX is a relative newcomer on the OS scene, but the rapid adoption of LINUX by the open-source community, as well as the large range of developers for LINUX from the open-source community, has allowed LINUX to mature rapidly. As of 2007, LINUX remains an emerging platform for enterprise-scale database processing, though it has seen rapid adoption for departmental level applications, and is gaining strength rapidly. Major products, such as MySQL, DB2, and Oracle, all support LINUX. AIX, Solaris, and HP are enterprise-scale operating systems. All of these have lost some market share to LINUX in recent years though HP appears to be the hardest hit.

All of the major database vendors support execution on Windows. However, SQL Server produced by Microsoft does not support any of the UNIX platforms. Therefore, if SQL Server is your database of choice, your choice of operating system is made for you—Windows is your only option.

Another factor in operating system choice is the "one-stop shop" factor.[3] Purchasing multiple components from a single vendor reduces the complexity of managing and servicing the complete database solution. For example, if you purchase the operating system and the database from the same company, any questions or problems relating to file caching have a clear target for who should be able to answer your questions. When the database and operating system are purchased from distinct vendors there are more vendors to work with and vendors can more easily evade responsibility for problems by pointing a finger at another component in the system. Purchasing an operating system and a database from the same vendor is currently possible with SQL Server on Windows, DB2 on AIX, and Teradata on NCR (strictly a warehousing solution).

13.6   Storage Systems

Throughout this book we have discussed the value of physical database design in reducing input/output (I/O) requirements for database systems. Intelligent and careful use of indexes, materialized views, data clustering, and range partitioning can all help reduce the I/O burden. However, despite the very best application of physical database design features, unless all the database data can be cached simultaneously in main memory, I/O will be required. Most databases used for online transaction processing (OLTP) and decision support systems (DSS) the I/O requirements remain very significant. It is common for databases larger than 500 GB pre-load data to be I/O bound[4] when they go into operation. This means that although the user has paid for significant CPU capacity they aren't able to make use of it, because the CPU is waiting for I/O. Database vendors

---

[3] Or occasionally known as the "one throat to strangle" factor. Buying multiple components from a single vendor reduces the number of vendors to deal with when there are questions or defects.

[4] Author's experience.

are now trying to help alleviate this problem by selling systems with a pre-configured balance between storage bandwidth and CPU capacity. These pre-configured systems are often called a data warehouse appliance. An example of this is the IBM Balanced Configuration Unit (BCU). Even so, minimizing the amount of I/O a database must perform to execute a workload remains a vital strategy. Ken Rudin said much the same thing in 1998 when he published an article in *DM Review Magazine*:

> Denormalization and advanced indexing techniques are highly effective for improving the performance of your data warehouse and other applications. But, regardless of how effectively you use these techniques, you will still need to frequently execute large and complex queries. To get good query response times, you need (among other things) high performance and scalability out of your I/O subsystem. By using scalable and parallel I/O techniques, you can push your system components (disks, controllers, CPUs, and memory) to the limits of their capacity, thereby fully utilizing your hardware's capabilities.

13.6.1 Disks, Spindles, and Striping

Disks are slow. Very slow. At least when compared to access by the CPU to local memory or the CPU cache. The most standard technique to improve the performance of disk access is to exploit multiple disks (or multiple spindles) in parallel, by spreading data across these disks so that fragments of the database can be accessed in parallel. This spreading of the data across devices is called "data striping." Data striping is generally performed in a round-robin algorithm, though there are variants. Using a round-robin algorithm, the first chunk of data goes to the first storage device, the second chunk to the second device, etc., and once every device has received a chunk of data, the *N*+1th chunk is stored on the first device, and the process continues until all the data has been allocated to disk. The chunks are usually a constant size, anywhere from 4B K to 1 MB, though sizes ranging from 32 KB to 256 KB are the most typical. There are several ways that striping is implemented: hardware striping, operating system striping (file system), and database striping.

Hardware striping is implemented by disk arrays that are purchased as a unit. Inside the storage device a set of disks act as a unit and the device itself manages the allocation and striping of data across the disks, independent of the operating system or the database. As a result a single file stored on the disk array will be automatically striped across multiple devices. This strategy wins for ease of use, but lacks control (more difficult for the administrator to intervene). Also, disk arrays are expensive, though they have become massively popular in recent years, especially for enterprise database systems where reliability is a key consideration because they are well suited to RAID. Striping can be performed at the operating system level, and has been done there for decades. In this strategy multiple storage devices (disks) are grouped together into "volumes." The operating system will create file systems on these volumes and data stored in the file system will automatically be striped across the devices. This strategy is fine, but requires a skilled system administrator to set up the volume groups. Finally, the database itself can perform data striping across storage devices by storing chunks of each table, index, and materialized view across the devices that are available to the database. However, because database striping is implemented above the file system, the allocation of chunks to each device generally requires at least as many files as storage devices per logical file.

In other words, consider a system with 16 disks: while a database file can be stored on these disks using disk array or volume groups as a single-file system file, a database would create 16 files in order to implement data striping at the database layer. This can lead to more than an order of magnitude increase in the number of file system handles required to be opened and managed while the database is executing. Since the database management system takes care of handling all these fragments and the file handles it doesn't matter as much to the users or the administrators, but it can lead to restrictions when the number of these file handles approaches systemwide limits, which can happen with complex databases.

Mixed striping strategies can lead to serious skew when the striping sets line up in the worst possible combination resulting in several chunks of data being mapped to the same devices, and other devices being relatively unused. This is a somewhat unlikely turn of events but has been known to happen in real systems. As disk arrays become more popular, people will depend increasingly less on database striping, reducing the chances of conflicting concurrent striping algorithms.

13.6.2 Storage Area Networks and Network Attached Storage

Two networking strategies for attaching storage via networked connections are radically changing (or have changed) the way we traditionally think about storage for database servers. In the past (pre-2000) storage devices were generally dedicated to the database server and directly attached via a device controller to the server. This traditional form of storage is known as DAS or direct access storage. In the earlier 2000s in order to consolidate storage devices and use storage space more efficiently, vendors introduced the concept of storage devices that were attached to servers via a network and perhaps shared by several servers at once. This consolidation greatly reduced the administrative burden for a large company that may have dozens or hundreds of servers. Using the DAS strategy it became virtually impossible to efficiently predict how much storage each server would require. The result was that some servers typically got an over allocation of storage while other servers were starved for storage space. Networked storage strategies help to solve this problem by allowing many servers to share a pool or storage. The two primary technologies in vogue are networked attached storage (NAS) and storage area networks (SAN). Increasingly, companies are using these strategies in combination to achieve even greater efficiencies and benefits than either one alone could provide.

SAN and NAS are similar in many ways and both often attach RAID disk arrays to servers over a network. The most important difference between them is the protocols. Some history: NAS evolved from the notion of file servers, which provided a service for file access and file management on a network. NetWare and Microsoft had file server products that were dominant in the market. Over time, vendors realized that a specialized server with a storage-specific operating system could be sold that was dedicated to the problems of file management on a network. This dedicated file management system was called "storage appliance," which grew into the NAS market, earning over seven billion dollars per year. While NAS focused on file management, SAN was focused much more on access patterns and the network traffic that data access generates. SAN separates the storage drives from the server and connects them via a Fibre Channel connection, supporting a many-to-many connection topology. Recently SANs have evolved to include other transport technologies including Gigabit Ethernet and SCSI over IP. Gartner predicted that sales of SAN and NAS technology by 2007 would be 10.3 billion U.S.$ and 2.8 billion U.S.$, respectively.

Contrasting the physical differences can be useful in understanding the differences (Table 13.2).

The next generation of technology for networked storage is driving the merging of SAN and NAS technologies, including convergence ideas such as file systems for SAN, Ethernet network support for SAN, NAS Gateways that connect distinct SANs via an Ethernet gateway, and NAS gateways that improve the ability to add capacity to NAS systems. Products exist for all of these today, though adoption is evolving.

13.7   Making Storage Both Reliable and Fast Using RAID

13.7.1 History of RAID

The development of high-performance reliable computing has been the philosopher's stone of computing systems since the development of the first computers. The first production-ready electronic computer, ENIAC, used vacuum tubes for electronic switching and had several failures per day. Most of us have experienced the frustration of having our computer fail (usually just before giving a presentation, or halfway through writing an important document!). As long as computer systems have moving parts they will develop failures. Even machines without moving parts are subject to breakage. Even so, reducing the likelihood of an outage from a device failure remains a high priority for the industry and the introduction of RAID storage devices represented a massive leap forward in the reliability of storage systems. RAID stands for reliable array of inexpensive disks, though the "inexpensive" adjective is highly debatable. RAID devices are designed to offer performance and reliability through a combination of parallelism striping, redundancy, and parity.

Table 13.2   SAN and NAS Differences

Attribute	SAN	NAS
Physical connection	Fiber Channel, Gigabit Ethernet, SCSI over IP	TCPIP networks. Including Ethernet, FDDI, ATM
Protocols	Encapsulated SCSI	TCPIP, NFS, CIFS, HTTP
Limitations on the connected servers	Fiber Channel currently has a limit of 10 km distance	Any machine connected to the LAN
Addressing	Data is addressed by disk block ID	Data is addressed by file name and byte offset
Sharing and concurrency	File sharing depends on the OS capabilities	Generally supports file sharing
BACKUP access	Data is backed up by block, generally less efficient than file level BACKUP	Data is backed up by file
BACKUP intrusion	BACKUP can be performed on a distinct network from the LAN used by the accessing data servers, making the BACKUP process non-intrusive in terms of network overhead	BACKUP typically performed on the same network used by the attached data servers, so network bandwidth must be shared
Performance	Significantly better	Significantly worse
Ease of administration	Worse	Better (no need for switches or network adaptor devices)
Capacity	Higher	Lower
Cost	Higher	Lower

The theoretical beginnings of RAID began at IBM in the late 1970s, when Normal Ouchi filed a patent for the "system for recovering data stored in failed memory unit." The basic concepts of Ouchi's patent describe the most important ideas of RAID 5. RAID was later formalized for storage systems in the 1988 SIGMOD paper by Patterson et al. [1988]. Patterson et al.'s paper was considered the seminal paper introducing the RAID concept, and the disk array industry expanded rapidly after its publication. Patterson, a professor of computer engineering at Berkley, is generally regarded as one of the industry's leading authorities on systems architecture, in part for his work on RAID, as well as his work on memory architecture and multiprocessor systems.

The original concept for RAID was to replace expensive high-performance devices with arrays of lower cost disks, and achieve similar performance by use of parallelism. However, since parallelism can be applied to both cheap and expensive disks, 10 expensive high-performance disks in parallel will still out perform 10 cheap ones. So the "inexpensive" part of RAID is somewhat historical, and RAID is widely used for disk arrays of all speeds, including high adoption for high-performance enterprise arrays.

The standard RAID levels now include RAID 0, RAID 1, RAID 2, RAID 3, RAID 4, RAID 5, RAID 6, RAID 0+1, RAID 10, RAID 10+0, and RAID 5+0. We will describe these briefly and discuss a few other proprietary RAID levels while indicating which are generally adopted for database use.

13.7.2 RAID 0

RAID 0 refers to simple striping across a set of disks. The collection of disks is known as the "stripe set," and data is simply written to the disks in a round-robin fashion. The first block is stored on the first disk, the second block on the second disk, etc. As shown in Figure 13.5 the stripe set in this example is 2. RAID 0 improves efficiency of read access because it allows multiple disks to operate in parallel. However, it does little to improve reliability. Also, if the disks are different sizes, the capacity of the array is going to be limited to the smallest disk in the array. In fact, RAID 0 arrays are actually less reliable than single-disk storage systems, because each disk in the array adds to the likelihood that a disk error will occur. For example, assume the mean time to failure (MTTF) for a single disk is once per year, and the MMTF for each disk in a storage array is once every two years. A storage array with eight disks will have an MTTF of four times per year, significantly worse than the single disk solution.

Note that block striping was not introduced by RAID 0. It's an old concept, implemented through software by many file systems before the formalization of RAID 0. Even so, the term RAID 0 is generally reserved for implementations with storage arrays (in particular storage arrays that can be sold and configured with multiple RAID strategies).

13.7.3 RAID 1

RAID 1 arrays introduce the notion of mirroring to improve reliability. Each block that is stored on disk is stored exactly twice, so that every disk in the system has a mirror image. As a result, if a disk fails, its mirror is available to continue processing (Figure 13.6). Notice that RAID 1 requires twice the storage space for a single data set.

A variation of RAID 1 allows for a disk array of any width where adjacent disks are used for mirroring. This method is known as RAID 1E, shown below in Figure 13.7.

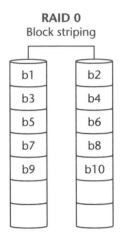

Figure 13.5   Simple RAID 0 striping.

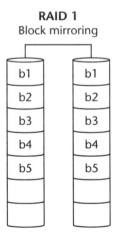

Figure 13.6   RAID 1.

13.7.4 RAID 2 and RAID 3

In RAID 0 and RAID 1 we discussed storing blocks of data. In contrast, RAID 2 introduced the idea of storing data by bits, and streaming the bits in parallel into a demultiplexer that would combine the streams (Figure 13.8). This requires the disks to operate in perfect synchronization. As a result this strategy is very good for single stream access, but bad for multi-user access where users may be interested in different parts of the data. Hamming codes are typically used in RAID 2 to do error correction. A Hamming

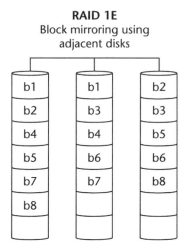

Figure 13.7   RAID 1E.

code is an error correction code (ECC). The ECC is recalculated each time data is modified. The ECC is usually stored in dedicated disks within the array. At read time the ECCs are read and matched to enforce that no data corruption has occurred during the read-write processing. In fact, because of the poor concurrency qualities, RAID 2 is virtually not used in practice.

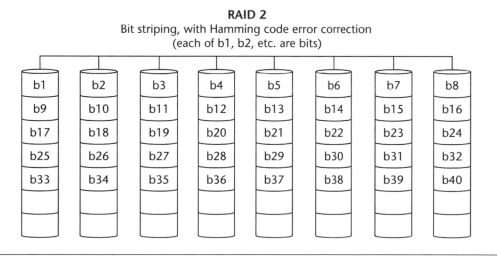

Figure 13.8   RAID 2.

RAID 3 is yet another variation that uses a finer granularity of data I/O than other RAID models, this time at the byte level. Bytes are written to disks in parallel (just like with RAID 2 it was bits written in parallel), and in order to do reasonable I/O on data (blocks) the disks need to be kept perfectly synchronized. Like RAID 2, this leads to very poor concurrency for multi-user access on the storage array since all disks within the array need to service a single request at the same time (working together). A disk is usually dedicated from within the array to serve as a parity disk.

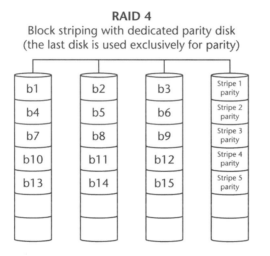

Figure 13.9   RAID 4.

13.7.5 RAID 4

RAID 4 stripes blocks of data across the storage array, and also introduces the use of a dedicated disk to store parity bits (Figure 13.9). This is similar in concept to RAID 3 except that the I/O to the disks is performed at the block level, not at the byte level. This is far more conducive to multi-user access.

13.7.6 RAID 5 and RAID 6

RAID 5 (Figure 13.10) is a variation of RAID 4 where the parity blocks are distributed across disks, instead of being stored on a dedicated parity disk. Most RAID 5 arrays include hardware support for the parity calculations. In general the combination of striping (parallelism) and parity bits makes RAID 5 one of the most popular RAID schemes for database systems.

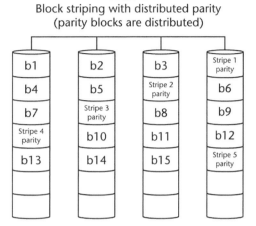

Figure 13.10   RAID 5.

RAID 6 (Figure 13.11) extends the ideas of RAID 5 by adding a second parity block within each data stripe on the storage array. The introduction of a second parity block for each stripe set allows RAID 6 to be particularly resilient to disk failure, being able to sustain two disk failures within the array and still operate normally. RAID 6 is not particularly efficient with a small number of disks because too high a percentage of the blocks are used for parity, increasing cost and decreasing performance. However, for wide arrays the overhead becomes more reasonable, and the benefits can become significant enough to make this a winning strategy. This is particularly important because as the stripe set becomes wider, the MTTF decreases, as discussed above.

13.7.7 RAID 1+0

RAID level can be used in combination and the main combinations are the combination of RAID 0 (striping) with either RAID 1 or RAID 5. Formally, the combination of RAID 1 and RAID 0 is denoted RAID 1+0, though the short form of RAID 10 has become popular. In RAID 10 data is mirrored and striped as shown in Figure 13.12.

13.7.8 RAID 0+1

A variation of RAID 10 is RAID 0+1, where data is striped and the striping sets are mirrored as shown in Figure 13.13.

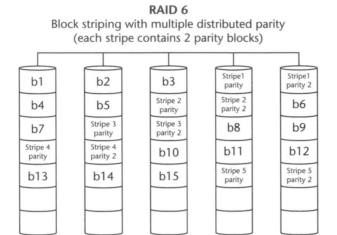

Figure 13.11   RAID 6.

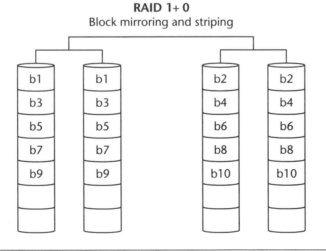

Figure 13.12   RAID 10.

13.7.9 RAID 10+0 and RAID 5+0

Common variations of RAID 10 and RAID 5 add additional striping, producing the configurations shown below in Figures 13.14 and 13.15, respectively, called RAID 10+0 and RAID 5+0 or RAID 100 and RAID 50 for short.

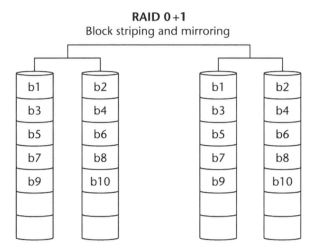

Figure 13.13   RAID 0+1.

The striping of RAID arrays together like this is sometimes referred to as "plaid RAID." This striping of RAID arrays can provide improved random access to data due to the increase in disks involved that can operate on data in parallel.

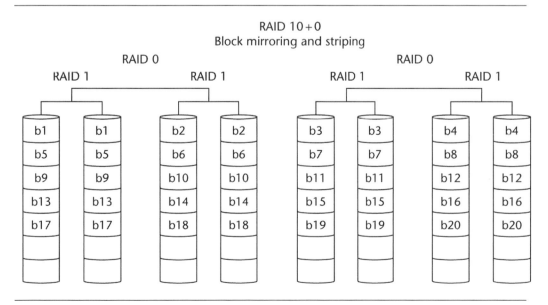

Figure 13.14   RAID 10+0.

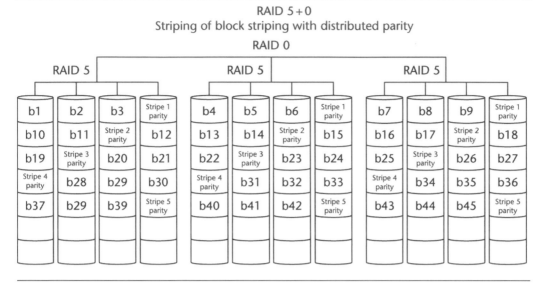

Figure 13.15   RAID 5+0.

13.7.10 Which RAID Is Right for Your Database Requirements?

Deciding which RAID strategy to use remains something of an art. However, the industry does appear to be converging around specific usage. RAID 5 is the dominant strategy for data stored within the database itself. It provides a reasonable balance between striping redundancy and recoverability and cost. RAID 10 is used as well, somewhat less commonly most likely because roughly half the disk is used for parity, making this a robust but expensive alternative.

However, in addition to the actual active data of the database, such as the data, the indexes, the materialized views, etc., the database designer needs to plan for the storage needs of the recovery logs (transaction logs). The transaction logs are needed to recover the database in the event of data corruption of disk failure on the devices storing the active database data. The industry typically uses RAID 5, RAID 10, or RAID 1E for transaction log storage.

13.8   Balancing Resources in a Database Server

Perhaps one of the least discussed but most practical problems of database server design is the relative proportion of resources required within the server: relative amount of disk storage, number of spindles, number and speed of the CPUs, RAM, etc. As a general rule of course, more is better for most resources, but cost climbs rapidly for some resources. And while CPUs are relatively inexpensive, large NUMA systems with complex bus architectures to efficiently support clusters of CPUs are dramatically more expensive than the simple sum of the cost of the CPUs they include might suggest. Several factors play into this problem:

1. The relative speed of disk access versus RAM.
2. The relative cost of CPU versus disk.
3. The relative cost of RAM versus disk.
4. The topology choice (e.g., shared nothing or shared everything).
5. The database access skew (how much of your data is really active).

There are no absolute rules that define what is right. However, there are some "best practices." What follows are some guidelines, which may not hold true in future generations of components.

Very generally, best CPU and I/O balancing appears to occur when CPU-to-data (GB) ratios are around 1:100, RAM-to-disk ratios are around 1:25, and CPU-to-disk ratios are 1:6. These are very approximate ratios that can vary quite widely based on component speeds. Because CPU speeds, memory speed, and disk capacity change significantly every year, these ratios can vary easily by a factor of 2 or 3. Even so, these ratios should serve as a somewhat useful guideline for the approximate range of relative capacity of components to compile when constructing a database server. These ratios have held their ground across many application types, including business intelligence systems (OLAP, DSS) and transaction processing systems (OLTP). See Table 13.3.

Table 13.3   Typical Resource Ratios

Resource ratio	Typical ratio
GB active disk per CPU	100:1 (+/− 200%)
RAM to active disk	1:25 (+/− 200%)
CPU per disk	1:6 (+/− 400%)

These ratios are likely reasonable for the next few years. Note that these ratios are based on the volume of active data. Many databases include a considerable amount of inactive data (rarely accessed). When considering the storage requirements for your server, you should calculate the total storage requirements for the system, and then determine what fraction of the data is active, and use only the active proportion in the ratio calculation.

13.9 Strategies for Availability and Recovery

Before discussing the strategies for data recovery and availability it's worth pausing to consider the degree to which this is at all needed. There are essentially two major scenarios. The first scenario concerns itself with the case that a database server fails for any reason including hardware fault or software crash, and while that server is being repaired we require a strategy that allows processing to continue. The second scenario is concerned with possible geographic disaster, where entire neighborhoods or cities can experience a serious disaster that would make the database unusable either because it has been destroyed or because connectivity to the region has been disruptive (a working database that nobody can connect to is less than useful). This would include major disasters such as New York City during the September 11 attacks, or the devastation caused by hurricane Katrina[5] that caused massive destruction.

The major strategies for database availability fall into six categories:

1. Application controlled multicast.
2. Replication.
3. Transaction log in-memory shipping.
4. Shared disk.
5. Cluster failover.
6. Flash copy or backup transfer.

With application-controlled standby server, the application applies all change in the database to two or more database servers. We've called this "application-controlled multicast" for want of a better term. As a result at any point in time there is more than one database that has all the required data. Should one database server fail, the remaining servers are available with all of the up-to-date data. The benefit of this strategy is that it is entirely within the control of the application designer, and no dependency is made on recovery features of the database server. However, there are several issues with this strategy. For example:

---

[5] The territory defined as a disaster zone by the United States government following Katrina covers an area of land approximately the size of the United Kingdom. Katrina caused mass destruction over much of the north-central Gulf Coast of the United States. Worst hit were New Orleans, Louisiana, and coastal Mississippi.

- Concurrency control becomes extremely difficult unless all clients update the servers in the same sequence. The asynchronous interleaving of transaction makes this difficult if not impossible to control, making this strategy impossible for several classes of applications.

- N times the server capacity is required to provide $N - 1$ redundancy, which is costly.

- The database application must perform N times the processing for each transaction or read request to the database. Thus, application performance is significantly impacted. If the bulk of the application performance is spent in database processing time, then a two-way solution would require 200% execution time in the application.

- When one of the replicas fails, a complex process is required to bring it back up to date with the remaining servers when it comes back online.

- A tremendous burden is placed on the application designer to manage this process, rather than placing the burden on the database software or at least specialized database administrators (DBAs).

The second strategy is to exploit data replication. All of the major database products support data replication allowing data to be moved from one system to another. Data replication can be configured to updates (inserts, updates, deletes) to the replicated database based on various configurable policies. These policies generally support a streaming and a batch model for applying the changes. The batch processing is considerably more efficient, but may require a time delay (second through hours) while a sufficient volume of data change occurs to motivate a batch apply process. Replication processing generally occurs asynchronously through a "capture and apply" process. The transaction log entries are read asynchronously (capture) and then these captured logs are flowed to the target system where they are replayed. This is a widely used strategy. Because the replication capture and apply processing are asynchronous the possibility of some data loss does exist with this method.

The third strategy to create standby database servers exploits memory-to-memory log shipping. This processing is similar in some ways to replication, which also applies to log changes, but there are major differences:

- The log shipping is memory to memory not disk to memory, and is therefore far more efficient.

- Unlike the replication-based scenario where control of the standby server is really unrelated to the replication process, in these memory-to-memory scenarios the technology is designed specifically for maintaining standby servers, and therefore in addition to moving data, these features also typically handle rerouting of the application connection to the standby if needed. Thus, if the database server fails, the application is automatically reconnected to the standby server.

- Again, unlike the replication-based scenario, setup and configuration of the standby system are partially automated usually through the help of software wizards.

The memory-to-memory log shipping strategy is used in Oracle Data Guard, Informix HDR, and DB2 HADR. These products can offer a range of control for the degree to which data is kept synchronous on the standby servers. For example, DB2 offers synchronous, near-synchronous, and asynchronous modes. This allows a common infrastructure to be used for both local failover and geographic failover, where a local standby server is kept synchronized through synchronous replication, while a remote server (which incurs latency due to its distance) can be updated asynchronously.

Depending on the product, the replicated database may or may not be available for query processing or write operations (insert, update, delete). When the standby server is available to share in the data processing, the overall solution is called "active-active" since both servers contribute processing power to transaction query processing. Conversely, when the standby database server is unavailable for processing unless the primary database has failed, the system is called "active-passive" processing.

All of the three strategies we have discussed so far are useful both for keeping data available when a local server has failed and for geographically remote failover in the case of site disaster. The site disaster is handled by keeping the standby server in a geographically remote location (perhaps another city). The geographic separation of the servers can incur time delay as well as some administrative burden since the DBA and system administrator can't be in the same location as both servers. For most administration functions, being in the same room or same city as the database server is not important, though there are obvious exceptions (e.g., inserting a CD or replacing a hardware component).

The fourth availability technology is "shared disk." The most popular of these are Oracle RAC and DB2 for zOS's Parallel Sysplex solution. With these strategies several computers share the same set of data on disk, but considerable handshaking is required to ensure consistency of the data that may be updated by any one of the servers. The major focus in shared-disk solutions is to ensure that the failure of any node in the system results in very little downtime and data loss for the entire system (as perceived by the connected applications). However, what shared-disk solutions do not focus on is the disk availability, which is assumed to be highly available through the use of RAID arrays, and their implied redundancy.

Oracle RAC (Figure 13.16) has become quite popular in recent years because of its ease of use and it is the only shared-disk solution in the open platform space (UNIX/ Windows). Database storage pages can be accessed by more than one server at a time using a technique known as "cache cohesion," which maintains integrity of data on

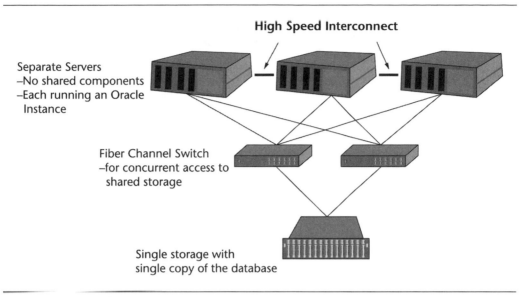

High Speed Interconnect

Separate Servers
–No shared components
–Each running an Oracle
  Instance

Fiber Channel Switch
–for concurrent access to
  shared storage

Single storage with
single copy of the database

Figure 13.16   Oracle RAC.

pages that are accessed by multiple servers. RAC has become the dominant availability solution for collocated servers today, largely because of its ease of use. However, as we will see, RAC is not without issues, and there are pros and cons to the major offerings in the market today. Oracle RAC does not support geographic failover.

RAC's shared-disk active-active solution has many benefits. It is easy to use. All servers in the configuration can be used for active work. However, there are some little discussed issues that are important to know about RAC related to the possibility of incorrect answer sets and log storage requirements.

Oracle RAC data consistency: Every Oracle data page has a system change number (SCN) that indicates the "time" the page was changed. The SCN is an ever-increasing number so that Oracle knows the order of the updates. Oracle uses this virtual "timestamp" to determine what data to return to a query. By default the current SCN is not broadcast to all other nodes for 7 seconds. This means a query can return the wrong results by default. Oracle can be configured to force the right results to be returned, though this incurs a significant performance penalty.

Oracle RAC has been used in industry-standard benchmarks, such as TPCC, to demonstrate its efficiency for use in OLTP workloads. The results of these benchmarks have shown that RAC appears to require an order of magnitude for more log storage than the non-RAC version of Oracle.

- Oracle 10g = 2,460GB of log per million tpmC
- Oracle 10g RAC = 20,676GB of log per million tpmC

Table 13.4   Pros and Cons for Various High-availability Strategies

Functionality	Transaction log in-memory shipping	Replication	Shared disk	Application controlled multi-cast	Cluster failover	Flash copy or backup transfer
Supports zero loss capability if a database server fails	✓		✓	✓		
Supports geographic failover (across sites or cities)	✓	✓		✓		✓
Active-active support	✓*	✓*	✓	✓	✓	
Replicate a subset of data		✓		✓		
Typically supports greater than 2 servers/nodes		✓	✓	✓		
Typically supports automatic client rerouting	✓		✓			
Monitoring	✓	✓	✓			
Simple reintroduction of previously failed server	✓	✓	✓		✓	
Supports software upgrades on the fly	✓	✓	✓			✓
Does not require rollforward (transaction replay) to bring failover server up to date	✓		✓	✓		
Rapid failover, including log replay etc.	✓		✓	✓		✓
Is not subject to large data loss (more than a few seconds worth)	✓		✓	✓		
Linear or less increase in log storage with number of nodes	✓	✓		✓	✓	✓

*Depending on the vendor. Active-active support is possible with this architecture though not all vendors support it

Table 13.5   Objectives and Solutions for High-availability Strategies

Objective	Best solution(s)
Zero data loss, fast failover	Transaction log in-memory shipping, shared disk
Zero data loss, geographic failover	Transaction log in-memory shipping
Fast failover, some data loss acceptable	Replication, Flash copy or backup transfer
Simplicity	Transaction log in-memory shipping, shared disk
Cost	Cluster failover
Control	Application controlled multi-cast
Active-active processing to maximize the use of all available servers during regular processing	Shared disk

Which option to use? The selected solution should depend in part on your objective. The answer will vary depending on your needs for cost, zero data loss, recovery speed, etc. Also, if you have already selected your database server you may be locked into a subset of alternatives since not all databases products support all recovery schemes.

13.10 Main Memory and Database Tuning

13.10.1 Memory Tuning by Mere Mortals

There are several major memory uses within a relational database system. The challenge for the database designer is that these memory areas are often configurable (designable) but have very little to do with each other. Some are used to reduce system I/O, while others are used to reduce CPU consumption or improve network usage efficiency. This makes tuning these heaps very difficult. The relative need for memory by each of these areas is critical to understand because the database server will have a fixed amount of real memory (RAM) to be shared by all of them. The server may be used for multiple databases, and possibly other middleware and applications, depending on your environment. This makes it impossible to simply give each memory heap as much memory as it would need to optimize its own resource goals. As a result, memory tuning is really defined as an art of tradeoffs. Wise tradeoffs lead to the best performance; poor tradeoffs give memory where it is not especially needed and starve the high-pressure areas, resulting in poor performance. The performance impact of good versus poor memory design can lead to performance differences measuring an order of magnitude or more. First let's discuss what the major memory areas are in modern database systems, and then examine some of the manual and automated methods for their tuning.

The following are generic terms for the main memory areas used by most modern database systems. Individual products may use different terminology for the same things. Also note that not all database systems include all of these heaps. In some cases the heaps exist internally within the database but are not exposed for external tuning.

Hand-tuning memory heaps is increasingly becoming a thing of the past simply because it really is too hard for most people to do well. However, for the time being many database systems are hand tuned for memory usage. Here are some high-level ideas on how to approach these for a few of the major memory heaps that are common.

Buffer pools (data cache). In general the buffer pool(s) are the primary data cache for the database. It's usually the heap that requires the most memory, and is second most important to performance (not size) only to the locking structures. Contention on the locks leading to escalations causes more serious performance issues than increased I/O, which is why we call the the buffer pools the second most important not the first. Fortunately the locking structures don't usually require a high percentage of the system memory. Most database systems dedicate the majority of the available memory to the buffer pools. However, there is no value at all in making the buffer pools larger than the data they can hold. For example, there is no value in making a buffer pool larger than 1 GB if the entire database, including indexes, views, and temporary tables will never exceed 1 GB. The key metrics to watch when tuning the buffer pool are the logical page reads in the database and the page hit rate. For extremely random access, increasing the buffer pool size may not significantly improve hit rates. So more memory in the buffer pools doesn't always help, but in general it does. In most cases memory for buffer pools is more than 80% of available memory on OLTP systems and more than 65% of memory on decision support systems.

Compiled query cache. This area is not tunable on all database products. It's a cache of recently executed SQL statements. If the compiled statement is cached, then the next time it's needed the compile time is saved. The savings are predominantly CPU, but there are some I/O savings as well as access to system catalogs that would normally occur during compilation. To tune this area, give some thought to how many unique statements your database receives per week, and the average size of each, and multiply by three for database control overhead that also needs to be in the cache (at a minimum the database will store the SQL text and the query execution plans). However, since the savings are predominantly CPU, also consider whether your database is under CPU constraint. On an I/O bound system the memory may be better used in the buffer pools. This heap usually represents less than 10% of total database memory, but on systems with large varied workloads there can be very distinct exceptions.

Sort memory. Sort memory is very challenging to tune. As sorts get large, if they fail to fit into memory, they will spill to disk, and the disk is used as extended virtual memory. This is usually implemented through temporary tables. Some sorts are so large that avoiding the spill to disk is impossible. Other sorts are so small that the size of sort memory is really irrelevant. The major metrics to watch for are the rate of sort spills, and the size of the spills. If sorts are spilling and the spill size is small enough that the spill could be avoided by simply increasing the size of sort memory, then increasing the sort memory is a good idea. The time spent in I/O is costly, and avoiding sort spills is usually more important than savings in I/O achieved through reduced page misses in the buffer pool. "Usually" is a loose terms in this case, and this is another area where automated tuning is really needed to do a good job. In most cases memory for hash joins is less than 5% of available memory on OLTP systems and less than 30% of memory on decision support systems.

Hash join memory. Hash joins are a remarkably efficient method for joining tables, producing the hashing structures to fit in memory. When they don't the result is an iterative spilling scheme known as "hash loops." The negative performance consequences of hash loops are far more severe than spilled sorts. The metrics to watch are the number and size of hash loops in the system. They are more important than spilled sorts, and therefore usually more important than buffer pools. However, "usually" is a very strict term. In most cases memory for hash joins is less than 5% of available memory on OLTP systems and less than 15% of memory on decision support systems.

Communications buffers. Memory for communications, if constrained, injects a huge latency into the system. As a general rule you'll want to feed this heap enough memory so that none of the executing transactions or queries are stalled waiting for a communication buffer to be available. Fortunately this memory is usually self-tuned. For the databases where this matters the vendors provide monitoring data you can view to determine how much time is being spent waiting for this memory, and if the number is high the heap should be increased. This is not usually a large percentage of the system memory.

Lock memory. When lock memory is constrained the result can be catastrophic, resulting in lock escalation and lock wait. Lock escalation means that due to the inability to obtain further row locks, the database will start locking data at a much more coarse level of granularity, such as locking ages or perhaps the entire table. When locks escalate the impact on system concurrency is disastrous. In many databases this memory is self-tuned, but if you need/want to tune it by hand the main metrics to watch are the number and frequency of lock escalations and the amount of time transactions and queries are spending waiting for locks (lock waits). If there is any significant degree of lock wait occurring, you will usually need to increase the allocation of memory to the lock structures. In most cases memory for locking structures is less than 7% of available system memory, though to protect against peak requirements, this allocation can temporarily need to be as high as 20% or more.

13.10.2 Automated Memory Tuning

This feature addresses the following main obstacles to end-user performance tuning:

1. *Inadequate knowledge of the product's memory use.* The documentation for a database product as sophisticated as DB2 V9.1 can seem overwhelming to an inexperienced DBA. In fact, even database product developers and technical leaders are frequently at a loss about how to allocate database memory, apart from the traditional trial-and-error approach. With this new functionality in DB2 V9.1, the DBA will be relieved of the need to invest time in understanding how the database uses memory before tuning can begin.

2. *Uncertain memory requirements for a given workload.* In some cases, even experienced DBAs can find it difficult to tune a database's memory because the workload characteristics are unknown. With the introduction of this new feature, the system will now be able to continuously monitor database memory usage and tune when necessary to optimize performance based on the workload characteristics. As a result, the user will require no knowledge of the workload for the memory to be tuned well.

3. *Changing workload behavior.* For many industrial workloads, no single memory configuration can provide optimal performance because, at different points in time, the workload can exhibit dramatically different memory demands. If STMM is running and the workload's memory demands shift, the system will recognize the changing needs for memory and adapt the memory allocation accordingly. As a result, the user will rarely (if ever) need to manually change the affected memory configuration parameters to enhance performance.

4. *Performance tuning is time consuming.* Tuning a database's memory to achieve high levels of performance is extremely costly and can take days or weeks of experimentation. STMM solves this problem by iterating toward the optimal memory distribution as the workload runs. As a result, the user will no longer be required to collect and analyze monitor output from workload runs. This should save a great deal of time and effort on the part of the DBA while at the same time achieving performance levels similar to that of an expertly tuned system. The net effect is a reduction in the product's total cost of ownership.

To further motivate the problem, we first discuss memory tuning of a relational database management system (RDBMS) that does not have automatic memory tuning functionality.

The academic investigation of the database memory tuning problem has produced many interesting papers. The papers, however, suffer from two problems that prevent their implementation in a commercial database product.

The first problem with many of these papers is that their approaches are not practical enough to be implemented in industrial database products. For example, in the research focused on buffer pool tuning, many of the approaches require the user to set response-time goals on sets of queries. While this is reasonable in theory, in practice, the task of setting response-time goals may be just as difficult as manually tuning the database's memory.

The previous buffer pool research is also problematic because it relies on heuristic hit rate estimation. In cases where the hit rate estimation is incorrect, suboptimal tuning will occur. Compounding the problem is the fact that even if hit rate estimation is accurate, hit rates alone fail to account for the potentially uneven cost of page misses. Depending on the disk from which the page must be read, certain page reads may be dramatically more expensive than others since page reads from hotly contested disks will take longer than page reads from idle disks.

The second problem with the academic approaches is that, to our knowledge, they all deal with only one aspect of the memory tuning problem. For instance, a great deal of work has been done on approaches to buffer pool tuning. Similarly, there is a considerable amount of research into optimizing the sort and hash join memory usage of a database system. The trouble with these approaches is that there is no clear method of integrating the separate components into a comprehensive database memory tuning system that can optimize all (or even most) of the database's memory.

Oracle, SQL Server, and DB2 all have introduced self-tuning memory management in recent releases to help address these issues. Tuning of database memory can be divided into two design problems:

- How much memory should be allocated to the database.
- How should this memory be divided among the various needs of the database for caching, sorting, locking, etc.

It's very important to bear in mind that the tuning of database memory is a zero-sum game:[6] there are many uses for the memory, but the total resource is finite, and usually not sufficient to optimize the performance requirements of all the memory usages.

SQL Server and DB2 both tune total database memory by exploring the availability of memory on the system. Special allowances are made for the file systems file cache so

---

[6] Zero-sum games involve situations where one player's gains are the result of another player's losses. Benefit is neither created nor destroyed. Memory tuning can be viewed as a zero-sum game if you consider memory allocation to each heap as "gains." Total cumulative memory is fixed, or "zero sum." John von Neumann and Oskar Morgenstern showed in 1944 that a zero-sum game involving multiple players is actually a generalized form of a zero-sum game for two players. Interestingly, they also showed that a non-zero-sum game for n players is reducible to a zero-sum game for $n + 1$ players where the $n+1$th player represents the overall non-zero gain.

as not to double count caching between the file system and the database. In situations where the database server appears to have a beneficial need for more memory and memory is available on the server, the RDBMS simply consumes more memory. The situation is more complicated when multiple databases are operating on the same server. In these cases the aggressiveness of the memory consumption is biased by the relative needs of each database. Databases that have a larger performance need for memory will consume memory more aggressively (with a lower goal for the amount of free memory to leave on the system). As each database competes for memory, the more aggressive memory consumers consume enough memory so that the free memory on the server is less than the free memory objective of the less needy databases, which indirectly forces the less needy databases to reduce their memory consumption. At this time Oracle does not yet support automatic tuning of total memory allocation.

The more difficult problem is determining how to wisely distribute memory in a zero-sum game for the database's many varied purposes. SQL Server uses a strategy that is largely effective in normal database operational domains, as follows:

- Lock memory is allocated up to a reasonably large maximum, to avoid lock escalations.

- Sort memory is allocated based on the projected needs of each sort operated as predicted by the query optimizer's cost modeling, provided the sort is small enough to fit in memory. If a spill is expected, the larger memory allocations for sort have very marginal gains, so a minimal amount of memory is given to the sort.

- The remaining tunable memory is given to the primary data cache.

This strategy works well in many scenarios, but can lead to over allocation of lock memory, and does not tune the most complex environments for business intelligence and data warehousing where optimizer estimates can be off by an order of magnitude and ad hoc workloads are common. SQL Server 2000 and beyond have also included self-tuning memory capabilities, using an approach that is based on backpressure from the operating system to determine total database memory allocation. Further details on how SQL Server chooses to distribute memory to various heaps within the database kernel have not yet been published in detail.

To solve the tuning problems in more complex environments, Oracle and DB2 use simulation techniques to model the benefit of adding memory to sort, hash join, or buffer pools (the data caches). Oracle performs this simulation on regular intervals. From product documentation and Oracle-published white papers, it is evident that Oracle 10g has an automated memory tuning feature. The Oracle Automatic Shared Memory Management feature is able to determine values for several configuration parameters including the "shared pool," the "buffer cache," and the "Java pool." It also is advertised that the feature works adaptively to modify memory distribution based on workload characteristics. The DB2 technology tunes the buffer pools, sort and hash join memory, lock memory, and the cache size for compiled SQL statements "package cache."

DB2 adaptively determines how frequently to tune a used system stability test. Because DB2 contains some of the most advanced strategies for memory management, we will present some of the DB2 techniques here to highlight the techniques. A particularly novel strategy of the DB2 approach is the incorporation of classical control theory with feedback for memory tuning.

There are two main functional differences between the IBM Self-tuning Memory Manager (STMM) feature and the Oracle Automatic Shared Memory Management (ASMM) feature. The primary difference is that ASMM requires the user to put a limit on the total amount of shared memory that the database can consume, a task that can be nontrivial in the presence of multiple databases running on the same machine. STMM, on the other hand, is able to adaptively determine the proper amount of memory that each database should consume, thus alleviating the need for the user to calculate a total memory value for every database. The second difference is that ASMM is unable to tune two critical memory consumers that are automatically configured by STMM. These consumers are sort and any buffer pools that store pages larger than 4 KB.

The approach by Storm et al. [2006] is the only industrially implemented approach that combines total database memory tuning and a comprehensive memory distribution algorithm with cost-benefit analysis and control theory techniques. We are reprinting much of the approach described in that paper with permission of the original authors and the VLDB Endowment.[7]

13.10.3 Cutting Edge: The Latest Strategy in Self-tuning Memory Management

This section describes in some detail the latest technology for self-tuning memory described by Storm et al. [2006]. The principal component of the STMM feature is the memory controller (Figure 13.17). During each tuning cycle, the memory controller (or memory tuner) evaluates the memory distribution and determines if system performance can be enhanced through the redistribution of the database memory. To do this, the controller uses cost-benefit data as input into a control model whose output is an improved memory distribution. The control model also determines an appropriate tuning frequency, typically between 30 seconds and 10 minutes, based on the workload characteristics (as defined through the input cost-benefit data).

---

[7] The self-tuning strategy described is protected under several U.S. and international patents filed prior to this publication. Publication here, and in other academic papers, does not provide legal right for other vendors to reuse these methods where they are currently protected under patent law.

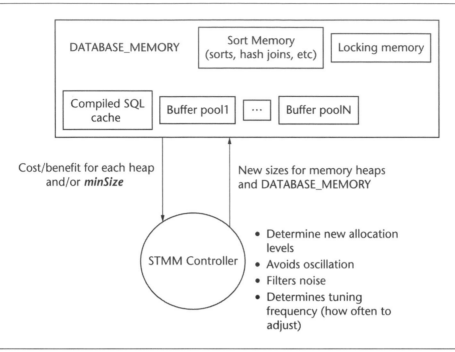

Figure 13.17   STMM overview.

In the remainder of this section, we first discuss STMM's cost-benefit analysis. We then discuss how STMM classifies memory and describes the control algorithms that are used to prevent tuning oscillation. Finally, we discuss STMM's memory transfer algorithm, how it tunes total database memory usage and determines the tuning frequency.

Cost-benefit Analysis

One of the main obstacles to developing a databasewide memory tuning algorithm is that each of the memory consumers (i.e., sort, buffer pool, etc.) has a different use for memory. For instance, the buffer pools use memory to cache data, index, and temporary pages. When buffer pool memory is insufficient, pages are evicted from the cache and must be reread upon the next access. A common performance metric used to track buffer pool performance is the cache hit ratio, which indicates the ratio of page accesses that require disk reads. Conversely, for the compiled SQL cache, which also uses hit ratios as its performance metric, misses incur a CPU penalty when evicted queries must be recompiled. The difference between these two seemingly similar metrics makes comparing their need for memory difficult. Clearly, if there was a common metric for all memory consumers, trading memory would be much simpler.

Since the database memory is predominantly used to increase system performance either by reducing latency, decreasing I/O, or decreasing contention, all of which can be expressed as a time benefit, a common metric of saved system time per unit memory was chosen. Determining how much disk and/or CPU time a given amount of memory would save each of the consumers produces a common metric that can then be used to determine relative need for memory across all of the consumers. For the rest of this document, the cost-benefit time/unit memory metric will often be referred to only as the cost benefit (or the cost-benefit metric).

The STMM memory model varies dramatically from other database memory tuning strategies in the published literature because it models the cost benefit on a system-wide level over the course of a time interval. The cost benefit is accumulated as savings in processing time for each memory consumer with which a database agent (the OS process performing the query operation) interacted during query processing. The aggregation of agent time savings implicitly models concurrency, since the time savings are directly measuring saved system time within the current observation window (tuning interval), and are subject to agent interactions and inefficiencies caused by system concurrency.

Space constraints in this book prohibit a detailed description of how the benefit data is obtained through simulation for each memory area. Very briefly, a distinct method was created for each memory consumer. These methods are all based on runtime simulations of cost.

Benefit Determination for Buffer Pools

The objective of the benefit model is to determine, with reasonable accuracy, the amount of agent processing time that would be saved if additional memory were allocated to the memory consumer. In the case of the buffer pool, this saving is almost exclusively a savings in I/O. The algorithm to determine the benefit does the following tasks:

- Maintains some extra space, called the "simulated buffer pool extension" (SBPX). The SBPX is large enough to store a significant percentage (10% or more) of the page identifiers of the buffer pool. Since the page identifiers are only 128 bytes long, and pages in the buffer pools are 4 KB, 8 KB, 16 KB, or 32 KB, the SBPX represents at most a 3% memory overhead per simulated page.

- When a page is victimized from the buffer pool, its identifier is stored in the SBPX and a page identifier is removed from the SBPX using a victimization algorithm similar to that of the actual buffer pool.

- When a new logical page read occurs, the following events take place:

— If the page is not found in the buffer pool, the SBPX is consulted. This searching of the SBPX is very efficient since its page identifiers are stored in the buffer pool and marked accordingly.

— If the page was not found in the buffer pool but was found in the SBPX, then STMM can reasonably say that if the SBPX were actual pages and not just simulated pages, the page miss being incurred would have been a hit.

— Once it is determined that a disk access is necessary, a victim page in the buffer pool is chosen, the victimized page is moved into the SBPX, and the desired page is read into the buffer pool from disk. This operation (victimizing the buffer pool page and bringing the desired page in from disk) is timed so that STMM will know the total time penalty that is due to the page miss. This time is then added to the "cumulative saved time" for the given buffer pool. Timing the operation is critical to the method since disk read times may vary dramatically if the load across all disks is not uniform.

• At the end of the tuning interval, the cumulative saved time is then normalized by the number of pages in the SBPX (since this is the maximum number of additional pages required to save the disk read) to determine the benefit/page metric.

The algorithmic details reveal the two major differences between this approach and previously proposed hit-rate estimation approaches. The first difference is that while in the past, hit rates have been estimated, however, in this approach STMM precisely simulates the page read behavior that will arise when memory is added to the buffer pool. Furthermore, this approach explicitly times the reads that will be saved, which allows for increased accuracy in the presence of nonuniform disk load.

Figure 13.18 shows how cost benefit is determined for increased buffer pool memory. This is an example of the above-described process where pages 1, 2, and 3 have been read from disk at various times. The read of page 3 resulted in the victimization of page 1, at which point page 1's identifier was transferred to the SBPX. When a read request occurs for page 1 at a future time, the page is not found in the buffer pool but is found in the SBPX. STMM therefore knows that had the buffer pool been larger, the I/O to read page 1 would have been avoided.

Benefit Determination for the Compiled SQL Statement Cache

The system time saved by increasing the size of the compiled SQL cache is different from that of the buffer pools. In the case of the buffer pools, the savings were predominantly I/O time reductions, whereas growth in the compiled SQL cache yields a reduction in the number of query compilations, which saves CPU time.

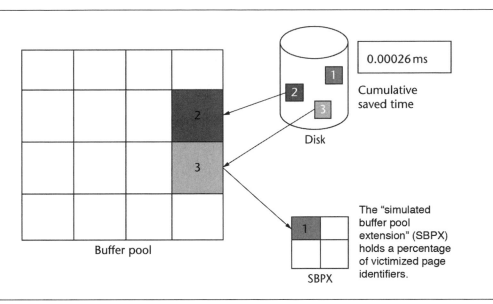

Figure 13.18   Estimating buffer pool benefit.

To produce a benefit value for the compiled SQL cache, STMM uses a cache simulation model similar to what was described for the buffer pool, where a simulation area holds identifiers for victimized objects. The following differences apply:

- Compiled statements in the Simulated SQL Cache Extension (SSCX) are represented by a generated checksum that uniquely identifies the SQL statement.

- When a cache miss occurs, but the statement is found in the SSCX, the statement compilation is timed, and added to the cumulative saved time for the SQL Cache.

- The benefit data is normalized to benefit/page based on the number of pages that would be required to store the compiled statements in the SSCX. This is different from the buffer pool computation since compiled statements vary in size while buffer pool pages for a given buffer pool are of a constant size.

The resulting benefit metric measured in seconds/page is directly comparable to the benefit metric calculated for the buffer pool, even though the former represents savings due to reduced I/O processing and the latter represents savings in CPU processing.

Memory Controller

For each memory consumer, in most cases, the saved system time decreases when the amount of memory allocated to the consumer increases. Additionally, at some point, when the memory consumer has a sufficient amount of memory, the addition of more memory produces no more saved system time.

For example, adding more memory for the buffer pools will see diminishing returns when the whole database, or the set of active pages, fits in memory or when the data accesses, beyond the set that is kept in memory, are random. Alternatively, for sort, the diminishing returns occur when there is enough memory to perform all sorts in memory.

This nonlinear relationship can be modeled as an exponential function $x_i = a_i \left(1 - e^{-b_i u_i}\right)$. The maximum total saved system time can be achieved when the partial derivative for each memory size is equal, that is,

$$\frac{\partial f}{\partial u_i} = \frac{\partial f}{\partial u_j},$$

13.3

where $i,j = 1...N$. This results is used as the memory tuning objective, namely, to equalize the cost-benefit metrics for all memory consumers.

Varying the Memory Transfer Limits

To achieve the memory tuning objective without excessive oscillations, the memory tuner varies the amount of memory by which each consumer can increase or decrease in a given interval. To compute these amounts, the memory tuner uses the following two algorithms:

MIMO controller. The multi-input multi-output (MIMO) controller uses a model-based control theory approach to determine the direction and step size of memory tuning. A MIMO model is first constructed (and continually revised to capture system and workload changes) to model the relationship between the memory size and the benefit value. After the model quality is verified, the MIMO control algorithm uses this model information and the integral control law to determine the proper tuning actions required to equalize the benefits for all memory consumers.

Oscillation dampening controller. When a MIMO model is not available (i.e., before the first model can be constructed), a fixed-step algorithm is used. In the fixed-step algorithm, all memory resizes are sized using a fixed percentage of the consumer's size, regardless of the benefit value. Since this can lead to significant size oscillation, an oscillation avoidance algorithm is introduced to reduce the memory tuning size once oscillating patterns are observed. The fixed-step tuning combined with the oscillation reduction is referred to as the oscillation dampening controller (or OD controller).

Figure 13.19 shows the STMM controller and the interaction between the MIMO and OD controllers.

The OD controller is used in only two scenarios: (1) when a database is starting up and lacks a tuning history, and (2) in the presence of large system noise. Because of

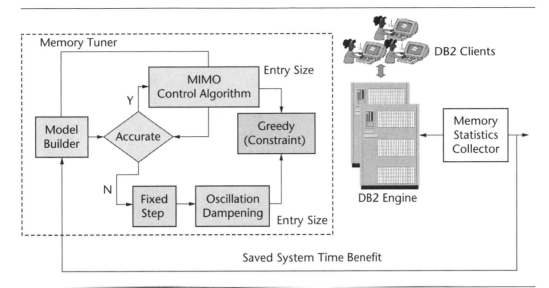

Figure 13.19 STMM controller.

space constraints, we have chosen to describe only the MIMO controller in detail since it is the algorithm that is most often used.

Determining how frequently to tune is a key consideration for a memory controller. An OLTP workload with thousands of short-running transactions can reasonably be tuned every few seconds, while a complex query environment may require several minutes or hours before a representative window of activity has occurred in order to make informed tuning decisions. The range of reasonable tuning rates varies by orders of magnitude depending on the system workload. To our knowledge, no research team or vendor has yet published a technique for determining the tuning rate for memory allocation in an RDBMS. The few publications that discuss this topic used fixed time intervals.

STMM determines the tuning interval by observing the signal-to-noise ratio in the benefit data from the memory consumers and finding a time interval over which the signal-to-noise ratio is within 70%. The sample interval is determined by considering the confidence of the benefit data. Using *P* measured benefit samples *benefit(i)*, *i=1, 2, …, P*, a sample mean, *mean_benefit*, and a sample standard deviation, *std_benefit*, are computed. The desired sample interval size is then calculated using the following equation:

$$\left(\frac{T \times std\_benefit}{desired\_confidence\_range} \right)^2 \times current\_sample\_interval, \qquad 13.4$$

where *desired_confidence_range* is an accuracy measure on the desired maximum difference between the measured sample benefit and the statistically "real" mean benefit, and *current_sample_interval* is the sample interval that is currently used to collect benefit data. The constant T is used to compensate for the estimated benefits and is selected from the student distribution table. Its value depends on two factors: the desired confidence level (for which STMM uses 70% in this design) and the number of measured benefit samples (where $T = 1.156$ if 5 measured benefit samples are used, and $T = 1.093$ if 10 samples are used).

In evaluating a database memory tuning feature, the most convincing result would be to show that the tuner is able to take an "out-of-the-box" configuration and tune it to an "optimal" configuration in a reasonable amount of time. The main problem with conducting such a test is that typically there is no easy way to determine the optimal memory configuration for a given workload.

Experimental Results for STMM

The experimental results using this technique were impressive. Three experimental results were published showing the technology's ability to:

- Tune a huge number of memory heaps, using an OLTP database with 14 buffer pools.
- Respond to workload shifts within a complex query workload.
- To readjust total memory between multiple databases.

In the multiple heap experiment STMM initially takes the system from the default configuration to a configuration within 10% of the hand-tuned result. In the second phase of tuning, the buffer pools are finely tuned to arrive at the desired final configuration. Finally, in the third phase, STMM makes only very minor adjustments to the system.

The performance of the system, as shown in Figure 13.20, can be seen in the same three phases. In the first phase, STMM takes the system from 47,029 to 139,110 transactions per minute. In the second phase, while STMM is fine tuning the configuration, performance oscillates around 140,000 transactions per minute. Finally, in the third phase, performance stabilizes at 143,141 transactions per minute. This shows the dramatic impact that STMM can have on a workload, improving performance in this case by over 300%, most of which is achieved in the first hour and a half of tuning.

To determine how close the final configuration was to the hand-tuned result a second run was performed using the final memory configuration and turning STMM off (also removing any small effect that tuning might have on the system). In this second run the STMM-generated configuration resulted in an average transaction rate of 145,391 transactions per minute compared to the baseline configuration of 145,156

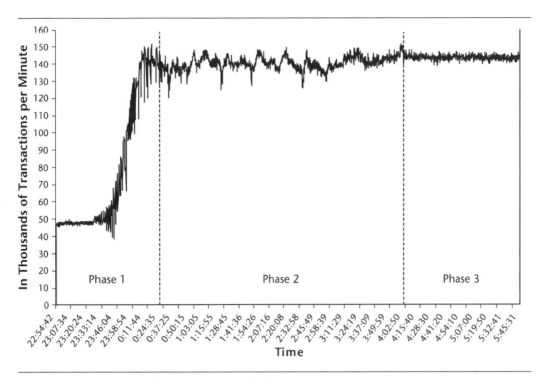

Figure 13.20   System performance during STMM tuning.

transactions per minute (a difference of 0.16%, which is within the interrun variability of the workload on the test machine). The results of this second run illustrate how STMM is able to converge to the optimal configuration when started from an out-of-the-box configuration. The results also show that even with STMM actively tuning a system, the performance can be within 1.4% of a hand-tuned result.

For the second experiment, to simulate such an environment an experiment was devised where the database began by running one type of query and then, once the memory configuration stabilized, the workload shifted to more complex queries. At first the experiment ran 16 concurrent streams of TPC-H query 13, a decision-support query with low requirements for sort memory. Then, once the memory configuration stabilized, the workload was changed to 16 concurrent streams of TPC-H query 21, which is substantially more complex, contains multiple subqueries, and has much higher requirements for sort memory. This shift from query 13 to query 21 places considerable pressure on the sort memory and should force the memory to be dramatically reallocated.

Figure 13.21 shows the memory distribution shift over the course of the run. Once the streams of query 13 stop and query 21 starts running, a dramatic increase in the amount of sort memory allocated to the database occurs. By the time the system has

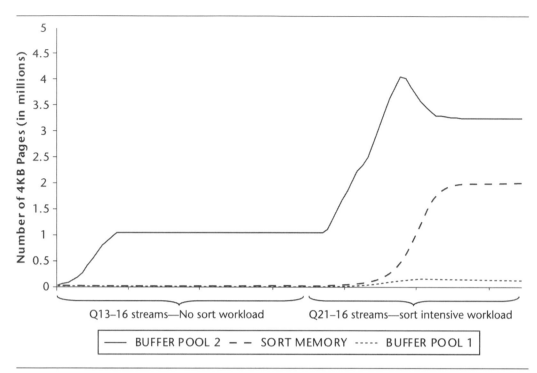

Figure 13.21   Workload shift—memory distribution.

converged, the database has reserved more than 8 GB of memory for sorting. As is illustrated in Figure 13.22, this memory distribution shift has a dramatic effect on the workload performance.

Figure 13.22 shows the workload performance during the run. In the first stage of the run, the memory distribution is stable as the 16 streams of query 13 complete consistently in about 280 seconds. Once the workload shifts, however, it is clear that the system's memory is not properly configured for query 21. At this point, STMM begins redistributing the database memory and the resultant dramatic effect on performance can be observed as quickly as the second run of the queries, at which point performance has already improved by 74%. After several more runs, the query response time stabilizes and a performance improvement of 254% can be observed when compared to the first execution of query 21. This not only shows how critical sort memory can be to a database system, but also how effective STMM can be at supplying the sort memory when necessary.

Finally, to test STMM in an environment where multiple databases are competing for a single system's memory, an experiment was performed with two identical databases running the same workload. In building the databases, it was necessary to ensure that both databases had the same physical design, resided on the same number of disks, and

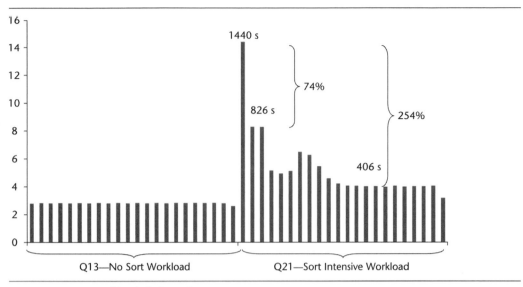

Figure 13.22 Workload shift performance.

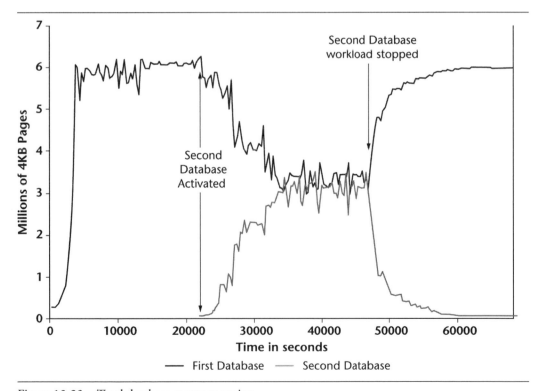

Figure 13.23 Total database memory tuning.

that the disks were of the same speed, since even the slightest difference in any of these variables could have skewed the memory requirements for the databases. The workload being run by each of the databases consisted of four clients, each running the 22 queries used in the TPC-H benchmark.

Figure 13.23 shows the database memory usage for the two databases during the 20-hour run. The first database is activated with the default configuration and the workload is started. In the first hour, STMM gives all of the system memory to this database as there are no other applications running on the system. After six hours of running, the second database is activated with the default configuration and begins running the same workload. As expected, two hours later both databases are sharing the system memory equally. A few hours after the memory is evenly distributed, the second database stops running the workload but remains activated. The dramatic difference in relative database activity that follows causes STMM to take memory from the second database and give it back to the first database.

TIPS AND INSIGHTS FOR DATABASE PROFESSIONALS

- **Tip 1. Do some capacity planning in advance.** Because of the growth in technology for both CPU and disk, you should expect your hardware to become somewhat obsolete every two years. It's a good strategy to plan for this, using Moore's Law, and start with capacity that is sufficient for three years of system use and growth.

- **Tip 2. For data-intensive processing having a lot of RAM and large CPU cache sizes is extremely important.** Storage is very slow compared to RAM, and RAM is very slow compared to the CPU cache. Given the choice, spend money in this priority: CPU cache, RAM, disk.

- **Tip 3. When purchasing storage, opt for more spindles rather than larger spindles.** Striping is king for improving the performance of your storage system, especially for highly concurrent systems. But in order for striping to be effective you need a plethora of disks.

- **Tip 4. Try to balance CPU and disk reasonably well.** A general rule of thumb is 150 GB raw data per 4 GB RAM, or 150 GB raw data per CPU, whichever is larger.

- **Tip 5. If your database supports automated memory tuning, use it.** Memory tuning is very hard, and the new self-tuning techniques do a better job than most human designers can. However, beware of the limitations of these self-tuning methods. There are clearly cases where self-tuning is not appropriate. The two major cases are: (1) dramatic but short-term workload shift (such as running a report for two minutes). Most self-tuning memory strategies won't be able to adapt in time to a short but sudden change like that, and by the time they have adapted the report is finished! (2) Intentional data caching, where you want to keep data hot by placing it in its own data cache (buffer pool). If this data is rarely accessed but highly urgent when it is accessed, a self-tuning memory scheme will probably have come to the conclusion the data is not important and will purge it from main memory long before the urgent access arrives. To avoid this problem, turn self-tuning off for the buffer pool you want to keep hot, if the RDBMS supports that. If not, you'll need to make a decision on whether the benefits of keeping that data hot outweigh your ability to tune memory on your system by hand. That will be a difficult call, and many DBAs would probably convince themselves falsely they can manually tune the memory heaps good enough. In the end the benefits they achieve from the hot buffer pool may be undone by the suboptimal memory tuning in all other areas of the DBMS.

- **Tip 6. Protect your on-disk data by using a RAID array.** Almost everyone does these days and for good reason. RAID 5 is dominant for database purposes.

- **Tip 7. All machines eventually break, so expect and plan for breakage.** At the very least make a backup every now and then. But for more serious recoverability make sure you have system failover of some kind in place. The best option will depend on your goals, and keep in mind that every option on the market today, including buzzwords like Oracle RAC and DB2 HADR, has disadvantages.

- **Tip 8. Scale-up versus scale-out.** Throughout this text we introduced a number of ideas in scale-out like adding more machines to help work on problems in parallel. We discuss shared nothing, and shared disk, etc. However, as you add servers you also add administration costs and increase the number of components in your system. More components mean an increase in likelihood that something will fail within the year. However, scale-up to very large servers with dozens of CPUs is costly. A general rule: Stick with mid-range servers with two to eight CPUs. When a single mid-range server doesn't suffice, only then start scaling out.

- **Tip 9. Ask the question, "Do we need geographic failover?"** How concerned are you about and entire building or city where you operate suffering a disaster that either destroys your primary database servers or at least makes them temporarily unavailable to the rest of the world? Like home insurance, it's costly and you hope you never need it. But should you ever (heaven forefend) need it, you'll be kicking yourself if you don't have it.

13.11 Summary

This chapter has covered a lot of ground and admittedly none of it as deeply as a database designer really needs to know. Even so the major concepts in CPU, multiprocessors, storage (SAN, NAS, RAID), high availability, and memory management have been touched with enough depth to provide you with the tools to walk the walk and talk the talk of database design at the machine layer.

13.12 Literature Summary

Adler, R. M. Distributed Coordination Models for Client/Sever Computing. *Computer,* 28(4), April 1995: 14–22.

Dickman, A. Two-Tier versus Three-Tier Apps. *InformationWeek,* 553, Nov. 13, 1995: 74–80.

Diao, Y., Hellerstein, J. L., and Storm, A. J., Surendra, M., Lightstone, S., Parekh, S. S., and Edelstein, H. Unraveling Client/Server Architecture. *DBMS,* 7(5), May 1994: 34(7).

Gallaugher, J., and Ramanathan, S. Choosing a Client/Server Architecture: A Comparison of Two-Tier and Three-Tier Systems. *Information Systems Management Magazine,* 13(2), Spring 1996: 7–13.

Garcia-Arellano, C. Incorporating Cost of Control into the Design of a Load Balancing Controller. IEEE Real-Time and Embedded Technology and Applications Symposium, 2004, pp. 376–387.

Garcia-Molina, H., and Polyzois, C. A. Issues in Disaster Recovery. *COMPCON,* 1990: 573–577.

Gibson, G. A., Hellerstein, L., Karp, R. M., Katz, R. H., and Patterson, D. A. Failure Correction Techniques for Large Disk Arrays. *ASPLOS,* 1989: 123–132.

Hennessy, J. L., and Patterson, D. A. *Computer Architecture: A Quantitative Approach,* 2nd ed. San Francisco: Morgan Kaufmann, 1996.

Hester, P. 2006 Technology Analyst Day, *AMD,* June 1, 2006

Lightstone, S., Storm, A., Garcia-Arellano, C., Carroll, M., Colaco, J., Diao, Y., and Surendra, M. Self-tuning Memory Management in a Relational Database System. Fourth Annual Workshop on Systems and Storage Technology, December 11, 2005, IBM Research Lab, Haifa University campus, Mount Carmel, Haifa, Israel.

Patterson, D. A. Latency Lags Bandwidth. *ICCD,* 2005: 3–6.

Patterson, D. A. Terabytes—Teraflops or Why Work on Processors When I/O Is Where the Action Is? (Abstract.) ACM Conference on Computer Science, 1994, p. 410.

Patterson, D. A., Gibson, G. A., and Katz, R. A. A Case for Redundant Arrays of Inexpensive Disks (RAID). SIGMOD Conference, 1988, pp. 109–116.

Pruscino, A. Oracle RAC: Architecture and Performance. SIGMOD Conference, 2003, p. 635.

Ramakrishnan, R., and Gehrke, J. *Database Management Systems*, 3rd ed. New York: McGraw-Hill, 2003.

Rudin, K., "Scalable Systems Architecture: Scalable I/O, Part I: Disk Striping," *DM Review Magazine*, May 1998.

Schulze, M., Gibson, G. A., Katz, R. A., and Patterson, D. A. How Reliable Is a RAID? *COMPCON*, 1989: 118–123.

Schussel, G. Client/Server Past, Present, and Future [online]. http://www.dciexpo.com/geos 1995.

Shelton, R. E. "The Distributed Enterprise (Shared, Reusable Business Models the Next Step in Distributed Object Computing)." *Distributed Computing Monitor* 8, 10 (October 1993).

Silberschatz, A., Galvin, P., and Gagne, G. *Operating System Concepts*, 6th ed. New York: John Wiley, 2002.

Storm, A. J., Garcia-Arellano, C. M., Lightstone, S., Diao, Y., and Surendra, M. Adaptive Self-tuning Memory in DB2 UDB, VLDB 2006, Seoul, South Korea.

Zikopoulos, P. C., and Eaton, C. Availability with Clicks of a Button Using DB2's HADR, at http://www.dbazine.com/db2/db2-disarticles/zikopoulos19.

Physical Design for Decision Support, Warehousing, and OLAP

The Store may be considered as the place of deposit in which the numbers and quantities given by the conditions of the question are originally placed, in which all intermediate results are provisionally preserved and in which at the termination all the required results are found.
—Charles Babbage, 1837

The concept of using a data storage area to support the calculations of a general-purpose computer date back to the mid-nineteenth century. The year 1837 is not a mistake for the above quotation! The source is a paper titled "On the Mathematical Powers of the Calculating Engine," published by Charles Babbage in 1837. This paper details the Analytical Engine, a plan for a mechanical computer. The organization of the Analytical Engine became the inspiration for the ENIAC more than one hundred years later. The ENIAC was the first general-purpose electronic computer, which in turn influenced the organization of computers in common use today.

Surprisingly, this quote from well over 150 years ago is descriptive of the current data warehousing and online analytical processing (OLAP) technologies. The original data is placed in the fact tables and dimension tables of a data warehouse. Intermediate results are often calculated and stored on disk as materialized views, also known as Materialized Query Tables (MQT). The materialized views can be further queried until the required results are found. We focus on two decision support technologies in this chapter: data warehousing and OLAP. We detail the physical design issues that arise relative to these decision support technologies.

14.1   What Is OLAP?

Online analytical processing (OLAP) is a service that typically sits on top of a data ware-house. The data warehouse provides the infrastructure that supplies the detailed data. Data warehouses often contain hundreds of millions of rows of historical data. Answer-ing queries posed directly against the detailed data can consume valuable computer resources. The purpose of OLAP is to answer queries quickly from the large amount of underlying data. The queries posed against OLAP systems typically "group by" certain attributes, and apply aggregation functions against other attributes. For example, a manager may be interested in looking at total cost, grouped by year and region. Most OLAP systems offer a graphical representation of the results (see Figure 14.1).

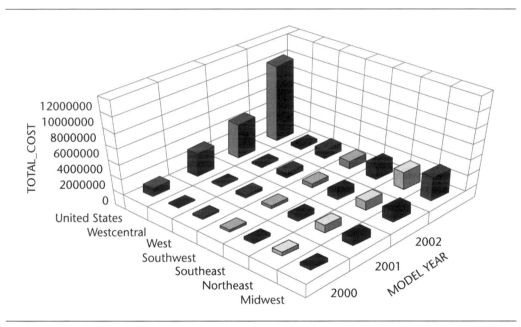

Figure 14.1   Graph example produced from Cognos PowerPlay.

Figure 14.1 includes two-dimensional attributes, namely location and model year, organized orthogonally. The third axis represents the magnitude of the measure of inter-est—the total cost. We are looking at a subset of the possible dimensions and measures for this data set. The database used to generate this graph contains six dimension attributes available for "group by," and four measures available for aggregation. The schema for this database is discussed further in Sections 14.2 and 14.3. The user selected the location at the region level and the model year dimensions along with the total cost in order to view the graph shown in Figure 14.1. The data space can be conceptualized as a hyperdimensional cube, with dimension values slicing across each dimension. Each cell of the cube contains values for the measures corresponding to the dimension values at that cell.

OLAP systems are organized for easy manipulation. Dimensions are easily added, replaced, or removed from the display. For example, we can replace the location dimension with the problem dimension using a simple drag-and-drop action, quickly changing the view to observe the total cost grouped by problem and model year. Likewise, we can change the measure to examine the sum of labor costs, if we decide to focus on labor. If we spot a dominant problem, we can double-click on the column of interest, and "drill-down" into more detailed data. OLAP systems make exploring large amounts of data easy and quick.

How exactly is this service accomplished? Most OLAP systems rely on saving summary results in materialized views. Since the materialized views are summary data, they are usually much smaller than the tables containing the detailed information. When a query is posed, the materialized views are utilized to obtain a quick response, avoiding calculating the results from the huge amount of underlying data. We covered the use of materialized views to speed up query responses in Chapter 5. An OLAP system automatically decides which views to materialize to achieve good performance.

There are three general categories of storage mechanisms in OLAP systems: relational OLAP (ROLAP), multidimensional OLAP (MOLAP), and hybrid OLAP (HOLAP). ROLAP uses standard relational tables to store data, typically using the dimensions as a composite primary key. Each row represents a cell of the data cube. Empty cells are not explicitly represented in ROLAP. MOLAP stores data on disk organized by location in the cube. Each cell is represented by a fixed, calculable location. Empty cells consume space in MOLAP representations. It is possible to utilize compression techniques to reduce the wasted space in MOLAP. It is generally recognized that ROLAP is better when the data is sparse, and MOLAP is good when the data is dense. Sparsity and density of the data can be measured in terms of the number of distinct keys in the data, compared to the number of possible key combinations. Let's illustrate with a simple example, and then discuss HOLAP.

Imagine a grocery store that tracks customer sales. The customer presents a membership card, and receives discounts for participating. The store tracks the customer ID, the items, and the date sold. Figure 14.2 illustrates a small portion of the data, showing the fruits bought by a single customer during one week. An X in a cell means that a transaction took place for the given combination of dimension values. The customer bought apples and bananas on Monday, and bought oranges and strawberries on Wednesday. The table can be thought of as four separate views. The upper left box contains the most detailed data. The weekly subtotals for each fruit are contained in the upper right box. The fruit subtotals for each day are contained in the lower left box. The grand total is contained in the lower right box. The data density of the most detailed data, weekly subtotals, fruit subtotals, and the grand totals, are 0.12, 0.4, 0.8, and 1.0, respectively. Generally, aggregating data from one view into another view increases the data density.

The difference in data density from the core data to summary views can be very marked. Extending our grocery store example, let's say that the store has 3,000 items available, and the average customer buys 30 distinct items per visit, shopping once a week. The data density of the core data is $(30/3,000)(1/5) = 0.002$. However, if we summarize the data across all customers, then it would not be unreasonable to have a data density of say 0.95 (i.e., most items have some units sold on any given day). Since ROLAP performs well for sparse data, and MOLAP performs best for dense data, a useful strategy might be to store the sparse data using ROLAP, and the dense data using MOLAP. This hybrid approach is called HOLAP. Some OLAP systems offer ROLAP, MOLAP, and HOLAP options.

	M	Tu	W	Th	F	Week
Apples	X					X
Bananas	X					X
Oranges			X			X
Strawberries			X			X
Kiwis						
Fruits	X		X			X

Figure 14.2 Aggregation increases data density.

14.2 Dimension Hierarchies

The ability to view different levels of detail is very useful when exploring data. OLAP systems allow "drill-down" operations to move from summary to more detailed data, and "roll-up" operations to move from detailed to summary data. For example, the user viewing the graph in Figure 14.1 may be curious to find out more detail on the large amount of cost in the Midwest region. Drilling down on the Midwest region shows summary data for states in the Midwest. Perhaps Michigan dominates costs in the Midwest. The user may wish to further drill-down on Michigan to view data at the city or dealership level. The location information can be stored in a dimension table named "Location." The levels of the location dimension may be represented as attributes in the location table. Figure 14.3 is a simple UML class diagram, showing the attributes of the location table, supporting a location hierarchy. We indicate the primary key using the stereotype "«pk»."

```
              Location
        «pk» loc_id
        dealership
        city
        state-province
        region
        country
```

Figure 14.3   Example dimension table with hierarchy.

Notice that this dimension table is not normalized. Data warehouse design is driven by efficiency of query response and simplicity. Normalization is not the driving factor as it is in the design of databases for daily transactions. Dimensional modeling is the dominant approach utilized for designing data warehouses. The companion book on logical design [Teorey, Lightstone, and Nadeau 2006] includes an overview of the dimensional modeling approach. Kimball and Ross [2002] is an excellent and detailed resource covering the dimensional modeling approach for data warehousing.

Figure 14.4 illustrates two date dimensions implemented as views. The Production_Date dimension and the Repair_Date dimension are similarly structured, with the same underlying data. Following the recommendations of Kimball and Ross [2002], in such cases we implement one underlying table, and use a view fulfilling each role, presenting separate date dimensions.

```
     «table»                    «view»                     «view»
  Date_Dimension          Production_Date              Repair_Date

 «pk»date_id            «pk»prod_date_id          «pk»Repair_date_id
 date_desc             prod_date_desc            repair_date_desc
 week                  prod_week                 repair_week
 month                 prod_month                repair_month
 quarter               prod_quarter              repair_quarter
 yr                    prod_year                 repair_year
```

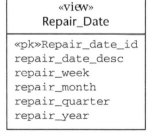

Figure 14.4   Example date dimensions with hierarchies.

14.3   Star and Snowflake Schemas

The dimension tables are used to group data in various ways, offering the user the freedom to explore the data at different levels. The measures to be aggregated are kept in a central table known as a *fact table*. The fact table is surrounded by the dimension tables.

The fact table is composed of dimension attributes and measures. The dimension attributes are foreign keys referencing the dimension tables. Figure 14.5 illustrates what is commonly known as a *star schema*. The Warranty_Claim table is the fact table, and the six surrounding tables are the dimension tables. Star schemas are the dominant configuration in the context of data warehousing.

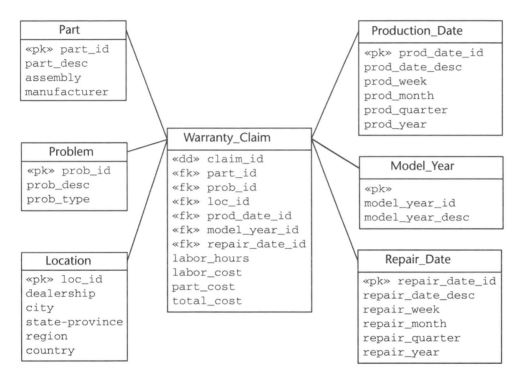

Figure 14.5   Example star schema.

The foreign keys are indicated using the "«fk»" stereotype. Notice also the "«dd»" stereotype on the claim_id attribute. This signifies a degenerate dimension. The claim_id is included in order to maintain the granularity at the claim level in the fact table. Degenerate dimensions do not have any associated dimension table. The dimension attributes form a superkey to the fact table, because the values of the dimension attributes uniquely identify a cell in the data cube, and therefore determine the values of the measures associated with the cell. Sometimes the set of dimension attributes also forms the primary key of the fact table. It is possible for a proper subset of the dimension attributes to form a candidate key. Such is the case in Figure 14.5, where claim_id by itself determines all other attributes in the table, making it a candidate key.

The star schema is an efficient design in the context of data warehousing. We led gradually into the star schema in Chapter 5; Figure 5.6 is actually a star schema with only two dimensions. The calculations in Chapter 5 demonstrated the performance gains possible with a star schema when the environment is dominated by reads. This is exactly the case in a data warehouse environment. Since the data is mostly historical, the reads predominate, and the star schema is a winner.

The snowflake schema is another configuration that sometimes arises in data warehouse design. If you normalize the dimension tables in a star schema, you end up with a snowflake schema. Figure 14.6 shows the snowflake schema equivalent to the star schema of Figure 14.5. As you can see, there are many more tables. Most queries require many joins with the snowflake schema, whereas the dimension tables in the star schema are only one step away from the fact table. Most database systems implement an efficient "star join" to support the star schema configuration. The efficiency and simplicity are the primary reasons why the star schema is a common pattern in data warehouse design.

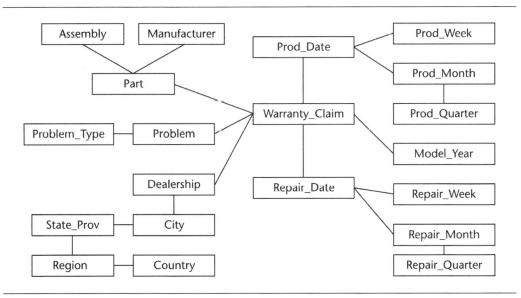

Figure 14.6   Example snowflake schema.

14.4 **Warehouses and Marts**

Data warehouses typically contain large amounts of historical data. Data can feed into the data warehouse from multiple databases. For example, a large company may have many plants, each with their own database for managing day-to-day operations. The company may wish to look for overall trends across the data from all plants. Each plant may have a different database schema. The names of the tables and attributes can differ between source databases. A plant in the United States may have an attribute named "state" while another plant in Canada may use an attribute named "province." The values of corresponding attributes may vary from plant to plant. Maybe one plant uses "B" as an operational code specifying a "blue" widget, and another plant uses "B" to specify "black." The pertinent data needs to be extracted from the feeder database into a staging area. The data is cleaned and transformed in the staging area. Corresponding attributes are mapped to the same data warehouse attribute. Disparate operational codes are replaced with consistent surrogate IDs. Terminology is standardized across the company. Then the data is loaded into the data warehouse. Moving data from the feeder databases into the data warehouse is often referred to as an *extract, transform, and load (ETL) process*. Data in the warehouse can then be explored in a variety of ways, including OLAP, data mining, report generators, and ad hoc query tools. Figure 14.7 illustrates the overall flow of data.

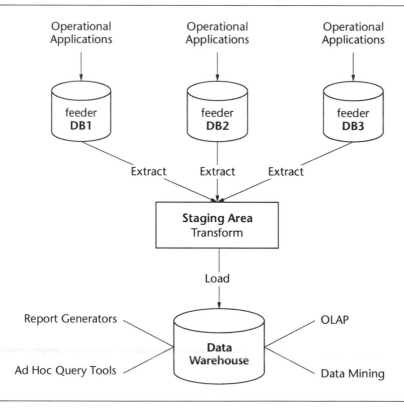

Figure 14.7   Basic data warehouse architecture.

Data warehouse schemas are typically arrived at through the dimensional modeling approach. The business processes of interest are determined. For example, a company may be interested in exploring data from scheduling, productivity tracking, and job costing. The data from each business process is destined to become a star schema. Some of the business processes may share dimensions. For example, the Cost_Center dimension is meaningful for scheduling, productivity tracking, and job costing. A useful tool for capturing the commonality of dimensions between business processes is the data warehouse bus. Table 14.1 shows a data warehouse bus where each row represents a business process and each column represents a dimension. Each x indicates that the

Table 14.1   Example Data Warehouse Bus

	Shape	Color	Texture	Density	Size	Estimate Date	Win Date	Customer	Promotion	Cost Center	Sched Start Date	Sched Start Time	Sched Finish Date	Sched Finish Time	Actual Start Date	Actual Start Time	Actual Finish Date	Actual Finish Time	Employee	Invoice Date
Scheduling										x	x	x	x	x	x	x	x	x		
Productivity Tracking										x					x	x	x	x	x	
Job Costing	x	x	x	x	x			x	x	x										x

given dimension is applicable to the business process. The dimensions that are shared across business processes should be "conformed." That is, each dimension and its levels should be known by the same names and have the same meanings across the entire enterprise; likewise for the values contained by said dimension levels. This is important so that data can be compared across business processes where meaningful, and people can discuss the data in the same terms from department to department, facilitating meaningful communication. The dimension data can be thought of as flowing through the data warehouse bus.

The data warehouse schema can contain multiple star schemas, with shared dimensions as indicated by the data warehouse bus. Figure 14.8 illustrates the data warehouse schema corresponding to the data warehouse bus shown in Table 14.1. The attributes are elided since we are focusing on the fact tables and dimensions. We have marked the fact tables using a «fact table» stereotype, whereas the tables that are not marked are dimension tables. The configuration of multiple star schemas in a data warehouse forms a constellation.

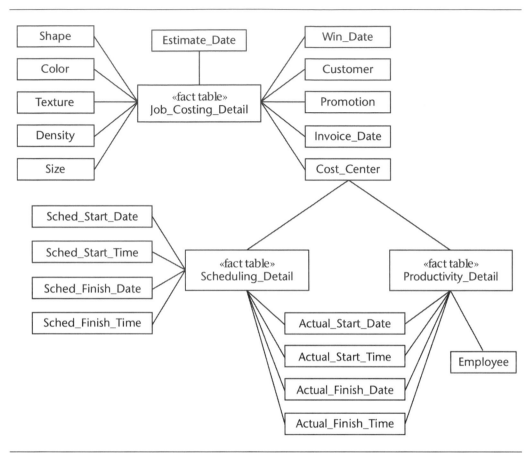

Figure 14.8   Example data warehouse constellation.

Even though the constellation forms a united schema for the data warehouse, the people analyzing each business process may be interested only in their piece of the puzzle. A scheduler will naturally focus on the scheduling star schema. Each star schema can be thought of as a data mart for the corresponding business process. It is possible to deploy data marts on physically different machines. Perhaps the scheduling department has their own dedicated computer system that it prefers. When deploying data to physically distinct data marts, it is still very important for the data to be conformed, so that everyone is communicating meaningfully.

14.5 **Scaling Up the System**

Horizontal table partitioning is common to many commercial systems, allowing the storage of a large table in meaningful pieces, according to the dimension values. The most common dimension for partitioning is time, but other dimensions can also be good candidates for partitioning, depending on the query processing required. For the time dimension, one option is to divide the data by month over n years and have $12 \times n$ partitions. The union of these partitions forms the whole table. One advantage of horizontal partitioning is that new data often only affects one partition, while the majority of the partitions remains unchanged. Partitioning can focus updates on a smaller set of data, improving update performance. Another advantage of horizontal partitioning is that the partitions can be stored on separate devices, and then a query can be processed in parallel, improving query response. Multiple CPUs can divide the work, and the system is not input/output (I/O) bound at the disks, since partitioning permits the number of disks to scale up with the amount of data. Chapter 7 discusses range partitioning in detail, which can be used to horizontally partition data.

To achieve parallel processing gains many data warehouses and data marts exploit shared nothing partitioning, as discussed in Chapter 6. This is the strategy used by IBM's DB2 and NCR's Teradata products. Shared nothing partitioning horizontally partitions data into multiple logical or physical servers by hashing each table record to a partition. The technique has been massively successful, though there are design complexities that are introduced. See Chapter 6 for a full discussion.

Vertical table partitioning allows dividing a table physically by groups of columns. This has the advantage of putting rarely used columns out of the mainstream of query processing, and in general it helps match the processing requirements with the available columns. Some overhead is incurred because the table key must be replicated in each partition.

Pushing the query processing down toward the disks is a recent interesting innovation that allows scalability through parallelism. Netezza Corporation has patented technology (see Hindshaw et al.) that utilizes active disks in a massively parallel processing (MPP) architecture. Figure 14.9 illustrates the general concept. Clients pose queries to the database over a communications network. The central database operation processor parses and optimizes the query, producing an execution plan where the query operations are broken into "snippets." Each snippet is assigned to a snippet processing unit (SPU). A SPU is composed of a SPU controller coupled with a storage device, typically a disk drive. Database tables can be distributed across the disk drives, either as redundant copies or sectioned with records assigned to specific SPUs. The SPU controller executes query processing of the snippet locally. Data can be streamed from the disk, and processed without materializing the raw data in memory. Only the processed data is sent back to the central database operation processor, thereby reducing the demand on bandwidth. Netezza's approach exploits proprietary hardware. Other companies, like DATAllegro are currently attempting to deploy similar data warehouse appliance tech-

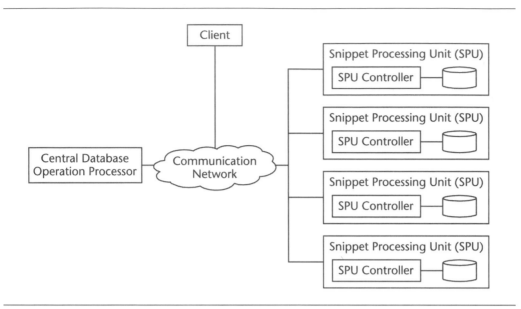

Figure 14.9   Netezza's assymetric massively parallel processing architecture.

nology using commodity components. The Netezza approach is based on massive I/O parallelism, and one of their claims is that the technique obviates the need for index and materialized view design. After all, do you need indexes when you can scan more than a Terabyte per minute? On the flip side, Netezza has no caching, no indexing. Every data request requires access to disk. The strategy is best suited to query processing needs, and may not be ideal for active data warehousing, a current trend in data warehousing where data warehouses are becoming increasingly near real time. Active data warehouses include a larger and more frequent amount of inserts and update activity. This interesting technology is emerging, and the next few years will be telling in terms of its success. There are major gains in scalability from the parallelism obtained by distributing the query processing.

14.6 DSS, Warehousing, and OLAP Design Considerations

Use the star schema approach rather than querying from normalized tables. The facts are central to the star schema, and the dimensions are only one step away. The star schema is efficient, as shown in Chapter 5. The snowflake schema requires more joins, and is less intuitive to navigate. The dimension tables of the star schema contain redundant data, but they are small compared to the fact table. Databases support efficient star joins.

Index each dimension attribute of the fact table. The dimension tables are used to select and group rows of the fact table. The dimension tables are the entrance into the fact table. Indexing each dimension attribute of the fact table is crucial for performance. Use bitmap indexes for each dimension attribute having a small cardinality of distinct values. Bitmap indexes are very fast and small compared to B+tree indexes, when the number of distinct values is low. A bitmap index is implemented with a bitmap for each distinct value of the attribute. Every bitmap has one bit for each row in the table. Each bit indicates if the given row contains the given value. When conditions are specified by the user on multiple dimensions, conjunction operations using the bitmaps are very fast, determining exactly which rows need to be fetched from the fact table.

Don't use views, with the exception of a dimension table fulfilling multiple roles. Views store a defining query rather than data. Every time a query is issued against a view, the underlying query for the view is run to obtain the data. This can lead to excessive processing. A web design company, unfamiliar with data warehouse and OLAP technology, attempted to design an OLAP application for one of their clients. The fact table was designed as a view built on base tables in normalized form. Every time the fact table (actually a view in this case) was accessed, the underlying query was run, leading to joins of huge tables. The OLAP system could not process the initial load of the cube. The system would hang endlessly. The gains of the data warehouse and OLAP are based on reusing results. The use of views defeats the gains, by processing the same query with each use. As mentioned, there is a possible exception to the rule. If multiple dimensions have the same underlying data, but are used for different roles, then views can be used to rename the underlying table and attributes. For example, the production and repair dates of Figure 14.4 both rely on the same underlying date dimension. Some designers eschew the use of views even in this case, copying the data to multiple dimension tables. Kimball and Ross [2002] recommend using one underlying table. In this instance, views reduce the resources required to maintain the dimensions. Changes only need to occur once in a single underlying dimension table. The heavier use of the single underlying table could also lead to better buffer pool performance. The cost of using views to fulfill roles is very small, since renaming operations require very little system resources.

14.7 Usage Syntax and Examples for Major Database Servers

We give a few concrete examples utilizing specific commercial products in this section, to illustrate the implementation of some of the concepts we've discussed. Recommendations for more complete coverage of specific products are given in the Literature Summary section at the end of the chapter.

14.7.1 Oracle

Oracle offers many ways of partitioning data, including by range, by list, and by hash value. Each partition can reside in its own tablespace. A tablespace in Oracle is a physical location for storing data.

Partitioning by range allows data to be stored in separate tablespaces, based on specified value ranges for each partition. For example, we may want to separate historical data from recent data. If recent data changes frequently, then isolating the recent data in a smaller partition can improve update performance. The following is the definition of a materialized view for labor costs by repair date, partitioned into historical and recent data, with 2006 acting as the dividing point.

```
CREATE MATERIALIZED VIEW mv_labor_cost_by_repair_date
PARTITION BY RANGE(repair_year)
(PARTITION repair_to_2006 VALUES LESS THAN (2006)
TABLESPACE repairs_historical,
PARTITION repair_recent VALUES LESS THAN (MAXVALUE)
TABLESPACE repairs_recent)
AS
SELECT w.repair_date_id, repair_year, sum(labor_cost)
FROM warranty_claim w, repair_date r
WHERE w.repair_date_id=r.repair_date_id
GROUP BY w.repair_date_id, repair_year;
```

If the values of a column are discrete, but do not form natural ranges, the rows can be assigned to partitions according to defined lists of values. Here is a definition for a materialized view that partitions the rows into east, central, and west, based on value lists.

```
CREATE MATERIALIZED VIEW mv_labor_cost_by_location
PARTITION BY LIST(region)
(PARTITION east VALUES('Northeast','Southeast')
TABLESPACE east,
PARTITION central VALUES('Midwest','Westcentral')
TABLESPACE central,
PARTITION west VALUES('West','Southwest')
TABLESPACE west)
AS
SELECT w.loc_id, region, sum(labor_cost)
FROM warranty_claim w, location l
WHERE w.loc_id=l.loc_id
GROUP BY w.loc_id, region;
```

Often, it is desirable to divide the data evenly between partitions, facilitating the balancing of loads over multiple storage devices. Partitioning by hash values may be a good option to satisfy this purpose. Here is a materialized view definition that divides the labor cost by repair date rows into three partitions based on hashing.

```
CREATE MATERIALIZED VIEW mv_labor_cost_by_repair_date
PARTITION BY HASH(repair_date_id)
PARTITIONS 3 STORE IN (tablespace1, tablespace2,
tablespace3)
AS
SELECT repair_date_id, sum(labor_cost)
FROM warranty_claim
GROUP BY repair_date_id;
```

Partition by hash may not work well in the case where the distribution of values is highly skewed. For example, if 90% of the rows have a given value, then at least 90% of the rows will map to the same partition, no matter how many partitions we use, and no matter what hash function the system utilizes.

14.7.2 Microsoft's Analysis Services

Microsoft SQL Server 2005 Analysis Services currently supports OLAP and data mining operations. The Analysis Manager is used to specify a data source. Many options are supported for the data source, including Open DataBase Connectivity (ODBC) data sources. A database connection can be established to a Microsoft SQL Server database (or any other ODBC-compliant database). The dimension tables and fact tables are specified using GUI screens, and the data cube is then built. There are a series of options available including ROLAP, HOLAP, and MOLAP. There are also several options for specifying limits on the use of aggregates. The user can specify a space limit.

Figure 14.10 shows a screen from the Storage Design Wizard. The wizard selects views to materialize, while displaying the progress in graph form. Note that Microsoft uses the term "aggregations" instead of materialized views in this context. OLAP systems improve performance by precalculating views and materializing the results to disk. Queries are answered from the smaller aggregations instead of reading the large fact table. Typically, there are far too many possible views to materialize them all, so the OLAP system needs to pick strategic views for materialization. In Microsoft Analysis Services, you have several options to control the process. You may specify the maximum amount of disk space to use for the aggregates. You also have the option of specifying the performance gain. The higher the performance gain, the more disk space is required. The Microsoft documentation recommends a setting of about 30% for the performance gain. Selecting a reasonable performance gain setting is problematic, since the gain is

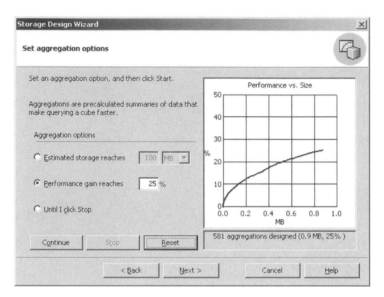

Figure 14.10   Print screen from Microsoft Analysis Services, Storage Design Wizard.

highly dependent on the data. The views are picked for materialization using a greedy algorithm, so the graph will indicate a trend toward diminishing returns. You can watch the gain on the graph, and click the stop button anytime you think the gain is not worth the disk space and the associated update costs. Also, if your specified gain is reached, and the curve is not leveling out, you can reset the gain higher, and continue if you wish.

TIPS AND INSIGHTS FOR DATABASE PROFESSIONALS

- **Tip 1. The dimensional design approach is appropriate for designing a data warehouse.** The resulting star schemas are much more efficient than normalized tables in the context of a data warehouse.

- **Tip 2. Use star schemas rather than snowflake schemas.** Star schemas require fewer joins, and the schemas are more intuitive for users.

- **Tip 3. Conform dimensions across all business processes.** Discussions between different groups of users are more fruitful if terms carry the same meaning across the entire enterprise.

- **Tip 4. Index dimension attributes with bitmap indexes when the attribute has a small to medium cardinality of distinct values.** The bitmap indexes are efficient for star joins.

- **Tip 5. Use materialized views when advantageous for speeding up throughput.** Chapter 5 contains more discussion on the topic of selecting views for materialization. Note that OLAP systems automatically select views for materialization.

- **Tip 6. Use appropriate update strategies for refreshing materialized views.** Typically this means incremental updates during a designated update window each night. However, company requirements may dictate a real-time update strategy. Occasionally, when the nature of the data leads to changes of large portions of a materialized view, it may be more efficient to run a complete refresh of that materialized view.

- **Tip 7. If your OLAP system offers both ROLAP and MOLAP storage options, use MOLAP only if the data is dense.** ROLAP is more efficient when the data is sparse. ROLAP is good overall, but MOLAP does not scale well to large, sparse data spaces.

- **Tip 8. When data sets become huge, utilize partitioning and parallel processing to improve scalability.** Chapter 6 discusses shared nothing partitioning. Shared nothing systems are massively parallel processing platforms that have become extremely popular for data warehousing. In general, once a data warehouse or data mart grows larger than ~500GB of raw data (size before loading into the database) shared nothing architectures will generally provide a superior architectural platform compared to scale-up solution that simply grow the database server resources within a single box.

- **Tip 9: Don't go nuts with dimension tables.** Additional tables in the system add complexity to the query execution plan selection process. Simply put, every table that needs to be joined can be joined in multiple ways (hash join, nested loop join, merge join, etc.). As the number of tables to join grows the join enumeration grows and therefore so does the compilation complexity. As a result a large number of dimension tables can cause increased complexity (and opportunity for error) within the query compiler. Therefore, for very narrow dimension tables, 20 bytes wide or less, consider denormalizing them. This is one of the practical trade-offs between design purity and real world practicality.

14.8 Summary

The decision support technologies of data warehousing and OLAP are overviewed in this chapter. Some of the physical design issues are described and some of the solutions illustrated with examples. The use of materialized views for faster query response in the data warehouse environment is discussed. The different general categories of OLAP storage are described, including relational (ROLAP), multidimensional (MOLAP), and hybrid (HOLAP), along with general guidelines when one may be more appropriate than the others, based on data density. The dimensional design approach is covered briefly, with examples illustrating star and snowflake schemas. The usefulness of the data warehouse bus is demonstrated with an example, showing the relationship of conformed dimensions across multiple business processes. The data warehouse bus leads to a data warehouse constellation schema with the possibility of developing a data mart for each business process. Approaches toward efficient processing are discussed, including some hardware approaches, the appropriate use of bitmap indexes, various materialized view update strategies, and the partitioning of data.

Data warehousing offers the infrastructure critical for decision support based on large amounts of historical data. OLAP is a service that offers quick response to queries posed against the huge amounts of data residing in a data warehouse. Data warehousing and OLAP technologies allow for the exploration of data, facilitating better decisions by management.

14.9 Literature Summary

The books by Kimball et al. offer detailed explanations and examples for various aspects of data warehouse design. The book *The Data Warehouse Toolkit: The Complete Guide to Dimensional Modeling* is a good starting point for those interested in pursuing data warehousing. The extract-transform-load process is covered in *The Data Warehouse ETL Toolkit*.

Product-specific details and examples for Oracle can be found in *Oracle Data Warehouse Tuning for 10g* by Powell. *SQL Server Analysis Services 2005 with MDX* by Harinath and Quinn is a good source covering Microsoft data warehousing, OLAP, and data mining.

The Patent Office website takes some getting used to, but the effort can be well worth it if you want to learn about emerging technology. Be prepared to sift, since not every patent is valuable. You may discover what your competition is pursuing, and you may find yourself thinking better ideas of your own.

Harinath, S., and Quinn, S. *SQL Server Analysis Services 2005 with MDX*. New York: John Wiley, 2006.

Hindshaw, F., Metzger, J., and Zane, B. Optimized Database Appliance, Patent No. U.S. 7,010,521 B2, Assignee: Netezza Corporation, Framingham, MA, issued March 7, 2006.

IBM Data Warehousing, Analysis, and Discovery: Overview: IBM Software, at http://www.306.ibm.com/software/data/db2bi/.

Kimball, R., Reeves L., Ross, M., and Thornthwaite, W. *The Data Warehouse Life Cycle Toolkit*, New York: John Wiley, 1998.

Kimball, R., and Ross, M. *The Data Warehouse Toolkit: The Complete Guide to Dimensional Modeling*, 2nd ed. New York: John Wiley, 2002.

Kimball, R., and Caserta, J. *The Data Warehouse ETL Toolkit*, 2nd ed. New York: John Wiley, 2004.

Microsoft SQL Server: Business Intelligence Solutions, at http://www.microsoft.com/ sql/solutions/bi/default.mspx.

Netezza Corporation, at netezza.com.

Oracle Business Intelligence Solutions, at http://www.oracle.com/solutions/business_intelligence/index.html.

Patent Full-Text and Full-Page Image Databases, at www.uspto.gov/patft/index.html.

Powell, G. *Oracle Data Warehouse Tuning for 10g*. Boston: Elsevier, 2005.

Teorey, T., Lightstone, S., and Nadeau, T. *Database Modeling and Design: Logical Design*, 4th ed. San Francisco: Morgan Kaufmann, 2006.

Denormalization 15

At the time, Nixon was normalizing relations with China.
I figured that if he could normalize relations, then so could I.
—Ted Codd (1923–2003)

The phrase "smaller, faster, cheaper" has long been the credo of the builders of computer chips, personal digital assistants (PDAs), quantum computers, and even printers. It is well known to be a difficult task to optimize all three at the same time, and most of the time there are important tradeoffs that need to be addressed. A similar phrase, "faster, better, cheaper," was used in NASA, but came into serious question after several critical losses in the past decade, including the infamous Mars Climate Orbiter with its disastrous mix of English and metric units in the same system. In database design we would very much like to optimize performance (fast queries), maintainability (fast updates), and integrity (avoiding unwanted deletes) if we can, but the reality is that there are often serious tradeoffs in these objectives that need to be addressed.

First it is important to distinguish the difference between normalization and denormalization. *Normalization* is the process of breaking up a table into smaller tables to eliminate unwanted side effects of deletion of certain critical rows and to reduce the inefficiencies of updating redundant data often found in large universal tables. Sometimes, however, normalization is taken too far and some queries become extremely inefficient due to the extra joins required for the smaller tables. *Denormalization* is the process of adding columns to some tables to reduce the joins, and is done if the integrity of the data is not seriously compromised. This chapter explains these tradeoffs with some simple examples.

15.1 Basics of Normalization

Database designers sometimes use processing requirements to refine the database schema definition during the physical design phase or as a method for tuning the database if there are real performance bottlenecks. Schema refinement, or denormalization, is often used in online transaction processing (OLTP) if meaningful efficiency gains can be made without loss of data integrity, and if it is relatively easy to implement. Denormalization is also very common in online analytical processing (OLAP) through the use of the star schema.

Relational database tables sometimes suffer from some rather serious problems in terms of performance, integrity, and maintainability. For example, when the entire database is defined as a single large table, it can result in a large amount of redundant data and lengthy searches for just a small number of target rows. It can also result in long and expensive updates, and deletions in particular can result in the elimination of useful data as an unwanted side effect.

Such a situation is shown in Figure 15.1, where products, salespersons, customers, and orders are all stored in a single table called "sales." In this table we see that certain product and customer information is stored redundantly, wasting storage space. Certain queries, such as "Which customers (by customer number) ordered vacuum cleaners last month?" would require a search of the entire table. Also, updates, such as changing the address of the customer Galler, would require changing multiple rows. Finally, deleting an order by a valued customer, such as Fry (who bought an expensive computer), if that is his only outstanding order, deletes the only copy of his name, address, and credit rating as a side effect. Such information may be difficult (or sometimes impossible) to recover.

If we had a method of breaking up such a large table into smaller tables so that these types of problems would be eliminated, the database would be much more efficient and reliable. Classes of relational database schemes or table definitions, called *normal forms*, are commonly used to accomplish this goal. The creation of a normal form database table is called *normalization*. It is accomplished by analyzing the interdependencies among individual attributes associated with those tables and taking projections (subsets of columns) of larger tables to form smaller ones.

Let's look at an alternative way of representing the same data of the sales table in two smaller tables—productSales and customer—as shown in Figure 15.2. These two tables can be derived (displayed) from the sales table by the following two SQL queries:

```
SELECT orderNo, productName, custNo, date AS productSales
    FROM sales;
```

sales

productName	orderNo	custNo	custName	custAddress	creditRat	date
vacuum cleaner	1300	45	Galler	Chicago	6	1-3-06
computer	2735	13	Fry	Plymouth	10	4-15-05
refrigerator	2460	27	Remley	Ann Arbor	8	9-12-04
DVD player	1509	34	Honeyman	Detroit	3	12-5-04
iPod	2298	55	Jagadish	Ann Arbor	9	6-2-06
radio	1986	91	Antonelli	Chicago	7	5-10-05
CD player	1817	43	Arden	Dexter	8	8-3-02
vacuum cleaner	2902	91	Antonelli	Chicago	7	10-1-04
vacuum cleaner	1885	63	Karmeisool	Mt. Clemens	5	10-31-98
refrigerator	1943	45	Galler	Chicago	6	1-4-04
television	2315	39	Patel	Chelsea	8	7-31-06

Figure 15.1   Single table database for "sales."

```
SELECT custNo, custName, custAddress, creditRat AS customer
    FROM sales;
```

These queries shows that they are nothing more than projections of the sales table over two different sets of columns. If we join the two tables, productSales and customer, over the common attribute custNo, they will produce the original table, sales. This is called a *lossless join* and shows that the two tables are equivalent to the single table in terms of meaningful content.

The two smaller tables, productSales and customer, have nice performance and storage properties that the single table, sales, doesn't have. Let's revisit the problems in the sales table mentioned above.

1. In the sales table we see that certain product and customer information is stored redundantly, wasting storage space. The redundant data is custNo, custName, custAddress, and creditRat. In the two-table equivalent, there is only redundancy in custNo. Attribute values for custName, custAddress, and creditRat are only stored once. In most cases, as is the case here, this separation of data results in smaller tables.

productSales

orderNo	productName	custNo	date
1300	vacuum cleaner	45	1-3-06
2735	computer	13	4-15-05
2460	refrigerator	27	9-12-04
1509	DVD player	34	12-5-04
2298	iPod	55	6-2-06
1986	radio	91	5-10-05
1817	CD player	43	8-3-02
2902	vacuum cleaner	91	10-1-04
1885	vacuum cleaner	63	10-31-98
1943	refrigerator	45	1-4-04
2315	television	39	7-31-06

customer

custNo	custName	custAddress	creditRat
45	Galler	Chicago	6
13	Fry	Plymouth	10
27	Remley	Ann Arbor	8
34	Honeyman	Detroit	3
55	Jagadish	Ann Arbor	9
91	Antonelli	Chicago	7
43	Arden	Dexter	8
63	Karmeisool	Mt. Clemens	5
39	Patel	Chelsea	8

Figure 15.2   Two table databases, "productSales" and "customer."

Certain queries (such as "Which customers (by customer number) ordered vacuum cleaners last month?") would require a search of the entire sales table. In the two-table case, this query still requires a search of the entire productSales table, but this table is now much smaller than the sales table and will take a lot less time to scan.

2. Updates, such as changing the address of the customer Galler, would require changing multiple rows. In the two-table equivalent, the customer address appears only once in the customer table, and any update to that address is confined to a single row in the customer table.

3. Deleting an order by a valued customer, such as Fry (who bought an expensive computer), if that is his only outstanding order, deletes the only copy of his name, address, and credit rating as a side effect. In the two-table equivalent, Fry's order can still be deleted, but his name, address, and credit rating are all still maintained in the customer table.

In fact, the two-table equivalent is in third normal form (3NF), and actually a stronger form of 3NF, called Boyce-Codd normal form (BCNF). It has the property that only the key of the table uniquely defines the values of all the other attributes of the table. For example, the key value for 45 for custNo in the customer table determines that the customer name, Galler, is the only value that can occur in the same row as the customer number 45. The custNo value also uniquely determines the customer address and the credit rating. This property of uniqueness is useful in keeping tables small and nonredundant. These unique properties can be expressed in terms of functional dependencies (FDs).

```
sales table
orderNo -> productName, custNo, custName, custAddress,
creditRat, date
custNo -> custName, custAddress, creditRat

productSales table
orderNo -> productName, custNo, date

customer table
custNo -> custName, custAddress, creditRat
```

In the customer and productSales tables, only the key uniquely determines the values of all the nonkeys in each table, which is the condition necessary for 3NF. In the sales table, you have a nonkey, custNo, which uniquely determines several attributes in addition to the key, orderNo. Thus, the sales table does not satisfy 3NF, and this dependency on nonkeys is the source of the loss of integrity and multiple updates in a nonnormalized database.

15.2 Common Types of Denormalization

Denormalization is often used to suggest alternative logical structures (schemas) during physical design and thus provides the designers with other feasible solutions to choose from. More efficient databases are the likely outcome of evaluating alternative structures. This process is referred to as denormalization because the schema transformation can cause the degree of normalization in the resulting table to be less than the degree of at least one of the original tables.

The two most common types of denormalization are two entities in a one-to-one relationship and two entities in a one-to-many relationship.

15.2.1 Two Entities in a One-to-One Relationship

The tables for these entities could be implemented as a single table, thus avoiding frequent joins required by certain applications. As an example, consider the following two tables in 3NF and BCNF:

```
CREATE TABLE  report
    (reportNum        INTEGER,
     reportName       VARCHAR(64),
     reportText       VARCHAR(256),
     PRIMARY KEY (reportNum));

CREATE TABLE reportAbbreviation
    (abbreviation   CHAR(6),
     reportNum        INTEGER NOT NULL UNIQUE,
     PRIMARY KEY (abbreviation),
     FOREIGN KEY (reportNum) REFERENCES report);
```

The functional dependencies for these tables are:

- Table report: reportNum -> reportName, reportText
- Table reportAbbreviation: abbreviation -> reportNum
- reportNum -> abbreviation

Example Query 15.1

```
SELECT r.reportName, ra.abbreviation
    FROM report AS r, reportAbbreviation AS ra
    WHERE r.reportNum = ra.reportNum;
```

In this relationship we denormalize report by defining report2 to include abbreviation and thus eliminate the abbreviation table completely. The new entry in report2 is shown in boldface.

```
CREATE TABLE  report2
    (reportNum      INTEGER,
     reportName     VARCHAR(30),
     reportText     VARCHAR(256),
     abbreviation   CHAR(6),
     PRIMARY KEY (reportNum));
```

The functional dependencies for the new report table are:

*   Table report2: reportNum -> reportName, reportText, abbreviation, abbreviation -> reportNum

The revised table report2 is also in 3NF and BCNF, so there can be no loss of data integrity due to deletes involving reportNum or abbreviation. If a report is deleted, both its report number and abbreviation are deleted, so neither one is left orphaned in the database.

15.2.2 Two Entities in a One-to-many Relationship

Sometimes logical design results in very simple tables with very few attributes, where the primary key is a foreign key in another table you want to join with. In such cases, when a query wants data from both tables, it may be more efficient to implement them as individually named columns as an extension of the parent entity (table).

Let's look at the following example. The table department is the "parent" table and emp is the "child" table since one department can have potentially many employees and each employee (emp) is in only one department.

```
CREATE TABLE department
    (deptNum    INTEGER,
     deptName   VARCHAR(30),
     PRIMARY KEY (deptNum));

CREATE TABLE emp
    (empNum    INTEGER,
     empName   VARCHAR(30),
     manager   VARCHAR(30),
     deptNum   INTEGER,
```

```
        PRIMARY KEY (empNum),
        FOREIGN KEY (deptNum) REFERENCES department);
```

The functional dependencies for these two tables are:

- Table department: deptNum -> deptName
- Table emp: empNum -> empName, manager, deptNum

Example Query 15.2

```
SELECT e.empName, d.deptName
    FROM emp AS e, department AS d
    WHERE d.deptNum = e.deptNum;
```

In this relationship we denormalize emp by defining emp2 to include deptName from the department table. The new attribute deptName in emp2 is shown in boldface.

```
CREATE TABLE department
    (deptNum      INTEGER,
     deptName     VARCHAR(30),
     PRIMARY KEY (deptNum));
```

```
CREATE TABLE emp2
    (empNum       INTEGER,
     empName      VARCHAR(30),
     manager      VARCHAR(30),
     deptNum      INTEGER,
     deptName     VARCHAR(30),
     PRIMARY KEY (empNum),
     FOREIGN KEY (deptNum) REFERENCES department);
```

The functional dependencies for these two tables are:

- Table department: deptNum -> deptName
- Table emp2: empNum -> empName, manager, deptNum
- deptNum -> deptName

Table department is still in 3NF, but table emp2 has lost normalization to below 3NF. To compensate for the lost normalization in emp2, we could keep department as a redundant table. The cost of this redundancy is in storage space and increased update time since updates involving deptName will have to be made to both tables. A third

Table 15.1   Comparison of Denormalization Options for Query 15.2

Option	Normalization	Query Time	Update Time	Storage Space
1–emp2 only	Less than 3NF, delete anomaly possible	Low, no joins needed	Low, no redundancy	Potentially higher
2–emp2 and department	3NF	Low, no joins needed	Lower due to redundancy	Highest
3–emp and department	3NF	Higher, join required	High, only hurt if deptNum is changed	Original

option is to leave the two original tables unchanged. Let's summarize the tradeoffs for these three options based on Query 15.2 (see Table 15.1).

- Option 1: Consolidate into one table, emp2.
- Option 2: Consolidate into one table, emp2, and retain department as redundant.
- Option 3: No change to emp and department.

The analysis of these three options goes as follows:

- *Option 1 (emp2):* This is pure denormalization. It optimizes the query time and usually improves the update times. Storage space can be higher or lower, depending on the relative sizes of the department and emp tables. The normalization definitely is less, leaving a potential delete anomaly and loss of integrity if the last record containing a particular deptNum and deptName combination is deleted. If this is not an issue, then denormalization is definitely a winning strategy. Query and update times are usually more important than storage space.

- *Option 2 (emp2 and department):* This is denormalization with redundancy to prevent the delete anomaly between deptNum and deptName. This strategy should only be used if the loss of integrity is a real issue here. Like pure denormalization, it greatly improves query time at the expense of update time and storage space.

- *Option 3 (emp and department):* This is the original database schema, which should be kept if the query and update times are acceptable. To denormalize would require a reorganization of the database schema and repopulation of emp2, a potentially significant overhead.

In summary, the key effects of denormalization are:

1. A definite improvement (decrease) in query time.
2. A potential increase in update time.
3. A potential increase in storage space.
4. A potential loss of data integrity due to certain deletions.
5. The necessity for program transformations for all relevant queries.
6. The overhead needed to reorganize one or more tables (e.g., emp to emp2).

These effects require careful consideration. The example in Section 15.3 goes into more details of this analysis.

Many database systems have software that provides data synchronization between redundant data and base data, and thus supports the concept of denormalization using redundancy. For instance, software such as DB2 Everyplace, Oracle Data Hubs and Oracle Streams, and SQL Server Compare (Red-Gate Software) and SQL Server Everywhere Edition, all provide such critical data synchronization services.

15.3 Table Denormalization Strategy

A practical strategy for table denormalization is to select only the most dominant processes to determine those modifications that will most likely improve performance. The basic modification is to add attributes to existing tables to reduce join operations. The steps of this strategy for relational databases follow.

1. Minimize the need for denormalization by developing a clear and concise logical database design, including tables that are at least 3NF or BCNF. This establishes the requirement of an accurate representation of reality and flexibility of the design for future processing requirements. If the original database does not meet performance requirements, consider denormalization as one of the options for improving performance.
2. Select the dominant queries and updates based on such criteria as high frequency of execution, high volume of data accessed, response time constraints, or explicit high priority. Remember this rule of thumb: Any process whose frequency of execution or data volume accessed is 10 times that of another process is considered to be dominant.

3. Define extended tables with extra columns, when appropriate, to reduce the number of joins required for dominant queries.

4. Evaluate total cost for storage, query, and update for the database schema, with and without the extended table, and determine which configuration minimizes total cost.

5. Consider also the data integrity due to denormalization. If an extended table appears to have lower storage and processing (query and update) costs and insignificant data integrity problems, then use that schema for physical design in addition to the original candidate table schema. Otherwise use only the original schema. Also, try very hard to use database management system (DBMS) features to keep the redundant data in sync with the base data.

15.4 Example of Denormalization

The following example illustrates how to proceed through the database life cycle, in a practical way, for a simple relational database. We will see how denormalization extends a logical design methodology to attain significant improvements in performance, given that the available access methods are known.

15.4.1 Requirements Specification

The management of a large retail store would like a database to keep track of sales activities. The requirements for this database lead to the following six entities and their unique identifiers:

Entity	Entity ID	ID length (average, in bytes)	Cardinality
Customer	custNum	6	80,000
Job	jobTitle	24	80
Order	orderNum	9	200,000
Salesperson	salesName	20	150
Department	deptNum	2	10
Item	itemNum	6	5,000

The following assertions describe the data relationships:

- Each customer has one job title, but different customers may have the same job title. (Note: Consider this a special database where customer job titles are important.)

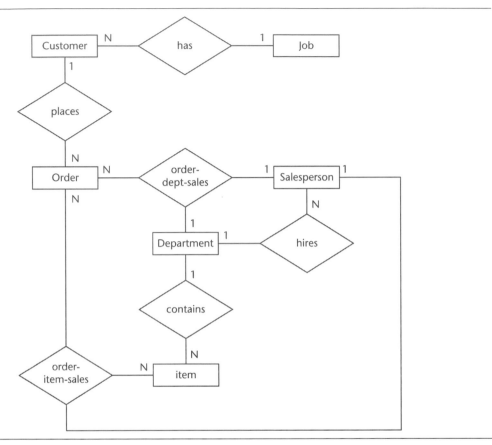

Figure 15.3   ER diagram for a simple database.

- Each customer may place many orders, but only one customer may place a particular order.

- Each department has many salespeople, but each salesperson must work in only one department. (Note: This may not be a realistic constraint for some retail businesses.)

- Each department has many items for sale, but each item is sold in only one department (item means item type, like IBM PC).

- For each order, items ordered in different departments must involve different salespeople, but all items ordered within one department must be handled by exactly one salesperson. In other words, for each order, each item has exactly one salesperson, and for each order, each department has exactly one salesperson.

15.4.2 Logical Design

An ER diagram and a set of FDs to correspond to each of the assertions are given below. Figure 15.3 presents the ER diagram. Normally the ER diagram is developed without knowing all the FDs, but in this example the nonkey attributes are omitted so that the entire database can be represented with only a few statements and FDs. The result of this analysis, relative to each of the assertions given, follows.

ER Construct	FDs
Customer(many): Job(one)	custNum -> jobTitle
Order(many): Customer(one)	orderNum -> custNum
Salesperson(many): Department(one)	salesName -> deptNum
Item(many): Department(one)	itemNum -> deptNum
Order(many): Item(many): Salesperson(one)	orderNum,itemNum-> salesName
Order(many): Department(many): Salesperson (one)	orderNum,deptNum-> salesName

The tables needed to represent the semantics of this problem can be easily derived from the constructs for entities and relationships. Primary keys and foreign keys are explicitly defined.

```
CREATE TABLE customer (custNum    CHAR(6),
    jobTitle    VARCHAR(256),
    PRIMARY KEY (custNum),
    FOREIGN KEY (jobTitle) REFERENCES job);

CREATE TABLE job (jobTitle    VARCHAR(256),
    PRIMARY KEY (jobTitle));

CREATE TABLE order (orderNum   CHAR(9),
    custNum     CHAR(6) not null,
    PRIMARY KEY (orderNum),
    FOREIGN KEY (custNum) REFERENCES customer);

CREATE TABLE salesperson (salesName VARCHAR(256),
    deptNum     CHAR(2),
    PRIMARY KEY (salesName),
    FOREIGN KEY (deptNum) REFERENCES department);
```

```
CREATE TABLE department (deptNum CHAR(2),
    PRIMARY KEY (deptNum));

CREATE TABLE item (itemNum   CHAR(6),
    deptNum    CHAR(2),
    PRIMARY KEY (itemNum),
    FOREIGN KEY (deptNum) REFERENCES department);

CREATE TABLE orderItemSales (orderNum   CHAR(9),
    itemNum    CHAR(6),
    salesName  varCHAR(256) not null,
    PRIMARY KEY (orderNum, itemNum),
    FOREIGN KEY (orderNum) REFERENCES order,
    FOREIGN KEY (itemNum) REFERENCES item,
    FOREIGN KEY (salesName) REFERENCES salesperson);

CREATE TABLE orderDeptSales (orderNum   CHAR(9),
    deptNum    CHAR(2),
    salesName  VARCHAR(256) not null,
    PRIMARY KEY (orderNum, deptNum),
    FOREIGN KEY (orderNum) REFERENCES order,
    FOREIGN KEY (deptNum) REFERENCES department,
    FOREIGN KEY  (salesName) REFERENCES salesperson);
```

Further logical design can be done to minimize the number of 3NF tables [Teorey 2005]. However, we will assume the tables defined here are complete and focus on the database refinement using denormalization to increase the efficiency for executing queries and updates.

15.4.3 Schema Refinement Using Denormalizaton

We now look at the quantitative tradeoffs of the refinement of tables to improve processing efficiency. Assume that each of the following transactions are to be executed once per fixed time unit.

Example Query 15.3

Select all order numbers assigned to customers who are computer engineers.

```
SELECT o.orderNum, c.custNum, c.jobTitle
    FROM   order AS o, customer AS c
    WHERE  c.custNum = o.custNum
    AND    c.jobTitle = 'computer engineer';
```

Example Update 15.4

Add a new customer, a painter, with number 423378 and the customer's order number, 763521601, to the database.

```
INSERT INTO customer (custNum, jobTitle) VALUES
('423378','painter');
INSERT INTO order (orderNum, custNum) VALUES
('763521601','423378');
```

Analysis of Example Query 15.3

The system query optimizer can choose from a number of different ways to execute the transaction, Query 15.3. Let us first assume that the tables are all ordered physically by their primary keys. We use the sort-merge join strategy for the first transaction: Sort the order table by custNum, then join tables order and customer with a single scan of each, and select only rows that have jobTitle of computer engineer. We then project on order-Num to answer the query. To simplify the analysis we assume that a sort of nb blocks takes $2 \times nb \log_3 nb$ block accesses (see Chapter 3) and that computer engineers make up 5% of the customers and orders in the database.

All row accesses are sequential in this strategy. For simplicity we have a block size of 4 KB (4,096 bytes) and a prefetch buffer size of 64 KB, as done in DB2. We can estimate the input/ouput (I/O) service time by first computing the effective prefetch blocking factors for the tables order, customer, orderCust, and compEngr: 4,369 (64 KB/15 bytes per row), 2,176, 1,680, and 1,680, respectively. We assume an IBM U320 146 GB hard drive with an average seek of 3.6 ms, an average rotational delay of 2 ms (for 15,000 RPM), and a transfer rate of 320 MB/sec.

I/O time for a block access in a table scan = rotational delay
+ transfer of a prefetch buffer
  = 2 ms + 64 KB/320 MB/sec
  = 2.2 ms.

Block accesses = sort order table + scan order table
    + scan customer table + create orderCust table
    + scan orderCust table + create compEngr table
    + project compEngr table
  = $(2 \times 4,369 \log_3 4,369) + 4,369 + 37 + 120 + 120 + 6 + 6$
  = $2 \times 4,369 \times 7.63 + 4,658$
  = 71,329.

I/O time = 71,329 block accesses × 2.2 ms
  = 156.9 seconds.

Analysis of Update 15.4

The strategy to execute the second transaction, Update 15.4, using the same schema, is to scan each table (order and customer) and rewrite both tables in the new order.

> Block accesses = scan order table + scan customer table
> + rewrite order table + rewrite customer table
> = 4,369 + 37 + 4,369 + 37
> = 8,812.

> I/O time = 8,812 block accesses × 2.2 ms
> = 19.4 seconds.

Defining the Denormalized Table orderCust

If we combine the customer and order tables to avoid the join in Query 15.3, the resulting schema will have a single table orderCust, with primary key orderNum and nonkey attributes custNum and jobTitle, instead of separate tables order and customer. This not only avoids the join, but also the sort needed to get both tables ordered by custNum.

```
CREATE TABLE orderCust (orderNum CHAR(9),
    custNum    CHAR(6) not null,
    jobTitle   VARCHAR(256),
    PRIMARY KEY (orderNum);
```

The strategy for Query 15.3 is now to scan orderCust once to find the computer engineers, write the resulting data on disk, and then read back from disk to project the resulting temporary table, compEngr, to answer the query.

> Block accesses = scan orderCust + write 5% of orderCust on disk
> + project 5% of orderCust
> = 120 + 6 + 6
> = 132.

> I/O time = 132 block accesses × 2.2 ms
> = .3 second.

The strategy for Update 15.4, using this refined schema, is to scan orderCust once to find the point of insertion and then to scan again to reorder the table.

> Block accesses = scan orderCust + scan orderCust
> = 120 + 120
> = 240.

I/O time = 240 block accesses × 2.2 ms
   = .5 second.

Common to both strategies is the addition of an order record to the tables order-ItemSales and orderDeptSales. For the sake of simplicity, we will assume these tables to be unsorted, so the addition of a new order will require only one record access at the end of the table and, thus, negligible I/O time.

The basic performance and normalization data for these two schemas and the two transactions given previously are summarized in Table 15.2. The refined schema dramatically reduces the I/O time for the query transaction and the update, but the cost is storage space and significant reduction in the degree of normalization. The normalization is reduced because we now have a transitive FD: orderNum -> custNum -> jobTitle in table orderCust. The implication of this, of course, is that there is a delete anomaly for jobTitle when a customer deletes an order or the order is filled (in particular, when the jobTitle value deleted is the last instance of that jobTitle in the database).

The significance of these performance and data integrity differences depends on the overall objectives as well as the computing environment for the database, and it must be analyzed in that context. For instance, the performance differences must be evaluated for all relevant transactions, present and projected. Storage space differences may or may not be significant in the computing environment. Integrity problems with the deletion commands need to be evaluated on a case-by-case basis to determine whether the side effects of certain record deletions are destructive to the objectives of the database. In summary, the database designer now has the ability to evaluate the tradeoffs among query and update requirements, storage space, and integrity associated with normalization. This knowledge can be applied to a variety of database design problems.

Table 15.2   Comparison of Performance and Integrity of Original Tables and Join Table

	Original Schema (order and customer tables)	Denormalized Schema (orderCust table)
Query time	156.9 sec	0.3 sec
Update time	19.4 sec	0.5 sec
Storage space (relevant tables)	5.4 MB	7.8 MB
Normalization	3NF	Less than 3NF

TIPS AND INSIGHTS FOR DATABASE PROFESSIONALS

- **Tip 1. Normalize first, then consider denormalizing if performance is poor.** You can maximize the probability of a good logical design by carefully creating a conceptual model using the entity-relationship (ER) approach or UML. These modeling methods tend to result in relational databases that are close to being or are already normalized. Normalization tends to reduce redundancy and provides a high level of integrity to the database. When the actual tables are not conducive to good performance (e.g., when they are so small that dominant queries must do extra joins on them each time they are executed), then consider merging two tables to avoid the join and reduce I/O time. If the benefit of this merge (and possible denormalization) in I/O time saved is greater than the cost in I/O time for the redundancy of data needed to avoid a delete anomaly, in terms of updates, then go ahead with the merge.

- **Tip 2. Denormalize addresses whenever possible.** Addresses can be very long and cumbersome to access, so it is often useful to store addresses separately and access them through joins only when explicitly needed. Furthermore, addresses are often stored redundantly across the database, so if one copy gets deleted, it can be recovered elsewhere. Usually the performance gains of avoiding joins most of the time and avoiding extra bytes in a query are worth the redundancy and the extra updates needed. Addresses are usually fairly static and don't change often.

- **Tip 3. Make use of existing DBMS-provided software to synchronize data between redundant data to support denormalization and the base data.** Examples of data synchronization software include DB2 Everyplace, Oracle Data Hubs, Oracle Streams, SQL Server Compare (Red-Gate Software), and SQL Server Everywhere Edition.

15.5 Summary

In this chapter we explored an in-depth definition and example for the use of denormalization to enhance performance of a relational database. The example reviews the life cycle steps of logical design before the denormalization step of schema refinement to increase efficiency for query processing.

15.6 Literature Summary

The idea for extending a table for usage efficiency came from Schkolnick and Sorenson [1980], and practical advice on denormalization is given in Rodgers [1989].

Ramakrishnan, R., and Gehrke, J. *Database Management Systems*, 3rd ed. New York: McGraw-Hill, 2004.

Rodgers, U. Denormalization: Why, What, and How? *Database Programming and Design,* 2(12), Dec. 1989: 46–53.

Schkolnick, M., and Sorenson, P. Denormalization: A Performance-Oriented Database Design Technique. In *Proceedings from the AICA 1980 Congress*, Bologna, Italy. Brussels: AICA, 1980, pp. 363–377.

Shasha, D., and Bonnet, P. *Database Tuning*. San Francisco: Morgan Kaufmann, 2003.

Silberschatz, A., Korth, H. F., and Sudarshan, S. *Database System Concepts,* 5th ed. New York: McGraw-Hill, 2006.

Teorey, T., Lightstone, S., and Nadeau, T. *Database Modeling and Design: Logical Design*, 4th ed. San Francisco: Morgan Kaufmann, 2006.

Distributed Data Allocation

All men are caught in a network of mutuality.
—Martin Luther King, Jr. (1929–1968)

The first electronic computer was arguably the ABC computer designed and built by John V. Atanasoff and Clifford E. Berry at Iowa State University in 1938 to solve sets of linear equations. The first general-purpose electronic computer, the ENIAC, was completed eight years later in 1946, and could solve a larger and much more general set of mathematical problems. The subsequent lawsuit involving patent rights between Atanasoff and the lead designers of the ENIAC, John W. Mauchly and J. Presper Eckert, resulted in a court decision in November 1971 that gave Atanasoff credit for inventing regenerative memory using a rotating drum and electronic adders, ruling the ENIAC patent for these components invalid. Much of the testimony in this trial focused on several meetings between Mauchly and Atanasoff in Atanasoff's laboratory in 1941 [Burks 1988, Burks 2003]. The ENIAC developers were awarded credit for many other features, however, and its speed improvement over the ABC computer was enormous. These two computers, along with several others of note, marked the beginning of the electronic computing era. Centralized computer systems then developed quickly with the invention of compilers, linkers and loaders, operating systems, and file systems during the 1950s and 1960s.

During the 1960s the concepts of multiple computer systems and computer networks were developed. Along with these systems, an important paper on data allocation in distributed file systems was written in 1969 by Wesley Chu, at Bell Labs, and then a professor of computer science at University of California–Los Angeles. When distributed database systems came to prominence in the 1980s, file allocation gave way to database (table) allocation. Other issues, such as system compatibility and integrity, however, became more important, and the database allocation problem is now just one of many problems that need to be resolved in such systems.

In this chapter we first look at the current technology in heterogeneous distributed (federated) databases and then examine the key database design issue—table allocation methods, particularly for replicated data.

16.1 Introduction

Information management has many new challenges today that are caused by the multiplicity, heterogeneity, and geographic distribution of important data sources.

A distributed or federated database management system is a software system that supports the transparent creation, access, and manipulation of interrelated data located at the different sites of a computer network. Each site of the network has autonomous processing capability and can perform local applications. Each site also has the potential to participate in the execution of global applications, which require network communication. The main goal of a federated database system is to improve the accessibility, compatibility, and performance of a federated database while preserving the appearance of a centralized database management system (DBMS).

Because of the nature of a loosely coupled network of computers, the database design issues encountered in federated database systems differ from those encountered in centralized database systems. In centralized databases, access efficiency is achieved through local optimization by using complex physical structures. In federated databases, the global optimization of processing, including network communication cost, is of major concern. The total cost to run an application is a function of the network configuration: the total user workload at that moment, the data allocation strategy, and the query optimization algorithm.

Federated database systems are very complex systems that have many interrelated objectives. For example, the IBM WebSphere Federation Server is an example of a federated database system that sets the following six objectives [Betawadkar-Norwood 2005]:

1. *Transparency:* A federated system is transparent if it gives the user the capability to code and use applications as though all the data resides on a single database. Thus, all the physical differences and language implementations of the underlying data sources are masked from the user, including the physical location of all data, and the user should see a uniform interface.

2. *Heterogeneity:* This means the system can accommodate different hardware, network protocols, data models, query languages, and query capabilities. They might be as similar as two versions of Oracle or SQL Server, or as diverse as relational databases, websites running XML, or special applications with other types of databases.

3. *Autonomy:* There is an absence of restrictions being enforced at the remote data source, thus allowing it to remain autonomous. It is highly desirable to have the federated database system not change the local operation of an existing data source.

4. *High degree of function:* A federated database system should allow applications to exploit not only the high degree of function provided by the federated system, but also the special functions unique to the variety of individual data sources. Typical federated systems run on SQL to make it easy to use relative to the individual local systems.

5. *Extensibility and openness:* Federated systems need to be able to evolve over time, and thus need the flexibility to seamlessly add new data sources to the enterprise. A *wrapper* module is used to provide the data access logic for each data source. In fact, it is common to supply wrappers for a set of known data sources like Oracle, Sybase, and XML files, plus some generic ones like Open Database Connectivity (ODBC). The IBM WebSphere Federation Server provides a wrapper development kit so customers can write their own wrappers to their own proprietary data sources that cannot be accessed by the native wrappers.

6. *Optimized performance:* The query optimizer of a relational database system is the component that determines the most efficient way to answer a given query. In a federated system the optimizer must also determine whether the different operations in a query (join, select, union, etc.) should be done by the federated server or by the local system at each data source. To do this, the optimizer not only needs to have a cost model for each data source as well as the overall network, but also it tries to figure out whether the query semantics are identical if a query operation is pushed down (in a query rewrite) versus whether the operation is performed locally. The latter decision is based on information specific to the data source. Once an operation is identified to be remotely executable, then the optimizer can use cost-based optimization to determine whether pushing it down is the right decision.

None of these objectives explicitly depends on a data allocation strategy. In federated systems, data allocation (or data distribution) is done largely at the discretion of the database designer or database administrator. Sometimes it involves homogeneous data sources, but usually it is heterogeneous (DB2, Oracle, SQL Server, etc.). Once the allocation decision has been made and the replicated data loaded into the system, the federated system can use its optimizer to maximize the efficiency of the reallocated database. This implies that the updating of multiple heterogeneous sites will have some sort of transaction support, like two-phase commit. This type of support is currently available in some systems.

In the next few sections we illustrate how data allocation decisions can be made with a simple model of performance.

16.2 Distributed Database Allocation

The conditions under which data allocation strategies may operate are determined by the system architecture and the available federated database system software. The four basic data allocation approaches are

- Centralized approach
- Partitioned approach
- Replicated data approach
- Selective replication approach

In the centralized approach, all the data is located at a single site. The implementation of this approach is simple. However, the size of the database is limited by the availability of the disk storage at the central site. Furthermore, the database may become unavailable from any of the remote sites when communication failures occur, and the database system fails totally when the central site fails. This is clearly the least desirable approach in terms of data accessibility and overall performance.

In the partitioned approach, the database is partitioned into its base tables, and each table is assigned to a particular site, without replication. This strategy is only appropriate when local secondary storage is limited compared to the database size.

The completely replicated data approach allocates a full copy of the database (all tables) to each site in the network. This completely redundant allocation strategy is only appropriate when reliability is extremely critical, disk space is abundant, and update inefficiency can be tolerated.

The selective replication approach partitions the database into critical use and non-critical use tables. Noncritical tables need only be stored once, while critical tables are replicated as desired to meet the required level of availability and performance. In general, this is the preferred approach since it balances data availability, query performance, and update efficiency.

The cost/benefit of the replicated database allocation strategy can be estimated in terms of storage cost, communication costs (query and update time), and data availability. Figure 16.1 briefly illustrates the tradeoff by showing the data replication on the horizontal axis and costs on the vertical axis. The following can be seen from Figure 16.1:

- The query communication cost decreases as the number of copies of tables increases because most data can be found at local sites, thus eliminating the need for communication calls.

- The update communication cost increases with the number of table copies because duplicated data will need to be updated.

- The storage cost and local processing cost increase as the number of table copies increases.

- The read availability increases with the number of table copies in the system, while the write availability generally decreases; a write requires most or all copies of a table to be available.

A general rule for data allocation states that data should be placed as close as possible to where it will be used, and then load balancing should be considered to find a global optimization of system performance.

Let's take a look at the basic table allocation problem and then investigate two easily computable methods, or strategies, for allocating tables in a federated database system.

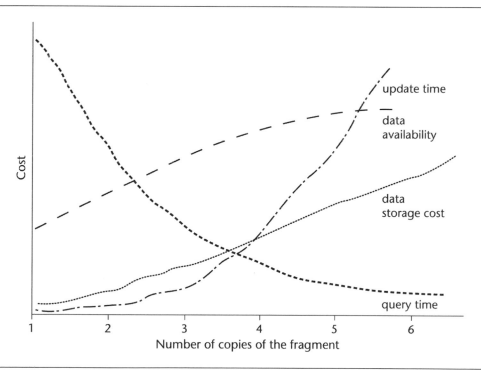

Figure 16.1   Tradeoffs in database allocation due to data replication.

16.3 Replicated Data Allocation—"All-beneficial Sites" Method

The "all-beneficial sites" method selects all sites for a table allocation where the benefit is greater than the cost for one additional copy of that table. You are assumed to start with no copy or one copy of each table.

The benefit for an additional copy of a given table tab0 at site S is measured by the difference in elapsed time between a remote query (i.e., no replicated copy) and a local query (i.e., replicated copy available), multiplied by the frequency of queries to table tab0 originating from site S.

The cost for an additional copy of a given table tab0 at site S is the total elapsed time for all the local updates for table tab0 from transactions originating at site S, plus the total elapsed time for all the remote updates of table tab0 at site S from transactions originating at other sites.

16.3.1 Example

Let us illustrate the application of this method with a simple example of a database schema and its processing characteristics. The average disk input/ouput (I/O) times are given for a query or update originating from the same site in the network (local) or combined disk and network service times from different sites (remote).

		System Parameters	
Table	*Size*	*Average Local Query (Update)**	*Average Remote Query (Update)**
tab1	300 MB	100 (150)	500 (600)
tab2	500 MB	150 (200)	650 (700)
tab3	1.0 GB	200 (250)	1,000 (1,100)

* *Time in milliseconds.*

User transactions are described in terms of their frequency of occurrence, which tables they access, and whether the accesses are reads or writes.

Transaction	Site(s)	Frequency	Table Accesses (Reads, Writes)
T1	S1, S4, S5	1	Four to tab1 (3 reads, 1 write), two to tab2 (2 reads)
T2	S2, S4	2	Two to tab1 (2 reads), four to tab3 (3 reads, 1 write)
T3	S3, S5	3	Four to tab2 (3 reads, 1 write), two to tab3 (2 reads)

Security: user transactions T1, T2, and T3 can either query or update (no restrictions).
Sources of data: all sites—S1, S2, S3, S4, and S5.
Sinks of data (possible locations of transactions): all sites—S1, S2, S3, S4, and S5.

Cost/Benefit Computations

The cost/benefit computations described in this section are summarized in Table 16.1.

Table tab1

Table tab1 at site S1 has the following cost: two remote updates (writes) by transaction T1 (frequency of one), one each from sites S4 and S5, multiplied by 600 milliseconds per write, totaling 1,200 milliseconds, plus one local update by T1 at site S1 at 150 milliseconds, for a grand total of 1,350 milliseconds. The benefit is from three queries (reads) by transaction T1 at site S1, multiplied by the difference between a remote and local query (500 − 100 = 400 milliseconds), totaling 1,200 milliseconds.

Table tab1 at site S2 has the cost of three remote updates by transaction T1 (frequency of one)—one each from sites S1, S4, and S5—multiplied by 600 milliseconds per write, totaling 1,800 milliseconds. The benefit is from two queries (reads) by transaction T2 at site S2 (frequency of two), multiplied by the difference between a remote and local query (400 milliseconds), totaling 1,600 milliseconds.

Table tab1 at site S3 has the cost of three remote updates by transaction T1 (frequency of one)—one each from sites S1, S4, and S5—multiplied by 600 milliseconds per write, totaling 1,800 milliseconds. There is no benefit, because no transaction accesses table tab1 locally at site S3.

Table tab1 at site S4 has the cost of two remote updates by transaction T1 from sites S1 and S5 (frequency of one), multiplied by 600 milliseconds per write, totaling 1,200 milliseconds, plus one local update by T1 at site S4 at 150 milliseconds, for a grand total of 1,350 milliseconds. The benefit is three queries by transaction T1 (frequency of one) and two queries by transaction T2 (frequency of two), multiplied by 400 milliseconds, totaling 2,800 milliseconds.

Table tab1 at site S5 has the cost of two remote updates by transaction T1 from sites S1 and S4 (frequency of one), multiplied by 600 milliseconds per write, totaling

Table 16.1   Cost and Benefit for Each Table Located at Five Possible Sites

Table	Site	Remote Update (Local Update) Transactions	No. of Writes* Freq* Time (milliseconds)	Cost (milliseconds)
tab1	S1	T1 from S4 and S5 (T1 from S1)	2*1*600 ms +1*1*150 ms	1350 ms
	S2	T1 from S1, S4, S5	3*1*600 ms	1800 ms
	S3	T1 from S1, S4, S5	3*1*600 ms	1800 ms
	S4	T1 from S1 and S5 (T1 from S4)	2*1*600 ms +1*1*150 ms	1350 ms
	S5	T1 from S1 and S4 (T1 from S5)	2*1*600 ms +1*1*150 ms	1350 ms
tab2	S1	T3 from S3 and S5	2*3*700 ms	4200 ms
	S2	T3 from S3 and S5	2*3*700 ms	4200 ms
	S3	T3 from S5 (T3 from S3)	1*3*700 ms +1*3*200 ms	2700 ms
	S4	T3 from S3 and S5	2*3*700 ms	4200 ms
	S5	T3 from S3 (T3 from S5)	1*3*700 ms +1*3*200 ms	2700 ms
tab3	S1	T2 from S2 and S4	2*2*1100 ms	4400 ms
	S2	T2 from S4 (T2 from S2)	1*2*1100 ms +1*2*250 ms	2700 ms
	S3	T2 from S2 and S4	2*2*1100 ms	4400 ms
	S4	T2 from S2 (T2 from S4)	1*2*1100 ms +1*2*250 ms	2700 ms
	S5	T2 from S2 and S4	2*2*1100 ms	4400 ms

Table	Site	Query (Read) Sources	No. of Reads* Frequency* (Remote–Local Time)	Benefit (milliseconds)
tab1	S1	T1 at S1	3*1*(500–100)	1200 ms
	S2	T2 at S2	2*2*(500–100)	1600 ms
	S3	None	0	0
	S4	T1 and T2 at S4	(3*1 + 2*2)*(500–100)	2800 ms
	S5	T1 at S5	3*1*(500–100)	1200 ms
tab2	S1	T1 at S1	2*1*(650–150)	1000 ms
	S2	None	0	0
	S3	T3 at S3	3*3*(650–150)	4500 ms
	S4	T1 at S4	2*1*(650–150)	1000 ms
	S5	T1 and T3 at S5	(2*1 + 3*3)*(650–150)	5500 ms
tab3	S1	None	0	0
	S2	T2 at S2	3*2*(1000–200)	4800 ms
	S3	T3 at S3	2*3*(1000–200)	4800 ms
	S4	T2 at S4	3*2*(1000–200)	4800 ms
	S5	T3 at S5	2*3*(1000–200)	4800 ms

1,200 milliseconds, plus one local update by T1 at site S5 at 150 milliseconds, for a grand total of 1,350 milliseconds. The benefit is three queries by transaction T1 (frequency of one), multiplied by 400 milliseconds, totaling 1,200 milliseconds.

In summary, for table tab1 benefit exceeds cost only at site S4; thus, only one copy of tab1 is allocated to this network.

Tables tab2 and tab3

With similar computations we obtain the results for tables tab2 and tab3 as shown in Table 16.1. In summary, for table tab2, benefit exceeds cost at sites S3 and S5. For table tab3, benefit exceeds cost at all sites except S1.

Allocation Decision

Figure 16.2 presents the allocation decision. Allocate table tab1 to site S4. Allocate table tab2 to sites S3 and S5. Allocate table tab3 to sites S2, S3, S4, and S5.

In the cases where benefit and cost are equal, consider whether either cost or benefit (or both) is likely to change in the near future or if greater availability is important. Adjust the allocation accordingly. If cost exceeds benefit at all sites for a given table, then pick the site for a single allocation where the difference between cost and benefit is minimized.

Note that there exist many more elaborate data allocation strategies than are covered here, however, this text has highlighted the major issues to provide a simple method when quick analysis is needed.

The all-beneficial sites method can be derived from exhaustive enumeration of total cost for the initial allocation configuration and the total cost for a new allocation configuration after the replication of a table at a given site. The decision is made to replicate the table if the total cost after replication is lower than the total cost before replication.

For example, let table tab1 be initially allocated to site S1. We need to decide whether to replicate tab1 at site S2. Let query Q1 and update U1, both originating at site S1, access tab1; and let query Q2 and update U2, both originating at site S2, also access tab1.

Total-cost$_1$ (initial allocation of tab1 to S1) = Q1(local) + U1(local)
  + Q2(remote) + U2(remote)

Total-cost$_2$ (after replication of tab1 at S2) = Q1(local) + U1(local)
  + U1(remote) + Q2(local) + U2(local) + U2(remote),

where queries Q1 and Q2 are made to the closest copy of tab1, and updates U1 and U2 must be made to both copies of tab1. We allow tab1 to be replicated at S2 if the following condition holds:

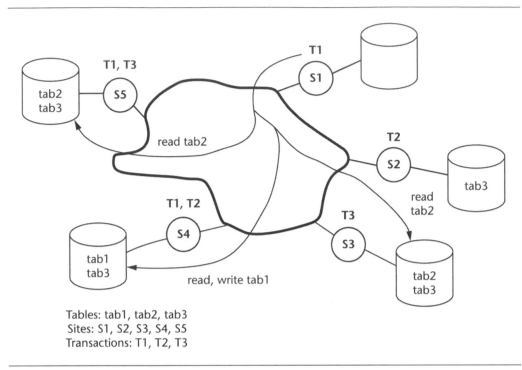

Tables: tab1, tab2, tab3
Sites: S1, S2, S3, S4, S5
Transactions: T1, T2, T3

Figure 16.2   All-beneficial sites method for data allocation, showing remote query and update for transaction T1 originating at site S1.

$$\text{Total-cost}_2 < \text{Total-cost}_1.$$

Expanding terms and simplifying, we get in succession:

Q1(local) + U1(local) + U1(remote) + Q2(local) + U2(local)
    + U2(remote) < Q1(local) + U1(local) + Q2(remote) + U2(remote)
U1(remote) + Q2(local) + U2(local) < Q2(remote).

Q2(remote) − Q2(local) > U1(remote) + U2(local),

which is the relationship that defines the all-beneficial sites method, in other words, the benefit is the difference between a remote and local query time to tab1, and the cost is the sum of the local and remote update times for the new copy of tab1.

16.4 **Progressive Table Allocation Method**

A practical extension of the all-beneficial sites method, called the *progressive table allocation method*, allocates the first copy of each table on the basis of maximum value of benefit-cost. It remembers where that copy is, and bases the next allocation decision on the location of that first copy and the maximum value of benefit-cost for the remaining sites. This procedure is continued, one allocation at a time, until benefit no longer exceeds cost for any of the remaining sites. Note that for this method, cost stays constant for each decision because the update for an additional table is independent of previous allocations. However, benefit does not stay constant; it decreases each time a new copy is allocated that is closer to a given site than the previous set of allocations. The decrease in the benefit at a given site, which must have at least one query to this table, is measured by the decrease in propagation delay between the former closest copy and the proposed new copy of the table, relative to that given site. In the worst case, when a new copy is no closer than any previous copies, the benefit does not increase.

This approach gives a more realistic allocation, based on a progressive set of allocations, rather than a set of independent allocation decisions. It is also a fast method because sites where benefit is less than cost need no longer be evaluated in future iterations.

As an example, let us assume that two tables, tab1 and tab2, are to be allocated to either or both sites S1 and S2. The costs and benefits are computed to be:

```
tab1    S1 cost = 150    benefit = 200
        S2 cost = 170    benefit = 175
tab2    S1 cost = 60     benefit = 30
        S2 cost = 50     benefit = 45
```

Using the all-beneficial sites method, tab1 is allocated to both S1 and S2 because benefit exceeds cost at both sites, and tab2 is allocated to S2 because it minimizes the amount by which cost exceeds benefit. Note: It must be allocated at least once, regardless of costs and benefits.

Using the progressive table allocation method, tab1 is initially allocated to site S1 where benefit exceeds cost by the greatest amount; and tab2 is initially allocated to site S2 where the differential between benefit and cost is minimized, even though cost exceeds benefit at all sites. After this initial mandatory allocation, let us assume the benefit of tab1 at S2 is decreased due to the presence of a copy of tab1 at S1:

```
tab1    S2 cost = 170    benefit = 165
```

At this point no further allocations can be made for tab1 (beyond site S1) because cost now exceeds benefit. This decision is based on more precise data than the all-beneficial sites method, and is more accurate.

Both I/O time and network delay time for these data allocation methods can be accurately estimated using the simple mathematical estimation models given in Appendix A.

TIPS AND INSIGHTS FOR DATABASE PROFESSIONALS

- **Tip 1. Determine when to replicate data across a network on a simple basis of cost and benefits.** Benefits occur when you can save network delay time and I/O time by placing a copy of the data closer to the source of a query. Costs occur when the extra copy of data must be updated every time the original data is updated. Benefits and costs are both estimated in terms of elapsed time (network delay time plus I/O time). In general you want to add a copy of data to a site when the benefit exceeds the cost.

- **Tip 2. When benefits and costs are approximately equal, decide whether to replicate data based on greater availability.** When you have multiple copies of data, the availability of data is greater. This could be a major concern when remote sites go down unexpectedly and you have high-priority queries to satisfy. Analyze the benefits of greater availability and make your decision about data replication based on both tangible and intangible benefits.

- **Tip 3. When the workload is very complex, use the dominant transaction approach.** One of the disadvantages of the data allocation methods presented in this chapter is the use of averages for query times and update times. This does not take into account the possibility of dominant transactions whose I/O specifications are known, and in an environment where the network configuration and network protocol details are given. Under such circumstances, the actual I/O times and network delay times can be estimated for individual dominant transactions instead of averages across all transactions. A dominant transaction is defined by criteria such as high frequency of execution, high volume of data accessed, tight response time constraints, and explicit priority.

16.5 Summary

Distributed database design requires one more step of analysis than centralized databases, but there exists a set of basic principles we can use for everyday design decisions. Replicated data allocation methods can be simply expressed and implemented to minimize the time to execute a collection of transactions on a distributed database. The methods take into account the execution times of remote and local database transactions for query and update and the frequencies of these transactions. Good estimating techniques for average I/O time and network delay costs can easily be applied to these methods.

16.6 **Literature Summary**

An excellent textbook on distributed database systems was written by Ozsu and Valduriez [1999]. The file allocation problem in computing networks was first addressed by Wesley Chu in 1969 [Chu 1984]. Earlier allocation resolutions were simple, but later methods were actual design methodologies that utilize the allocation techniques for one of the decisions [Ceri, Pernici, and Wiederhold 1987]. The "all-beneficial sites" method was originally defined by Ceri and Pelagatti [1984], and the progressive table allocation scheme was derived by Janakiraman et al. [1991]. White papers on the WebSphere Federation Server (IBM) are given in websites for Haas [2002] and Betawadkar-Norwood [2005].

Betawadkar-Norwood, A., Lin, E., and Ursu, I. Using Data Federation Technology in IBM WebSphere Information Integrator: Data Federation Design and Configuration. *developerWorks*, part 1 of 2, June 2005, at http://www-128.ibm.com/developerworks/db2/library/techarticle/0203haas/0203haas.html.

Burks, A. R., and Burks, A. W. *The First Electronic Computer: The Atanasoff Story.* Ann Arbor: University of Michigan Press, 1988.

Burks, A. R. *Who Invented the Computer? The Legal Battle That Changed History.* Amherst, New York, Prometheus Books, 2003.

Ceri, S., and Pelagatti, G. *Distributed Databases: Principles and Systems.* New York: McGraw-Hill, 1984.

Ceri, S., Pernici, B., and Wiederhold, G. Distributed Database Design Methodologies. *Proceedings of the IEEE*, May 1987, pp. 533–546.

Chu, W. W. Optimal File Allocation in Multiple Computer System. *IEEE Transactions on Computers*, Oct. 1969, pp. 885–889.

Chu, W. W. Distributed Data Bases. In *Handbook of Software Engineering*, eds. C. R. Vick and C. V. Ramamoorthy. New York: Van Nostrand Reinhold, 1984.

Fisher, P., Hollist, P., and Slonim, J. A Design Methodology for Distributed Databases. *Proceedings of the IEEE Conference on Distributed Computing*, Sept. 1980, pp. 199–202.

Haas, L., and Lin, E. IBM Federated Database Technology. *developerWorks*, Mar. 2002, at http://www-128.ibm.com/ developerworks/db2/library/techarticle/Dm-0506lin/index.html.

Haas, L., Lin, E, and Roth, M. Data Integration through Database Federation. *IBM Systems Journal*, 41(4), 2002: 578–596.

Janakiraman, J., Warack, C., Bhal, G., and Teorey, T. J. Progressive Fragment Allocation. Proceedings 10th International Conference on the Entity Relationship Approach, San Mateo, CA, Oct. 23–25, 1991, pp. 543–560.

Josifovski, V., Schwarz, P., Haas, L., and Lin, E. Garlic: A New Flavor of Federated Query Processing for DB2. ACM SIGMOD Conference, 2002, pp. 524–532.

Ozsu, T., and Valduriez, P. *Principles of Distributed Database Systems*, 2nd ed. Englewood Cliffs, NJ: Prentice-Hall, 1999.

A Simple Performance
Model for Databases

Performance is your reality. Forget everything else.
—Harold Geneen

This appendix presents a simple performance cost model for evaluating physical design methods and tradeoffs among various designs. The model includes estimations for input/output (I/O) time and network delays.

A.1 I/O Time Cost—Individual Block Access

A block (or page) has been traditionally the basic unit of I/O from disk to fast memory (RAM). It can range in size from 2 to 16 KB, although 4,096 bytes (4 KB) is the most typical size in many systems. Blocks usually include many rows in a table, but occasionally a large row can span several blocks. In recent years, prefetch buffers have been used more often in operational systems to increase I/O efficiency. Prefetch buffers are typically 64 KB (in DB2, for instance). In some systems the disk track is the I/O transfer size of choice.

Block access cost
    = disk access time to a block from a random starting location
    = average disk seek time + average rotational delay + block transfer.   A.1

Disk access time is becoming much faster with new technologies, and currently we can estimate the access time to a 4 KB block to be well below 10 ms in a shared-disk environment. For example, an IBM U320 146 GB hard drive has an average seek time of 3.6 ms, average rotational delay of 2 ms for a half rotation (at 15,000 RPM), and a transfer rate of 320 MB/sec. For this disk, the expected block access cost in a shared-disk environment is:

I/O time (4 KB block access in a shared disk)
  = 3.6 ms + 2 ms + 4 KB/320 MB/sec = 5.6 ms.

I/O time (64 KB prefetch buffer in a shared disk)
  = 3.6 ms + 2 ms + 64 KB/320 MB/sec = 5.8 ms.

In a dedicated disk environment, the disk-seek component is rarely needed, so the time is considered negligible.

I/O time (4 KB block access in a dedicated disk)
  = 2 ms + 4 KB/320 MB/sec = 2.0 ms.

I/O time (64 KB prefetch buffer access in a dedicated disk)
  = 2 ms + 64 KB/320 MB/sec = 2.2 ms.

A.2 I/O Time Cost—Table Scans and Sorts

Disk technologies that create higher speeds plus special prefetching hardware can also make table scans and sorting operations extremely efficient. The total I/O time for a full table scan is computed simply as the I/O time for a single block or prefetch buffer, whichever applies, times the total number of those I/O transfers in the table.

Sorting, which is a part of many queries, especially those needing a sort-merge join, has progressed well beyond the simple two-way sorts of the past. The estimated cost of an M-way sort is approximately $2 \infty nb \infty \log_M nb$, where nb is the number of blocks in the table to be transferred to memory from disk [O'Neil 2001, Silberschatz 2006]. In the examples in this book, we use $M = 3$ to represent three-way sorts.

A.3 Network Time Delays

Network delays can be significant compared to I/O delays, and when data is accessed across a network, the following model can be used, which is very similar to the disk I/O model.

$$\text{Network delay = propagation time + transmission time,} \qquad A.2$$

where

$$\text{Propagation time = network distance/propagation speed,} \qquad A.3$$

and

$$\text{Transmission time = packet size/network transmission rate.} \qquad A.4$$

The propagation speed is estimated to be 200,000 km/sec, which is approximately two-thirds of the speed of light, taking into account normal degradations of transmission media from the theoretical speed of light of approximately 300,000 km/sec. The network distance is given in kilometers (km). If the network media you are using has a known propagation delay, then substitute the known value for 200 km/ms in the equation. Rough approximations are considered reasonable here to get "ballpark" estimates of total time.

The transmission time for a packet on a network is the time to get the packet on or off the network to or from the controlling device in the local computer system. It is analogous to the transfer time for a block on a disk. The transmission rate is given in bits/second and packet size is given in bytes. We assume an 8-bit per byte conversion factor.

For example, the time to send one packet of 1,500 bytes (let's say its one block of data) over an Ethernet with a transmission rate of 1 Gb/sec in a wide area network (WAN) at a network distance of 1,000 kilometers would be:

Network time = 1,000 km/200,000 km/sec + 1,500 bytes
      × 8 bits/byte/1 Gb/sec
  = .005 sec + .000012 sec
  = .005012 sec (or 5.012 ms).

For a local area network (LAN) with a network distance of .1 km, we get:

Network time = .1 km/200,000 km/sec + 1,500 bytes
      × 8 bits/byte/1 Gb/sec
  = .0000005 sec + .000012 sec
  = .0000125 sec (or .0125 ms).

Putting these numbers in perspective, higher-speed Ethernet networks have very small transmission times, and for longer distances of WANs, the total network time is dominated by the propagation time. In this case, the typical values for network time (that is, the propagation time) are in the same range as disk I/O times, and need to be considered in the estimate of total response time.

For LANs where network distances may be less than .1 km, the dominating delay is transmission time, but neither time in this example is significant compared to typical disk I/O times. Thus, in LANs we can consider network delays to be negligible unless there are extremely large packets or trains of packets.

A.4 CPU Time Delays

CPU time delays are mainly dependent on the processing required by the database application, and are largely independent of the I/O operations. Those CPU delays caused by the software to manage the I/O are usually negligible compared to the I/O times, and are even further diminished when they overlap the I/O operations. Our model assumes database systems to be I/O-bound and considers CPU delays as negligible.

Technical Comparison of DB2 HADR with Oracle Data Guard for Database Disaster Recovery

Oracle Data Guard is a feature of 10g Enterprise Edition that allows for the creation of standby databases that can be kept transactionally consistent with a primary database. To achieve this, Oracle ships log buffers (or log files in some configurations) from the primary server to the standby server where the log records are replayed on the standby database. A Data Guard standby comes in two "flavors": logical standby and physical standby. In logical standby mode, log records are converted to SQL statements and replayed on the standby database. This more closely resembles DB2's SQL Replication and Q Replication capabilities and as such will not be discussed here. In physical standby mode, log records are applied using redo logic, which applies the records much in the same fashion as would occur when rolling forward a database through log files.

In this mode, both the primary and standby databases are exact physical copies of each other and the application of log buffers is similar to that of IBM's HADR. However, there are many differences that appear when you look just below the surface that make HADR a superior solution to Data Guard for high-availability scenarios. A summary of the differences, each of which will be described in detail, follows.

Both IBM's HADR and Oracle's Data Guard protect from failures, such as software failure, primary server failure, storage failure, or even primary site failure. In both cases the configuration can include a second complete copy of the database in a remote location to protect from any or all of these forms of failure. It should be noted that Oracle Real Application Cluster (RAC) only protects from server and software failure on a node in the cluster and has no protection for storage or site failure. To cover more fail-

Note: Used with permission from Chris Eaton.

ure scenarios, Oracle would likely recommend a combination of both Oracle RAC and Data Guard, though the user should be cautious of the increased cost of the solution.

IBM HADR allows for fix packs (patch sets) and OS level fixes to be applied in a rolling fashion. For example, the following steps can be deployed to maintain maximum availability while patches are applied:

1. Stop HADR on the standby.
2. Apply the DB2 fix or OS fix on the standby.
3. Start HADR on the standby—database will automatically resynchronize.
4. Perform a switch-roles takeover.
5. Stop HADR on the new standby (old primary).
6. Apply the DB2 fix or OS fix to this server.
7. Start HADR on the new standby (old primary)—database will automatically resynchronize.

At this point, since HADR is intended to be a peer-to-peer HA solution, you can leave the roles as they are above. Alternatively, you can perform a takeover to switch roles again to get back to the original primary/standby configuration. With Oracle Data Guard, a physical standby database does not support rolling upgrades. Both primary and standby servers must be using the same patch set.

B.1 Standby Remains "Hot" during Failover

The following sequence of events occurs on the standby during an HADR takeover:

1. Last log buffer is replayed (if not already done).
2. Undo of in-flight transactions occurs—note that the buffer pool on the standby is likely full of all the recent updates so there is likely little to no random data page I/O during undo recovery.
3. New transactions are allowed to access the database. Note that the buffer pool and all other memory structures remain allocated.

With Data Guard, in order to convert a standby into a primary (during either failover or when switching roles) the standby database must be shutdown and started up again. This results in buffer caches, catalog caches, and package caches (library caches) being torn down and recreated. Therefore, a significant "brown out" period would follow a Data Guard failover. According to a presentation given by Angelo Pruscino, Principal Architect, Oracle Corporation, there is an issue with warming the buffer cache on a cold failover that can take "5+ minutes" to resolve.

B.2 Subminute Failover

HADR has been demonstrated with a failover of a database supporting 600 concurrent SAP users and was achieved in only 11 seconds. Clearly HADR is capable of supporting subminute failover.

One of the issues with Data Guard is that you must stop and restart the instance during failover, which negatively impacts availability. The following quote is from a case study on Oracle's own internal processing systems, which use Data Guard. It is significant to note that this system does not deliver subminute failover.

B.3 Geographically Separated

Both HADR and Data Guard use TCP/IP to send log buffers from the primary server to the standby site. As such, both allow for the servers to be separated by a large distance. In addition, both products offer asynchronous buffer transmission so that very large distances do not adversely affect the performance of the primary server.

B.4 Support for Multiple Standby Servers

With the first release of HADR, DB2 supports one primary and one standby database. The key objective is to provide the highest levels of availability possible. An issue with multiple standby servers is that the impact on the primary server becomes too great to efficiently support synchronous mode. Therefore, in order to support multiple standby servers, the use of asynchronous mode is more appropriate. IBM's solution for asynchronous multisite standby servers is Q Replication, with which you can have multiple targets for a given source database. The tradeoff to consider when looking at asynchronous modes to multiple standby servers is the potential transaction loss in comparison to HADR in synchronous or near-synchronous modes.

B.5 Support for Read on the Standby Server

Oracle Data Guard allows for the log replay to be suspended on the standby server so that the database can be opened in read-only mode. This, however, elongates the failover times as the standby server cannot be both in read-only mode and be replaying logs at the same time. In some reports, delaying the log apply can add 15 minutes to the failover times. If read on standby is a higher priority, then DB2 Q Replication would be a better alternative. Q Replication allows for read and write on the remote databases. Combined with automatic client reroute, this solution provides "instant" failover as there is no need to recover in-flight transactions after a failover.

B.6 **Primary Can Be Easily Reintegrated after Failover**

In the event of a failure on the primary server, the standby server can be forced into the primary role. With DB2, the command is called "takeover by force," in which the standby does not need to communicate with the primary prior to taking over the role as the primary database. With DB2 it is possible to reintegrate the old primary into the cluster as a standby. When in synchronous (SYNC) mode, DB2 ensures that the logs on both servers are identical so reintegration only requires an HADR start command on the old primary in order for it to become the new standby. In the case of NEARSYNC, the only possible loss of transaction is if the primary and standby fail simultaneously. If this is not the case then a simple HADR start on the old primary will reintegrate that server as a new standby.

In the case of ASYNC, there is the possibility that the failover to the standby occurred before log records made it to the database on that server. However, it is still recommended that the HADR start command be issued on the old primary after that server comes back up. DB2 will automatically check the log streams on both sites to determine if there were any transactions lost. If no transactions are missing, the old primary will automatically be reintegrated as a standby. If there are missing transactions, IBM Recovery Expert can be used to list the missing transactions and the new standby can be rebuilt from a backup of the new primary. In Oracle Data Guard, a failover requires the original primary to be rebuilt, which adds additional work and elongates the time required to revert back to the original primary server. Following is a quote from the 10gR1 Data Guard Concepts and Administration manual:

> During failovers involving a physical standby database: In all cases, after a failover, the original primary database can no longer participate in the Data Guard configuration. To reuse the old primary database in the new configuration, you must recreate it as a standby database using a backup copy of the new primary database.

Glossary

access path: Another term for index structures, which provide a well-defined path through which data can be located and accessed by the database management system.

access plan: See query execution plan.

attribute: A primitive data element that provides descriptive detail about an entity; a data field or data item in a record. For example, lastname would be an attribute for the entity customer. Attributes may also be used as descriptive elements for certain relationships among entities.

automated design tool: A software tool to help the database designer or database administrator design an optimal or near-optimal set of physical design parameters: indexing, materialized views, partitioning, and clustering.

autonomic computing: A term formally coined by IBM in 2001. Its ultimate aim is to create self-managing computer systems overcoming the rapid growth in IT systems management complexity. Self-managing systems reduce administrator responsibility by introducing self-configuring (setup), self-optimizing (performance), self-healing (error avoidance), and self-protecting (security) capabilities. Automated physical database design is one of the major themes in autonomic computing.

base tables: SQL tables that are defined from the original database design; materialized views are derived from the base tables.

BID: Block identifier or block ID, the disk address of the physical block.

bitmap index: A collection of bit vectors.

block: The basic unit of data input/output from disk to RAM. It can range from a single record to millions of records. Usually large blocks are the most efficient way for sequential search of large databases.

blocking factor: The number of records in a block (assuming fixed record size).

B-tree: A data structure that generalizes a binary tree in which two or more branches can be taken from each node. Each node contains pairs of records and pointers, so queries are completed as soon as the target record is reached in the tree.

B+tree (or B*tree): An efficient variation of the B-tree with each nonleaf and leaf node containing key-pointer pairs, and the leaf nodes point to block addresses of target records in the database. Each record search has the same number of steps due to a balanced tree format. The basis for indexes in virtually all major database systems.

candidate key: Any subset of the attributes (data items) in a superkey that is also a superkey and is not reducible to another superkey.

CASE tool: Computer-aided software engineering tool, or software design tool to assist in the logical design of large or complex databases. For example, ERwin Data Modeller or Rational Rose using UML.

client server architecture: The term *client server* was introduced in the 1980s to describe the relationship between computers on a network. The term gained broad adoption in the 1990s and is widely used to refer to processing performed between a series of remote computers with a larger, more powerful central computer, usually through a message-based communication protocol, such as TCP/IP. The server provides services to one or more clients, such as access to database data.

clustered index: Any index structure having the data accessed be sorted in the same way the index is organized so that data with similar or the same key values is stored (clustered) together. These tend to be very efficient for certain queries.

clustering: See data clustering.

coarsification: The granularity of clustering along a dimension. One can cluster by day of year, or week of year, or month, quarter, etc.

composite index (or concatenated index): An index made up of composite keys.

composite key (or concatenated key): Any search key made up of the concatenation of existing attributes (fields or columns).

conceptual data model: An organization of data that describes the relationships among the primitive data elements. For example, in the ER model, it is a diagram of the entities, their relationships, and their attributes.

counting: The process of recording counts of the number of rows in tables that meet certain criteria as important statistics used in index design, and estimating database volume and potential materialized view volume, for example. Counting can be done by using common SQL operators such as COUNT and DISTINCT.

covering index: An index that covers certain queries, that is, an index with enough information to answer the query by merely accessing the index and not the target table.

DAS: Direct attached storage, the preferred storage medium for small networks and small databases, where all storage (e.g., internal hard disks, tape drives) is controlled by the server.

DASD: Direct access storage device, a general term for a magnetic disk used in a personal or business computer system.

database: A collection of interrelated stored data that serves the needs of multiple users; a collection of tables in the relational model.

database administrator (DBA): A person in a software organization that is in charge of designing, creating, and maintaining the databases of an enterprise. The DBA makes use of a variety of software tools provided by a DBMS.

database life cycle: An enumeration and definition of the basic steps in the requirements analysis, logical design, physical design, creation, and maintenance of a database as it evolves over time.

database management system (DBMS): A generalized software system for storing and manipulating databases, for example, Oracle, IBM's DB2, or Microsoft SQL Server or Access.

data clustering: The process of storing data (records) near each other on disk because they have the same or similar key values, to obtain maximum query efficiency. Clustering applies to indexes as well, to coordinate the fast access to clustered data on disk.

data item: The basic component of a data record in a file or database table; the smallest unit of information that has meaning in the real world, for example, customer last name, address, and identification number.

data mart: A special-purpose, typically smaller data warehouse; sometimes derived from an existing data warehouse.

data mining: A way of extracting knowledge from a database by searching for correlations in the data and to present promising hypotheses to the user for analysis and consideration.

data model: An organization of data that describes the relationships among the primitive and composite data elements.

data partitioning: See partitioning.

data warehouse: A large repository of historical data that can be integrated for decision support.

DBA: See database administrator.

denormalization: The consolidation of database tables to increase performance in data retrieval (query), despite the potential loss of data integrity. Decisions on when to denormalize tables are based on cost/benefit analysis by the DBA.

dense index: An index in which each record in the target database has a pointer to it. Clustered indexes may or may not be dense. Nonclustered indexes are always dense.

dimension: Those entities the users want to group by when exploring data in a data warehouse, such as time, location, product type, etc. Dimensions are typically represented by tables in a star schema.

dimension block index: A B+tree index (in DB2) used to access clustered dimension blocks.

dimension table: The smaller tables used in a data warehouse to denote the attributes of a particular dimension such as time, location, customer characteristics, product characteristics, etc.

disaster recovery: Part of a DBMS (recovery manager) that provides log data of all transactions executed since the last checkpoint or beginning of the current set of active transactions. When a failure of some sort occurs, either hardware or software, the log can be used to return to the same state of the committed transactions before the failure occurred, thus allowing the committed transactions to survive. Typically, uncommitted transactions are undone and must be restarted.

distributed data allocation: Strategies concerning where to place fragments of data in a system distributed over a computer network, including decisions about whether to replicate the data and how much to replicate.

fact table: The dominating table in a data warehouse and its star schema, containing dimension attributes and data measures at the individual data level.

failover: The ability for a secondary server to take over the processing responsibilities or service requests that were previously directed to a primary server in the event the primary server goes offline. When a primary server fails and a secondary takes over, the primary is said to have "failed over" to the secondary. Failover processing is a major theme in high-availability computing.

federated database management system: A database system that supports the transparent creation, access, and manipulation of heterogeneous interrelated data located at different sites of a computer network.

file: A collection of records of the same type. For example, an employee file is a collection of employee records.

foreign key: Any attribute in an SQL table (key or nonkey) that is taken from the same domain of values as the primary key in another SQL table and can be used to join the two tables (without loss of data integrity) as part of an SQL query.

global schema: A conceptual data model that shows all the data and its relationships in the context of an entire database.

GRID computing: A "function shipping" architecture for massive computational scale-out, whereby distinct problems are shipped to any number of participating computers on a network. Each node on the GRID (a participating computer) computes a solution for the problem it receives. This allows a massive number of computers to collectively solve pieces of a problem with little communication between the systems. The most well known example of GRID computing is the Internet-connected computers in the search for extraterrestrial intelligence (SETI).

hash join: An efficient method of searching two tables to be joined when they have very low selectivity (i.e., very few matching values). Common values are matched in fast memory, then the rest of the data record is obtained using hashing mechanisms to access the disk only once for each record.

hash table index: An index method that maps primary key values to block addresses in the database for otherwise unordered data. The record containing that key value is stored in the block address mapped to by the hashing function. This produces very efficient access to specific records based on primary key values.

index: A data organization set up to speed the retrieval of data from tables. An index typically contains pairs of key values and pointers to blocks of data containing the records that have those same key values.

indexed join: An efficient method of searching two tables to be joined when they have low selectivity (i.e., very few matching values). For each value in one (usually much smaller) table, an index is used to quickly find matching values in the other (usually much larger) table.

interdependence problem: The different methods of physical database design, such as indexing, materialized views, shared-nothing partitioning, multidimensional clustering (MDC), and range partitioning, are somewhat dependent on each other to be applied purely in sequence. The interdependencies must be taken into account to determine an overall plan for design.

I/O time: The time required to complete the I/O operations for a particular transaction or application. I/O cost is another term for I/O time.

join selectivity: A measure of the volume of matching data values between two tables that are to be joined, based on statistical analysis of the tables. High-selectivity joins have a high volume of potential matches, and low-selectivity joins have a low volume of potential matches. Different access methods are useful depending on the selectivity values.

key: A generic term for a set of one or more attributes (data items) that, taken collectively, allows one to identify uniquely an entity or a record in an SQL table; a superkey.

L1 cache, L2 cache: A CPU cache is a memory directly inside the central processing unit (CPU) of a computer to reduce the average time (latency) to access memory in RAM. Most modern CPU architectures have adopted a multilevel cache design, with two or three levels of cache inside the CPU. Each level is larger and slower than the next, though all are faster to access than main system memory (RAM).

logical database design: The step in the database life cycle involved with the design of the conceptual data model (schema), schema integration, transformation to SQL tables, and table normalization; the design of a database in terms of how the data is related, but without regard to how it will be stored.

logical data model: An SQL schema or definition of tables; the result of a transformation from the conceptual data model.

materialized view: A table formed by querying one or more base tables and permanently storing the result. In data warehouses it refers to the storage of aggregate data from other tables and speeds up certain queries based on aggregate results.

materialized query table (MQT) [IBM]: Materialized views or aggregates of data saved for future use to reduce future query times.

MDC: See multidimensional clustering.

measure: Columns in a table that contain values to be aggregated when rows are grouped together. Examples of measures are estimated hours, hourly rate, estimated cost, price, etc.

merge join: An efficient method of joining two tables when they are both sorted on the same key with high selectivity. The method simply does a sequential search of each table once, comparing attribute data values between the two tables that are from the same domain of values.

mirroring: The duplication of data on multiple disks; a form of redundancy used to speed up queries. It has the side effect of making updates slower because of the multiple copies.

monotonicity: Functions are monotonic (or monotone) if the order of data after transformation has the same order as the data prior to transformation. A function f is monotonic if whenever $x \leq y$, then $f(x) \leq f(y)$.

multicore CPU: Combines two or more independent processors into an integrated circuit allowing the combined chip to provide the computing power of several CPUs. Multicore CPUs offer thread-level parallelism (TLP). Each core in the chip has its own level 1 memory cache, and often the higher level caches and the bus interface are shared between the cores.

multidimensional clustering (MDC): A technique by which a table can be created by having key attributes in a related base table designated as dimensions, so data can be clustered by dimensions in the database. Each dimension consists of one or more columns (attributes), and the clusters are formed to take advantage of known and anticipated workloads.

multidimensional OLAP (MOLAP): An OLAP system that uses multidimensional arrays to store multidimensional data efficiently. An alternative to relational OLAP systems that use fact tables to store data.

NAS: Network-attached storage, a disk array connected to a controller that provides file access services over a network.

nested-loop join: An algorithm that contains a pair of nested for loops to search the contents of two tables to be joined, matching one key value in a record in one table with all the key values in records of the other table, then repeating the step for each record in the first table. It has a complexity of n1 ∞ n2 record accesses, where n1 and n2 are the number of records (rows) in the two tables.

nonunique index (or secondary index): An index having each entry consist of a key value—pointer pair—but the key values are not unique and may have several entries, one for each record that contains that value; an inverted file.

normalization: The process of breaking up a table into smaller tables to eliminate problems with unwanted loss of data (the egregious side effects of losing data integrity) from the deletion of records, and inefficiencies associated with multiple data updates.

OLAP: Online analytical processing, a query service that overlays a data warehouse by creating and maintaining a set of summary views (materialized query tables) to allow for quick access to summary data. Related architectures include relational online analytical processing (ROLAP) and multidimensional online processing (MOLAP).

OLAP hierarchy: For each dimension defined for data in an OLAP system, the attributes of each dimension can be structured as a hierarchy. For example, time can be broken down into years, months, weeks, days, etc. Each level in the hierarchy can be used to group data into materialized views.

OLTP: Online transaction processing; the preferred method for database processing before data warehouses.

partitioning: An algorithm for reducing the workload on any one hardware component (like an individual disk) by dividing the data fairly evenly over several components. This has the effect of balancing the workload across the system and minimizing bottlenecks.

physical block: See block.

physical database design: The step in the database life cycle involved with the physical structure of the data, that is, how it will be stored, retrieved, and updated efficiently. In particular, it is concerned with issues of table indexing, partitioning, and clustering on secondary storage devices (e.g., disks).

primary key: A key that is selected from among the candidate keys for an SQL table to be used to create an index for that table.

query execution plan (QEP) (or query plan): An extended relational algebra tree specifying the set of precise relational algebra operations (in a specific order) needed to complete a query.

query execution plan selection: In query optimization, alternative query execution plans are evaluated for estimated cost (usually in I/O time) and the plan with the minimum estimated cost is selected for execution.

query optimizer: Software within a DBMS that determines the fastest way to execute a query through the analysis of query execution plans and that estimates the I/O time needed to execute each candidate plan.

query response time: The real time between the last keystroke of a query and the last character displayed in the response; it is typically composed of the I/O time, CPU time, and network time, including delays, and often overlapped.

RAID: Reliable array of inexpensive disks. Replacement of expensive, high-performance devices with arrays of lower cost disks to achieve similar high performance and reliability by the use of parallelism, striping, redundancy, and parity.

range partitioning: The partitioning of a table by selecting ranges of attribute values such that the table can be divided into nearly equal numbers of records. Each range of records is stored on a separate disk to help balance workloads and maximize parallelism.

range query: Any query that targets records with a closed range of attribute values (e.g., $18 \leq age \leq 29$).

RDBMS: Relational database management system.

record: A group of data items treated as a unit by an application; a row in a database table.

referential integrity: A constraint in an SQL database that requires that for every foreign key instance that exists in a table, the row (and thus the primary key instance) of the parent table associated with that foreign key instance must also exist in the database.

replication (or mirroring or redundancy): The act of storing multiple copies of tables or fragments of tables on another part of a disk, on separate disks, or possibly on devices at separate sites.

requirements specification: A formal document that defines the requirements for a database in terms of the data needed, the major users and their applications, the physical platform and software system, and any special constraints on performance, security, and data integrity.

RID: Record identifier, or record ID, uniquely identifies a record and provides the address of the record on disk.

R*index: An index based on an R*tree structure.

row: A group of data items treated as a unit by an application; a record; a tuple in relational database terminology.

R*tree: An R-tree is a balanced tree structure adapted from the B+tree to handle spatial data, such as line segments, rectangles, and other polygons. Each node of the tree is defined by a bounding box (rectangles) that contain one or more geometric objects. An R*tree is a variant of the R-tree that reduces overlapping bounding boxes and query times.

sampling: The process of collecting sample data from selected tables in the database to use to estimate volumes and distributions of data across the entire database or data warehouse. SQL supports sampling through the TABLESAMPLE clause. Applications include estimating the sizes of materialized views before they are created, as well as design for indexes, multidimensional clustering, and shared-nothing partitioning.

SAN: Storage area network, a network that links servers to disk arrays, typically over a gigabit network such as Gigabit Ethernet.

schema: A conceptual data model that shows all the relationships among the data elements under consideration in a given context; the collection of table definitions in a relational database.

secondary index: An index structure that allows an efficient search to be made to a table, given a Boolean search criterion, usually involving nonkey data (i.e., data values that are not unique).

sequential search method: A simple search mechanism that searches every record in a file or database.

shared-nothing partitioning: Database systems based on relatively independent servers that work cooperatively on subsets of a problem for high efficiency. When they need to share data, it is passed between servers over a high-speed interconnect. They are particularly useful in analyzing large complex data sets.

slice: A block containing a single value of one dimension in a multidimensional database.

sparse index: An index in which each target data block or page has exactly one pointer to it. Only clustered indexes can be sparse.

star schema: The basic form of data organization for a data warehouse, consisting of a single large fact table and many smaller dimension tables.

striping (or data striping): A technique for distributing data that needs to be accessed together across multiple disks to achieve a greater degree of parallelism and query efficiency.

superkey: A set of one or more attributes (data items) that, taken collectively, allow one to identify uniquely an entity or a record in a relational table.

table: In a relational database, the collection of rows (or records) of a single type (similar to a file).

third normal form (3NF): The most common form of a table considered to be sufficiently normalized (broken up into smaller tables) to eliminate problems with unwanted loss of data from the deletion of records (rows) and inefficiencies associated with multiple data updates due to redundant data. A table in 3NF has one or more keys such that all nonkey attributes have exactly one value associated with each key value.

unique index: An index based on pairs of primary key values and pointers; each pointer is the address for a block containing the unique record that has that specific key value.

what-if analysis: A technique of estimating the time or cost to execute a given work-load with a particular hardware configuration, data structure, and/or software method by varying each measurable parameter one at a time and analyzing the result compared to previous results from using other values.

Bibliography

Acharya, S., Gibbons, P., Poosala, V., and Ramaswamy, S. Join Synopses for Approximate Query Answering. In Proceedings of 1999 SIGMOD. New York: ACM Press, 1999, pp. 275–286.

Adler, R. M. Distributed Coordination Models for Client/Server Computing. *Computer,* 28(4), April 1995: 14–22.

Agrawal, S., Agrawal, V., and Yang, B. Integrating Vertical and Horizontal Partitioning into Automated Physical Database Design. Proceedings of ACM SIGMOD, 2004.

Agrawal, S., Chaudhuri, S., Kollar, L., Maranthe, A., Narasayya, V., and Syamala, M. Database Tuning Advisor for Microsoft SQL Server 2005. International Conference on Very Large Databases (VLDB), Toronto, 2004, pp: 1110-1121.

Agrawal, S., Chaudhuri, S., and Narasayya, V. R. Automated Selection of Materialized Views and Indexes in SQL Databases. International Conference on Very Large Databases (VLDB), Cairo, 2000, pages 496–505.

Agrawal, S., Gehrke, J., Gunopulos, D., and Raghavan, P. Automatic Subspace Clustering of High-dimensional Data for Data Mining Applications. Proceedings of ACM SIGMOD International Conference on Management of Data, 1998, pages 94–105.

Ailamaki, A., DeWitt, D. J., Hill, M. D., and Skounakis, M. Weaving Relations for Cache Performance. International Conference on Very Large Databases (VLDB), Rome, 2001: 169–180.

Ailamaki, A., DeWitt, D. J., Hill, M. D., and Wood, D. A. DBMSs on a Modern Processor: Where Does Time Go? *VLDB,* 1999: 266–277.

Alhamed, A., and Lakshmivarahan, S. A Clustering Approach to Multimodel Ensemble Analysis Using SAMEX Data: Preliminary Results. Proceedings of the 2000 ACM Symposium on Applied Computing, 1, 2000: 111–116.

Asami, S., Talagala, N., and Patterson, D. A. Designing a Self-maintaining Storage System. IEEE Symposium on Mass Storage Systems, 1999, pp. 222–233.

Baluja, S., and Caruana, R. Removing the Genetics from the Standard Genetic Algorithm. *Technical Report No. CMU-CS-95-141.* Pittsburgh, PA: Carnegie Mellon University, 1995.

Barucci, E., Pinzani, R., and Sprug-noli, R. Optimal Selection of Secondary Indexes. *IEEE Trans. on Software Engineering,* 16(1), Jan. 1990: 32–38.

Bayer, R., and McCreight, E. Organization and Maintenance of Large Ordered Indexes. *Acta. Inf.,* 1(3), 1972: 173–189.

Bell, G., and Gray, J. What's Next in High-performance Computing? *Commun. ACM,* 45(2), 2002: 91–95.

Bernstein, P., Brodie, M., Ceri, S., DeWitt, D., Franklin, M., Garcia-Molina, H., Gray, J., Held, J., Hellerstein, J., Jagadish, H. V., Lesk, M., Maier, D., Naughton, J., Pirahesh, H., Stonebraker, M., and Ullman, J. The Asilomar Report on Database Research. *SIGMOD Record,* 27(4), Dec. 1998, at http://www.acm.org/sigs/sigmod/record/issues/9812/asilomar.html.

Betawadkar-Norwood, A., Lin, E., and Ursu, I. Using Data Federation Technology in IBM WebSphere Information Integrator: Data Federation Design and Configuration. *developerWorks,* June 2005.

Bhattacharjee, B., Padmanabhan, S., Malkemus, T., Lai, T., Cranston, L., and Huras, M. Efficient Query Processing for Multi-Dimensionally Clustered Tables in DB2. International Conference on Very Large Databases (VLDB), Berlin, 2003, pp. 963–974.

Blasgen, M. W., Astrahan, M. M., Chamberlin, D. D., Gray, J., King III, W. F., Lindsay, B. G., Lorie, R. A., Mehl, J. W., Price, T. G., Putzolu, G. R., Schkolnick, M., Selinger, P. G., Slutz, D. R., Strong, H. R., Traiger, I. L., Wade, B. W., and Yost, R. A.: System R: An Architectural Overview. *IBM Systems Journal* 38(2/3), 1999: 375–396.

BMC Index Advisor, at http://www.bmc.com.

Bornhövd, C., Altinel, M., Mohan, C., Pirahesh, H., Reinwald, B. Adaptive Database Caching with DBCache. *IEEE Data Eng. Bull.,* 27(2), 2004: 11–18.

Brown, K. P., Carey, M. J., and Livny, M. Goal-Oriented Buffer Management Revisited. ACM SIGMOD, Montreal, 1996, 353–364.

Brown, K., Carey, M, and Livny, M. Managing Memory to Meet Multiclass Workload Response Time Goals, International Conference on Very Large Databases (VLDB), Dublin, 1993, 328–341.

Brown, K., Mehta, M., Carey, M., and Livny, M. Towards Automated Performance Tuning for Complex Workloads. International Conference on Very Large Databases (VLDB), Santiago, 1994.

Bruno N., and Chaudhuri, S. Physical Design Refinement. The Merge-Reduce Approach. Proceedings of the 2006 EDBT Conference, Munich, 386–404.

Bruno, N., and Chaudhuri, S. Automatic Physical Design Tuning: A Relaxation-based Approach. Proceedings of the ACM SIGMOD, Baltimore, MD, 2005.

Burks, A. R. *Who Invented the Computer? The Legal Battle That Changed History.* Amherst, New York, Prometheus Books, 2003.

Burks, A. R., and Burks, A. W. *The First Electronic Computer: The Atanasoff Story.* Ann Arbor: University of Michigan Press, 1988.

Burleson, D. K. *Physical Database Design Using Oracle.* Boca Raton, FL: Auerbach Publishers, 2004.

Callahan, P. B., and Kosaraju, S. R. A Decomposition of Multidimensional Point Sets with Applications to k-nearest Neighbors and n-body Potential Fields. *Journal of the ACM,* 42(1), 1995: 67–90.

Capara, A., Fischetti, M., and Maio, D. Exact and Approximate Algorithms for the Index Selection Problem in Physical Database Design., *IEEE Transactions on Knowledge and Data Engineering*, 7(6), Dec. 1995: 955–967.

Ceri, S., Negri, M., and Pelagatti, G. Horizontal Data Partitioning in Database Design. Proceedings of ACM-SIGMOD International Conference on Management of Data, Orlando, FL, June 2–4, 1982, pp. 128–136.

Ceri, S., and Pelagatti, G. *Distributed Databases: Principles and Systems.* New York: McGraw-Hill, 1984.

Ceri, S., Pernici, B., and Wiederhold, G. Distributed Database Design Methodologies. Proceedings of the IEEE, May 1987, pp. 533–546.

Chan, T. F., Golub, G. H., and LeVeque, R. J. Algorithms for Computing the Sample Variance: Analysis and Recommendation. Amer. Statist., 37, 1983: 242–247.

Chaudhuri, S., Christensen, E., Graefe, G., Narasayya, V., and Zwilling, M. Self-Tuning Technology in Microsoft SQL Server. *IEEE Data Engineering Bulletin,* 22(2), June 1999: 20–26.

Chaudhuri, S. Dageville, B., Lohman, G. M. Self-managing Technology in Database Management Systems. International Conference on Very Large Databases (VLDB), Toronto, 2004: 1243.

Chaudhuri, S., Das, G., Datar, M., Motwani, R., and Narasayya, V. R. Overcoming Limitations of Sampling for Aggregation Queries. In Proceedings of the 17th International Conference of Data Engineering, IEEE Computer Society Press, 2001, pp. 534–542.

Chaudhuri, S., Gupta, A., and Narasayya, V. Workload Compression. Proceedings of ACM SIGMOD, 2002.

Chaudhuri, S., Motwani, R., and Narasayya, V. R. On Random Sampling over Joins. In Proceedings of 1999 SIGMOD. New York: ACM Press, 1999, pp. 263–274.

Chaudhuri, S., Motwani, R., and Narasayya, V. R. Random Sampling for Histogram Construction: How Much Is Enough? SIGMOD Conference, 1998, pp. 436–447.

Chaudhuri, S., and Narasayya, V. AutoAdmin What-if Index Analysis Utility. Proceedings of the 1998 ACM SIGMOD Conference, Seattle, 1998, pp. 367–378.

Chaudhuri, S., and Narasayya, V. Microsoft Index Tuning Wizard for SQL Server 7.0. Proceedings of the 1998 ACM SIGMOD Conference, Seattle, 1998, pp. 553–554.

Chaudhuri, S., and Narasayya, V. An Efficient Cost-driven Index Selection Tool for Microsoft SQL Server. *VLDB*, 1997, pp. 146–155.

Chaudhuri S. and Narasayya V., "Index Merging," Proceedings of 15th International Conference on Data Engineering, Sydney, Australia 1999.

Chen, J., DeWitt, D. J., and Naughton, J. F. Design and Evaluation of Alternative Selection Placement Strategies in Optimizing Continuous Queries. *ICDE,* 2002: 345–356.

Chen, P. M., Lee, E. K., Drapeau, A. L., Lutz, K., Miller, E. L., Seshan, S., Shirriff, K., Patterson, D. A., and Katz, R. H. Performance and Design Evaluation of the RAID-II Storage Server. *Distributed and Parallel Databases,* 2(3), 1994: 243–260.

Chen, P. M., and Patterson, D. A. A New Approach to I/O Performance Evaluation—Self-scaling I/O Benchmarks, Predicted I/O Performance. *ACM Trans. Comput. Syst.,* 12(4), 1994: 308–339.

Cheng, C. H., Fu, A. W., and Zhang, Y. Entropy-based Subspace Clustering for Mining Numerical Data. Proceedings of the 5th ACM SIGKDD International Conference on Knowledge Discovery and Data Mining, 1999, pp. 84–93.

Choenni, S., Blanken, H. M., and Chang, T. On the Selection of Secondary Indices in Relational Databases., *Data & Knowledge Engineering*, 11(3), 1993: 207–233.

Christensen, R. *Analysis of Variance, Design, and Regression: Applied Statistical Methods*. New York, Chapman & Hall, 1996.

Chu, W. W. "Distributed Database Systems," Chapter 14 in *Software Engineering Handbook*, eds. C. R. Vick and C. V. Ramamoorthy. New York: 1984.

Chu, W. W. Optimal File Allocation in Multiple Computer System. *IEEE Transaction on Computers,* Oct. 1969: 885–889.

Chung, J., Ferguson, D., Wang, G., Nikolaou, C., and Teng, J. Goal-oriented Dynamic Buffer Pool Management for Data Base Systems. *IEEE ICECCS,* 1995: 191–198.

Clark, J., and Downing, D. A. *Forgotten Statistics: A Self-teaching Refresher Course*. Hauppauge, NY, Barrons Educational Series, ISBN: 0812097130, 1996.

Cochran W. G. Sampling Techinques, 3rd ed. New York: John Wiley, 1977.

Codd, E. F. *The Relational Model for Database Management*, 2nd ed. Reading, MA: Addison-Wesley, 1990.

Codd, E. F. A Relational Model of Data for Large Shared Data Banks (Reprint). *Commun. ACM, 26*(1), 1983: 64–69.

Codd, E. F. Extending the Data Base Relational Model to Capture More Meaning (Abstract). SIGMOD Conference, 1979, p. 161.

Codd, E. F. A Relational Model of Data for Large Shared Data Banks. *Commun. ACM,* 13(6), 1970: 377–387.

Dageville, B., Das, D., Dias, K., Yagoub, K., Zaït, M., and Ziauddin, M. Automatic SQL Tuning in Oracle 10g. *VLDB*, 2004: 1098–1109.

Dageville, B., and Zaït, M. SQL Memory Management in Oracle9i. *VLDB*, Hong Kong, 2002, pp. 962–973.

Date, C. J. *An Introduction to Database Systems*, vol. 1, 8th ed. Boston: Addison-Wesley, 2003.

Date, C. J. Defining Data Types in a Database Language—A Proposal for Adding Date and Time Support to SQL. *SIGMOD Record,* 17(2), 1988: 53–76.

Date, C. J. A Critique of the SQL Database Language. *SIGMOD Record, 14*(3), 1984: 8–54.

Date, C. J. Database Usability (Abstract). SIGMOD Conference, 1983, p. 1.

Date, C. J. Referential Integrity, *VLDB,* 1981: 2–12.

Davison, D., and Graefe, G. Memory Contention Responsive Hash Join. VLDB, Santiago, Chile, 1994.

DB2 Database, at http://www-306.ibm.com/software/data/db2/udb/.

DB2 UDB: The Autonomic Computing Advantage, at http://www.db2mag.com/epub/autonomic/.

Deigin, Y. DB2 UDB Query Execution Plans: Up Close and Personal. DB2 Information Management Technical Conference AGENDA, Orlando, FL, Sept. 12–16, 2005.

Devroye, L. Non-Uniform Random Variate Generation. New York: Springer-Verlag, 1986.

DeWitt, D. J., and Gray, J. Parallel Database Systems: The Future of High-Performance Database Systems. *Commun. ACM,* 35(6), 1992: 85–98.

DeWitt, D. J., Naughton, J. F., Schneider, D. A., and Seshadri, S. Practical Skew Handling in Parallel Joins. International Conference on Very Large Databases (VLDB), Vancouver, 1992: 27–40.

Diao, Y., Hellerstein, J. L., and Storm, A. J., Surendra, M., Lightstone, S., Parekh, S. S., and Garcia-Arellano, C. Incorporating Cost of Control into the Design of a Load Balancing Controller. IEEE Real-Time and Embedded Technology and Applications Symposium, 2004, pp. 376–387.

Diao, Y., Hellerstein, J. L., and Storm, A. J., Surendra, M., Lightstone, S., Parekh, S. S., and Garcia-Arellano, C. Using MIMO Linear Control for Load Balancing in Computing Systems. American Control Conference, 2004.

Diao, Y., Wu, C. W., Hellerstein, J. L., Storm, A. J., Surendra, M., Lightstone, S., Parekh, S. S., Garcia-Arellano, C., Carroll, M., Chu, L., and Colaco, J. Comparative Studies of Load Balancing with Control and Optimization Techniques. 24th American Control Conference (ACC), Portland, OR, June 8–10, 2005.

Dias, K., Ramacher, M., Shaft, U., Venkataramani, V., and Wood, G. Automatic Performance Diagnosis and Tuning in Oracle. *CIDR,* 2005.

Dickman, A. Two-Tier versus Three-Tier Apps. *InformationWeek*, 553, Nov. 13, 1995: 74–80.

Dröge, G., and Schek, H. J. Query-Adaptive Data Space Partitioning Using Variable-Size Storage Clusters. SSD, Singapore, 1993, pp. 337–356.

Edelstein, H. Unraveling Client/Server Architecture. *DBMS*, 7(5), May 1994: 34(7).

Elmasri, R., and Navathe, S. B. *Fundamentals of Database Systems*, 4th ed. Boston: Addison-Wesley, 2004.

Epter, S., and Krishnamoorthy, M. A Multiple-resolution Method for Edge-centric Data Clustering. Proceedings of the 8th International Conference on Information Knowledge Management, 1999, pp. 491–498.

Falkowski, B. J. Comments on an Optimal Set of Indices for a Relational Database. *IEEE Trans. on Software Engineering*, 18(2), Feb. 1992: 168–171.

Ferhatosmanoglu, H., Agrawal, D., and El Abbadi, A. Clustering Declustered Data for Efficient Retrieval. Proceedings of the 8th International Conference on Information Knowledge Management, 1999, pp. 343–350.

Finkelstein, S., Schkolnick, M., and Tiberio, P. Physical Database Design for Relational Databases. *ACM Transactions on Database Systems*, 13(1), Mar. 1988: 91–128.

Fisher, P., Hollist, P., and Slonim, J. A Design Methodology for Distributed Databases. Proceedings of the IEEE Conference on Distributed Computing, Sept. 1980, pp. 199–202.

Flajolet, P., and Martin, G. N. Probabilistic Counting Algorithms for Database Applications. *Journal of Computer and System Sciences*, 31, 1985: 182–209.

Frank, M. R., Omiecinski, E. R., and Navathe, S. B. Adaptive and Automated Index Selection in RDBMS., International Conference on Extending Database Technology (EDBT), Vienna, Austria, Mar. 1992, pp. 277–292.

Fushimi, S., Kitsuregawa, M., Nakayama, M., Tanaka, H., and Moto-oka, T. Algorithm and Performance Evaluation of Adaptive Multidimensional Clustering Technique. Proceedings of the 1985 International Conference on Management of Data, Austin, TX, May 1985, pp. 308–318.

Gallaugher, J., and Ramanathan, S. Choosing a Client/Server Architecture. A Comparison of Two-Tier and Three-Tier Systems. *Information Systems Management Magazine*, 13(2), Spring 1996: 7–13.

Ganguly, S., Gibbons, P. B., Matias, Y., and Silberschatz, A. Bifocal Sampling for Skew-resistant Join Size Estimation. In Proceedings of the 1996 SIGMOD. New York: ACM Press, 1996, pp. 271–281.

Ganti, V., Gehrke, J., and Ramakrishnan, R. CACTUS—Clustering Categorical Data Using Summaries. Proceedings of the 5th ACM SIGKDD International Conference on Knowledge Discovery and Data Mining, 1999, pp. 73–83.

Garcia-Arellano, C. M., Lightstone, S., Lohman, G., Markl, V., and Storm, A. Autonomic Features of the IBM DB2 Universal Database for Linux, UNIX, and Windows. IEEE Transactions on Systems, Man, and Cybernetics: Special Issue on Engineering Autonomic Systems, 2006.

Garcia-Arellano, C. M., Lightstone, S., and Storm, A. A Self-managing Relational Database Server: Examples from IBM's DB2 Universal Database for Linux, Unix, and Windows. IEEE Transactions on Systems, Man, and Cybernetics: Special Issue on Engineering Autonomic Systems, 2005.

Garcia-Molina, H., and Polyzois, C. A. Issues in Disaster Recovery. *COMPCON, 1990*: 573–577.

Garcia-Molina, H., Ullman, J., and Widom, J. *Database Systems: The Complete Book.* Englewood Cliffs, NJ: Prentice-Hall, 2001.

Gibson, G. A., Hellerstein, L., Karp, R. M., Katz, R. H., and Patterson, D. A. Failure Correction Techniques for Large Disk Arrays. *ASPLOS*, 1989: 123–132.

Goldstein J., and Larson, P. Optimizing Queries Using Materialized Views: A Practical, Scalable Solution. In Proceedings of the ACM SIGMOD International Conference on Management of Data, 2001.

Gonick, L., and Smith, W., *The Cartoon Guide to Statistics.* New York: HarperCollins, 1994.

Gray, J. A "Measure of Transaction Processing" 20 Years Later. *IEEE Data Eng. Bull.,* 28(2), 2005: 3–4.

Gray, J. Distributed Computing Economics CoRR cs.NI/0403019, 2004.

Gray, J. The Next Database Revolution. SIGMOD Conference, 2004, pp. 1–4.

Gray, J. The Revolution in Database System Architecture. ADBIS (Local Proceedings), 2004.

Gray, J. Where the Rubber Meets the Sky: The Semantic Gap between Data Producers and Data Consumers. *SSDBM*, 2004: 3.

Gray, J. Review—Benchmarking Database Systems: A Systematic Approach. *ACM SIGMOD Digital Review,* 1, 1999. See: http://www.informatik.uni-trier.de/~ley/db/indices/a-tree/g/Gray:Jim.html and http://dblp.uni-trier.de/rec/bibtex/journals/dr/Gray99.

Gray, J. Super Servers: Commodity Computer Clusters Pose a Software Challenge. *BI W*, 1995, pp. 30–47.

Gray, J., and Shenoy, P. J. Rules of Thumb in Data Engineering. *ICDE,* 2000: 3–12.

Gray, P., and Watson, H. J. *Decision Support in the Data Warehouse.* Englewood Cliffs, NJ: Prentice-Hall, 1998.

Grosshans, D. *File Systems Design and Implementation.* Englewood Cliffs, NJ: Prentice-Hall, 1986.

Gupta, H., Harinarayan, V., Rajaraman, A., and Ullman, J. D. Index Selection for OLAP. Proceedings of the International Conference on Data Engineering, Birmingham, UK, April 1997, pp. 208–219.

Haas, L., and Lin, E. IBM Federated Database Technology. *developerWorks,* March 2002: 1–11. See http://www-128.ibm.com/developerworks/db2/library/techarticle/0203haas/0203haas.html.

Haas, L., Lin, E, and Roth, M. Data Integration through Database Federation. *IBM Systems Journal,* 41(4), 2002: 578–596.

Haas, P. J. The Need for Speed: Speeding Up DB2 Using Sampling. *IDUG Solutions Journal,* 10, 2003: 32–34.

Haas, P. J., and Hellerstein, J. M. Ripple Joins for Online Aggregation. In Proceedings of the 1999 SIGMOD. New York: ACM Press, 1999, pp. 287–298.

Haas, P. J., and K^nig, C. A Bi-level Bernoulli Scheme for Database Sampling. In Proceedings of the 2004 SIGMOD. New York: ACM Press, 2004, pp. 275–286.

Haas, P. J., Naughton, J. F., Seshadri, S., and Stokes, L. Sampling-based Estimation of the Number of Distinct Values of an Attribute. International Conference on Very Large Databases, Zurich, 1995.

Haas, P. J., Naughton, J. F., Seshadri, S., and Swami, A. N. Selectivity and Cost Estimation for Joins Based on Random Sampling. *J. Comput. Sys. Sci.,* 52, 1996: 550–569.

Haas, P. J., Naughton, J. F., and Swami, A. N. On the Relative Cost of Sampling for Join Selectivity Estimation. *PODS,* 1994: 14–24.

Haas, P. J., and Stokes, L. Estimating the Number of Classes in a Finite Population. *Journal of the American Statistical Association (JASA)*, 93, Dec. 1998: 1475–1487.

Harbron, T. R. *File Systems Structures and Algorithms.* Englewood Cliffs, NJ: Prentice-Hall, 1988.

Harinarayan, V., Rajaraman, A., and Ullman, J. D. Implementing Data Cubes Efficiently. Proceedings of the 1996 ACM-SIGMOD Conference,1996, pp. 205–216.

Harinath, S., and Quinn, S. *SQL Server Analysis Services 2005 with MDX*. New York: John Wiley, 2006.

Hellerstein, J. L., Diao, Y., Parekh, S., and Tilbury, D. M. *Feedback Control of Computing Systems*. New York: John Wiley, 2004.

Hellerstein, J. M., Haas, P. J., and Wang, H. J. Online Aggregation. In Proceedings of the 1997 SIGMOD. New York: ACM Press, 1997, pp. 171–182.

Hennessy, J. L, and Patterson, D. A. *Computer Architecture: A Quantitative Approach*, 2nd ed. San Francisco: Morgan Kaufmann, 1996.

Hester, P. 2006 Technology Analyst Day. AMD, June 1, 2006. See http://www.amd.com/us-en/Corporate/InvestorRelations/0,,51_306_14047,00.html and http://www.amd.com/us-en/assets/content_type/DownloadableAssets/PhilHesterAMDAnalystDayV2.pdf.

Hindshaw, F., Metzger, J., and Zane, B. Optimized Database Appliance, Patent No. U.S. 7,010,521 B2, Assignee: Netezza Corporation, Framingham, MA, issued March 7, 2006.

Hoffer, J. A., Prescott, M .B., and McFadden, F. R. *Modern Database Management*, 8th ed. Englewood Cliffs, NJ: Prentice-Hall, 2007.

Holland, J. H. *Adaptation in Natural and Artificial Systems*. Ann Arbor: University of Michigan Press, 1975.

Hou, W., Ozsoyoglu, G., and Taneja, B. Statistical Estimators for Relational Algebra Expressions. In Proceedings of the 7th ACM SIGACT-SIGMOD-SIGART Symposium. Principles of Database Systems. New York: ACM Press, 1988, pp. 276–287.

Hu, Q., Lee, W., and Lee, D. Indexing Techniques for Wireless Data Broadcast under Data Clustering and Scheduling. Proceedings of the 8th International Conference on Information Knowledge Management, 1999, pp. 351–358.

Hua, K., Lang, S., and Lee, W. A Decomposition-based Simulated Annealing Technique for Data Clustering. Proceedings of the 13th ACM SIGACT-SIGMOD-SIGART Symposium on Principles of Database Systems, 1994, pp. 117–128.

Hubel, M. A Simple Approach to DB2 Index Redesign. *IDUG Solutions Journal*, 8(3), 2001.

IBM Data Warehousing, Analysis, and Discovery—Overview—IBM Software, at http://www.306.ibm.com/software/data/db2bi/.

Ioannidis, Y. E., and Poosala, V. USA Balancing Histogram Optimality and Practicality for Query Result Size Estimation. Proceedings of the 1995 ACM SIGMOD International Conference on Management of Data, San Jose, CA , May 1995, pp. 233–244.

Ip, M. Y. L., Saxton, L. V., and Raghavan, V. V. On the Selection of an Optimal Set of Indexes, *IEEE Transactions on Software Engineering*, 9(2), Mar. 1983: 135–143.

SQL 2003. ISO/IEC 9075-2:2003, Information Technology—Database Languages—SQL: Part 2: Foundation (SQL/Foundation). See http://www.iso.org/iso/en/CatalogueDetailPage.CatalogueDetail?CSNUMBER=34133.

Jagadish, H. V., Lakshmanan, L. V. S., and Srivastava, D. Snakes and Sandwiches: Optimal Clustering Strategies for a Data Warehouse. Proceedings of the 1999 International Conference on Management of Data, 1999, pp. 37–48.

Jain, A. K., Murty, M. N., and Flynn, P. J. Data Clustering: A Review. *ACM Computing Survey*, 31(3), Sept. 1999: 264–323.

Jaisingh, L. R. *Statistics for the Utterly Confused*. New York: McGraw-Hill, 2000.

Janakiraman, J., Warack, C., Bhal, G., and Teorey, T. J. Progressive Fragment Allocation. Proceedings of the 10th International Conference on the Entity Relationship Approach, San Mateo, CA, Oct. 23–25, 1991, pp. 543–560.

Keim, D. A., and Hinneburg, A. Clustering Techniques for Large Data Sets—From the Past to the Future. Tutorial Notes for ACM SIGKDD 1999 International Conference on Knowledge Discovery and Data Mining, 1999, pp. 141–181.

Kimball, R., and Caserta, J. *The Data Warehouse ETL Toolkit*, New York: John Wiley, 2004.

Kimball, R., Reeves L., Ross, M., and Thornthwaite, W. *The Data Warehouse Life Cycle Toolkit*, 2nd ed. New York: John Wiley, 1998.

Kimball, R., and Ross, M. *The Data Warehouse Toolkit: The Complete Guide to Dimensional Modeling*, 2nd ed. New York: John Wiley, 2002.

Kolovson, C. P., and Stonebraker, M. Indexing Techniques for Historical Databases. *ICDE*, 1989: 127–137.

König, A., Nabar, S., Scalable Exploration of Physical Database Design. Proceedings of 22th International Conference on Data Engineering, Atlanta, GA, 2006.

Koopman, J. Introduction to Oracle 10g's New SQL Tuning Advisor. *Database Journal*, July 29, 2004.

Kotidis, Y. and Roussopoulos, N. "DynaMat: A Dynamic View Management System for Data Warehouses," in ACM SIGMOD Conference, Philadelphia, 1999, 371–382.

Kurzweil, R. *The Age of Spiritual Machines*. Penguinbooks, New York, 1999.

Kwan, E., Lightstone, S., Schiefer, B., Storm, A., and Wu, L. Automatic Configuration for IBM DB2 Universal Database: Compressing Years of Performance Tuning Experience into Seconds of Execution. 10th Conference on Database Systems for Business, Technology, and the Web (BTW), University of Leipzig, Germany, Feb. 26–28, 2003.

Larsen, R. P. Rules-based Object Clustering: A Data Structure for Symbolic VLSI Synthesis and Analysis. Proceedings of the 23rd ACM/IEEE Conference on Design Automation, 1986, pp. 768–777.

Larson, P., and Graefe, G. Memory Management during Run Generation in External Sorting. SIGMOD, Seattle, WA, 1998.

Lee, J. H., Kim, D. H., and Chung, C. W. Multidimensional Selectivity Estimation Using Compressed Histogram Information. Proceedings of the 1999 ACM SIGMOD International Conference on Management of Data, Philadelphia, PA, May 31–June 3, 1999, pp. 205–214.

Lehner, W., Cochrane, R., Pirahesh, H., and Zaharioudakis, M. Fast Refresh Using Mass Query Optimization. *ICDE*, 2001: 391–398.

Li, W. S., Zilio, D. C., Batra, V. S., Subramanian, M., Zuzarte, C., and Narang, I. Load Balancing for Multi-tiered Database Systems through Autonomic Placement of Materialized Views. *ICDE*, 2006: 102.

Lightstone, S., and Bhattacharjee, B. Automating the Design of Multi-dimensional Clustering Tables in Relational Databases. Proceedings of VLDB, Toronto, Canada, 2004.

Lightstone, S., Hellerstein, J., Tetzlaff, W., Janson, P., Lassettre, E., Norton, C., Rajaraman, B., and Spainhower, L. Towards Benchmarking Autonomic Computing Maturity. IEEE Workshop on Autonomic Computing Principles and Architectures (AUCOPA), Banff AB, Aug. 2003.

Lightstone, S., Lohman, G., and Zilio, D. Toward Autonomic Computing with DB2 Universal Database. *SIGMOD Record*, 31(3), 2002: 55–61.

Lightstone, S., Schiefer, B., Zilio, D., and Kleewein, J. Autonomic Computing for Relational Databases: The Ten-year Vision. IEEE Workshop on Autonomic Computing Principles and Architectures (AUCOPA), Banff AB, Aug. 2003.

Lightstone, S., Storm, A., Garcia-Arellano, C., Carroll, M., Colaco, J., Diao, Y., and Surendra, M. Self-tuning Memory Management in a Relational Database System. Fourth Annual Workshop on Systems and Storage Technology, December 11, 2005, IBM Research Lab, Haifa University, Mount Carmel, Haifa, Israel.

Lindgren, B. W. *Statistical Theory*, 3rd ed. New York: MacMillan, 1976.

Liou, J. H., and Yao, S. B. Multi-dimensional Clustering for Database Organizations. *Information Systems*, 2, 1977: 187–198.

Lohman, G., Valentin, G., Zilio, D., Zuliani, M., and Skelly, A. DB2 Advisor: An Optimizer Smart Enough to Recommend Its Own Indexes. Proceedings of the 16th IEEE Conference on Data Engineering. San Diego, CA, Feb. 2000.

Manku, G. S., Rajagopalan, S., and Lindsay, B. G. Random Sampling Techniques for Space Efficient Online Computation of Order Statistics of Large Datasets. SIGMOD Conference, 1999, pp. 251–262.

Markl, V., Popivanov, I., Lightstone, S., Raman, V., Aboulnaga, A., Haas, P., and Lohman, G. Automated Statistics Collection in DB2 Stinger. Proceedings of VLDB, Toronto, Canada, 2004.

Markl, V., Ramsak, F., and Bayer, R. Improving OLAP Performance by Multi-dimensional Hierarchical Clustering. Proceedings of IDEAS '99, Montreal, Canada, 1999.

Martin, P., Li, H., Zheng, M., Romanufa, K., and Powley, W. Dynamic Reconfiguration Algorithm: Dynamically Tuning Multiple Buffer Pools. *DEXA*, 2000: 92–101.

McCallum, A., Nigam, K., and Ungar, L. H. Efficient Clustering of High-dimensional Data Sets with Application to Reference Matching. Proceedings of the 6th ACM SIGKDD International Conference on Knowledge Discovery and Data Mining, 2000, pp. 169–178.

Mehta, M., and DeWitt, D. J. Data Placement in Shared-nothing Parallel Database Systems. *VLDB*, 6(1), 1997: 53–72.

Mehta, M., and DeWitt, D. J. Managing Intra-operator Parallelism in Parallel Database Systems. *VLDB,* 1995: 382–394.

Mehta, M., and DeWitt, D. Dynamic Memory Allocation for Multiple-Query Workloads. International Conference on Very Large Databases (VLDB), Dublin, 1993.

Microsoft SQL Server Home, at http://www.microsoft.com/sql/default.mspx.

Microsoft SQL Server: Business Intelligence Solutions, at http://www.microsoft.com/sql/solutions/bi/default.mspx.

Miller, R. G. *Beyond ANOVA, Basics of Applied Statistics.* New York: John Wiley, 1986.

Mitchell, M. "An Introduction to Genetic Algorithms." MIT Press, Cambridge, MA, 1996.

Moravec, H. *Mind Children: The Future of Robot and Human Intelligence.* Boston: Harvard University Press, 1988.

Nadeau, T. P., and Teorey, T. J. A Pareto Model for OLAP View Size Estimation. *Information Systems Frontiers*, 5(2), 2003: 137–147.

Nadeau, T. P., and Teorey, T. J. Achieving Scalability in OLAP Materialized View Selection. Proceedings of DOLAP '02, 2002, pp. 28–34.

Nag, B., and DeWitt, D. J. Memory Allocation Strategies for Complex Decision Support Queries. *CIKM, 1998*: 116–123.

Netezza Corporation, at www.netezza.com.

Nievergelt, J., Hinterberger, H., and Sevcik, K. C. The Grid File: An Adaptable, Symmetric Multikey File Structure. *ACM Transactions on Database Systems (TODS),* 9(1), Jan. 1984: 38–71.

O'Neil, P., and Graefe, G. Multi-table Joins through Bitmapped Join Indices. *SIGMOD Record,* 24(3), Sept. 1995: 8–11.

O'Neil, P., and O'Neil, E. *Database: Principles, Programming, and Performance*, 2nd ed. San Francisco: Morgan Kaufmann, 2001.

Olken, F. Random Sampling from Databases. Ph.D. Dissertation, University of California, Berkeley, 1993.

Oracle Business Intelligence Solutions, at
http://www.oracle.com/solutions/business_intelligence/index.html.

Oracle Database, at http://www.oracle.com/database/index.html.

Oracle 9*i* Memory Management, at
http://www.oracle.com/technology/products/oracle9i/daily/apr15.html.

Oracle—SQL Tuning Advisor, at
http://www.oracle-base.com/articles/10g/AutomaticSQLTuning10g.php.

Ozsu, M. T., and Valduriez, P. *Principles of Distributed Database Systems*. Englewood Cliffs, NJ: Prentice-Hall, 1991.

Padmanabhan, S., Bhattacharjee, B., Malkemus, T., Cranston, L., and Huras, M. Multi-dimensional Clustering: A New Data Layout Scheme in DB2. ACM SIGMOD/PODS 2003 Conference, San Diego, CA, June 9–12, 2003, pp. 637-641.

Palmer, C. R., and Faloutsos, C. Density-biased Sampling: An Improved Method for Data Mining and Clustering. Proceedings of the 2000 ACM SIGMOD on Management of Data, 2000, pp. 82–92.

Pang, H., Carey, M., and Livny, M. Partially Preemptible Hash Joins. SIGMOD, Washington, DC, 1993,

Patent Full-text and Full-page Image Databases, at www.uspto.gov/patft/index.html.

Patterson, D. A. Latency Lags Bandwidth. *ICCD*, 2005: 3–6.

Patterson, D. A. Latency Lags Bandwith. *Commun. ACM,* 47(10), 2004: 71–75.

Patterson, D. A. Hardware Technology Trends and Database Opportunities, SIGMOD Conference 1998 Keynote Speech. *Video ACM SIGMOD Digital Symposium Collection,* 1(2), 1999.

Patterson, D. A. Terabytes—Teraflops or Why Work on Processors When I/O Is Where the Action Is? (Abstract.) ACM Conference on Computer Science, 1994, p. 410.

Patterson, D.A., Gibson, G. A., and Katz, R.A. A Case for Redundant Arrays of Inexpensive Disks (RAID). SIGMOD Conference, 1988, pp. 109–116.

Pendse, N., Creeth, R., "The OLAP Report," http://www.olapreport.com/.

Powell, G. *Oracle Data Warehouse Tuning for 10g.* Boston: Elsevier, 2005.

Pruscino, A. Oracle RAC: Architecture and Performance. SIGMOD Conference, 2003, p. 635.

Ramakrishnan, R., and Gehrke, J. *Database Management Systems,* 3rd ed. New York: McGraw-Hill, 2003.

Rao, J., Lightstone, S., Lohman, G., Zilio, D., Storm, A., Garcia-Arellano, C., and Fadden, S. DB2 Design Advisor: Integrated Automated Physical Database Design, International Conference on Very Large Databases (VLDB), Toronto, 2004.

Rao, J., Zhang, C., Megiddo, N., and Lohman, G. Automating Physical Database Design in a Parallel Database. Proceedings of the 2002 ACM SIGMOD/PODS Conference, Madison, WI, June 3–6, 2002, pp. 558–569.

Rees, S. Index Design for Performance. IDUG 2004—North America.

Rodgers, U. Denormalization: Why, What, and How? *Database Programming and Design,* 2(12), Dec. 1989: 46–53.

Roussopoulos, N. View Indexing in Relational Databases. *ACM Trans Database Systems,* 7(2), 1982: 258–290.

Rudin, K. Scalable Systems Architecture: Scalable I/O, Part I: Disk Striping. *DM Review Magazine,* May 1998: 1–3.

Runapongsa, K., Nadeau, T. P., and Teorey, T. J. Storage Estimation for Multidimensional Aggregates in OLAP. *Proceedings of the 10th CASCON Conference,* Toronto, 1999, pp. 40–54.

Runkler, T. A., and Glesner M. Multidimensional Defuzzification—Fast Algorithms for the Determination of Crisp Characteristic Subsets. Proceedings of the 1995 ACM Symposium on Applied Computing, Nashville, TN, Feb. 26–28, 1995, pp. 575–579.

Sarndal, C.-E., Swensson, B., and Wretman, J. *Model Assisted Survey Sampling.* New York: Springer-Verlag, 1992.

Schiefer, B., and Valentin, G. DB2 Universal Database Performance Tuning. *IEEE Data Engineering Bulletin,* 22(2), June 1999: 12–19.

Schkolnick, M., and Sorenson, P. Denormalization: A Performance-Oriented Database Design Technique. In *Proceedings of AICA 1980 Congress, Bologna, Italy.* Brussels: AICA, 1980, pp. 363–377.

Schulze, M., Gibson, G. A., Katz, R. A., and Patterson, D. A. How Reliable Is a RAID? *COMPCON,* 1989: 118–123.

Schussel, G. Client/Server Past, Present, and Future, at http://www.dciexpo.com/geos/, 1995.

The Self-managing Database: Automatic SGA Memory Management. Oracle White Paper, Nov. 2003, at http://www.oracle.com/technology/products/manageability/database/pdf/twp03/TWP_manage_self_managing_database.pdf.

Selinger, P. G., Astrahan, M. M., Chamberlin, D. D. Lorie, R. A., and Price, T. G. Access Path Selection in a Relational Database Management System. ACM SIGMOD Conference, 1979, pp. 23–34.

Shasha, D., and Bonnet, P. *Database Tuning: Principles, Experiments, and Troubleshooting Techniques.* San Francisco: Morgan Kaufmann, 2003.

Sheikholeslami, G., Chang, W., and Zhang, A. Semantic Clustering and Querying on Heterogeneous Features for Visual Data. Proceedings of the 6th ACM International Conference on Multimedia, 1998, pp. 3–12.

Shekhar, S., and Chawla, S. *Spatial Databases.* Englewood Cliffs, NJ: Prentice-Hall, 2003.

Shelton, R. E. The Distributed Enterprise (Shared, Reusable Business Models the Next Step in Distributed Object Computing. *Distributed Computing Monitor,* 8(10), Oct. 1993.

Shukla, A., Deshpande, P., Naughton, J., Ramasamy, K., Storage Estimation for Multidimensional Aggregates in the Presence of Hierarchies. International Conference on Very Large Databases, Mumbai (Bombay), 1996.

Silberschatz, A., Galvin, P., and Gagne, G. *Operating System Concepts,* 6th ed. New York: John Wiley, 2002.

Silberschatz, A., Korth, H. F., and Sudarshan, S. *Database System Concepts,* 5th ed. New York: McGraw-Hill, 2006.

Sinnwell, M., and Konig, A. C. Managing Distributed Memory to Meet Multiclass Workload Response Time Goals. *ICDE*, 1995: 87–94.

Sipper, M. A Brief Introduction to Genetic Algorithms, at http://lslwww.epfl.ch/~moshes/ga.html.

Son, E. J., Kang, I. S., Kim, T. W., and Li, K. J. A Spatial Data Mining Method by Clustering Analysis. Proceedings of the 6th International Symposium on Advances in Geographic Information Systems, 1998, pages 157–158.

Special Issue on Heterogeneous Databases. *ACM Computing Surveys*, 22(3), Sept. 1990: 173–293.

SQL Server Architecture: Memory Architecture, at http://msdn.microsoft.com/library/default.asp?url=/library/en-us/architec/8_ar_sa_4rc5.asp.

Stohr T., Martens, H., and Rahm, E. Multidimensional Aware Database Allocation for Parallel Data Warehouses. Proceedings of VLDB, 2000.

Stonebraker, M. Outrageous Ideas and/or Thoughts While Shaving. *ICDE,* 2004: 869–870.

Stonebraker, M. Too Much Middleware. *SIGMOD Record,* 31(1), 2002: 97–106.

Stonebraker, M., Sellis, T. K., and Hanson, E. N. An Analysis of Rule Indexing Implementations in Data Base Systems. Expert Database Conference, 1986: 465–476.

Storm, A. J., Garcia-Arellano, C. M., Lightstone, S., Diao, Y., and Surendra, M. Adaptive Self-tuning Memory in DB2 UDB, International Conference on Very Large Databases (VLDB), Seoul, 2006.

Sun, J., and Grosky, W. I. Dynamic Maintenance of Multidimensional Range Data Partitioning for Parallel Data Processing. Proceeding of the ACM First International Workshop on Data Warehousing and OLAP, Washington, DC, Nov. 3–7, 1998, pp. 72–79.

Szalay, A. S., Gray, J., and vandenBerg, J. Petabyte Scale Data Mining: Dream or Reality? CoRR cs.DB/0208013, 2002.

Telford, R., Horman, R., Lightstone, S., Markov, N., O'Connell, S., and Lohman, G. Usability and Design Considerations for an Autonomic Relational Database Management System. *IBM Systems Journal*, 42(4), 2003: 568–581.

Teorey, T. J. Distributed Database Design: A Practical Approach and Example. *SIGMOD Record*, 18(4), Dec. 1989: 23–39.

Teorey, T., and Fry, J. *Design of Database Structures*. Englewood Cliffs, NJ: Prentice-Hall, 1982.

Teorey, T., Lightstone, S., and Nadeau, T. *Database Modeling and Design: Logical Design*, 4th ed. San Francisco: Morgan Kaufmann, 2006.

Thompson, M. E. *Theory of Sample Surveys*. Chapman & Hall, 1997.

Thomsen, E. *OLAP Solutions*. New York: John Wiley, 1997.

Tian, W., Powley, W., and Martin, P. Techniques for Automatically Sizing Multiple Buffer Pools in DB2. CASCON, Toronto, Canada, 2003.

Transaction Processing Performance Council, at http://www.tpc.org.

Uchiyama, H., Runapongra, K., and Teorey, T. "Progressive View Materialization Algorithm," DOLAP, Kansas City, MO, 1999, 36–41.

Valentin, G., Zuliani, M., Zilio, D., and Lohman, G. DB2 Advisor: An Optimizer That Is Smart Enough to Recommend Its Own Indexes. Proceedings of ICDE, 2000.

Wan, S. J., Wong, S. K. M., and Prusinkiewicz, P. An Algorithm for Multidimensional Data Clustering. *ACM Transactions on Mathematical Software,* 14(2), June 1988: 153–162.

Wang, J. T. L., Wang, X., Lin, K. I., Shasha, D., Shapiro, B. A., and Zhang, K. Evaluating a Class of Distance-mapping Algorithms for Data Mining and Clustering. Proceedings of the 5th ACM SIGKDD International Conference on Knowledge Discovery and Data Mining, 1999, pp. 307–311.

Weikum, G., Hasse, C., Moenkeberg, A., and Zabback, P. The COMFORT Automatic Tuning Project. *Information Systems,* 19(5), 1994, pp 381–432.

Whang, K. Y. Index Selection in Relational Databases., Proceedings of the International Conference on Foundations on Data Organization (FODO), Kyoto, Japan, May 1985, pp. 369–378. Reprinted in *Foundations of Data Organization*, eds. S. P. Ghosh, Y. Kambayashi, and K. Tanaka. Tokyo, Japan, Plenum Press, New York, 1987, ISBN 0-306-42567-X, pp. 487–500.

Wiederhold, G. *File Organization for Database Design*. New York: McGraw-Hill, 1987.

Zaman, K. A., and Padmananbhan, S. An Efficient Workload-based Data Layout Scheme for Multidimensional Data. *IBM Technical Report*, July 2000.

Zhang, T., Ramakrishnan, R., and Livny, M. BIRCH: An Efficient Data Clustering Method for Very Large Databases. Proceedings of the 1996 ACM SIGMOD International Conference on Management of Data, 1996, pp. 103–114.

Zhang, W., and Larson, P. Dynamic Memory Adjustment for External Merge Sort. VLDB, Athens, Greece, 1997.

Zikopoulos, P. C., and Eaton, C. Availability with Clicks of a Button Using DB2's HADR, at http://www.dbazine.com/db2/db2-disarticles/zikopoulos19.

Zilio, D. C. Physical Database Design Decision Algorithms and Concurrent Reorganization for Parallel Database Systems, Ph.D. Thesis, University of Toronto, Toronto, Canada, 1998.

Zilio, D., Lightstone, S., and Lohman, G. Trends in Automated Database Design. IEEE Workshop on Autonomic Computing Principles and Architectures (AUCOPA), Banff AB, Aug. 2003.

Zilio, D., Lohman, G., Zuzarte, C., Ma, W., Lightstone, S., Cochrane, B., and Pirahesh, H. Recommending Materialized Views and Indexes by IBM's DB2 Design Advisor. International Conference on Autonomic Computing (ICAC), New York, May 17–18, 2004.

Zilio, D. C. Rao, J., Lightstone, S., Lohman, G. M., Storm, A. J., Garcia-Arellano, C., and Fadden, S. DB2 Design Advisor: Integrated Automatic Physical Database Design. International Conference on Very Large Databases (VLDB), Toronto, 2004, pp. 1087–1097.

Zilio, D.C., Lightstone, S., Lohman, G. Trends in Automating Physical Database Design", Proceedings IEEE International Conference on Industrial Informatics, 2003. INDIN 2003, 21–24 Aug, pp. 441–445

Index

About the Authors

Sam Lightstone is a Senior Technical Staff Member and Development Manager with IBM's DB2 product development team. His work includes numerous topics in autonomic computing and relational database management systems. He is cofounder and leader of DB2's autonomic computing R&D effort. He is Chair of the IEEE Data Engineering Workgroup on Self Managing Database Systems and a member of the IEEE Computer Society Task Force on Autonomous and Autonomic Computing. In 2003 he was elected to the Canadian Technical Excellence Council, the Canadian affiliate of the IBM Academy of Technology.

He is an IBM Master Inventor with more than 25 patents and patents pending; he has published widely on autonomic computing for relational database systems. He has been with IBM since 1991.

Toby Teorey is a Professor Emeritus in the Electrical Engineering and Computer Science Department and Director of Academic Programs in the College of Engineering at The University of Michigan, Ann Arbor. He received his B.S. and M.S. degrees in electrical engineering from the University of Arizona, Tucson, and a Ph.D. in computer science from the University of Wisconsin, Madison. He has been active as program chair and program committee member for a variety of database conferences.

Tom Nadeau is the founder of Aladdin Software (aladdinsoftware.com) and works in the area of data and text mining. He received his B.S. degree in computer science and M.S. and Ph.D. degrees in electrical engineering and computer science from The University of Michigan, Ann Arbor. His technical interests include data warehousing, OLAP, data mining, and machine learning. He won the best paper award at the 2001 IBM CASCON Conference.